WITHDRAWN

Middle Class Radicalism in Santa Monica

Middle Class

Radicalism in

Santa Monica

Mark E. Kann

Temple University Press · Philadelphia

Temple University Press, Philadelphia 19122

Published 1986

Printed in the United States of America

Library of Congress Cataloging-in-Publication Data

Kann, Mark E.
    Middle class radicalism in Santa Monica.

    Bibliography: p.
    Includes index.
    1. Radicalism—California—Santa Monica—History.
2. Middle classes—California—Santa Monica—Case studies. I.
Title.
HN90.R3K35   1986   322.4′4   85–22230
ISBN 0–87722–414–5

To Simon Michael Kann

May you inherit your mother's wisdom

And grow up in the world of your father's dreams

A Fable

Once there was a town
that had a stagnant pond in its center.

People tried not to notice the foul, murky thing
and almost learned to live with it . . .
except that every few months someone fell in
and had to be fished out.

Some people even drowned.

This went on for years and years.
Warning signs didn't help; fences got knocked
   down.
Nothing ever worked for long.

People gave up.

Finally one day someone said,
Who says we have to live with this?
Why don't we simply drain the pond?

At first this seemed radical but they finally agreed.
So they joined together and drained the pond
And were elated to discover that they had power
over their lives after all.

California Campaign for
Economic Democracy poster

Contents

Preface

Why would affluent, middle class citizens give an electoral mandate to leftist radicals? Why should privileged, middle class youth seek a radical mandate? What can middle class citizens and radical politicians do to implement a radical agenda in one U.S. city and promote it nationwide? And what does the merging of "middle class" and "radicalism" mean for our understanding of these concepts and for the future of American politics? These are some of the questions raised by recent events in what local bumperstickers proclaim as "The People's Republic of Santa Monica, California."

Santa Monica is a prosperous oceanside city just west of Los Angeles. Beginning in the early 1970s, it hosted a growing grassroots movement that struggled to protect and enhance the local quality of life against business interests promoting growth and development. By 1979, the movement had garnered enough citizen support to pass one of the most radical rent control laws in the United States. In 1981, activists moved from rent control to political control when Santa Monicans elected a radical city council majority that started to experiment with building a "human scale community" founded on principles of "participatory democracy" and priorities putting "people ahead of profits." The next year, residents reaffirmed their support for the leftist agenda by sending Campaign for Economic Democracy (CED) leader Tom Hayden to the California State Assembly. Clearly, the radicals were in power.

Santa Monica activists believed that they were constructing a model of leftwing government that would install radical democracy in their municipality and also be emulated by leftists in other cities. According to several scenarios, widespread urban radicalism would help to build the base for an enduring national movement that would change the Democratic party and have considerable influence in Washington, D.C. The opposition saw the Santa Monica experiment either as a CED conspiracy against basic American values and institutions or as an adolescent politics that was transforming the city into what one gentleman called "Santa Moronica." Meanwhile, journalists from the national media descended on Santa Monica to report on its odd marriage between affluent middle class citizens and young radical politicians.

In one sense, the union was unusual. Cities such as Cleveland, Ohio, or San Antonio, Texas, or Berkeley, California, had experimented with radical governments. But their experiments were infused with the working class, minority, or student politics that traditionally are the base for radical movements. Santa Monica stood out because its grassroots base was strictly "Main Street," composed almost exclusively of successful, white, "bourgeois" citizens who normally ignore or oppose radicals. Furthermore, activists in other cities, though often themselves from the middle class, identified their goals with the exploited, subjugated, impoverished, and dispossessed people of American society. Santa Monica activists, as we will see, redefined radicalism. They self-consciously identified with their own privileged class; and they hoped to extract from middle class culture the roots of an indigenous American radicalism, more moral and political than economic, that would appeal to the prosperous as well as the poor.

In another sense, Santa Monica's convergence of affluence and radicalism was odd only insofar as it was an exemplary chapter in a larger American story. That narrative concerns the evolution of the American middle class in the twentieth century, particularly its growing ambivalence toward conventional institutions and politics as well as its manifest interest in exploring alternatives. The larger story also involves changes in the values and strategies of the American left. Activists who participated in the student movement of the 1960s and explored alternative institutions and politics in the 1970s became more sympathetic to the emerging dilemmas of middle class life and more interested in solving them. Middle class radicalism in Santa Monica was both a manifestation of these trends and an effort to pioneer their potential contribution to democratic change in the United States.

Part 1 of this book is an analysis of the historical roots of middle class radicalism in both Santa Monica and the United States. Its object is to locate the point where middle class versions of the American Dream intersect with radical visions of the American future. Part 2 describes and assesses the practice of middle class radicalism in the exemplary Santa Monica case. It examines the tensions between radicals' principles and their pragmatic politics as they appeared in grassroots organizing, electioneering, and running city hall. Part 3 evaluates the promise of middle class radicalism to contribute to democratic change in the United States. It looks at the gap between the radicals' dreams and practices to understand whether middle class radicalism can mobilize mainstream America in the cause of democratic reform, empower people and undermine dominant elites, and shift the nation's political agenda toward greater human autonomy and equality. Let me state from the outset that I am sympathetic to the dream, skeptical of the practice, and ambivalent about the promise.

The idea for this book originated at a dinner party that took place in 1981. The party was in a lovely home in Pacific Palisades, a wealthy section of Los Angeles that borders Santa Monica. The table was set with fine china, silverware, and crystal and the cuisine was continental. My hosts were college professor Kitty Kovacs and film producer Steve

Kovacs, and the guests included Santa Monica mayor Ruth Yannatta
Goldway and Santa Monica planning commissioner Derek Shearer. In
this quintessential "bourgeois" setting, we middle class Americans spent
the evening discussing the prospects of radical politics in Santa Monica
and the United States. The idea that middle class and radicalism were
not necessarily mutually exclusive terms was planted though I had no
notion that it would grow into a book.

A few months later, Elizabeth Rapoport suggested that I write an
article for *Socialist Review* on Santa Monica politics. I took up her sug-
gestion and began doing taped interviews with people involved in Santa
Monica politics. I began with Goldway and Shearer, whom I already
knew, and then spoke with city councilmembers Dolores Press, James
Conn, Dennis Zane, Kenneth Edwards, Christine Reed, and William
Jennings. I also interviewed city manager John Alschuler, city attorney
Robert Myers, city liaison officer Vivian Rothstein, and assistant city
planner Christopher Rudd. Finally, I set up formal talks with activists
involved with different political groups or neighborhood organizations
in the city, including Maurice Zeitlin, Roger Thornton, Allan Heskin,
Judy Abdo, Fred Allingham, and Herman Rosenstein. During the next
few years, I spoke informally with many of these people as well as with
other activists and city officials. Conrad Melilli and Laurie Lieberman
were particularly helpful. I also carried on continuous conversations with
friends living in Santa Monica or simply interested in it. They were
Judith Stiehm, Harlan Hahn, Larry Berg, Olga Matich, Zan Steiner,
and Carl Boggs.

These interviews yielded two results. First, they were the basis for several articles on radicals in power in Santa Monica. My initial approach
was to use the Santa Monica experiment to test some of the claims of
what scholars were calling "the new populism" against some of the older
but revised claims of neo-marxists. Still, I was uncomfortable with this
approach because Santa Monica events seemed so bourgeois compared
to the concerns of both new populists and neo-marxists for the exploited
classes in America. Second, the interviews kept reaffirming my earlier
dinner party idea. Santa Monica residents, activists, politicians, and
bureaucrats all betrayed the distinctive signs of middle class background
and culture. They were generally affluent, highly educated, articulate,
cosmopolitan, self-confident, and effective. They lived the American
Dream and yet they sought to fulfill radical dreams. Perhaps there was a
connection.

Like most American scholars, unfortunately, I needed to encounter
some European theorists to understand what was happening on this
side of the Atlantic Ocean. My own "Tocquevilles" included Antonio
Gramsci and George Orwell. Prior work on Gramsci alerted me to the
public ambivalence that coexists with elite hegemony. This ambivalence,
manifested among professionals who are torn between success in the

marketplace and empowering other people, helped to explain middle class support for radicalism in Santa Monica. Then, some research, writing, and teaching on Orwell provided me with a good example of middle class radicalism. Orwell intermittently attacked and defended the marketplace in the hope of promoting radical democracy. His own ambivalence was remarkably similar to the attitudes of radicals in Santa Monica. With the artificial self-confidence that derives from being able to draw on noted European superstars, I began to reanalyze Santa Monica's middle class and its radicalism in terms of their systematic connection.

Several colleagues in the academic community provided encouragement and comment on portions of this manuscript. Booth Fowler and Judith Stiehm, as always, patted me on the back and then pointed out problems to nurture improvements. Ben Agger, Peter Clecak, Philip Green, Jennifer Hochschild, Jane Mansbridge, and Maurice Zeitlin provided invaluable criticism and advice. My ideas were sharpened considerably by discussions and disagreements with Carl Boggs. Temple University Press reviewers Harry C. Boyte and Craig Reinarman did an excellent job of pointing out the manuscript's shortcomings. And Carol Thompson and Nora Hamilton were an immense help, restraining my optimism of will with their pessimism of intellect.

Much of this book is based on taped interviews that I conducted, transcribed, and inserted into the text. I have tried to adhere as closely as possible to context and exact wording in citations from the interviews, though it was sometimes necessary to insert an article or verb when converting the spoken word into written prose. Obviously, I did not interview everyone involved in Santa Monica politics, which means that some viewpoints may have been shortchanged. I tapered the interviewing process when it seemed to become repetitious, at that point relying more on informal discussions and the day-to-day reporting of Santa Monica's local newspaper, the *Outlook*. I assiduously read and clipped the *Outlook* for several years and developed a great respect for the local reporters, who did an outstanding job of chronicling local politics despite the fact that their employer was at the forefront of the opposition to the radical experiment. I also drew on Santa Monica's radio station KCRW, which produced weekly broadcasts of city council meetings, saving me from driving the seventy-five-mile roundtrip between my home and Santa Monica.

I acknowledge the generous help of all of these people. I thank them for the time, resources, and wisdom that they put at my disposal. Finally: Kathy and Simon, I love you.

Mark E. Kann

San Pedro, California
1985

Part 1
The Dream

Until an independence is declared, the continent
will feel itself like a man who continues putting
off some unpleasant business from day to day,
yet knows it must be done, hates to set about it,
wishes it over, and is haunted with the thoughts of
its necessity.

Thomas Paine

1

Where the Rainbow Ends

Santa Monica is probably the last place in the world where you'd expect to find "the revolution." For the most part, it's just a drowsy beachfront suburb of about 86,000 people nestled between Los Angeles and the Pacific Ocean, the kind of place where Californians would say the rainbow ends.

Its politics were pretty much conventional until about a year ago. That's when the local elections swept into power a group on "the far left." Suddenly, this community woke up to find itself polarized. The radicals, or the progressives as they call themselves, haven't renamed Santa Monica "Ho Chi Minh City" but if they did, the people who used to rule here—the conservatives, the landlords, the developers, the business people—wouldn't be at all surprised.

CBS "60 Minutes Report" [1]

Generations of Americans have traveled west on Route 66 in search of
the middle class dream. They wanted a decent environment for raising
their families, jobs that might be parlayed into homeownership, and
maybe some sunshine to warm their later years. Those who took "the
Main Street of America" to its end found themselves in Santa Monica,
California. They had arrived.

But affluence was not enough. It was one thing to profit from the
growth of the nation but quite another to have to live with the growing
pains. Santa Monicans felt those pains in the 1970s when it became
clear that their town was becoming a mere extension of the Los Angeles
megalopolis. Paradoxically, the cure was for middle class residents to
vote radicals into power.

Santa Monica

Route 66 ends at Santa Monica's Palisades Park. The park is landscaped
with wide-leafed palm trees and bird-of-paradise plants that symbolize
Southern California beauty. It is located on a bluff overlooking the Pacific
Ocean, whose constant sea breezes cleanse the air and moderate tem-
peratures to a near perfect seventy degrees throughout the year. Just
below the park are miles of broad sandy beaches that provide virtually
unlimited recreational possibilities for people of all ages. The horizon af-
fords scenic vistas that include Malibu and the mountains to the north,
the Palos Verdes peninsula on the south, and brilliant Pacific sunsets
directly west. Most filmgoers and television buffs have unknowingly seen
Palisades Park because it is a regular location for shooting movies, programs, and commercials.

The park recently served as a starting point for a ten-kilometer race
that capsulized Santa Monica life. The more than 2,000 entrants looked
affluent. They were mostly young white people wearing expensive running clothes and shoes from specialty sporting-goods stores as well as
healthy tans that came from outdoor living. The race course wound its
way through the "north of Montana" neighborhood where half-million-
dollar homes (and up) and Mercedes in driveways were common sights.
The last two and a half miles gently sloped downhill, encouraging runners to achieve their "personal bests," which were recorded by high tech
timing devices at the finish line. Every finisher was applauded; everyone
was a winner. The event, like Santa Monica itself, epitomized middle
class success.

That success can be gleaned from some basic statistics. In 1980, the
average Santa Monica home sold for a hefty $203,600—slightly more
than in nearby Beverly Hills. The mean income for Santa Monica families was $28,825, a respectable middle class figure that would be higher if
accumulated and invested wealth were added. Nearly 78 percent of the

residents were white, 60 percent of the adult women employed, and fully 43.5 percent of all residents engaged in professional and managerial careers.[2] Relatively unusual for American communities, more than 70 percent of Santa Monicans rented their homes but the renters were almost as affluent as the homeowners. A random survey of tenants revealed that 87 percent were white, over 50 percent had household incomes above $20,000, and 51 percent were in professional, managerial, or business careers.[3] In addition, 17 percent of the Santa Monica population was black or Hispanic, and less than 14 percent was working in manufacturing.[4]

These statistics confirm what any visitor can see. Santa Monica has a few bona fide mansions and slum buildings. But its geography is mostly defined by the costly single-family houses, modern condominiums, and well-trimmed apartment complexes that are badges of middle class affluence. Santa Monica is the kind of place where the upwardly mobile seek residence.

Residents' affluence feeds into the city's thriving commercial economy. Merchants peddle more than goods and services; they also sell shopping experiences. One can bicycle down to old Main Street and be transported back to the 1890s by its wooded storefronts and stained glass windows, Victorian restorations, period restaurants, and sidewalk vendors. The prospective buyer can also return to the precorporate 1950s by strolling through the open-air downtown mall and chatting with the owners of the modest family-run businesses there. The shopper fond of the countercultural 1960s has no problem finding the food coops and health food stores, unique bookshops, or artisan outlets that dot the city. The more contemporary consumer can choose between Santa Monica Place, a new indoor center featuring major chain outlets, chic boutiques and galleries, and lots of roofed-in greenery designed by a famous local architect, or the finer specialty stores that are now colonizing Montana Avenue in competition with Beverly Hills' Rodeo Drive. The Santa Monica jetsetter can now stay at home with the opening of Colorado Place, with its European atmosphere, shops, and restaurants. Santa Monica is an 8.3 square mile island of consumer delights that has yet to suffer from the waves of recession that have swept across the United States in the past decade.[5]

One item regularly produced and consumed in Santa Monica is culture. Simply living in Santa Monica is a form of cultural enrichment. One's neighbors are likely to be interesting if not important people in the world of ideas and the arts. The city houses an incredible concentration of scientists, professors, journalists and writers, architects, designers, doctors, and lawyers as well as producers and directors, actors, dancers, sculptors, painters, and artisans. These "captains of culture" for the Southern California region and beyond form a critical mass of support for public and commercial performances. Many of them contribute time, talents, and money to city cultural affairs and many patronize the experimental theaters that germinate there. Furthermore, their avocational interests compose the demand that attracts an abundant supply of private schools and lessons that cater to middle class hobbyists.

The source for Santa Monica's middle class affluence, consumption, and culture is marketable intellectual skills. Santa Monicans have "earned" their slice of the American Dream not by inheritance or manual labor but by getting the education, credentials, and experience that foster upward social mobility. They know the importance of investing in their children's education to ensure generational continuity and, even in the era of tax rebellions, they overwhelmingly vote to increase education expenditures. Santa Monica youth matriculate into a fine school system that includes an alternative elementary school stressing freedom and creativity plus a noted high school whose campus resembles an ivy-trimmed university and whose graduates often feed into Ivy League schools. Students not able to make the leap from Santa Monica High School to Harvard can spend a few years at Santa Monica College before going to nearby universities such as the University of California at Los Angeles or the University of Southern California. Local educational offerings are enhanced by an excellent municipal library system, numerous private tutoring opportunities, and, of course, an array of high tech computer outlets with the latest in hardware, software, how-to manuals, free introductory lessons, and computer camp brochures. Santa Monica youth are assured a head start in tomorrow's race for middle class success.

Despite pockets of extraordinary wealth and modest poverty, Santa Monica is a city where the affluent middle class enjoys its success. A stereotyped view of such success might have it that local politics would be informed by smug contentment. Residents would demand from city government decent public services and protection against the riff-raff; merchants would use city government as a vehicle for attracting tourists and consumers; and political conflicts would be limited to questions such as: Should cyclists or runners have the right of way on beachfront paths? As with many stereotypes, this one is partially accurate. But recent events suggest that middle class success and smug contentment do not necessarily come wrapped in a single package.

In the early 1970s, Santa Monica became a center of considerable grassroots activism across a range of issues. By 1979, activists had initiated and won popular support for the most stringent rent control law in the United States. In 1981, a group of "radicals" won control of city government, including the mayor's office, the city council majority, the city manager's office, the city attorney's office, the rent control board, the planning commission majority, the redevelopment agency majority, citizen task forces and advisory commissions, key posts in the bureaucracy, and an annual $90 million budget. Local leaders hailed their victory as a move from "tenant power to political power" and announced their intention to "show the nation what local government can do when government is no longer in the service of business."[6] If success breeds contentment, then why did Santa Monica's affluent middle class vote radicals into power?

When the CBS "60 Minutes" commentator said that Santa Monica is the last place in the world where one would expect to find "the revolution," he was echoing conventional wisdom. American scholars, journalists, and leftwing analysts agree that the middle class—the bourgeoisie—is wedded to the capitalist system and opposed to the radical movements that promise to undermine it. What happened in Santa Monica was not supposed to happen because middle class joggers cannot be revolutionaries.

Joggers Cannot Be Revolutionaries

American scholars tell a story about how the middle class has immunized the nation against the radical movements that pervade European history. Their first chapter has America being founded amidst relative equality and the absence of sharp class conflicts. The eventual result, according to Louis Hartz, "was to electrify the democratic individual with a passion for great achievement and to produce . . . the hero of Horatio Alger."[7] From the mid-nineteenth century onward, Americans developed an individualism informed by a get-rich-quick compulsion that inspired the poor and needy to strive for middle class success in the capitalist marketplace, and motivated the middle class to defend that marketplace. Scholars are sometimes hesitant to defend individual acquisitiveness and materialism, preferring to read American history in terms of loftier goals, but they consistently justify the efforts of entrepreneurs as far superior to the historical alternative of working class socialism.[8]

Chapter two tells of the triumph of middle class capitalism over working class socialism. Why is there not a serious socialist movement in the United States? Why does this country lack a European-style social democratic party or a radical labor movement that will stand up for collective ownership of the means of production? Werner Sombart in 1906 summarized what has become the core of scholarly wisdom: "All socialist utopias came to nothing on roast beef and apple pie."[9] On the one hand, Americans' entrepreneurial efforts resulted in incredible economic growth in the late nineteenth century, producing a substantial number of middle class individuals whose interests were tied to capitalist expansion. On the other hand, the bourgeois ideology linking individual mobility to capitalist expansion muted class conflict. Workers could believe that their individual efforts would win them middle class prosperity or at least an education for their children, who would achieve upward mobility in the next generation. Thus, the middle class defended the capitalist system and the working class experienced "embourgeoisement," pinning material hopes on entrance into the middle class rather than on collective opposition to capitalism.[10]

The third chapter focuses on the flexibility of the American political system, its ability to absorb reforms that tame discontents and stabilize capitalism. Between the 1880s and the 1930s, populists, socialists, labor radicals, and progressives mobilized people in behalf of reforms intended to transform government into a positive force for social cooperation and equality. This political activism helped to bring about the welfare state. The federal government promised to oversee the prosperity, enhanced individual opportunities, full employment, a social safety net, and fair mediation of business-labor relations that were to dilute, institutionalize, and moderate radicalism. Meanwhile, the federal government also promised to use new regulatory powers to rationalize the marketplace and smooth the way for capitalists to enter into international competition. And the government's regulatory machinery—its growing bureaucracy, civil service, public and quasipublic agencies, and so forth—provided massive employment opportunities for emerging middle class professionals and managers. Social welfare and economic regulation combined with the prosperity following World War II seemingly confirmed the flexibility of the political system as a cure for radicalism: the leftwing activists of the 1930s were isolated in the 1940s, easily routed out of the Congress of Industrial Organizations, redbaited by Senator Joseph McCarthy and his middle class supporters, and burned out by cold war fever. By the 1950s, notable American scholars were convinced that abundance and reform had all but eliminated radicalism.[11]

There are serious problems with this storybook history. It neglects the significant degree of class conflict that was manifest in early America. It ignores the fact that middle class Americans sometimes have been attracted to radical values and politics. For example, Edward Bellamy's vision of a technologically efficient socialist society, portrayed in his book *Looking Backward*, which sold more than a million copies and spawned more than one hundred clubs in the later decades of the nineteenth century, appealed to the middle class sense of order and intelligence. Other radicals such as Henry George had some success in calling on science and religion as a means of courting middle class support. Furthermore, working class Americans did not all buy into the dream of individual mobility within the capitalist system. Embourgeoisement was uneven. And many workers continued to react to immiseration, poor working conditions, and the destruction of their crafts and communities with considerable militancy. As for the flexibility of the political system, one ought not to forget the use of public and private violence as a continuing mechanism for curtailing the radicalism that did not get absorbed. And, of course, American radicalism was not eliminated by the 1950s because it reemerged forcefully, to the surprise of many scholars, in the 1960s.

What is striking, however, is that many of the critics who pointed out these problems nonetheless agreed with the main storyline: middle class America and the workers who identified with it comprised the main social barrier to radical change. C. Wright Mills and Herbert Marcuse, the two most prominent leftwing scholars of the postwar period, argued that the mass of American people had been integrated into the capitalist system.[12] The middle class thrived on it and workers were being sold on its norms: individual paths to the American Dream, a home in the suburbs, two cars in the garage, and a new television set. The minority of workers that were unionized sought better wage and benefit packages instead of social ownership of the means of production or worker control on the shopfloor. Labor leaders had largely become middle class bureaucrats, more comfortable hobnobbing with management than dirtying their hands among common workers. By the time the new left entered onto the American stage, diminishing numbers of radicals accepted the orthodox marxist expectation that the working class would be in the vanguard of change; too often, it was in the vanguard of the rednecks and hardhats who opposed the civil rights and antiwar movements.

Many new left scholars still looked on middle class America as the major social barrier to change. It was complicit in unresponsive big government, corporate growth and monopolies, imperialism, environmental degradation, institutionalized racism and sexism, as well as bureaucratism, impersonality, and psychological repression. While some activists explored new ways to build a working class opposition and others identified with Third World revolutionaries such as Mao, Fidel, and Ho, many new left thinkers sought to pioneer a new opposition. They looked to potentially militant minorities who existed on the fringes of capitalist society and had yet to develop a stake in middle class America; to student intellectuals whose moral idealism and advanced education helped them to transcend their own middle class backgrounds; and to the youth counterculture whose spontaneism, experimentalism, and liberationist ethic could be seen as a profound alternative to the bourgeois Protestant Ethic.[13] This search for a new sociology of radicalism, however, did not dispense with earlier visions of working class socialism. Marcuse, for example, hoped that minority, student, and counterculture radicalism would spark a larger working class movement.[14] Intellectually, the battle lines were all too familiar.

For many scholars, the struggles of the 1960s produced the predictable outcomes of the 1970s: the American political system absorbed some reforms that placated the discontented. The radicals were not only isolated but also ripe for conversion to "bourgeois narcissism," translating their quest for social justice into an individual quest for egocentric fulfillment. Christopher Lasch, whose *The Culture of Narcissism* popularized the latest trends in psychoanalytic theory, quoted former radical Jerry Rubin as an example: "In five years from 1971 to 1975, I directly embraced est, gestalt therapy, bioenergetics, rolfing, massage, jogging, health foods, tai chi, Esalen, hypnotism, modern dance, meditation, Silva Mind Control, acupuncture, sex therapy, Reichian therapy, and More House—a smorgasbord course in New Consciousness." [15] On this view, the personalization of politics during the "Me Decade" was profoundly conservative. Individuals fine-tuned the art of buying (therapy, health food, roller skates, etc.) while corporations fine-tuned the art of selling (goods, services, television politicians, peace of mind, etc.). The radical sensibility of the 1960s had given way to a middle class obsession with personal lifestyles in the 1970s.

Again, there are problems of oversimplification with these stories of the recent past but, for our purposes, the main problem is that they make no sense when applied to Santa Monica, California. Santa Monica has an affluent middle class and an expanding capitalist economy that *theoretically* insulates the municipality from the appeals of radicals. Local residents are the beneficiaries of state and federal government reforms intended to enhance middle class opportunities and ease working class discontents. Santa Monica's own working class population is quite small, if not politically insignificant, and often channels its discontents into conservative politics. The city's black minority is also quite small (4 percent of the population) and usually conservative while the Hispanic population (13 percent) demonstrates considerable skepticism if not apathy toward radicals. Santa Monica has no discernible core of university students who might transcend their middle class upbringing to fuel radical politics and its countercultural core evidences more interest in protecting its Ocean Park neighborhood than in promoting a radical liberationist ethic. And one can easily imagine Christopher Lasch pointing to Santa Monica's consumer culture, replete with trendy shops and jogathons, as an ideal example of conservative bourgeois narcissism. By all scholarly rights, Santa Monica should be a wasteland for leftwing organizing. Instead, it proved to be extraordinarily fertile.

What do scholars do when their pet theories conflict with historical realities? Usually, they try to save their theories by reinterpreting realities. Suppose that Newton's theory of gravity conflicts with the actual path of a planet. Scientists can save Newton's theory in three ways. First, they can write off the errant planet as an unimportant quirk that will eventually be eliminated by theoretical refinements. Second, they can assume the problem is one of measurement and work to develop a bigger, better telescope to show that the planet really is on its prescribed Newtonian course. Third, they can simply own up to a conflict between theory and reality, and then continue to support Newtonian physics until a better theory comes along. [16] Each method allows them to live comfortably with Newton, their colleagues, and their own research, at least until Einstein appears.

The conventional wisdom of scholars regarding the antagonism between the American middle class and radicals is shared by journalists who research, analyze, and communicate the news to American audiences. The fact that conventional wisdom was at odds with experience in Santa Monica made local politics newsworthy. The idea of middle America going to bed with leftwing radicals had great human interest value. But how was one to explain it? Like the scientists who would write off an errant planet as an unimportant quirk, the major media that covered Santa Monica politics treated it as an example of Southern California crackpotism.

Southern California Crackpotism

Southern California is noted for its flair for the new, untried, and idiosyncratic if not plain faddishness, a tendency, says Carey McWilliams, "dismissed by all observers as 'crackpotism,' still another vagary of the climate, a byproduct of eternal sunshine."[17] When major media observers came to Santa Monica, they generally saw the relationship between its affluent middle class and local radicals as still another byproduct of too many hours in the sun. Nonetheless, the media accidently hit upon a major clue to the relationship.

CBS's "60 Minutes," the highly rated and much-watched television news magazine with a flair for the sensational, turned Santa Monica into a microcosm of the cold war. On one side stood this strange alliance between affluent American voters and radicals associated with "the revolution," "the far left," and "Ho Chi Minh." Little effort was made to investigate why the affluent supported the radicals but the "60 Minutes" staff did its best to extract statements about the redistribution of wealth from radicals. On the other side stood the conservative opposition. The staff succeeded in unearthing Santa Monica's rightwing fringe. They quoted one Santa Monican, a Soviet sphere refugee, who said that the communists had once again caught up with her; they also quoted a gentleman who told of an historical revolutionary blueprint first used by Napoleon, then refined by Hitler, and now practiced by the Santa Monica left. The result was a story about middle class crazies lusting after a piece of the political pie while replaying the conflict between capitalism and socialism.

The reputable *Wall Street Journal* ran an article entitled "Santa Monica's Suburban Radicals" that mostly followed the "60 Minutes" scenario.[18] The title juxtaposed "suburban" and "radical" to suggest something like a spoiled middle class wanting more topping for its ice cream. The article portrayed the Santa Monica left as "apostles" of economic democracy, "a vaguely defined anti-capitalist, local action platform which depicts big business as the source of most evil." The between-the-lines message was that the radicals could as easily have been the apostles of Jim Jones or any other cult leader. Why would successful middle class people be attracted to such radical cultism? "The secret of the radical breakthrough is the relentless exploitation of rent control." The left used this issue as "a means of buying votes by a forced redistribution of wealth" as part of its larger war against capitalism; thus, the radicals duped the middle class public. Fortunately, the article continued, some Santa Monicans had not been deceived. Stavisa Milsavljevic, a disabled Yugoslav immigrant whose father's Belgrade apartment building was expropriated by Tito's communists and whose own six-unit Santa Monica building was now imperiled by local radicals, had joined other "mom and pop" landlords to fight back in the press, the courts, and the polling place.

How would the battle end? The *Wall Street Journal* suggested that the leftwing crackpots were almost certain to fail because their redistributive policies would backfire, putting the squeeze on small landlords and businesses that would be forced to sell out to big-time speculators and developers. The result would be not economic democracy but a further concentration of wealth. Thus the article's conclusion: "One can argue that the experiment should be left alone . . . if only to be an example for the rest of the nation."

Other newspapers more or less followed the same line. The Detroit *News* portrayed the contest as one pitting radicals and their supporters, engaged in an "experiment in socialism" pointing toward a "worker paradise," against large corporate developers whose eighty-two ongoing projects, valued at $251 million, were imperiled by the socialist onslaught.[19] The Baltimore *Sun* reduced Santa Monica politics to a single-issue rent control struggle, asking whether this California craze was "the wave of the future."[20] The most serious analysis was a *Village Voice* piece called "About-Face in Santa Monica" that nonetheless succumbed to amusement by captioning an inset "Tomorrow the World?"[21]

To my knowledge, not one member of the major media seriously investigated the relationship between the middle class and the radicals. It may be naive to expect the media to do indepth analysis, but its absence forced journalists to take conventional wisdom for granted and to distort facts to fit it. Briefly, Santa Monica's affluent middle class did not suffer from crackpotism and did not suffer deception. To the contrary, it was an extraordinarily educated and self-conscious population that knowingly supported the radicals. Furthermore, the Santa Monica left never had the ideological cohesion attributed to it by the media. At most, it contained a handful of socialists who were the first to suggest that local events had nothing to do with the revolution, the far left, Ho Chi Minh, apostolic politics, socialist experimentation, a worker paradise, or shaping the world's future. It did have a few advocates of economic democracy in leading positions but they neither agreed among themselves on policy priorities nor represented the majority of activists in the city. Finally, the major opposition in Santa Monica had little to do with rightwing fanaticism, anticommunism, or even the enshrinement of private property; it was a complex and disorganized group. England's Manchester *Guardian* piece on Santa Monica suggested, "In Southern California, the idea of restricting property rights sounds remarkably like an excerpt from the Communist Manifesto."[22] In fact, this statement is far more descriptive of how the media saw Santa Monica politics than of actual events.

The media did hit upon one interesting quirk. Article after article pointed out that Santa Monica's radicals did not look like radicals. In fact, they looked like conventional middle class people. The *Wall Street Journal*, for example, attributed some of their success to the fact that they did not look very threatening to young professionals. Their leaders included a mother of four, a Methodist minister, a college professor, and even Tom Hayden and Jane Fonda, who owned an "unpretentious two-story house near the beach."[23] Either the radicals were out to deceive people by passing as members of the middle class much as the Progressive Labor party of the 1960s tried to pass as members of the working class, or they did not recognize the contradiction between their appearances and their politics.

Newsweek ran an article called "Santa Monica Tilts Left" that noted a local contest over who would be considered Santa Monica's "top reformers."[24] The implicit notion that radicals, who support egalitarian cooperation, would engage in middle class competition suggested an oddity. Two Santa Monica couples were typed as the rivals: Tom Hayden and Jane Fonda versus Ruth Yannatta Goldway and Derek Shearer. The accompanying photos showed a thoughtful Tom Hayden wearing a coat and tie, and a mildly smiling Ruth Yannatta Goldway sitting amidst papers piled high on her mayoral desk. These folks did not look very radical; rather they looked like serious, hardworking people.

Hayden and Fonda have biographies that make them perpetual human interest stories in the media. Hayden was a leading 1960s radical, best known for his founding role in Students for a Democratic Society (SDS) and his courtroom role as defendant in the Chicago Seven trial that followed the 1968 national Democratic party convention. In the 1970s, Hayden put on a coat and tie and began to work within the political system. He made an impressive run for California's Democratic party nomination for U.S. senator in 1976, founded the Santa Monica-based Campaign for Economic Democracy (CED) the next year, served on several state commissions under Governor Jerry Brown, and was elected to represent the Santa Monica area in the California State Assembly in 1982. Hayden is a prolific writer, a regular interviewee, and a common center of controversy. When he went to the State Assembly, newspapers reported both surprise among his colleagues that he was a team player and the expected accusations of groups that wanted him impeached for having aided the enemy during the Vietnam war.

Hayden is married to Jane Fonda. She was born into the Hollywood Fonda family, who undoubtedly helped her into the business when she launched her acting career as a sex bombshell. She eventually earned recognition as a fine actress in her own right, making social consciousness films that stirred controversy and stimulated box office success. Her fame meant easy access to public platforms from which she has promoted liberal to radical causes, including economic democracy. Her immodest income from acting and her various "workout" industries (books, salons, etc.) have helped to finance Hayden, CED, and other leftist groups. In a review entitled "Stretch Marx," a *New Republic* critic suggested that *Jane Fonda's Workout Book*, coming amidst America's fitness craze, may be "the basis for an authentic American socialism: body worship." How?

> It manages the acrobatic feat of linking every wooly trend imaginable: acupuncture, "natural" medicine, anticorporatism, chiropractic, nutrition, a new feminism ("our right to physical as well as economic, political, and social equality"), cancer phobia, economic democracy, lean thighs, community control, and an aversion to sugar. The only thing missing is a call to nuclear disarmament. Not to worry. The *Workout* came out just before that wave crested. Look for it in the revised edition.[25]

Ironically, the critic praised Fonda's sense of entrepreneurship. She knows how to profit by catering to exercise as the new middle class hobby even as she preaches a fad-oriented "Adidas socialism."

According to *Newsweek*, Hayden and Fonda's rivals for top reformer honors were Ruth Yannatta Goldway and Derek Shearer, Santa Monica's first family from 1981 to 1983. Goldway received her first dose of political recognition in 1973, when she spearheaded a national meat boycott as chair of a group called Fight Inflation Together. She went on to direct a nonprofit consumer organization, serve in Governor Brown's Department of Consumer Affairs, run for a State Assembly nomination, and direct the Center for New Corporate Priorities. In 1979, she was elected to the Santa Monica city council; in 1981, the radical council majority appointed her mayor. A former Ph.D. candidate in English, Goldway is articulate as well as outspoken, making her the key figure on the city's most controversial issues. That she is also physically attractive made her an ideal object of media attention. The Los Angeles *Herald Examiner* did a profile on her called "Goldway: A Dragon Lady or a Pussycat?"[26] The article contrasted her "steely self-confidence" as a radical mayor facing opposition to her softer, more conventional roles as middle class daughter, wife, and mother. It also provided a storybook account of her relationship with Derek Shearer. She met him at a Ralph Nader citizens group meeting; it was "love at first sight"; and marriage soon followed, officiated by James Conn, "a Santa Monica city councilmember and a hip-looking blue-jeaned Methodist minister"—a kind of leftwing Harlequin romance.

Derek Shearer, whose photo has graced the cover and inner pages of *Mother Jones* magazine, was described there as an individual whose "wholesome looks and penchant for LaCoste shirts give him more the appearance of a young, ambitious Reagan official than a radical economist."[27] Shearer's roots came out in most stories: his father is *Parade Magazine* editor Lloyd Shearer. Son Derek is a Yale-educated urban planner and college professor who has worked with Tom Hayden and Ralph Nader and has also served as a presidential appointee on Jimmy Carter's National Consumer Cooperative Bank. He is perhaps best known as coauthor of a must-read book for American leftists, *Economic Democracy: The Challenge of the 1980s.* Shearer is often considered the key intellectual strategist for the Santa Monica radicals; he cochaired their most successful electoral campaign and served on the city planning commission, eventually becoming its chairman. Given his way with words, Shearer may be the most quoted person within the Santa Monica left; certainly the press has continuously sought him out for interviews.

The general function of the media portraits was to highlight the discrepancy between the radicals' apparently middle class personalities and their radical politics, in some cases, to undermine their credibility. When Hayden and Fonda remodeled their home with nonunion labor and were then picketed by local construction workers, the story went out over the wires. When Goldway and Shearer accepted complimentary tickets for a Laker Airlines trip to England, journalists labeled the shortlived controversy "Lakergate." The insinuation was that one cannot be both middle class and radical. Either these people should continue to lay claim to middle class prerogatives and suspend their radical rhetoric or they should give up their middle class fronts and live according to their radical values. They could not have it both ways.

One can draw a different message from the media portraits: Santa Monica's leftwing activists were both middle class and radical. They generally come from middle to upper middle class homes. They are highly educated and credentialed, extraordinarily articulate in the spoken and written word, and comfortable when dealing with major political figures, public audiences, and the media. Their grooming and clothing follow conventional if not stylish middle class fashions. They live fairly normal middle class lives: they marry, buy homes, raise children, and strive for success and attain it. They are professionals at what they do, well-connected to other professionals, and they rise to managerial positions in relatively large organizations. Their leaders have won public recognition as authors and politicians, recognition founded not on sudden popularity but on years of effort and hard work. One might say that these people are simply more successful and more political than other members of their class. And one must at least surmise that their middle class backgrounds, lifestyles, and successes are somehow sources of their radicalism rather than something alien to it. The media portraits begged this question but conventional wisdom stood in the way of asking it.

Of course, the question can be avoided by writing off the relationship between Santa Monica's affluent middle class and the radicals as a scientific measurement problem. The press may have gotten the right dimensions of Santa Monica's middle class activists but it completely misjudged their "radicalism." A more accurate reading might be that there is no relationship between the middle class and radicals because Santa Monica's activists were not *truly* radicals. Or as some leftwing critics put it sarcastically, they were "quiche and perrier" radicals. This was the predominant viewpoint of America's leftwing intellectual community.

Quiche and Perrier Radicalism

One might have expected events in Santa Monica to generate considerable interest among the American left intelligensia. Here was a rare example of success to be cherished. Perhaps one could learn some strategic lessons about mobilizing the American heartland. At the least, leftwing intellectuals might have been curious about the contrast between Santa Monica's shift to the left and neighboring Pacific Palisades' Ronald Reagan bringing new conservative energy to Washington, D.C. In fact, radical thinkers showed little interest in Santa Monica and those who did felt little of importance was happening there. The view from the left, overall, was that Santa Monica was another manifestation of liberal reformism that would be easily accommodated by the capitalist system.

Lack of leftwing interest was manifested in the fact that individuals directly involved in Santa Monica politics were the ones mainly responsible for getting out the word; left intellectuals were not flocking to the city. Further, these individuals did not doubt their own radical credentials and consequently did not shape their analyses to support them. Derek Shearer wrote an article for *Social Policy* that identified the local left as "progressives" and the movement as "urban populism."[28] Ruth Yannatta Goldway did a *Playgirl* piece—which did not endear her to local feminists—on women in politics in which she identified herself as a member of a coalition "designed to humanize the quality of human life."[29] CED activist Maurice Zeitlin reported on local events in *The Nation*, where he labeled the local left as a "progressive political coalition" and as a "liberal-radical coalition that works."[30] Allan Heskin, who set up a community development corporation in Santa Monica, coauthored an article for the Union for Radical Political Economics (URPE) *Newsletter* that relied on terms such as progressives, economic democrats, and social democrats.[31] Heskin later published a book on the Santa

movements to succeed on their own terms, they will end up *stabilizing* the very corporate power structure they ostensibly set out to oppose."[43] Santa Monica's "ostensible" radicals, alas, turned out to be flirting with counterrevolution.

The core insight in this leftwing analysis, never understood by the media, was that the Santa Monica left had no direct relationship to socialism or proletarian consciousness. Santa Monica was, in fact, too well endowed to serve as a model for the struggle between the captains of industry and the impoverished working class and, as far as I know, no one in Santa Monica saw themselves as experimenting with marxist upheaval. At most, one might project a possible link between Santa Monica events and some future movement for democratic socialism, but that is a projection that would have little basis in Santa Monica realities. The problem with this analysis is that it assumes that socialist revolutionism and working class activism are the measure of *true* radicalism in the United States.

Socialist revolution has rarely been a serious item on the American agenda. Many if not most of the leaders in the struggle between capital and labor in the United States have been middle class intellectuals who claimed to represent the interests of the working class. Harvey Goldberg's anthology of *American Radicals* includes writers, journalists, academics, politicians, and other largely middle class figures who became famous by embracing the working class cause.[44] But did the working class itself embrace it? Aileen Kraditor's study of the Socialist party, Socialist Labor party, and Industrial Workers of the World during the heyday of American socialism suggests that these groups "never enrolled more than a tiny proportion of the American working class."[45] Furthermore, a good many workers, with mixed feeling to be sure, admired the middle class rather than sought to dislodge it from power. "As perceived by real workers," write Richard Sennett and Jonathan Cobb, "cultured people do acquire in their eyes a certain right to act as judges of others, because society has put them in a position to develop their insides."[46] Within this historical context, "radicalism" comes to mean a debate among middle class intellectuals regarding the real interests of the working class—despite the working class's general lack of interest in the debate.

Why does radicalism as a middle class debate persist, given its isolation from everyday politics in the United States? Part of the reason is that American left analyses draw from a European dialogue dominated by thinkers such as Marx, Lenin, Luxemburg, Lukacs, Korsch, Gramsci, Benjamin, Adorno, Horkheimer, Marcuse, Habermas, Poulantzas, Althusser, Foucault, Miliband, Lacan, and other European "superstars" who are at least able to build theory on the foundation of actual socialist movements in their part of the world. More often than not, the Americans take the Europeans' ideas and apply them to the United States without concerning themselves about whether the ideas are appropriate on this side of the Atlantic. Thus, Stanley Aronowitz calls on Lukacs, Korsch, and Marcuse to frame his study of American working class consciousness; Alan Wolfe points to the brilliance of Lukacs and Benjamin and the creativity of Spanish, Italian, and French marxists to justify the teaching of marxism in American classrooms; and scores of leftwing American intellectuals, including Heskin and Boggs, have adopted Gramsci to inform their explorations of American politics, culture, and ideology.[47] Leftwing thinkers continue to debate socialism and the possibility of working class radicalism because their domestic isolation is partly alleviated by their identification with international scholarship.

One of the basic characteristics of major segments of the modern American middle class is precisely this identification with an international world of ideas that cuts across even iron and bamboo curtains. American scholars and scientists share ideas in international journals and conferences; American journalists easily move between the world's capitals; American writers and entertainers ply their trades anywhere that audience demand can be encouraged; and American engineers and managers supervise major construction projects that include refineries in reactionary Middle East countries and hotels in the communist People's Republic of China. Thus, American radicalism understood as a middle class debate can be seen as another manifestation of the internationalization of middle class intelligensia.

Consequently, one may draw from the leftwing analyses of Santa Monica two implications other than that the local left was not truly radical. First, what the American left takes as radicalism may tell us more about middle class intellectuals and European politics than about the political and ideological spectrum in the United States. Second, it is conceivable that radicalism in an American context has little to do with socialist revolution or proletarian consciousness. We do not know what an indigenous American radicalism is, but we can at least consider the marriage between Santa Monica's affluent middle class and its leftwing activists as a possible candidate. In fact, it is a very good candidate.

Indigenous Radicalism

Is the American middle class inextricably bound to capitalism, ensnared in rapacious individualism, and thus committed to defending the status quo against the claims of radicals? This is certainly the shared assumption of many American scholars, journalists, and leftwing intellectuals; and the pervasiveness of this assumption explains why the major media saw Santa Monica's liaison with leftwing activists as an idiosyncrasy; and why the left did not consider it particularly radical. I know of only one article that hinted that the middle class might be more complex than conventional stereotypes, that American radicalism might be more than socialism, and that Santa Monica events had a deeper significance. It is appropriate that the article appeared in *Mother Jones.*

Mother Jones is a monthly intended to combine middle class appeal and leftwing politics. Editor Deirdre English states that the magazine is aimed at "the first post-television generation (the median age of our readers is now a ripe-old 33)." Capturing this audience requires high tech journalism, including "grabby graphics, glossy paper, four-color printing, and a lot of laughs." The art director who "pioneered the packaging of *Mother Jones*," English continues, "insisted on a design concept that would lead 'to the coffee table, not the garbage can.'"[48] The magazine does personality profiles, stories on David-versus-Goliath conflicts, and investigative journalism of human interest value. Its writers avoid jargon and usually maintain a journalistic style that is smooth, easily understood, and concrete rather than abstract or philosophical. The magazine is generally leftist but has no discernible ideological line per se. Its content spans neoliberal economist Lester Thurow as well as *Socialist Review* perspectives, the politics of gender and love as well as debates over labor, nuclear disarmament, civil liberties, grassroots activism, and the vast range of issues that interest politically thoughtful people. One might measure its "success" by its ability to reach mass audiences and legitimate radical sensibilities that rarely surface in *Time* magazine.

Mother Jones did a one-page article on Santa Monica entitled "You *Can* Win City Hall."[49] Immediately below the title was a quarter-page picture of Ruth Yannatta Goldway and Derek Shearer, an all-American couple beaming with civic pride. The message, hinted at in the title, was articulated in the second paragraph: "It was no fluke; Santa Monica is mainstream, say Goldway and Shearer, and what worked here can work in cities across the country, or even on a national scale." Shearer was then quoted as saying, "I think that we are evidence that if you work hard enough on it, you can win." The author framed the rest of the story, "This is not a humble statement. Can it be true?" What followed was a brief history of Santa Monica politics, the left's electoral victories, and its accomplishments to date. No mention was made of the difficulties the Santa Monica activists encountered since their first day in office, implicitly suggesting that they could overcome all barriers. The author left us with no room for doubt: "As the sportswriters say, these people have come to play." In a single page, the reader was overwhelmed by middle class optimism, achievement, efficacy, self-confidence, and certainty that hard work is rewarded.

What were the rewards? The article dished out an ad hoc menu of leftwing causes in no particular order: consumerism, economic democracy, opposition to big money and corrupt government, rent control, decent neighborhoods, the new left, Democrats, feminism, environmentalism, trade unionism, seniors' rights, neighborhood organizing, antinuclear activism, El Salvador, and controlled development. If there was any doubt that the Santa Monica left was really radical, the author quelled it in his introduction of the opposition that "redbaited the lefties unmercifully and outspent them three to one." While leftwing intellectuals would point out the absence of theoretical coherence and the presence of reformist tendencies, middle class audiences were more likely to find some issues that directly concerned them and learn that their own participation could expand the range of political options in existence. A more accurate title for this story might have been "The Middle Class *Can* Win City Hall."

Unlike other coverage, the *Mother Jones* article implicitly recognized an anomaly between conventional wisdom and Santa Monica politics. Why should the middle class want to win city hall? Doesn't it already control it? The inference is that middle America is not all smug contentment because it is not in control. Why should the middle class ally itself with radicals to achieve victory? Aren't middle America's interests bound to conventional Democratic and Republican party politics? The article hinted that the middle class has a stake in broadening what it considers legitimate politics and in considering leftwing alternatives. However, the *Mother Jones* piece did no more than recognize, infer, and hint. Nor could it do otherwise unless there were an alternative to conventional wisdom that begins to explain a possible relationship between the American middle class and radicalism. Let me suggest the basis for such an alternative.

In her study of American beliefs on *What's Fair*, Jennifer Hochschild quotes an individual descended from a long line of affluent middle class professionals:

> On the one hand, the government should not hand everybody everything and say "Hey, here's your cupcake—be happy! What else do you want? I've just given you a cupcake." Good Lord! On the other hand, it should provide a level beneath which people should not be allowed to drop. Setting that level at mere survival is insufficient. Decency, humanity would say that you have to do more than that. "Minimal" to me would be enough support so that people could live with reasonable dignity. Dignity—that really says it. People are entitled to live with self-respect and the respect of other people. They're entitled to be free from the anxiety of a pauper state, a dependent state.[50]

At first glance, this statement nicely fits the capitalist mold of Protestant Ethic individualism, materialism, and perhaps welfare state reformism. One can reasonably assume that the speaker is antisocialist as well. I believe, however, that this reading is grossly simplistic.

The speaker is also concerned with serious moral issues that do not automatically lend support to capitalism or socialism and that do not assume that those two options are the only ones. He is concerned with the worth of labor, decency, dignity, self-respect, and independence as human entitlements. These values are as central to Jeffersonian liberalism as they are to Marxian socialism as they are to the mainstream of middle class American culture. Indeed, these are the same values that middle class scholars, journalists, and leftwing intellectuals draw on when they participate in the national pastime of criticizing crass materialism among the American bourgeoisie. George Orwell put it this way, "As for the word 'bourgeois,' it is used almost exclusively by people who are of bourgeois origin themselves."[51] If middle class intellectuals are somehow able to avoid the crass materialism of their own class (which is debatable regardless of their ideology) and validate moral norms, for example, that equate intelligence and public service with dignity and decency, then perhaps other members of their class can do the same.

Historically, the middle class that emerged with modern American capitalism at the turn of the century has from the start had an ambivalent relationship with the capitalist system. As we will see, middle class support for the capitalist marketplace has persisted alongside middle class claims to moral decency subverted by the marketplace. It is mostly true that middle class Americans have resolved their ambivalence in favor of prevailing power structures but they have usually done so in ways that preserve contradictory values. Where conventional wisdom errs is in its assumption that middle class Americans support some version of the status quo inevitably rather than as a function of specific historical forces. In the next chapter, I will trace the evolution of Santa Monica's affluent middle class to identify a more general American phenomenon: today's middle class is on the defensive, forced to tally the costs of its material success in terms of significant moral defeats. And one middle class response is to investigate radical political alternatives, both right and left.

Perhaps part of the reason that the American middle class has so long persisted in its ambivalent loyalty to prevailing power structures is that its own intellectuals have not developed relevant or coherent alternatives. As noted earlier, middle class intellectuals have usually identified middle class interests with capitalism, sometimes as a lesser evil, while leftwing intellectuals have portrayed the middle class as in the enemy's camp, in opposition to working class socialism. These alternatives offer little solace to a discontented middle class: it must live with its discontents under capitalism or suffer class suicide under socialism. More important, these alternatives are not particularly relevant to middle class discontents. Capitalism and socialism are primarily *economic* alternatives founded on issues that are crucial to owners who want to protect accumulated wealth and workers who have yet to accumulate wealth. But such economic perspectives may be secondary to an affluent middle class population whose most pressing concerns are moral and political. In Chapter 3, I will trace the growth of the Santa Monica left, again to identify a more general American phenomenon: the middle class has spawned its own version of radicalism that appeals directly to moral and political rather than economic values.

Once it is established that the terms "middle class" and "radicalism" are not mutually exclusive but are integrally related in modern American society, then we can investigate the nature of the relationship and its potential impact for social and political life in the years ahead. Conventional wisdom notwithstanding, we will see that the emergence of *middle class radicalism* in Santa Monica may indicate not "the revolution" but a peculiarly indigenous revolution brewing where the rainbow ends.

2

The Highest Bidder

At one o'clock we will sell at public outcry to the highest bidder, the Pacific Ocean, draped with a western sky of scarlet and gold; we will sell a bay filled with white-winged ships; we will sell a southern horizon, rimmed with a choice collection of purple mountains, carved in castles and turrets and domes; we will sell a frostless, bracing, warm, yet languid air, braided in and out with sunshine and odored with the breath of flowers. The purchaser of this job lot of climate and scenery will be presented with a deed of land 50 by 50 feet. The title to the ocean and the sunset, the hills and the clouds, the breath of life-giving ozone and the song of birds is guaranteed by the beneficent God who bestowed them in all their beauty.

Tom Fitch, announcing the auction of
the first Santa Monica lots in 1875 [1]

Southern California was founded on corporate promotion schemes that converted the climate into a marketable commodity and made rapid expansion the main business of the region. Santa Monica was also produced by corporate entrepreneurs who sought to control the city's future in order to reap monopolistic profits. But their bid failed, and early Santa Monica history is marked by a small town autonomy and a small business dominance that stood in sharp contrast to nearby burgeoning Los Angeles. Not until the post-World War II period was Santa Monica caught up in the maelstrom of regional growth. Local autonomy was eroded as the regional marketplace overspilled local boundaries; small business dominance was undermined by an influx of middle class professionals and managers, themselves escaping an unhappy existence in the metropolis. The result, by the 1970s, was a fragmented social structure and a political vacuum that created new opportunities for radicals who could appeal to middle class discontents.

Corporate Dreams

Local historians disagree about which entrepreneurs should be considered Santa Monica's official founders. The first candidates are Ysidro Reyes and Francisco Marquez, "enterprising harness makers" who won the favor of the king of Spain and were granted title to the 6,400-acre Rancho Boca de Santa Monica in 1838. A great great grandson claims that these founders started a hospitable community that was occasionally forced on the defensive by outsiders, marauding Indians and gringo bandits.[2] The Anglicized history begins with Colonel Robert S. Baker and Arcadia Bandini de Baker. Colonel Baker sought his fortune in the 1849 goldrush in Northern California but found it instead in the cattle and sheep trade. He invested in landholdings (Bakersfield, California, is named after him) and in 1872 purchased half of Rancho Boca de Santa Monica. He consolidated his Southern California empire when he married Arcadia Bandini de Stearns, whose deceased husband left her heiress to the largest individual landholdings in California history. Thus one local historian suggests that "Arcadia Bandini de Baker and Colonel Robert Baker were the real mother and father of Santa Monica."[3] Nonetheless, in 1874, the Bakers took on a partner in their Santa Monica Land and Water Company and it is the partner's bust as official city founder that now graces the Santa Monica Mall.

John P. Jones was a corporate dreamer worthy of the Robber Baron Age. He came to California in 1850 seeking wealth in silver rather than gold and eventually cashed in on Nevada's fabulous Comstock Lode. Jones moved to Nevada in 1868, a man of substantial wealth and influence, and was elected by the state legislature to the U.S. Senate in 1873. Jones "won" his Senate seat "at a reputed cost of $500,000."[4] With wealth, position, and ambition, he hatched a scheme to make himself one of the most powerful men in America.

Jones invested heavily in California's Panamint mines knowing that their full profit potential could not be realized until the silver could be easily transported to the ocean and shipped to major markets. His plan was to build an integrated corporate monopoly that would include his own mines, his own railroad to the ocean, his own seaport city, his own deep sea harbor, and thus his own control of West Coast shipping. Jones's major problem was that he would be in competition with the Southern Pacific Railroad, the fabled "Octopus" that wrote the book on integrated corporate monopoly west of the Mississippi River. The Southern Pacific owned the only rail line between Los Angeles and the Wilmington-San Pedro harbor twenty-five miles to the south, controlled the harbor facilities, and dominated regional shipping. It would not look kindly on Jones's competitive bid.

Jones's strategy was to bypass the Southern Pacific as much as possible. He could build a railroad between the Panamint mines and Los Angeles without raising too much fuss because the Southern Pacific was concentrating its expansion efforts on a line between Los Angeles and San Francisco. Once Jones's railroad reached Los Angeles, it would veer west toward the Santa Monica Bay rather than south in direct competition with the Southern Pacific line to the San Pedro harbor. Jones purchased from Colonel Baker a three-quarter interest in his Santa Monica landholdings, intending to transform what was essentially a weekend campsite into a major seaport city. Jones would then build a wharf with docking facilities for loading and unloading deep sea vessels off of the Santa Monica coastline; and he would use his political influence in the U.S. Senate to win a federal appropriation for a breakwater that would make Santa Monica the major deep sea harbor for all Southern California.

In 1875, Jones laid out the town of Santa Monica, registered it with the government, and hired noted auctioneer Colonel Tom Fitch to begin selling lots. He also began construction on his wharf and docking facilities, and on his Los Angeles and Independence Railroad that would link the Santa Monica harbor to Los Angeles and then to the Panamint mines. Before the year was out, his 1,740-foot wharf was operational, complete with warehouse and depot; excursion trains were running between Santa Monica and Los Angeles; and advertisements appeared in newspapers throughout the United States inviting West Coast steamers to dock at the new harbor and businessmen to invest in the new seaport city. The promotional literature called Santa Monica "the Zenith City by the Sunset Sea."[5]

The sun set on Jones's scheme almost immediately. The Southern Pacific cut its own rates and applied considerable pressure on shipping companies to continue to dock in San Pedro rather than Santa Monica.

Jones expected this and confidently predicted that he would "ruin" the other harbor and that Santa Monica would become the "logical metropolitan center of California."[6] Jones was losing money at the moment but figured that the growth of the shipping trade and the town of Santa Monica would convert temporary losses into long-term profits. What he did not figure on, however, was that his Comstock mines would crash, his bank would close, and his financial support would disappear in a statewide depression, or that his Panamint mines would fail and his construction on the railroad from the mines to Los Angeles would be stopped for lack of funds. By 1877, Jones's dream of an integrated corporate monopoly was shattered.

It was time to salvage his investment. He hoped to safeguard his Santa Monica holdings by selling his wharf and railroad to someone who would build a future for his new seaport city. He approached the county of Los Angeles but it feared offending the powerful Southern Pacific; he approached Jay Gould of the Union Pacific Railroad but Gould was not convinced that investments west of Los Angeles would pay off. Jones had no choice other than to deal with the Southern Pacific, which, having eliminated the threat of Jones's competition, had no particular interest in his wharf and railroad. However, Collis P. Huntington persuaded his Southern Pacific partners that they could get the railroad dirt cheap (at one-fourth of Jones's investment) and simultaneously "keep the Nevada legislator friendly, in view of his influence in the United States Senate."[7] Jones retained his land interests in Santa Monica, eventually acquired a local bank that his son would manage one day, but left the city's future to the Southern Pacific.

The Southern Pacific had no plans for Santa Monica; its purchase was largely a political one. In 1878, when Southern Pacific engineers determined that the wharf needed expensive repairs, the corporation decided that it was simply cheaper to dismantle the wharf. The Los Angeles and Independence Railroad, whose service had deteriorated during Jones's downfall, now ran on a reduced schedule, bringing weekend campers and beachgoers rather than silver, businessmen, and buyers who were to have made Jones's dream metropolis into a reality. What happened to the individuals who had invested in Santa Monica's future? "A pervasive gloom now settled over Santa Monica, and the town went into a 'slump.' Business failures were common, property values sank, and within a few months the population had dropped from 1000 to 350 citizens."[8] Santa Monica seemed to have become a silver miner's ghost town.

This fate was avoided, however, by a new twist in Southern California's railroad wars. In 1890, a powerful syndicate of St. Louis capitalists decided to challenge the Southern Pacific's hegemony by laying its own track to the San Pedro harbor and building its own docking facilities there. The Southern Pacific in essence resurrected Jones's old scheme as a competitive response. Collis Huntington drew up plans to construct a deep sea harbor off Santa Monica that it could monopolize by virtue of its ownership of Jones's Los Angeles and Independence Railroad. Huntington also began a campaign to discredit as unsafe the harbor facilities in San Pedro where the Southern Pacific had once had uncontested control. Ultimately, Southern California shipping would be shifted to the new harbor, and Santa Monica, once again, was slated as a high growth metropolis. By 1893, the Southern Pacific had completed construction of a new 4,500-foot Long Wharf just north of Santa Monica, bought up land throughout the area, and marshaled enough congressional support (including that of Senator John P. Jones and Senator Cornelius Cole, who also had land investments in Santa Monica) to prevent federal appropriations for a breakwater in San Pedro. Huntington meanwhile courted the support of the Los Angeles business community and other influential politicians to win federal appropriations for building a sheltered deep sea harbor off Santa Monica.

Huntington called the new harbor "Port Los Angeles" in the hope that Santa Monica would become the commercial gateway for Los Angeles and all of Southern California. He arranged tours of the Long Wharf for businessmen, buyers, and politicians; he ran excursions for tourists who were also potential investors. Ships once again began to dock at Santa Monica and the city itself went through its second wave of growth. Huntington's scheme might have worked were it not for the fact that the St. Louis capitalists had a major ally in the person of General Harrison Gray Otis, founder of the Los Angeles *Times* and the key single figure in the making of Southern California. Otis put together a coalition of powerful business interests and politicians (including California U.S. Senator Stephen White) to stop the Southern Pacific by ensuring that federal appropriations went to the San Pedro harbor. Otis's public posture was nicely summarized in this *Times* editorial of 1892:

> Is any individual or corporation to have a monopoly on this deep sea harbor when it is constructed? If it is found as a result of investigation that the Southern Pacific has taken in advance a mortgage (death grip) on the forthcoming artificial harbor at Santa Monica, then we say let us not give any assistance to the scheme. On the contrary, let us fight with all the self-respecting manhood we have. Better that the deep sea harbor be defeated altogether than that the government should be encouraged to appropriate $4 million or $5 million for the exclusive benefit of this already overgrown and too dictatorial corporation.[9]

In 1895, the Otis coalition founded the Free Harbor League, determined to win the battle for appropriations in favor of San Pedro, thereby breaking the Southern Pacific stranglehold in Southern California and, not coincidentally, elevating Otis to the position of regional powerbroker.

The struggle between the Huntington and Otis forces raged for nearly a decade, finally being settled on the floor of the U.S. Senate in favor of the Otis camp. Construction of a deep sea harbor at San Pedro began in 1899. A small city similar to Santa Monica, San Pedro would become the site of one of the busiest harbors in the world, a shipping, railroad, and trucking center, and a desirable location for commercial and industrial corporations as well as U.S. military installations that benefitted from proximity to the harbor. San Pedro would be annexed to Los Angeles within a decade of the Senate decision, its local business community intertwined with the large corporations staffed by professionals, rent by trade union struggles, and intermarried to regional, statewide, national, and international political interests. Santa Monica, by contrast, would remain a small, almost premodern town.

Again, those who had invested in Santa Monica's metropolitan future suffered when the Southern Pacific bubble burst. However, the various promotional schemes of Jones and Huntington had produced a steady stream of tourists and small businesses plying the tourist trade that were to outlast corporate dreams. By 1900, Santa Monica had become a "town whose image of itself had firmed into that of a year-round resort." [10] The Long Wharf was eventually dismantled only to be replaced by several amusement piers featuring theaters, ballrooms, auditoriums, roller coasters, arcades, and a famous merry-go-round where actors Paul Newman and Robert Redford would plot *The Sting* more than a half-century later. The Los Angeles and Independence Railroad was incorporated into the Pacific Electric Railway Company, whose excursion trains brought weekenders to Santa Monica for boat rides, balloon rides, picnicking, swimming, and dining. The trains also brought tourists to other oceanside resorts such as Venice and Redondo Beach, making Santa Monica one of several beach cities living off oceanfront amenities. Santa Monica's 1900 population was 3,000 residents, increasing to 7,800 by 1910, and growing gradually thereafter.

Two beliefs developed as part of the local culture. People who moved into Santa Monica assimilated those beliefs and others moved in because such beliefs were congenial to their values. First, Santa Monicans felt that being the plaything of big corporate entrepreneurs and power politics was unpleasant. The promotions and promises of outsiders resulted in bankruptcies and deteriorating property values for insiders. Santa Monicans developed something of a fortress mentality. Local autonomy became dear, protected by townspeople who were to withstand the Los Angeles annexationists who gobbled up neighboring cities in the 1920s. The abiding symbol of the Santa Monica community became the Municipal Pier or simply "The Pier," a reminder of the corporate machinations of the past and a rallying point against outside interests in the future. Second, Santa Monicans believed that gradual rather than rapid economic growth was consistent with community interests. Not only was gradual growth a foil to would-be corporate dreamers; it was also consistent with a resort economy dependent on an attractive local environment that would lure tourists wishing to escape the ferro-concrete rat race that Los Angeles was becoming. Santa Monica could survive, even thrive, as long as it offered an alternative to life in the neighboring marketplace.

In any case, these lessons became a part of Santa Monica's local folklore and are still manifest today. A recent article in the *Santa Monica Realtor*, a local trade publication, carries on the legacy:

> Santa Monica has always been noted for its strong community spirit. Surely the fact that it is an incorporated city, apart from the Los Angeles Metropolitan System, has contributed to this identity. But more important is that Santa Monicans believe their community has a character all its own. . . . What are the distinctive qualities that describe Santa Monica? Its location where the mountains meet the sea, its temperate weather. But as soon as we have named the natural givens, we begin to list the very elements of what one would call its history: the neighborhoods, each with a different development and atmosphere; personages who have lived here for many years and placed their stamp on the social life of the city; the familiar surroundings, the parks, long established stores.[11]

The city's cultural history is that of an independent small town protecting the virtues of an earlier age against the likes of monolithic, always-growing Los Angeles. And for the first half of the twentieth century, that history was guided by the politics of "conservative" small businessmen.

The Virtues of an Earlier Age

One notable Santa Monica small businessman was Harry C. Henshey, who started Henshey's Department Store in 1925. Henshey is fondly remembered as a store owner who "knew every employee in his store; he made a point to go around and talk to people." He is also remembered as a concerned citizen. Henshey was involved in the local chapters of the American Red Cross and the Boys' Club. He encouraged his employees to be active in the community and so they were, serving in voluntary associations and local politics. Herbert Spurgin, Henshey's operations manager as well as Santa Monica's former mayor, stated, "We feel that this store is a semi-civic institution. . . . We have a tremendous loyalty in our customers. The fourth generation of customers is coming in."[12] In 1985, Henshey's is one of the few independent department stores left in California.

Small businessmen such as Henshey remind us that the American Dream has a moral component as well as an economic one. Early dreammakers, including Horatio Alger, Andrew Carnegie, and Russell Conwell, were Christians. They promoted individualism, self-reliance and self-help, and personal responsibility as Christian virtues. Certainly the practice of these virtues might lead to wealth but wealth was not intended to serve greed or hedonism. Wealth was viewed as an instrument for doing good works, for promoting Christian stewardship, charity, and neighborly concern. Alger's heroes, for example, needed a helping hand on their roads to success and were expected to reciprocate by helping others take the same route.[13]

The same virtues reappeared in the more secular versions of the American Dream. Tenants hoped to become landowners and homeowners, partly for economic reasons but also to gain greater control over their working and living conditions. Lower class and working class people often wanted to become small businessmen for reasons beyond wealth. They admired small businessmen's ability to set their own hours, make their own workplace decisions, reap the full rewards of their labors, and thus shape their own futures; they also envied small businessmen's ability to take an active role in the community, perhaps serving as organizers of social activities, voluntary associations, or public life.[14] From below, small businessmen appeared to have succeeded in terms of wealth, autonomy, and social respect, and their status was not so distant that others could not imagine entering into their ranks.

In general, small businessmen were attached to the morality of the American Dream. Some viewed themselves as Christians practicing virtue in the pursuit and use of wealth; some had risen from the lower classes hoping to fulfill dreams of economic security, individual autonomy, and social service. Many came from religious, racial, ethnic, or neighborhood groups that supported their businesses and, in return, expected personalized service from their businessmen. The ability of small businessmen to sustain the moral side of the American Dream, however, was contingent on the nature of the marketplace in which they operated.

Traditionally, small businessmen have been located at the fringes of the marketplace where profit margins are slim and economic survival is uncertain. Their modest initial investments could be matched by others wishing to set up competing businesses, and new competition almost always meant trouble. Small businessmen who survived the competition and even thrived under its pressure soon faced a new dilemma. Their success invited emerging chain-store operations to set up in the neighborhood. Modest owners might meet the threat through considerable self-sacrifice involving hard work, longer hours, family loans, and personal financial losses to ensure the fiscal stability of the business. They might redouble their efforts to keep and attract customers by developing an extrasensitivity to the subtleties of their local clientele, providing specialized services and personalized attention. Or they might go out of their way to build a critical mass of customer loyalty, allowing their places of business to become neighborhood gathering spots, maybe offering convenient check-cashing services or immediately accessible sources of local credit.

Small businessmen may see growth in the local marketplace as a grave risk that attracts more powerful competitors and disrupts residential patterns of customer loyalty. But small businessmen can also gamble on growth in the hope of profiting from it. Win or lose, however, these businessmen discover that they may no longer be their own bosses. They need reliable information on the likely contours of growth, the services of accountants and lawyers to protect new investments, and maybe bank financing to get into the race for greater prosperity. Thus they must entrust their futures to others who may in fact prove untrustworthy. Reliable information in high growth areas is a dear commodity. Sometimes it must be bought at a price, such as playing according to the rules of major insiders, and sometimes it proves wrong, for example, when major players drop out at the last moment. Dependence on professionals is also chancy. They occasionally err, often get involved in conflicts of interest that usually benefit their largest clients, and almost certainly mire small businessmen in a world of jargon, clauses, and legalities that they cannot understand. Furthermore, small businessmen who mortgage their futures to banks and other financial interests sacrifice their autonomy as "independent" businessmen by transferring some of their decisionmaking power to large institutions that may be willing to sacrifice the little guy in order to turn a big deal. Should small businessmen gamble on growth, knowing that the returns are uncertain but the loss of autonomy is guaranteed?

In relatively small to moderate-sized towns, there is an added dimension to small businessmen's calculations. If they are truly gamblers, then why locate their businesses outside the major marketplaces of big cities such as Los Angeles? One reason is that they are born into these towns, involved in traditional networks of social relations that keep them there, and prefer to live and work in familiar surroundings. Another possibility is that they moved away from the metropolitan arenas in the hope of finding a community where people know one another, cooperate with one another, and live peacefully in proximity to one another. What can happen to their community when it is subjected to the forces of high growth capitalism? Garry Wills provides the answer in his *Confessions of a Conservative*:

> Capitalism is of its nature expansive, risk-taking, wanting new markets and materials and products. It has wrought more change in the modern world—often senseless change—than any revolutionary force. It overturns and runs on. It has of itself no sense of tradition. It tears down the old to keep building the new in a perpetual gamble on tomorrow. It is of all things the least worthy of the name conservative.[15]

Small businessmen who locate their sense of self-worth and social respect in traditional community relations will have serious hesitations when faced with the prospect of impersonal marketplace forces managed by professionals and big business types. Moreover, as community residents, they will be less than delighted with the prospect of a high growth revolution that promises a huge apartment complex next to their homes, more crime in their neighborhoods, and more traffic congestion on the way to their shops.

Given fears of economic risks, dependence, and disruption of community life, many small businessmen may opt for conserving traditional local life against the expanding marketplace. Nancy Eberle provides an example taken from Galena, Illinois.[16] Robert Buehler, president of a large corporation headquartered in Chicago, took up residence in the city and soon became the central figure in an effort to revitalize Galena's economy. He gained access to $2 million to underwrite economic redevelopment. His plan was put to a local referendum and was decisively defeated by a 1,363 to 340 margin. Some local businessmen told Buehler, "You're destroying our business," and they spearheaded a drive—complete with their own newspaper and door-to-door canvassing—that effectively mobilized Galena residents against the uncertainties and social erosion that would accompany growth.

Small businessmen's impulse to conserve the traditional fabric of local life—their "traditional" conservativism—is not easily articulated in the twentieth century when the *official* conservative creed involves support for an unrestricted free marketplace against government intervention. Nonetheless, it does get communicated. In his study of the middle class in medium-sized cities, C. Wright Mills interviewed small businessmen who almost automatically supported the free market. When pressed, however, they admitted, "Well, you see, in certain lines, it's no good if there are too many businesses." When pressed further, they sometimes stated that the survival of small businesses depends on having no competition at all. "In the dream life of the little businessman," Mills concluded, "the sure fix is replacing the open market."[17] Do small businessmen turn to government to conserve traditional virtues against encroaching market forces? Economist Lester Thurow puts it this way: "Political speeches are still offered up to the totem of unplanned, competitive economies, but at the first sign of trouble everyone runs to the government looking for protection."[18] Small businessmen are as likely as anyone else to employ political authority in their own behalf when they feel that their investments in the American Dream are endangered, even by the free market that they otherwise honor.

Santa Monica's business community was especially likely to harbor a streak of traditional conservative morality. If they did not remember the early corporate promotion schemes that caused business bankruptcies and social disruption, they were nonetheless involved in a resort economy that depended on conserving an attractive environment that distinguished the city from Los Angeles. Further, Santa Monica's small businessmen were always willing to work with government and accede to its intervention in the marketplace. They supported city-owned and operated amusement piers that helped the resort economy; they welcomed New Deal programs that enhanced the local environment, including a Federal Arts Project that placed a statue of the city's namesake in Palisades Park and a Federal Emergency Public Works Project that built Santa Monica's impressive city hall. Under their tutelage, Santa Monica residents carried on traditions of gradual economic growth, individual and community autonomy, and a pride in neighborhood that comes with a relatively stable population.

Santa Monica peacefully evolved from a small resort town into a middle-sized city of 50,000 residents by 1940. It was still fifteen miles away from central Los Angeles—too far to attract more than a gentle stream of new residents, businesses, investors, or tourists. A few Hollywood figures bought oceanfront homes on Santa Monica's Gold Coast and some Los Angeles garment workers retired to modest bungalows and apartments in Santa Monica's Ocean Park neighborhood. But rapid growth was not a threat as long as Santa Monica remained a distant outpost of the metropolitan Los Angeles market.

But how long could Santa Monica remain a remote community? As World War II approached, the relatively small Douglas Aircraft plant on the city's eastern extremity expanded to meet wartime demand, employing nearly 40,000 workers at the height of production. This wartime industry soon declined, relocating to other parts of the region along with the workers that it had hired. For some small businessmen, however, this experience hinted at new economic opportunities on the horizon, ones that could be mined by their enrollment in "the growth machine."

The Growth Machine

Opportunities for expansion were enthusiastically seized upon by the Babbitts of Santa Monica. George Babbitt was Sinclair Lewis's fictional model of the small businessman who outgrew traditional conservativism and gambled on growth.[19] Babbitt was a real estate broker whose code of ethics was the boosterism of personal self-aggrandizement; whose profits depended on entrepreneurialism, new developments, and continuous economic growth; and whose advocacy of economic progress exaggerated the modern conservative's promarketplace and antigovernment ideology. Babbitt represented the thorough materialist who discovered great poetry in advertising jingles. In the 1930s, he would have considered the New Deal to be a communist plot; in the 1980s, he might have told CBS "60 Minutes" reporters that the red menace had landed in Santa

Monica. Babbitt stood as a symbol of the American Dream stripped of all moral content.

Small businessmen like Babbitt are natural constituents of what Harvey Molotch calls "the growth machine" that came to dominate municipal economies and polities as the twentieth century moved forward.[20] Such small businessmen profit by the expansion of nearby basic industries, growth in the labor force, more retail and wholesale commerce, intensified land development, and expanding financial activities. Their own investments become more valuable when land and housing as well as goods and services are in high demand as a result of growth; their own economic opportunities are enhanced to the extent that they get in on the groundfloor decisions that bring growth. These entrepreneurs ally themselves with the business groups, banks, and developers that, taken together, engineer the growth machine.

The mechanism has several parts. It often includes service clubs and civic organizations that strive to make the local community more attractive, provide business contacts, and organize forums on local policy questions. A service club that runs a fund drive for a new youth recreation center, for example, helps to make the community more attractive to prospective homebuyers, who are also prospective consumers of local wares. The growth machine includes business agencies such as the Chamber of Commerce that specifically function to boost the local economy. These agencies may advertise the city as a good place to live, work, and raise a family; they may organize drives to lure investors; and they often serve as political pressure groups, kitchen cabinets, and training and recruitment centers for the next generation of municipal leadership. The growth machine may also be a steering mechanism for local government, pointing it toward favorable tax treatment for business and public expenditures that improve the municipal services basic to business expansion.

The small business constituents of the growth machine do not necessarily agree on what growth policies are in their common interest. A housing development here or a road expansion there may advantage some businesses but harm others. Usually, policy disagreements can be settled peacefully. The Chamber of Commerce may be the sounding board for studying options, forging compromises, and making trade-offs. Local newspapers can function as forums for defining issues, weighing contending possibilities, and pointing dialogue toward consensus. Especially stubborn policy disputes may be subject to binding arbitration processes that heal cleavages. Banks have the financial leverage to settle many conflicts and municipal governments have the political authority to make land use decisions to settle other disagreements; and both banks and governments generally try to strike an agreeable bargain among disputants to assure the continuing patronage and support of the entire business community.[21]

Local businessmen who distinguish themselves in growth machine activities sometimes become what Manuel Castells calls the "local notables" who link the municipality to "the regional system of class alliances and the power bloc of the nation as a whole."[22] The local notables may serve in regional political parties, statewide trade associations, and national business lobbies. Beyond greater social status, their service outside the local community can be quite profitable. It gives them access to considerable influence, resources, and business contacts as well as political pull that can be parlayed into new economic opportunities, more weight in local policy decisions, and perhaps growth in the home marketplace.

Unlike traditionalists, these "modern" conservatives are interested in conserving the free marketplace, its gambles and revolutionizing effects, against government constraints. Their ideology is the machismo of the entrepreneur. They view small business in terms of new initiatives, innovation, and knowhow tested in competitive struggles where the risks of losing enrich the self-satisfaction of winning. They look on government as a necessary evil, necessary to protect individual freedom in the marketplace but evil when it exercises control over the marketplace. Their modern conservativism is summarized in these remarks by the manager of a small business trade association: "Small business. . . . What is it? It is American Business. . . . It is the reason we have the American Way!"[23] Small business success is American success, proof positive that rugged individualism is superior to all forms of public or collective decisionmaking. Never mind the *fact* that small business in the twentieth century has become a diminishing component of American business.

Early Santa Monica history had its growth machine boosters who also believed in rugged individualism. They took the initiative to organize service clubs, civic organizations, and the Santa Monica Area Chamber of Commerce; they encouraged economic development in the city and boosted it as a good place to live and work, invest and visit. They guided city government, which, for its part, enacted exceptionally low business fees and lent public legitimacy to private growth ventures. The city's conservative newspaper, homegrown bankers, and local notables played their parts well, minimizing disputes within the business community and overseeing steady economic growth. Part of the reason that they could maintain unity within the business community was that their boosterism never produced enough growth to threaten the economic security, autonomy, and social values of the traditional conservatives in their midst.

When the alliance between the moralists and the materialists was actually tested by the high growth economy that followed World War II, its weaknesses became apparent. Shopkeepers would be unhappy with high growth that raised their overhead costs and increased their competition, but real estate speculators would enjoy high growth that inflated the value of their investments. Not only would fragmentation in the business community result but, ironically, the growth machine that reveled in the postwar boom would soon lose its grip on city politics.

Postwar Santa Monica

Joel Kotkin and Paul Grabowicz argue that "the transformation of California from lotus land to industrial giant began with the outbreak of World War II."[24] Between 1940 and 1944, more than $800 million was invested in 5,000 industrial plants that sprouted throughout Southern California. Los Angeles's west side was transformed almost overnight from the economic periphery to a major center of large corporations that were to fill more than one-fourth of government airplane orders during the war years. Companies such as Douglas, Hughes, and Northrup sowed the seeds of the region's high technology future while cultivating the growth of a thriving job market within minutes of Santa Monica. The boom inevitably affected Santa Monica, which experienced 40 percent population growth during the decade.

Southern California was also on the brink of the Automobile Age. In the 1930s, General Motors bought up the Pacific Electric Railway system to scrap it. The corporation replaced trains with diesel buses that it manufactured. The buses did not carry freight, so merchants were forced to buy or rent trucks that General Motors also manufactured. The buses were uncomfortable and unreliable, which encouraged Southern Californians to purchase automobiles that General Motors gladly sold to them. The corporation was convicted in 1949 of having conspired to replace municipal transit systems with products that it monopolized. The $5,000 fine, however, did not deter General Motors from continuing its practices or from putting its considerable weight behind the $70 billion Interstate Highway Act that reinforced consumer demand for automobiles by underwriting massive highway construction throughout the United States.[25]

For Santa Monica, the fallout from this corporate maneuvering was the construction of the Santa Monica Freeway in the mid-1960s. The city, already feeling the impact of regional economic boom and population explosion, was now *only* fifteen miles from central Los Angeles, that is, a fifteen-minute commute to the metropolitan marketplace. Furthermore, the freeway was an immediate conduit to the regional maze of freeways that linked all parts of Southern California. It was suddenly convenient for people to settle in a desirable city such as Santa Monica and drive to work in the new nearby industries, central Los Angeles, and even beyond.

The postwar combination of economic boom, population pressure, and automobile culture amounted to an external assault on the integrity of Santa Monica. The city was most vulnerable on the real estate front. Housing demand increased throughout Southern California but especially along the Pacific Ocean. Santa Monica experienced the extraordinary demand that invited rent gouging, arbitrary evictions, condominium conversions, demolition of low and moderate income housing to be replaced by luxury developments, the constant selling and buying of real estate, and skyrocketing prices for land and single-family homes. Santa Monica's growth machine rushed to the party, as did outside investors, developers, and speculators, who saw a chance for quick and easy profits. During a five-year period in the early 1970s, apartment vacancies fell below 5 percent for the first time while speculation in residential income property increased more than 1,000 percent.[26] The anarchy of the real estate market rippled throughout local life.

First, major shifts in Santa Monica's population base occurred. Beginning in the early 1940s, the city attracted more and more middle class professionals and managers who worked in nearby high growth, high technology industries. For these migrants, Santa Monica was a beachfront resort town with all the amenities of an autonomous community: a pleasing small town environment, good schools, parks, entertainment, the beaches, and so forth. Santa Monica's magnetic appeal grew, particularly when the Santa Monica Freeway provided easy access throughout the region and when rapid industrialization, congestion, pollution, and crime provided good reasons for leaving Los Angeles proper. The fact that Santa Monica real estate prices were higher than elsewhere was no deterrent to this affluent middle class population. Professionals and managers had incomes that outpaced inflation and they could even afford to profit from inflation by purchasing land, housing, and income property. Thus, in 1983, a remarkable 11 percent of residents in the city's more affluent neighborhoods owned rental property in the city.[27] By the 1970s, one need not have been an astute observer to see that Santa Monica was undergoing gentrification, that affluent newcomers were replacing less prosperous oldtimers.

Santa Monica's population stabilized in the 80,000s during the 1960s. Consequently, the continuous influx of professionals and managers necessarily meant the loss of older, more stable residents. The Santa Monica Freeway, for example, cut through the city's lower income neighborhoods, eliminating considerable numbers of minority residences. The retired people in the Ocean Park neighborhood, whose numbers had been augmented by the growth of a countercultural enclave, suffered a major redevelopment project that replaced older affordable housing with luxury oceanfront condominiums. Even the more affluent people in Santa Monica's central neighborhoods faced escalating property taxes and rents that pressured them to move elsewhere. In the 1970s alone, Santa Monica lost 3,187 households, "most of them with low, very low, and moderate incomes."[28] Santa Monica's small town reputation as an "All American City" with a population mix representative of the nation as a whole shifted toward the new status of being an intown suburb for the well-to-do.

Second, postwar Santa Monica experienced a significant transformation of its economy. For the city's rugged individualists, growth was a wonderful adventure, especially if one was involved in real estate and banking, had access to investment resources, and liked the risk of investing and getting out before the bubble burst. The real entrepreneur had a chance to grow with the city. However, economic growth proved perilous for Santa Monica's more traditional small businessmen. Shopowners faced higher rents and overhead costs, customer displacement and uncertainty, and new competition from the national chain-store operations that invaded the city. Family businesses on the Santa Monica Mall became more transient and seedy, a process accelerated by the development of a new shopping center in the next block and symbolized by some local residents who came to refer to the old one as "the Mexican Mall." City homeowners tended to be ambivalent about economic growth: it increased their housing values but also their property taxes while eroding their local quality of life as parts of the city became overdeveloped. Thus the 1960s witnessed the onset of a twenty-year battle between growth machine diehards, who wanted to protect and further develop the Santa Monica Airport, and the nearby homeowners, who wanted to limit air traffic and the development of airport land, and even to close down the facility. The local growth machine had increasing difficulty maintaining unity among many small businessmen and homeowners.

Simultaneously, the growth machine's economic might was diminishing. Boosters who invested in growth became more dependent on outside interests. Local entrepreneurs were pressured to sell out to corporate developers with regional, national, or international interests. The local entrepreneurs might feed at corporate troughs but it was the corporations that planned, designed, financed, constructed, and operated the new apartment, condominium, retail, and office complexes that appeared in Santa Monica in the 1960s and 1970s. Meanwhile, Santa Monica was becoming a desirable location for clean or high technology industries. The city had a growing concentration of professionals and managers who staffed these industries; and the city had the environmental amenities that might lure the personnel needed by these industries. A 1982 Chamber of Commerce profile reported that the leading characteristic of the local labor force was the "high proportion of professional, technical, managerial, and white collar" personnel in the area. It also listed Santa Monica's major employers as General Telephone (communications), St. John's Hospital (health care), Systems Development Corporation (computer software), Santa Monica Hospital (health care), Paper Mate (light manufacturing), Rand Corporation (research and policy think tank), Lear Siegler (aerospace), and Pennsylvania Life (insurance).[29] The influence of the local growth machine could have been neutralized by the economic power of the new personnel and corporations should they have decided to exercise it.

Finally, postwar Santa Monica evidenced the first traces of a shift in political attitudes. These new middle class professionals and managers who had migrated to the city were more liberal than the small business-men who ran it. Their liberal attitudes were first manifest in the 1972 presidential election, when they helped to provide a municipal majority for George McGovern. Nonetheless, city politics continued to be dominated by the growth machine despite its fragmented base and eroded economic hegemony. The modern conservatives were able to install a city council led by a bank vice president, two landlords, and three home-owners into the late 1970s. Part of the reason that the growth machine stayed in control so long was that the newer, more affluent migrants were ambivalent about their liberalism.

Ambivalent Liberalism

The rise of large corporations, symbolized in Santa Monica first by Southern Pacific and later by General Telephone, produced a sphere of work for a *new* middle class that Barbara and John Ehrenreich call the "professional managerial class." It now includes "such groups as scientists, engineers, teachers, social workers, writers, accountants, lower- and middle-level managers and administrators, etc.," who comprise roughly one-fourth of the U.S. workforce.[30] The members of this new middle class are primarily "mental" laborers who invest their energies in ideas rather than in the production and distribution of goods. They honor those who investigate new science and technology more than those who peddle for profit. They view themselves as experts who provide services that improve the human condition rather than as hucksters who feed off of it. Politically, the professional managerial class grew up alongside of New Deal liberalism, which was consistent with new middle class values and legitimated those values. This liberalism, however, is an ambivalent attachment to both idealism and materialism.

Ambivalent liberalism is rooted in the evolution of mental labor in the United States. In 1776 Philadelphia, science and rationality were the new revolutionary morality, "the principle expression of civic pride and enlightenment."[31] Ideally, science provided a social identity exclusive of corrupted European traditions; it informed a new politics intended to harmonize republican virtue and democratic freedom; it promised to unveil the relation between nature and civilization to produce a prosperous and egalitarian farm economy. Science would tame the wilderness and serve in the cause of human progress. In actuality, science was immediately put to more practical uses. Philadelphia scientists Benjamin Rush and David Rittenhouse, for example, left off their basic research during the Revolutionary War to develop a new munitions technology, a temporary expedient that would become a worldwide industry. Thomas Jefferson could foresee science being turned to inhuman endeavors, especially warning against the development of a manufacturing technology

that profits the few and "begets subservience and venality, suffocates the
germ of virtue, and prepares fit tools for the designs of ambition."[32] If science could serve human ideals, its technological offspring could serve economic domination.

From the Jacksonian to the Progressive Era, the nation's leading political figures learned to ignore possible tensions between scientific ideals and technological realities; the former were increasingly subordinated to the latter. Social Darwinism became the scientific justification for the industrial technologies of laissez-faire capitalism; Lester Frank Ward's new social science legitimated the social engineering techniques of an increasingly active federal government; and scientific socialism became the creed of radicals who wanted to combine technological abundance and revolution. Rank-and-file workers sometimes protested the "innovations" that cost them workplace autonomy, but their leaders "adopted an official posture of encouragement, accommodation, and acceptance."[33] Farmers often felt victimized by "innovations" that forced them off the land, but "so thoroughly had the cult of forward motion infused itself into the very structure of the American idiom that populists sometimes encountered great difficulty finding language that could convey their individual disenchantment."[34] America's entrance into the twentieth-century world of big armies, big government, and big business could hardly be disputed on grounds other than technological inefficiency; but the new scientific management movement of Frederick Taylor assured the nation that modern techniques could unite size and efficiency to serve the public interest.

The task of mediating moral ideals and material realities, as well as size and efficiency, fell to the new professional managerial class that rationalized and legitimated its role in its codes of ethics. "The professional," writes David Smith, "best serves humanity by preaching what he practices: dispassionate appraisal, skeptical rationality, a respect for facts and figures, and a steady devotion to working a personal synthesis of professional competence and humane values."[35] Professionals demanded the individual autonomy necessary to develop their expertise in the service of humanity; they engaged in theoretical inquiries founded on the separation of fact from fiction in order to provide a realistic assessment of human options for a better life. Professionals sacrificed many of their own pleasures in their dedication to serving their clients, countrymen, and species. Ideally, professionals contributed to "the method of cooperative intelligence" that John Dewey pinpointed as the most efficient means of harnessing knowledge to human progress.[36] Professional ethics promised a future in which the general public would enjoy greater individual happiness and dignity, mutuality, and equal opportunity to live the good life.

Professional ideals also informed a more modern version of the American Dream. According to Ira Shor, "Today, instead of the illusion of 'working for yourself,' the new ideal is promoted. . . . The *career* is the modern form of the Dream."[37] The professional career afforded most of the virtues associated with being a small businessman and avoided the irrationalities, exploitation, and money-grubbing associated with the competitive marketplace. Both independent and hired professionals would have the autonomy linked to expertise, the social respect that comes with advanced education, and the self-satisfaction of helping others capture their piece of the American Dream. They would use their knowledge rather than their competitive savvy to guide society; they would work in harmony with rather than in opposition to others in the name of universal happiness; and they would avoid cutrate, cutthroat competition and the degradations of advertising by allowing their professional associations to regulate their own marketplaces. Furthermore, the professional career was a cosmopolitan undertaking in contrast to the parochialism of small business. Professionals moved between the nation's metropolises, hobnobbing with the movers and shakers of society, politics, and the economy while enjoying the high culture that appeals to the intellect. Here was a more progressive, more civilized existence than that of the petty conservativism that defined life on Main Street.[38]

Professionals who viewed themselves as the avant garde of the future found a compatible politics in variants of New Deal liberalism that promised to improve the human condition by employing the nation's expertise.[39] Democracy would be enriched if all Americans had the opportunity to develop their intelligence and talents regardless of their race, creed, color, and (eventually) gender. Government should be professionalized to bring greater rationality and efficiency to the political process, now geared toward general social welfare and universal prosperity. Further, experts should bring to bear their intelligence on the nation's economy, regulating it in ways that ensure people their fair share and that stimulate the economic growth from which everyone can benefit. Indeed, the United States should become an example of democracy, rationality, and prosperity for other nations to emulate.[40]

This New Deal liberalism had to overcome obstacles before it could become a material reality. Conservatives still controlled much of the U.S. government and the constitutional system of checks and balances made it extraordinarily difficult for experts to carry out their plans without interference. But liberals were a political avant garde, unafraid to innovate or tinker with the political mechanism. Thus, "the modernizing elites" of the New Deal turned to the American presidency "to overcome or remove obstacles."[41] The executive branch would overwhelm congressional conservatives and neutralize the Supreme Court in its efforts to engineer social welfare and economic rationality. Professionals generally acceded to such political centralization as long as it seemed consistent with their own codes of ethics.

Professional idealism, however, *coexisted* with a professional materialism hinted at by the liberal avant garde's willingness to support a centralized government when it suited their interests. Within the U.S. political economy, professionals simultaneously believed in idealism and yet demonstrated great adeptness at purchasing their own autonomy, social respect, and self-satisfaction at the expense of those that they claimed to serve. For example, professionals were virtually all males who formed professional associations that resembled fraternities that systematically excluded women and reinforced efforts to help women to adapt to second class citizenship. In practice, professionals' most sophisticated skill may have been their ability to manage other people's lives.

First, professionals engineered the "deliberately mystifying jargon" that simultaneously excluded the public from their discussions and ridiculed "popular traditions of self-help as backward and unscientific."[42] Their management of specialized knowledge involved the development of vested interests in particular theories and modes of inquiry that implicitly authorized experts to distort, ignore, and even deceive the public when it served the "higher purposes" of their ideals, their professions, or their government and corporate employers.[43] The "helping professions" such as psychiatry promised to empower people to control their own lives but often functioned as "the most effective contemporary agents of social conformity and isolation."[44] And to the extent that private and public policymaking was "left to the experts," consumer and citizen choice was restricted. During the New Deal, suggests Sheldon Wolin, "democracy reemerged as dependence."[45]

Second, professional careers often encompassed middle management positions in big bureaucracies, big government, and big business. Professionals' jobs were to employ their expertise to administer centralized decisions by regulating subordinates' behavior. They experimented with positive and negative sanctions to ensure rule-abiding behavior; they pioneered time-motion studies and minute divisions of labor; they developed, studied, published, and applied new techniques to make labor more efficient and predictable. When their techniques proved unsatisfactory, they founded the sciences of human relations, public relations, and industrial psychology to bring the human element into line. The professionals-as-managers kept the bureaucratic engines humming by ensuring that what Harry Braverman called "the human machinery" was well oiled.[46] They also helped to engineer and administer the latest labor-saving technologies that made human "hands" expendable, leaving it to other professionals to manage unemployment, job retraining, and the psychic trauma of modernization. These professionals won the respect of their employers, colleagues, and communities by exploring the frontiers of social control.

Finally, professionals translated the promise of public service into a mystique of problem-solving. Once professionals had mastered the so-called scientific method or sophisticated problem-solving techniques of their own specialties, they became universal problem-solvers. The professional economist, for example, became an environmental expert simply by converting clean air and water into quantifiable commodities bought and sold in the marketplace and subject to government regulation.[47] The logic of this mystique pointed toward B. F. Skinner's *Walden Two*, a society that authorized engineers to shape reality and prepared citizens to enjoy it passively. What happened when experts failed to solve problems or when they produced solutions that simply generated new if not more dangerous problems? Armed with optimism, the professionals explained that more research, innovation, and time would certainly result in acceptable solutions. Thus, the experts could produce nuclear wastes that presented major storage problems, or pharmaceuticals with dangerous side-effects, and yet feel confident that the problems were only temporary obstacles on the road to more progress. From one vantage point, this notion of professional service amounts to authority without responsibility or what the Founding Fathers simply called tyranny.

How did professionals reconcile their professional ideals of autonomy, rationality, and public service with their material contribution to human dependence, social control, and even tyranny in the political economy? Beyond self-deception, they simply lived with ambivalence by adhering to myths that made it tolerable: They would educate workers, minorities, and women so that they could *eventually* share in the autonomous life; they would underwrite the rational ordering of society and *eventually* assure people the affluence and leisure to manage their own lives; and they would solve the problems of modernity so that all people would *eventually* have better opportunity to author their own happiness. This ideology of "the dream deferred but certain to be realized" made it possible for people in the new middle class to believe that the tensions between their idealism and materialism, professionalism and managerialism, science and technology would be resolved with the growth and diffusion of knowledge. And, sometimes, the tensions were resolved.

By 1940, professsional managerial class liberalism had seemingly triumphed in America. Small business conservatives were relegated to American backwaters while professionals claimed more wealth, status, and political power in major metropolises and the nation's capital. Roosevelt's New Deal succeeded not only in weathering the depression, taming radicalism, and preparing the nation for war against Nazi atrocities but also in leaving a liberal legacy powerful enough to win support among the Republican opposition. America's growing corporate economy was poised for economic recovery, reconciled to bargaining with organized labor, and ready to assert hegemony in the world marketplace after the war. The new middle class should have been supremely self-confident about its ability to shape a better future and yet it betrayed signs of self-doubt. One sign was that its members began to migrate from the modern metulopolises they had created to suburbs and satellite cities like Santa Monica.

Professional Self-Doubt

Both self-confidence and self-doubt explain the demographic movement of Americans from big cities to suburbs, small cities, and even rural areas after 1940. For some, migration was the fruit of professional managerial class success. According to Kirkpatrick Sale, "It is by and large the young, and more affluent, the professional and upper-echelon workers, who have led the migration out of the big cities, who have the confidence and money to move to areas they find more congenial and then go about seeking jobs."[48] For many, however, migration was a psychological necessity because big city life provided daily evidence that the liberal myths of progress bore little relationship to urban realities. Migration was an escape from "deteriorating cities, megalopolitan sprawls, stifling ghettos, overcrowding, traffic congestion, untreated wastes, smog and soot, budget insolvency, inadequate schools, mounting illiteracy, declining university standards, dehumanizing welfare systems, police brutality, overcrowded hospitals, clogged court calendars, inhuman prisons, racial injustice, sex discrimination, poverty, crime and vandalism, and fear."[49] If the nation's metropolises were supposed to be the future, where problems called forth solutions, then the future did not work.

Perhaps more important, it did not work for the professionals themselves. Would the big city school systems prepare *their* children adequately for the journey to professional credentials? Would the metropolitan police forces protect *their* families from the urban crime spawned by poverty and racism? Would *their* own economic opportunities be safeguarded in the regulated but nonetheless chaotic urban marketplaces? And who could the professionals turn to for help in solving *their* problems? On the one hand, the professionals prided themselves on their ability to help other people rather than on their willingness to be helped, making it less likely that they would seek other than individual solutions. On the other hand, professionals who did turn to politics for help were likely to discover the familiar myths that explained administrators' inability to help: It's complicated. It's a matter of time. Bear with us. Trust us.

One obvious alternative was a move to suburbs and nearby modest-sized cities where one could sustain the illusion that the future worked. One could reside in a homogeneous neighborhood where most people were educated, fairly self-sufficient, and affluent; where people supported schools and libraries, and city governments delivered basic services; where professional skills were appreciated by the corporations that began to locate their offices and industrial plants on the outskirts of big

perhaps liberal ideals actually contributed to material pain and suffering. Such doubt is manifest in the defensiveness of Anthony Fainberg, an experimental physicist on the staff of Brookhaven National Laboratory. Fainberg asks, "How much blame, if any, do scientists, past and present, deserve for wars, their causes and effects?" Why even ask this question?

> ... because of an attitude on the part of many nonscientists, often tacit, occasionally explicit, which is evident both in print and in private conversation. This attitude holds that scientists bear heavy responsibility for human suffering, at least in recent wars; that, having known sin, they as a class are morally beyond the pale or at the least suspect in all their societal dealings or pronouncements, particularly those of a technical nature. . . . Some [critics], how- ever, go further and generically, almost in a racist fashion, ascribe certain rather unpleasant personal and social characteristics to scientists: they are said to be insensitive, unfeeling, narrow, drawn to science as a means of escape from social contact, arrogant, and contemptuous of nonscientists. In other words, in most aspects, as has been said of Jews, they are supposed to be like everyone else, only more so.[55]

Fainberg wants to defend scientists but not in terms of their service to humankind. He admits that they have done their share to degrade the human condition. His defense is that scientists are no more blameworthy than other professionals who have also contributed to degradation.

Scientists' postwar experiences mirrored those of other professionals. The helping professions became more bureaucratized, overcrowded, regulated, and subjected to public distrust. Professionals educated to serve the welfare state bore the additional burden of an impending tax- payer revolt that portrayed public employees and retainers as mindless bureaucrats. Demand for professional services in the corporate world waned in a particular way. America's postwar oligopolies, facing little competition, were often more interested in guaranteed profits than in professional creativity, innovation, efficiency, or public service; they were sometimes more concerned with promoting managers able to oversee the pain resulting from runaway shops, conglomeration, and merger- mania than, for example, with employing professionals who might mod- ernize the nation's aging steel plants. For a while, it seemed as if the Master of Business Administration (MBA) was the practical college de- gree of the future, that is, until an overabundance of MBA recipients crowded into corporate personnel offices. Simultaneously, social critics hammered away at the professional managerial class, declaring it "guilty by association" with America's increasingly therapeutic society, its crisis- ridden state planning mechanisms, and its overheated economy grown too fat, flabby, and complacent. And the sour note sounded by critics rang true enough that the therapists, planners, and economic managers began to wonder if New Deal liberalism had outlived its promise.

The established professionals who moved to Santa Monica after World
War II had invested too much of their lives, careers, and ideals in the
modern American Dream to write off the New Deal liberalism associated with it. But they could not avoid some disenchantment with it.
They became more convinced of the durability of social problems and
more skeptical of the ability of their class and the welfare state to solve
them. Their evolving consciousness was reinforced when the revolution
of rising expectations took a feminist bent in the 1970s.[56] Professional
ideals demanded that women be admitted to the fold and rising divorce
rates prompted more and more middle class women to explore their
talents, seek professional credentials, and find fulfilling careers. Though
some middle class women were able to stake out a place in men's professional world, many could not find jobs in the depressed economy of the
1970s. Those who did often found ones where individual autonomy was
restricted, outlets for intelligence limited, and concern for public service
a luxury; moreover, the material rewards for women professionals were
far less than either what was expected or what was obtained by male
counterparts. For all their talk about equal opportunity and affirmative
action, politicians and planners had done remarkably little to improve
the career opportunities of most women. Meanwhile, professionals' children—male and female—frequently faced a trade-off between professionalism and material success. Those seeking professional careers might
discover that they could not match their parents' standard of living;
those recognizing professional careers as nothing special might opt for a
business occupation where education is secondary and material rewards
are primary; and many might simply struggle to get any job available
to support themselves.[57] The dream of finding a career that combined
public service and personal affluence was receding.

Rapid growth and development in Santa Monica forced some of this
disenchantment into the open as the city became more like metropolitan
Los Angeles. More residents, stores, office buildings, and mobility added
up to more traffic congestion. Santa Monica began to experience full-
scale rush hours, with long waits to get on a freeway that had become
the busiest in Southern California. The crime rate grew when freeway
accessibility marked Santa Monica as a good location for murder, bur-
glary, armed robbery, and rape. Homeless people wandered the streets
by day and slept at city parks and beaches during the night.[58] The professionals who turned to city government for help or who offered to
help city government solve problems ran into the growth machine, still
preaching the anachronistic politics of free market individualism and
limited government. This encounter clearly offended the professionals'
liberal sensibilities; but the professionals, their self-confidence shaken,
could offer no coherent alternative. They had become wary of government programs that promised rational regulation only to deliver policy
failures.[59] Very much like the Democratic party after 1968, Santa Monica's new middle class suffered the political paralysis that comes with

recognizing the problems with conservativism while being skeptical of the solutions posited by liberalism. Lacking a coherent alternative, they could not and did not contest the continuing power of the growth machine.

Middle Class Intersections

By the mid-1970s, Santa Monica's middle class strata felt some degree of discontent. The traditional small businessmen who wanted to conserve small town virtues were being victimized by the postwar invasion of the regional marketplace and rapid growth. The growth machine entrepreneurs prospered, to be sure, but their efforts to conserve entrepreneurialism and the free market were endangered by the influx of liberal professionals and more powerful corporations as well as by the growing fears of overdevelopment among homeowners and tenants. The professionals, many of whom had escaped the metropolis and visible evidence of liberal failures, now faced further urbanization and political impotence and perhaps even identity-shattering neoconservative doubts that problems can be solved. Despite the different sources, these middle class discontents intersected at three points where we can locate some middle class foundations for radicalism.

First, each segment of the middle class had reasons to distrust large corporations. Santa Monica's traditional small businessmen, though they did not recall the dealings of John P. Jones and Collis P. Huntington that nearly destroyed the city, were being squeezed out by large corporate developers and chain-store operations. Santa Monica's liberal professionals had mixed reasons to distrust corporate giants. They were part of a class that grew up with corporate America and thrived with it but, more recently, they had found themselves the objects of corporate management in their workplaces and the victims of corporate development in their residential community. The slowest learners, predictably, were the growth machine advocates, who supported the marketplace that gave birth to large corporations but who would soon discover that their free market version of growth did not necessarily coincide with progress as defined by corporations willing to do business in communist China, socialist Angola, and what they would soon call the People's Republic of Santa Monica.

Second, these middle class strata identified with versions of the American Dream that were potentially subversive of the free marketplace. Traditional small businessmen might value economic security, autonomy, and community respect more than the unregulated marketplace that assaults these values. Professionals have long espoused liberal ideals that demand market restrictions in the name of individual self-development, political rationality, and shared prosperity. Even laissez-faire conservatives might look to controlled markets if they were necessary for support-

ing entrepreneurship and competition against the forces of monopoly, or
if control were a lesser evil in circumstances where their power was eroding. Indeed, growth machine proponents might even show grudging respect for the regulators, who also demonstrated some entrepreneurship and competitive fiber of their own.

Third, the middle class strata became increasingly ambivalent about their political beliefs. Most traditional conservatives, modern conservatives, and New Deal liberals did not detach themselves from their respective ideologies when faced with disenchantment; but they often clung to those ideologies with diminishing tenacity, uncertain whether old dreams could in fact become modern realities. In her study of American political beliefs, Jennifer Hochschild catalogues the ways in which individuals cope with political ambivalence.[60] They may simply experience uneasiness and reticence toward getting involved; they may learn to live with the tension between ideals and material reality; they may abandon ideals and resign themselves to reality; they may suffer political paralysis and go along with the status quo for lack of alternatives; or they may seek to support their ideals by changing political-economic reality. In the 1970s, all these ways of coping were evident in Santa Monica but political paralysis seemed predominant.

However, a new generation of middle class Santa Monicans discovered that ambivalence could be a fertile ground for experimenting with alternatives that revitalized middle class ideals in ways that justified significant changes in political reality. The young Santa Monicans shared their parents' ideals but not their ideological loyalties or paralysis. They too wanted economic security, autonomy, and community; they too validated entrepreneurial innovation and competition as means for realizing their ideals; and they too sought outcomes that would not serve simply themselves and their community but also the nation and even humankind. They came from families that dreamed the American Dream and partly lived it; equally important, they came from families that were disenchanted because the Dream was not firmly in their grasp. The younger generation then matured into a society that no longer validated the old tickets to the future. Most of them grew up on the 1950s, when conservativism, traditional and modern, had been all but discredited by New Deal liberalism; they went to school and came into political consciousness in the 1960s, when liberal myths about the welfare state were being undermined by mass protests against racism and militarism; they went on job searches in the 1970s, when fulfilling careers were scarce, established politicians were caught engaging in corruption, and oil corporations reaped superprofits while customers suffered gasoline shortages. Half of them were young women who at some level understood that past ideological loyalties—right, center, and left—had ignored their dreams; many of them were becoming young parents, the first generation of parents to have grown up in the shadow of a mushroom cloud, who feared that a world of environmental disaster and nuclear catastrophe would be visited on their children. The younger generation was clearly of the middle class but not quite in its conventional political molds.

Sharing their parents' values and discontents, the younger people could appeal to them, experimenting with ideas of corporate distrust and regulated marketplaces that might fill the political vacuum founded on ambivalence. But having put some distance between their parents' ideologies and their own politics, the younger people would have to innovate, offer something radically different. In a sense, they were ideally situated to appeal to the affluent but disenchanted middle class with a vision of middle class radicalism.

I walked into Santa Monica city hall for the first time in 1982, when the "radicals" had been in power for one year. I did spot a few crusty old men in wide-lapeled suits looking as if they had spent too many years behind bureaucratic desks. For the most part, however, I encountered men and women in their thirties, some younger or a bit older, wearing casual clothes and full heads of hair only occasionally laced with gray. When I walked into outer offices, I was greeted by receptionists of both sexes; when admitted to inner offices, I spoke with roughly equal numbers of women and men city officials. This was the newest adult generation of the American middle class and it proved to be the highest bidder for control over Santa Monica's future.

3

Liking Middle America

Holly Near: It's very difficult for an artist like myself to decide whether to continue to play in small community-type places or whether to go out and become well-known in the mainstream. There's constantly the question as to whether I'm selling out. . . . I had in one of my songbooks a quote that Pete [Seeger] said when he was up in front of HUAC: "This music can be sung and I'll sing it for anybody who wants to listen to it." That's how I feel about my music. I think if Johnny Carson wants me on his show and wants millions of Americans to listen to it, I'll go on the Johnny Carson show. . . . I also happen to like middle America and I have every intention to sing to them.

Ronnie Gilbert: God, talk about living and learning! I never heard any militant activist say that, and it's the thing that I've been feeling for years. My travels and my living among people in middle America does not match the image that was put forth in the sixties, but I never had the courage to say it, and certainly not in the media.

Holly Near and Ronnie Gilbert [1]

American radicals have frequently been members of the middle class but have also consistently identified their aspirations and frustrations with other classes, particularly farmers and the working class. They generally condemned their own class as "bourgeois," either complicit in the social injustices that make for inequality or complacent in the face of social oppression begotten by elites and suffered by lower classes. Occasionally, American radicals such as Morris Hillquit of the old Socialist party believed that the proletarian struggle might absorb some middle class elements, but virtually no serious radical looked to the middle class itself as the social base for change in America.

The Santa Monica left, to the contrary, liked middle class America. It was sympathetic to the plight of traditional small businessmen; it appreciated the entrepreneurial ethic of innovators; and it stood behind both science and professionalism in the service of citizens. It differed, however, from earlier middle class generations in its attempt to extract from the middle class past those elements that might prefigure a more egalitarian future, what one might call a human scale future characterized by participatory democracy and a one class society.

Can such an enterprise be considered "radical"? I will locate the source of the Santa Monica left in the new left student movement of the 1960s and its undercurrents in the 1970s. I will then analyze how Santa Monica activists perceived social change in America and only then consider if their perceptions constituted a form of radicalism. Let me state from the outset that I believe the Santa Monica left represents one of the few indigenous forms of radicalism in the United States today.

From Port Huron

In 1962, a student named Tom Hayden drafted a statement of principles for the Students for a Democratic Society (SDS) at its convention in Port Huron, Michigan. Hayden's draft became the basis for the Port Huron Statement that guided SDS through the mid-1960s and provided a political identity for the early new left student movement.[2] The SDS document was an appeal to the aspirations and frustrations of white middle class youth in America.

"We are the people of this generation," it began, "bred in at least modest comfort, housed now in universities, looking uncomfortably to the world we will inherit." This middle class identification was augmented by an expressed faith in the American Dream. "Freedom and equality for each individual, government of, by, and for the people—these American values we found good, principles by which we could live as men." Unfortunately, these principles were not practiced in American society, where freedom and equality were eroded by problems ranging from racism to The Bomb. The problems could be solved, but only if Americans replaced their "complacency" and "apathy" with a pioneering spirit, a willingness to "experiment with living" and "seek new departures as well." The SDS analysis that followed was essentially that of neophyte professionals who felt stymied in their ethics and problem-solving abilities by the growth of managerial society in America.

"Men have unrealized potential for self-cultivation, self-direction, self-understanding, and creativity," but American institutions instead encourage "submission to authority." Universities were part of the problem. They too often ignored "the personal cultivation of the mind" and devoted energy to administration, bureaucracy, and enforced conformity. Modern science, "admittedly necessary to our complex technological and social structure," was regularly abused as "many social and physical scientists, neglecting the liberating heritage of higher learning, develop 'human relations' or 'morale-producing' techniques for the corporate economy while others exercise their intellectual skills to accelerate the arms race." Reason was no longer in the service of humankind. And the older generation was hypocritical to the extent that it preached service but resigned itself to administered existences. Students' parents were "in withdrawal from public life, from any collective effort at directing their own affairs." They had lost touch with traditional American optimism and knowhow by tolerating the "muddle through" of their politicians and the "pervading feeling that there are simply no alternatives."

The SDS document legitimated a new experiment in social change because the older methods had failed or at least not succeeded. Social change would not likely come from a labor movement that was "too quiescent to be counted on with enthusiasm." Nor was it likely to come from minorities who were "too poor and socially slighted." However, change might come by mobilizing the affluent white youth of the middle class who had the sense of efficacy to believe that "something *can* be done to change circumstances" and the potential power to make that change.

"We believe that universities are an overlooked seat of influence." Why the university? First, it was a strategic point of production in modern society. "Its educational function makes it indispensable and automatically makes it a crucial institution in the formation of social attitudes. In an unbelievably complicated world, it is the central institution for organizing, evaluating, and transmitting knowledge." Second, the university promised to nurture individual autonomy, rationality, and public service but failed to deliver minimal intellectual satisfaction, spawning an alienated student body and possibly "a new left with real intellectual skills, committed to deliberativeness, honesty, and reflection as working tools." Finally, the university had a critical mass of students who were an ideal vanguard for change because they had the intelligence to "transform modern complexity into issues that can be understood and felt close-up by every human being." Students were to form alliances with labor and minorities but, this time, the movement was to be founded on middle class norms and a middle class social base that would absorb the concerns of other classes.

The goals of the student movement as described in the Port Huron Statement were largely an amalgam of middle class concerns. The document called for "a democracy of individual participation, governed by two central aims: that the individual share in those social decisions determining the quality and direction of his life; that society be organized to encourage independence in men and provide the media for their common participation." This call for what soon became known as "participatory democracy" mainly reflected professional managerial class attitudes or, as Barbara and John Ehrenreich put it:

> The first wave of student activists typically came from secure professional managerial class backgrounds and were, compared to other students, especially well-imbued with the traditional professional managerial class values of intellectual autonomy and public service. Their initial radicalism represented an attempt to reassert the autonomy which the professional managerial class had long since ceded to the capitalist class.[3]

Whereas working class and minority activists focused mainly on issues concerning the distribution of wealth and related rights, the students focused on independence, participation, self-direction, and control over the quality of life. And even within the context of middle class concerns, SDS plotted a road to more democracy led by self-confident white students who could and did easily reproduce some managerial dominance in their own ranks. Dotson Rader remembered the student rebellion at Columbia University later in the decade: "As it worked inside Mathematics, where Hayden was in charge, participatory democracy was much like a town meeting where a highly organized minority, in firm agreement on objectives, is able to cow the unorganized, apolitical majority into acting against its better judgment."[4] SDS experienced a tension between membership demands for autonomy and leadership attempts to manage the organization throughout its existence.

When the Port Huron Statement did address economic issues, it did so half-heartedly. It envisioned an economy founded on the principle "that work should involve incentives worthier than money or survival" and gave precedence to the middle class desire for "meaningful" careers over the lower classes' demands for jobs, decent wages, better working conditions. Thus, the document stated, "the serious poet burns for a place, any place to work; the once-serious and never-serious poets work at the advertising agencies." The idea that intellectual careers may have been of little immediate interest to Americans in uncertain economic straits received little consideration beyond "a new left cannot rely only on aching stomachs to be the engine force of social reform." The SDS document also envisioned an economy whose "major resources should be open to democratic participation and subject to democratic social regulation," essentially begging the question of the economic future. Did a democratic economy refer to the "independence" of small business-men? Was it meant to invoke a "willingness to take risks" associated with innovative entrepreneurs? Was it pointing to public planning aimed at making corporations "publicly responsible" along New Deal lines? Or did it represent middle class intellectuals' flirtation with socialism for its "sense of thoroughgoing reforms" in the social ownership of the means of production? The document hinted at all of these possibilities but pro-vided no systematic support for any of them, setting the stage for future debates between those intent on democratizing capitalism and those wanting to scuttle it for some leftwing alternative.

The imprecision of the Port Huron Statement bothered Tom Hayden very little. He came to Port Huron, states SDS historian Kirkpatrick Sale, "more convinced than before of the need to set out a broad defini-tion of common values rather than a lot of narrow statements about this or that political or economic policy."[5] Hayden's broad definition of com-mon values was nicely summarized in the document's introduction: "The search for truly democratic alternatives to the present, and a commit-ment to social experimentation with them, is a worthy and fulfilling human enterprise, one which moves us and, we hope, others." Hayden had been criticized as too utopian but it was his call to an "ad hoc" sort of radicalism that legitimated the renewal of political dialogue and an openness to untried possibilities that captured the imagination of the first wave of middle class students who valued intelligence and experi-mentation enough to found the new left student movement. Indeed, Hayden's lack of specificity functioned as an invitation to discussion— not only among middle class students but also among their parents.

SDS and the other groups that made up the new left grew rapidly after 1962. A complete explanation would account for this growth in terms of a number of postwar trends, the civil rights movement, the Berkeley free speech movement, the Vietnam war, and military conscription. But the explanation would also have to account for the expanding student move-ment in terms of the resonant chord it struck in the lives of older profes-sionals who had lost much of their autonomy, rational self-sufficiency, and ability to service human ends. This resonance meant that many students could become activists while receiving reinforcement and a hearing at home; it meant that American society had a critical mass of parental tolerance that insulated student demonstrators from the overt violence and social sanctions advocated by their opponents; and it meant that students were relatively free to experiment with the limits of Ameri-can tolerance, new lifestyles, confrontational politics, and alternative eco-nomic institutions. A series of polls on middle America, commissioned by *Newsweek* magazine in the late 1960s, clearly identified the parental support.[6]

"What seems to be going on in middle America today," reported Richard Lemon in his analysis of the polling data, "is not so much a revolt as an agonizing reappraisal. The white American is upset about the quality of life in America." Many middle Americans blamed moral decay, political chaos, and social crises on civil rights activists and student protesters but their blame was marked by ambivalence. They complained about favoritism toward blacks and spoiled college kids but 54 percent of them agreed that "young people were not unduly critical of their country, and that cynicism is needed." The percentages rose rapidly when one examined the opinions of the most affluent, educated, and professional members of middle America, who were most confident that America could solve its problems, that experimental solutions were worth trying, and that "young people and college students involved in demonstrations and sit-ins" were in large degree "justified" in their deeds.[7] Had such support persisted, it is unlikely that the killings at Kent State would have occurred.

But the support did not persist when "large numbers of young people pushed professional managerial class radicalism to its own limits and found themselves, ultimately, at odds with their own class."[8] After 1967 or 1968, student politics changed. Those who once looked to the university as a source of leftwing promise began to mobilize against the university as an accomplice in warfare. Students who earlier looked to the intellect as an authoritative guide increasingly denied all authority, instead seeking "authenticity" in emotional spontaneity, drugs, and the counterculture. Activists who took for granted open discussion, democratic dissent, and peaceful protests soon encountered militants tired of talk and poised for direct, even violent confrontation. For student organizations such as SDS, these shifts were wrenching. Participatory democracy gave way to factional control by highly organized sects; discussions concerning economic experimentation gave way to a leftwing hero-worship of Third World socialism. As a result, writes Peter Clecak, "the Movement confronted the old options that its founders and its sympathetic critic-participants had intended to avoid: sectarianism, withdrawal, and assimilation."[9] And each option was certain to alienate middle Americans.

The leninist sects that took over some new left organizations were centralized, quasimilitaristic hierarchies replete with their own narrow ideologies and jargon; but middle class professionals would not support or show much tolerance for an extreme leftwing version of the same managerialism they suffered on the job, much less ideologies and jargon that were explicitly antibourgeois and anti-American. Those activists who withdrew into the counterculture preached a return to nature, simplicity, and the liberation of the id that hinted of a luddite attack on science, technology, expertise, and even education; but few professionals would go along with what amounted to a plea for professional managerial class suicide. The student activists who opted for assimilation, joining with Eugene McCarthy, Robert Kennedy, and then George McGovern, no longer offered an energizing vision significantly different or at least dissociated from New Deal liberalism; but professionals were already familiar with the promise of the New Deal and, more important, its failings. Suffering internal fragmentation and an erosion of its middle class base, the new left soon withered away. What persisted, however, was a generation of middle class activists who had graduated from college and were now entering the workforce as well as a disenchanted American middle class now entering a decade of economic instability.

To Santa Monica

New left graduates faced the immediate challenge of supporting themselves. Many of them channeled their desire for independence and social service into professional careers, somehow hoping to practice professional ethics without becoming either the object or the instrument of elite social control. More surprising, others bypassed their parents' career patterns and went back to their grandparents' search for autonomy and community in small businesses located on the fringes of the marketplace. Theirs was an older American Dream that they would now infuse with a new social ethic.

A trend toward what was called "the new professionalism" was manifested by the late 1960s, when student activists moved into teaching, journalism, social services, health care, law, and related professions. Initially, such career paths were attractive to youth with a social conscience because they still offered a degree of individual autonomy, intellectual challenge, and opportunity for public service—so-called free spaces for combining work and politics. When the young people encountered managerial constraints, they sometimes stuck to their ideals and sought to change their professions. In the early 1970s, they staged their own professional conferences, formed their own caucuses and organizations, sponsored their own journals, and published books such as *The New Professionals* or *Toward a New Public Administration*.[10] They attempted to redefine professionalism, first distinguishing it from bureaucratic domination and then associating it with leftwing politics.

Three principles stood out in their literature. First, they argued that greater professional autonomy was needed to enhance citizen autonomy. Michael Harmon, for example, suggested that professionals should be free to "self-actualize"—that is, to develop, express, and advocate meaningful social values in an uncertain world where "objective" professionals had failed to notice, much less solve, pressing social problems. The underlying assumption, as expressed by H. George Frederickson, was that the meaningful social values would include "social equity" defined as "activities designed to enhance the political power and economic well-

being" of disadvantaged Americans.[11] In theory, the disadvantaged would
not only be best served by committed professionals but would also be empowered to assume greater control over their own lives.

Second, the "radicals in the professions," as the Ehrenreichs call them, wanted to break down the barriers between experts and amateurs. "The rule of experts would be abolished—by the young experts."[12] The new professionals hoped to strip their specialties of mystifying jargon, use their knowledge to help people clarify their own choices, and invite lay people into their discussions, both to share skills with them and to learn from them. The young experts also hoped to break the monopolies of their professional associations. They contested the elitist credential systems that limited the supply of experts and inflated the costs of their services; they supported paraprofessional programs that promised to nurture expertise within the communities that most needed it.[13] Narrowing the distance between expert and amateur, they believed, would undermine professional authority as a means of social control.

Third, the new professionals generally argued that decentralization and democratization of decisionmaking was crucial to ridding the professions of their managerial functions and functionaries. They experimented with localized models of decisionmaking and community control that emphasized building a consensus among affected constituencies and creating institutions willing to confront vested elites.[14] These models would give voice to the silent, involve more and more people in shaping the use of knowledge, and generate solutions to problems at the level where they were felt and lived.[15] Public service would no longer be an abstraction conjured from textbooks but a personalized process of everyday interaction; and the tyranny of professional authority without responsibility would give way to a greater sense of community, mutuality, and shared commitment.

These principles surfaced in the major middle class political movements of the 1970s: environmentalism, feminism, and the antinuke, propeace movement. Reluctant to claim the social authority to make technical decisions for other people, the 1970s activists *began* to learn how to work with other people and recognize the autonomy, intelligence, and expressed needs of amateurs. Environmentalists learned that scientific solutions to environmental degradation must also take into account the workplace environment and possible job displacement.[16] Feminists housed in university women's studies programs discovered the need to deal with the high costs of public transportation confronting minority women in urban areas.[17] Peace proponents began speaking less of shutdowns and more of conversions of defense plants in response to people's fears of unemployment.[18] Many activists were torn, trusting their own solutions to social problems but not wanting to reclaim the prerogatives of their own class without renegotiating the social contract between education and democratic citizenship.

Even marxists, those perhaps most critical of American professions as bourgeois fraternities, entered into the ranks of the new professionals. Ellen Schrecker puts it this way:

> To the extent that academic status confers respect, American marxism is now respectable. Its practitioners teach and sometimes get tenure at Ivy League schools as well as community colleges. Their scholarship appears under the imprint of university presses and mainstream quarterlies. And, in certain fields, American history for example, marxism is the mainstream. Two recent presidents of the Organization of American Historians were marxists or at least *marxisantes*. The influence of radicals within other disciplines, though not as dramatic, is nonetheless evident. Just about every field, certainly every social science, has its own marxist journal and its own radical caucus or subgroup that competes or meets with the main professional organization. Together these groups have more than 12,000 members. . . . These people constitute the intellectual legacy of the new left, the political activists of the 1960s who turned to scholarship in the 1970s to make sense of their own experiences.[19]

Marxist academics also sound like new professionals. A popular book such as *Studies in Socialist Pedagogy* could be renamed *The New Marxist Professor*.[20] It advised marxist academics to use their teaching positions as a means to enhance teacher–student autonomy, destroy barriers between experts and amateurs, and cultivate mutuality rather than authority in the leftwing classroom.

Of course, many new left graduates did not opt for the new professionalism. Some thought it was still too constricting, affording little free space but lots of bureaucratic restraint. Others felt that it was politically ineffective. If elite power is centered in the business world, then radicals must either infiltrate the business world or provide egalitarian alternatives to it. In a 1972 article entitled "The New Businessman," Holly Henderson explored both alternatives.[21]

New left graduates could enter into the corporate world and hope to accomplish some political goals. With little hurrah or notice, activists had already established education and sensitivity programs, credit unions, daycare centers, and innovative investment programs that benefitted company employees, unions, minorities, women, consumers, and the general community. The opportunities for new business activists to make corporations socially responsible were untested and unlimited. The activists might help to organize white collar workers into unions or perhaps engineer innovative management-worker exchanges that point toward greater workplace democracy; they might use corporate laboratories to develop ecologically sound technologies or they might direct corporate charity money toward needed social services.

However, Henderson recognized that many political activists might feel that corporate jobs simply put people in the belly of the beast, and so she offered this advice: "You may want to build a business from scratch, employing only those who have a sense of business as an organism which must serve the interests of buyers as well as sellers—and those who can't afford to buy."[22] She cited the case of "one young entrepreneur" who felt that educational toys were too expensive for the children of the poor and who then established a large toy company able to market inexpensive educational toys.

The advantages of starting one's own business included the chance to create a concern with maximal freedom for oneself and one's employees while producing goods and services that are needed according to one's political ideals. Also, one could experiment with new forms of business, cooperative enterprises or worker-owned companies, that give greater weight to values like independence and community than to profits. Such experiments were potentially satisfying for those directly involved in them and they were also examples of a humane yet practical alternative to the corporate marketplace.

In fact, many activists from the 1960s entered into the business world in the 1970s, locating themselves in what Kirkpatrick Sale calls "the interstitial economy" where quality and community take precedence over the bottom line.[23] They became artisans, craftsmen, and entertainers plying the street and tourist trade. They started cottage industries in their homes and garages that sometimes developed, for example, into solar energy or recycling businesses. They sought to live as independent producers and sellers of books, articles, art, and films; and they began new bookstores, magazines, art galleries, and movie theaters. They also founded new social service agencies and nonprofit corporations that catered to pressing human needs for affordable health services, legal services, housing services, and so forth. They sometimes entered into the world of high finance with a women's bank or a socially conscious investment firm or consumer network like Co-op America, which offers comprehensive life insurance to community groups through a plan developed by an employee-owned insurance company that invests premiums in low income cooperative housing. And they often experimented with things like food, housing, or even bicycle cooperatives, editorial collectives, and community development corporations. According to Sale, these business ventures "are all pointing in a single direction, toward individual self-worth, community cooperation, harmony with nature, decentralization of power, self-sufficiency"—that is, toward the virtues of small businessmen that Santa Monica's Harry C. Henshey appreciated a half-century ago.[24]

Those who opted for the business world needed a large reservoir of entrepreneurial spirit and self-sacrifice. They had to tap relatives, friends, foundations, local support groups, and others for the capital and expertise necessary to set up their businesses. They then faced the constant tension of being savvy enough to survive and committed enough to maintain their political values. In many cases, the young entrepreneurs spent endless hours plotting their business strategies only to endure endless meetings with partners, consultants, employees, and neighbors advocating different priorities and strategies. Often, the business activists not only had to live on minimal wages but also had to persuade workers that the peculiar mix of business and politics required them to live at subsistence or "movement" wages too. In an odd way, the business activists were prepared for these challenges. They had been involved in political groups, like the Organization for a Better Austin on Chicago's west side, where funding was always a problem, endless meetings the stuff of everyday life, and movement wages a badge of honor; this meant that they were aware of the pitfalls of combining business and politics even though they were often unaware of how to avoid them.[25] Furthermore, they were of the middle class, heirs to the American Dream legacy that pronounced individual daring, intelligence, hard work, long hours, and self-sacrifice the key to success despite adverse odds.

More so than other leftists, Tom Hayden exemplified a continuing belief in struggling against the odds. His Port Huron idealism outlasted the 1960s and 1970s, showing up again in the conclusion to his 1980 *The American Future: New Visions Beyond Old Frontiers*: "Ours is a great and young nation, living in a yet richer and older world. It is not too late for a new beginning, no longer based on a hostile assessment of nature and others. . . . Hope and love still know no boundaries."[26] In fact, Hayden's political ideas had changed very little over the course of two decades. What had changed, however, was his understanding of the American middle class.

By the mid-1970s, Hayden not only recognized the transformation of student activists into new professionals and new business people; he also sensed that their ideals had rippled throughout middle America to produce "a great shift in consciousness which began in the sixties and continues in less-noticed ways in the seventies."[27] Whereas he had once feared middle America as a home for hawks or worse, he gradually came to realize that "our movement was not isolated and embattled on the fringe as we thought, but was instead flowing through the mainstream, filling up with GI's and vets, former Pentagon officials, POW's, a baby doctor, actors and actresses, gold-star mothers, dissenting Democrats, parents of campus revolutionaries." Middle America's complacency and apathy proved "skin-deep" and middle class activism swelled. "Today, middle Americans organize to protest meat prices, utility rate hikes, public employee lay-offs, childcare cutbacks, nuclear power plants, environmentally destructive land developments, arbitrary rent increases, redlining of neighborhoods, unsafe working conditions—and innumerable threats to everyday security and well-being." Confident that "what were once minority viewpoints have become majority viewpoints," Hayden attested to his faith in middle America by quoting a Holly Near song: "Oh America, I now can say your name / Without feeling bitter / Without feeling ashamed / I've traveled across your country / Your villages and your towns / And I've seen some friendly people / Who turned my head around." Hayden decided to seek the Democratic party nomination for the U.S. Senate in 1976 with the notion that the Port Huron Statement, now updated in a campaign booklet called *Make the Future Ours*, could appeal to affluent voters in places like Santa Monica.

The campaign booklet was an update in two senses. First, it was largely an orchestrated appeal to new professionals and new business people. It condemned corporate, government, and bureaucratic powers that eroded the prerogatives, for example, "of an elementary school teacher who does the tough classroom work." It suggested that professional wisdom would not fulfill its promise unless "those receiving it have some voice in shaping its content to their needs." It appealed to a new science and technology that can empower people to control their own lives, arguing that "our aerospace engineers and technicians need to be put to work immediately to develop solar systems" that provide people a decentralized source of energy. The campaign document also spoke out in behalf of small businesses, favoring family farms as "still the best form of agriculture," or "small independent timber companies" against the conglomerates, "the alternative press" above media giants, and "small firms" and "enterprising investors" against the energy corporations, and so forth. It also put in a good word for cooperative businesses that "could play a vastly expanded role in service areas such as schools, health care, aid to the disabled, community legal services, etc." Small was beautiful in the sense that it facilitated "individual invention and breakthrough" as well as "quality of services." Hayden wrote that "middle Americans find themselves more and more outside the promise and protection of the 'Dream,'" and his campaign for the U.S. Senate nomination was "an attempt to provide one way out of powerlessness for us all."

Second, *Make the Future Ours* was far more policy-specific than the Port Huron Statement. Hayden defined that specificity in these terms: "If being radical has its original meaning as *going to the root*, then we need more radicals because we are in dire need of getting to the roots of our problems and coming up with alternatives." The new left had been considered too utopian, pointing out problems but ignoring the concrete solutions necessary for making change. Hayden took this criticism to heart and his campaign document overflowed with concrete policy recommendations and alternatives on issues concerning corporate power, political processes, environmentalism, peace, feminism, minorities, labor, gays, seniors, disabled people, and more. In part, Hayden was appealing to the professional problem-solving and business pragmatism of the middle class; in part, he was following political expedience by casting his campaign net as wide as possible; and in part, he believed that different policy areas were ultimately interrelated in his notion of "economic democracy."

Taken separately, Hayden's policies were similar to ones proposed in Jack Newfield and Jeff Greenfield's 1972 *A Populist Manifesto* and Fred Harris's 1973 *The New Populism.*[28] But the separate policies were knit together in significantly different ways. On the one hand, the populists were associated with movements of America's disadvantaged and dispossessed, an association captured in Fred Harris's slogan, "Up with those who are down." But Hayden's intended constituency was not so much the disadvantaged and dispossessed as the advantaged and possession-laden middle class. On the other hand, Hayden's particular notion of economic democracy spoke directly to the concerns of the middle class. It emphasized people's right to control their lives and future, to assume mastery in their communities and workplaces, and to play a larger part in shaping the services that they produce, distribute, and consume. As Hayden recognized, *it was powerlessness not poverty at the root of middle class frustrations.*

One Hayden campaign goal was "building a lasting political organization that will go on whether I am elected or not." He was not elected. But he garnered an impressive 1.2 million votes in the primary, more than enough to suggest that his platform did have a social base in California and that a lasting political organization was needed to cultivate it. Undaunted by his 1976 setback in the political marketplace, Hayden manufactured in 1977 the Campaign for Economic Democracy (CED), a California "grassroots citizens' campaign to take back power over our lives—and create healthy individuals, families, communities, and workplaces."[29] Appropriately, Hayden located CED state headquarters in middle class Santa Monica. There it spawned a local chapter that defined the core ideology and organizational thrust of the Santa Monica left.

The Core Ideology

If the personal is political, then Dennis Zane's biography is a good indication of the Santa Monica left's core ideology. During the 1960s, Zane participated in the student antiwar movement, changing his college major from science to philosophy. He then went to Boston, where he fulfilled his fantasy of camping out on Henry David Thoreau's Walden Pond, worked as a teacher in a school for mentally retarded persons, and organized a degree of democratic self-management among employees in a restaurant where he worked nights. Zane eventually returned to Southern California to pursue graduate studies in philosophy and then urban planning but his politics took precedence. He secured a job teaching math and American history at a private school, which left him time to

work in Hayden's 1976 campaign, to help found the Santa Monica CED
chapter, and to become the key figure in mobilizing the Santa Monica left.[30] Local activists generally credited Zane with the energy behind organizing CED, the Santa Monica Fair Housing Alliance, and the city's Democratic Club into the Santa Monicans for Renters' Rights (SMRR) coalition and with masterminding SMRR's 1979 electoral victories. Zane himself was elected to a four-year city council term in 1981 and has since remained one of the most tireless activist–politicians in town.

Zane's journey, in rough outline, is similar to paths taken by the generation of Santa Monica activists in their thirties. James Conn, for example, worked in the civil rights and antiwar movements as a student in the 1960s, became an activist Methodist minister and community organizer in the 1970s, was deep into SMRR politics by the decade's end, and was elected to the city council at the same time as Zane. My interviews with activists in and out of city government revealed a fairly consistent pattern: personal stories about movement politics in the 1960s in places like Berkeley, a mixture of new professionalism and leftwing politics in the 1970s, and then increasing political involvement in Santa Monica toward the 1980s. Most of the activists were not CED members but almost all of them shared the experiences that gave rise to CED and the political values that were closely aligned with it.

A significant minority of older activists, however, had somewhat different biographies that rooted their values in New Deal and New Frontier traditions. Dolores Press was raised during the depression with a picture of Franklin Roosevelt gracing the family hearth, married her childhood sweetheart, who became a successful college fundraiser and administrator, and raised four children. Her fairly conventional middle class life was disrupted when her husband died in the mid-1970s. She took an office job with the Retail Clerks Union that rekindled her New Deal unionism. She also reported discovering her identity as an independent woman and feminist. Press got involved in local and state Democratic party politics and was drafted by SMRR as a successful unionist–feminist candidate for the rent control board and then the city council.

Kenneth Edwards, who holds an advanced degree in sociology, pioneered new frontiers as a community organizer in Venezuela in the mid-1960s. He then became a probation officer and social worker in the 1970s and spent most of that decade active in grassroots politics and municipal advisory groups, with a special concern for housing and crime issues in Santa Monica. He was elected as a SMRR councilmember in 1981 and chosen by the council as city mayor in 1983. Press, Edwards, and some other local activists were less closely attached to the visionary politics of the 1960s than to the programmatic politics of the liberal wing of the Democratic party. They tended to be issue-oriented, concerned with specific policies related to labor, feminism, housing, crime, seniors' rights, social services, and so forth; and they were joined by various city groups and individuals committed to single-issue politics. These people sometimes found CED and its policy alternatives attractive but they also had independent priorities that conflicted with both new left graduates and people pushing other issues.

Thus, the Santa Monica left had a core ideology but also a considerable range of disagreement. The core ideology is summed up in the general notion of "radical democracy" and in three concepts: human scale community, participatory democracy, and one class society. The general notion of radical democracy points toward a closer relationship between the people and power. The three concepts are somewhat ambiguous but nonetheless fulfill two functions. They speak to middle class aspirations and frustrations. And they legitimate a new social, political, and economic order for America.

In a huge tome criticizing growth and bigness in America, Kirkpatrick Sale explores an alternative:

> The other possibility . . . lies in exactly the opposite direction: toward decentralization of institutions and devolution of power, with the slow dismantling of all large-scale systems that one way or another have created and perpetuated the current crises, and their replacement by smaller, more controllable, more efficient, people-sized units, rooted in local circumstances and guided by local citizens. In short, the *human scale* alternative.[31]

In cities such as New York, Chicago, and Los Angeles, the human scale alternative would literally require a revolution, an overturning of trends and structures that have developed in the past century. In Santa Monica, however, the human scale alternative mostly required the conservation of community traditions, neighborhoods, political prerogatives, and small businesses, but also some restoration work to repair the recent ravages of the marketplace.

CED activist Maurice Zeitlin said that Santa Monica is "a great place to live. We don't have any kind of politics to want to preserve the place where we live."[32] Derek Shearer went a step further. "I never mind being called a conservative. Santa Monica is an almost uniquely balanced city and we want to conserve it."[33] The left's dedication to conserving human scale community took symbolic and tangible forms. Most city activists wanted to preserve the municipal pier against development as both a monument to the city's small town past and a reminder of what could be lost through growth and urbanization. They gave considerable support to parks, pedestrian walkways, and the arts, according to Dennis Zane, "to make the life of people better, more inviting, more community-oriented; the purpose of green space and art is to promote that kind of sense of community."[34] Other ways to promote that sense of community included rent control as a means of protecting the cur-

rent population mix against further gentrification, a moratorium on new
development to preserve the residential and commercial balance, and strict environmental guidelines to safeguard the local ecology. Relatedly, Santa Monica leftists supported neighborhood organizations and voluntary groups. Participation in them, said community liaison officer Vivian Rothstein, "builds community identification" and helps people "to know their neighbors."[35] The organizations and groups were also viewed as political levers that neighbors could use to preserve the unique qualities of their particular section of the city. "Santa Monica's biggest problem," Ruth Yannatta Goldway stated, "is that it is so desirable that people still want to develop it."[36]

The key to aborting overdevelopment was to maintain local political autonomy in opposition to the continuous centralization of political power that has characterized twentieth-century America. Most leftists appreciated the fact that Santa Monica is a charter city—a municipal corporation—with considerable legal power over local affairs; the city can pass laws and make policies with the general presumption that its actions will be upheld in the courts and legitimated by superior county and state agencies. However, the activists were also supersensitive to rightwing groups and politicians who lent verbal support to local power but also ran to the higher courts, assemblies, and executives to override local decisions they disputed. Commenting on a dispute concerning the Santa Monica Airport that pitted local government against federal government, Goldway remarked:

> There's no question that the Reagan Administration, in spite
> of its rhetoric about local control, wanted to have federal control
> in this. . . . The real conservative message is for government control
> in behalf of the business interests and the airport interests are
> very much a part of the business interests that Reagan thinks his
> government should work for.[37]

Santa Monica activists consistently spoke out for local control, for example, supporting lobbying efforts in Sacramento to ensure that no state law was passed that would override Santa Monica rent control. Some SMRR people thought it crucial to Santa Monica that supportive state and federal administrations be elected but their bottom line was to get administrations that "do not attack us."[38]

Local leftists also wanted to support the town's small business economy. Their views on conventional small businesses were, however, more mixed than their consistent advocacy of alternative small business ventures. Zane spoke highly of the "family-run businesses" on the Santa Monica Mall as "sensitive to the local market rather than the regional market" and as a "source of jobs for local people."[39] Zane also saw those businesses as potential allies against big businesses, but James Conn disagreed: "The small business people identify with General Motors, not

Tom Hayden, and that's just the way it is."[40] Shearer occupied the middle ground, simultaneously ruing Chamber of Commerce attacks on the left and suggesting that the Chamber really did not represent small businesses, that it was split and the left could still win small business support. Where all tended to agree was that small businesses should be supported, or in Shearer's words, "I think that people, progressives on the left, have to develop a strategy of pro-small business."[41] They tended to discuss policies such as commercial rent control that would save small businesses from escalating overhead costs, or redevelopment plans aimed at reinvigorating small businesses facing hard times.

Perhaps most crucial, SMRR people were especially endeared to the new business people that set up shop in Santa Monica and evidenced a significant community orientation. Goldway told this story:

> There was a bookstore on Main Street which was forced out by the landlord because it was supportive of the community organization. Well, it wasn't started through the community organization but the people who started it were clearly part of the community organization and there was a great deal of community support for it and fundraising for it; and they helped it when it moved to another location. . . . It was a center for various meetings and a wonderful place. Unfortunately, the new location made it impossible for it to survive.[42]

Such community-oriented businesses needed to be preserved and nurtured. And one way to do this was to "work cooperatively with the business community and the hotel industry to make Santa Monica an attractive tourist place, to increase tourist business," said Maurice Zeitlin.[43] Conserving Santa Monica's turn-of-the-century tourism traditions by reinforcing them would better enable community bookstores, coops, artists, entertainers, and others in the interstitial economy to survive, and would also generate tax revenues that could be used for other city projects.

Underlying activists' support for community, neighborhoods, local autonomy, and small businesses was a vision that synthesized the virtues of small town America and leftwing politics. Derek Shearer capsulized that vision in describing his own quality of life:

> In our hometown of Santa Monica, California, my family shops at Co-Opportunity, a food cooperative, where we save 10 percent to 20 percent on our monthly bill, purchase healthy food, and see our friends while we shop. Our children attend the Santa Monica Alternative School (SMASH), which is a public school, but run in a democratic manner with student and parent participation. I shop for books at the Midnight Special or Papa Bach, both run by political activists. The Liberty Hill Foundation, located in the nearby Ocean Park Church, gives donations to a variety of com-

munity action groups in the Los Angeles area. We take our children to hear benefit concerts by artists like Pete Seeger for *In These Times* or Jackson Brown to raise money for the statewide nuclear freeze campaign. *Mother Jones, Working Papers, democracy*, and other publications arrive at our house with news and political information.[44]

Human scale community, Santa Monica style, combined the neighborliness of Main Street, the educational and consumer options of suburbia, and the political discussions and commitments of leftwing America. There was something in it for older small businesses struggling in the marketplace and for professionals seeking an escape from the metropolis; but there was a lot in it for the new professionals and new business people who, trying to intermarry work and politics, settled in Santa Monica in the 1970s.

How was human scale community to be protected and nurtured? The consistent SMRR answer was participatory democracy. An old concept born again during the new left era, "participatory democracy connotes decentralization of power for the direct involvement of amateurs in authoritative decisionmaking."[45] It means people taking control over their own communities rather than allowing elites to exercise sovereignty. Certainly, decentralization and amateur involvement are consistent with human scale community but it is less obvious whether they are effective means for safeguarding or enhancing it. Perhaps people are not particularly interested in spending the time and energy necessary for participation; perhaps they feel that experts are more qualified to make the crucial decisions. For most of Santa Monica history, residents expended little political effort, trusting the few to look out for community interests; and even all of the hoopla of the 1970s did little to draw more than a few people into politics beyond the ballot box. Santa Monica activists usually believed that most people really do want to participate in politics and thereby develop the expertise to make wise decisions themselves; but the activists also believed that some political entrepreneurship and professional effort was needed to encourage people to take control.

Grassroots political movements depend on mobilizing large numbers of people for involvement but the mobilizations themselves depend on local leaders willing to put in considerable time and ingenuity. The leaders need what Ruth Yannatta Goldway called an "entrepreneurial spirit," which she described as a transference from "marketplace activity." She saw leaders as competitors, competing for people's ears, understanding, support, time, ideas, involvement, and commitment; and the opposition included not only other political organizers but also television, family activities, job commitments, apathy, skepticism, and related components of daily life that distance people from politics. "I hope," she continued, "that we have some of those people in our community groups and that they put that entrepreneurial spirit to work within the community."[46]

One aspect of the entrepreneurial spirit was a commitment to growth, not of the city but of mass-based political action. This involved constant recruitment of new members, coalition formation, petitioning and outreach work, networking, lobbying, envelope-licking, canvassing, and hours and hours of meetings. This also involved cultivating new generations of leadership as the movement grew. James Conn talked about "the leadership development process" whereby experienced leaders put new people into responsible roles that challenged them and cultivated their entrepreneurial skills to continue to "energize and enable and empower" more citizens.[47] Political entrepreneurship is exhausting and self-sacrificing, which is one reason why so many Santa Monica activists were single and childless.

The entrepreneurial spirit also involved toughness and shrewdness. Toughness is more than the ability to keep going past the point of burnout, to withstand poor political odds and setbacks, and to encourage others to do the same. It is also the ability to withstand success. As a movement grows, there is the chance that leadership will usurp power to ensure that its goals do not get devalued by new members. As a movement becomes a more serious political force for the opposition to reckon with, leadership might suffer a combination of personal attacks, investigations, redbaiting, libel, and so forth, as well as temptations to cooptation. Shrewdness, on the other hand, involves knowing when it is time to slow down, reassess goals, and perhaps accept compromises. Maurice Zeitlin noted this combination of toughness and shrewdness in Ruth Yannatta Goldway's dealings with the business community:

> When you have political power and you take political power seriously, and you are concerned about not dissipating it, and the businessmen know it, you then sit down and deal. . . . When it became clear to [businessmen] that that was the case, and Ruth is the pointperson on this—unquestionably unbending, unyielding, principled commitment to this—when that was clear to them that the mayor thought this way, that the movement thinks this way, that it's got political power and is very likely to continue to have that political power, then they sat down and said, "Okay, let's try to figure out what's reasonable." And they got into quite pragmatic discussions.[48]

Santa Monica activists took pride in knowing when a hard line or a soft compromise was most likely to enhance movement numbers and commitment; in this, they were very much like the savvy businessmen who know when to attack worldwide communism and when to market their goods in the People's Republic of China. Both appreciated the need for the iron fist and the velvet glove.

Still another aspect of the entrepreneurial spirit was the willingness to take risks, to innovate and experiment. The Santa Monica left self-consciously took the risk of transforming a relatively spontaneous grass-roots movement that protested against government policies into an organized electoral machine that captured government power; and, in the process, it professionalized its electoral politics and governmental power. The danger was that grassroots participation, initiative, and energy would dissipate as organizers and experts played an increasingly large role; the potential payoff was that the struggle for and achievement of newfound power would draw more people into the political arena. Most Santa Monica activists were aware of the danger but confident of the payoff.

At the very least, more participation meant more voters turning out for municipal elections. SMRR members believed they accomplished the increased turnout through a combination of grassroots organizing and "modern electoral techniques" such as "computer-aided targeting, direct mail literature appeals, and intensive Big League fundraising."[49] Both the organizing and the techniques became more professional over time. The core of part-time volunteer canvassers would be augmented first by paid full-time organizers and then by professional campaign consultants drawn from CED and elsewhere. Computer-aided targeting called for people with computer expertise, and the increasing use of local surveys called for professional pollsters. Direct mail appeals and door-to-door fundraising persisted but with more sophistication, and new devices such as $100-a-plate dinners run by professionals appeared. The common justifications for these trends included: first, political expedience in the face of an opposition with far greater resources; second, political catalysis in the sense that both grassroots organizing and modern electoral techniques provide means to communicate with more people and to get them involved; third, the involvement of increasing numbers of people, as evidenced by increasing voter turnout once SMRR entered into local campaigns; and, fourth, the fruits of electoral success—access to institutional powers that could be used to stimulate new avenues of popular participation.

In fact, as activist after activist pointed out, SMRR's electoral success put into office people committed to using government as a means of stimulating political dialogue and participation, especially among issues and groups that had too often suffered invisibility through silence. James Conn put it this way: "There are people in neighborhoods being represented in decision processes of this city; they were either patronized or ignored or shut out, and those channels are now open."[50] Among those channels were a host of citizen advisory commissions, task forces, affirmative action programs, municipal unionization efforts, informal meetings, well-attended city council meetings, and scores of public hearings that nurtured a highly charged political environment in Santa Monica. Leftists such as Conn felt that a broad spectrum of residents were now able to speak out and be heard, even if their message was not always what the radicals in city hall wanted to hear.

The process of encouraging participation by all groups in the city was also professionalized, especially by the SMRR-appointed city manager and his staff. John Alschuler brought to his office considerable experience and insight as a public administrator as well as a new professional commitment to enhance residents' power in local politics. He understood that "you get a kind of elitism by participation" in the sense that the people "able to put in the time are basically professional," leaving others outside the political process. But he was able to use his administrative skills to face the "difficulty in bringing into government, in an active way, working people, Hispanic people, and the black community."[51] He tried to show the city council how to redirect various federal funds into neighborhood organizations and projects, and he used his staff to encourage the growth and development of neighborhood organizations in parts of the city that traditionally had little or no voice in decisionmaking. Vivian Rothstein, the city manager's community liaison person, described her job:

> I have two parts to my job. One is to do outreach to the community, to try to organize them, to help build the kernel of new organizations, not necessarily to build the organization but to begin to get citizens together so that they can talk about the organization and a whole variety of issues. And the other is to develop mechanisms so that the people tuned to city issues know when the issues are coming up.[52]

When opposition forces alleged that city officials were using staff time and public resources to do what was tantamount to SMRR political organizing, the left looked to the expertise and new professionalism of SMRR-appointed city attorney Robert Myers and his staff for legal defense. An attorney in Myers' office told me, "The fact that we are directing certain attention to disadvantaged neighborhoods is hardly an indication that appropriate attention is not directed to the more affluent parts of the community."[53] The attorney went on to provide evidence for his assertion as if preparing a brief to defend city participation policy in court. In fact, Myers' office defended many city policies in court with remarkable success; as Dennis Zane suggested, "We've got a hot city attorney's office."[54]

Building participatory democracy, manifested in both entrepreneurial and professional politics in Santa Monica, may or may not have won a grudging respect from the opposition growth machine forces, as some activists suggested. But it certainly did have appeal for both the old and new professionals, who saw opportunities for enhanced control over their community, efforts to utilize political and governmental machinery efficiently, and the use of expertise to serve and involve society's less advantaged citizens. Born-again participatory democracy was also seen as born-again public service. However, the precise nature of that service, in economic terms, was not clear. The Santa Monica left spoke a lot about economic democracy but evidenced little interest in establishing it.

Economic democracy, according to CED's founding statement, is "an evolving system in which economic decisions are made with the involvement and consent of the people affected, rather than on the criterion of private profit for a remote few."[55] What such a system would look like in practice is vague. Martin Carnoy and Derek Shearer's *Economic Democracy* emphasized greater public control over ownership, production, and investment.[56] People's involvement and consent might be manifested in cooperatively owned housing and community development corporations, in public banks and investment institutions, or in publicly owned enterprises; popular control might also appear in greater leverage for unions, worker control and self-management, affirmative action in hiring and promotions, or perhaps worker and community representation on corporate boards. In this sense, economic democracy legitimates the general idea that people should have greater power over the production and flow of goods; and they should experiment with alternatives to the capitalists' unrestricted marketplace, which produces concentrated corporate power, as well as with alternatives to the socialists' state ownership, which results in centralized governmental power.

Some Santa Monica activists, especially the CED minority, wanted to take concrete steps toward economic democracy. They supported efforts to facilitate limited equity housing for low income people and community development corporations that would enhance neighborhood control over housing and needed social services. They stood behind the unionization of city employees, some degree of worker control within municipal agencies, and affirmative action throughout local government. They sometimes talked about enacting a local workers' bill of economic rights, sponsoring a municipally owned arts complex, and creating a municipal bank or public investment institution. However, they encountered two problems.

First, they could do very little on the local level either to enhance popular control over ownership, production, and investment or to take power from the "remote few" who run the corporate economy. A handful of housing cooperatives or community development corporations made virtually no dent in the marketplace; support for worker control within government bore little relationship to worker or community control in the corporate economy; and extensive municipal ownership or investment institutions were simply beyond the fiscal pale of city government. Thus, Dennis Zane liked the idea of a municipal bank but doubted that the city could amass enough capital to make the venture workable, and Maurice Zeitlin's interest in a Public Investment Reserve System was focused at the state level, where financing and legal support were conceivable.[57]

Second, there was little reason to believe that more than a few activists saw economic democracy as a significant item on the local agenda. They may have supported the idea of more economic power to the people but did not necessarily agree that this was either a top priority or the best route for local politics. Ruth Yannatta Goldway said, "I think I'm most disappointed in community groups when it comes to economic development; I guess it's because most people don't really expect to be able to participate and don't conceive of ways in which they can participate."[58] They had other interests. In February 1981, SMRR hammered out and adopted some "Principles of Unity" intended to establish movement priorities in the city.[59] Instead, the "Principles" promised something to everyone in the coalition, specifying neither priorities nor strategies that might define any systematic economic program much less economic democracy. In fact, the document provided no real evidence that economic democracy was of great moment to coalition members.

More indicative of activists' economic thinking is what C. B. Macpherson describes as "one class society."[60] This concept involves a leveling of economic independence rather than wealth. It is an updated version of Thomas Jefferson's idea that private property and ownership, great personal wealth, and a fair amount of economic inequality are justifiable as long as everyone has a measure of economic independence or self-sufficiency. For Jefferson, the wage laborer was not a wage slave to the boss if he was free to quit his job, obtain some land, and return to farming. For Santa Monicans, residents are not economically oppressed when they exercise some control over the fulfillment of their basic needs and living environment. And this greater equality of control could be accomplished through collective community leverage in the marketplace.

Santa Monica activists were not opposed to affluence. They barely blushed when their city councilmembers approved giving SMRR-appointed city manager John Alschuler a $2,440 raise and a $3,000 bonus on top of his $63,500 yearly salary and $14,000 yearly housing allowance; and Alschuler did not blush at receiving it, commenting to a reporter that it was "a fair raise, but it's on an inadequate base."[61] Nor did SMRR people express much dismay at the hefty salaries of other city professionals, including $60,000 per year for someone to manage the restoration of the storm-damaged municipal pier. Local leftists shared with the middle class the belief that hard work, education and expertise, and personal achievement should be rewarded handsomely. And the city's new professionals saw no reason why their own material rewards should be less than those of the old professionals. The left's objection was not to the marriage of effort and reward but, to the contrary, to the dependence of people who make an effort but do not receive their just dessert—often because a few people receive unearned wealth at their expense. This objection was especially apparent, historically and locally, in rent control struggles.

Early in U.S. history, tenant farmers argued that their inability to reap the full reward of their labors was due to the landlord "seen as not entitled to either property or rent because he does not earn them through work."[62] In Santa Monica, tenant activists felt that their inability to achieve their piece of the American Dream despite their efforts was due largely to landlords who extracted unearned windfall profits. The activists tended to be highly educated, career-oriented young men and women who wanted to buy their own homes; but they had suffered the escalating rents that limited their ability to accumulate a downpayment and the inflated housing prices that put the dream of homeownership beyond their perceived grasp.[63] Their inability to control their housing situation was punctuated by the threat and reality of arbitrary evictions and the demolition of rental units. Part of their problem stemmed from the difficulties of career advancement in the 1970s and 1980s, a cause of concern to economic democrats but one largely unsolvable at the municipal level. Another part of their problem was landlord behavior, but that could be modified by city rent control.

Robert Myers, author of Santa Monica's rent control law, agreed with activists who thought that landlordism could be an acceptable institution if owners worked to maintain their buildings and then recovered operation costs as well as modest returns on their investments.[64] But Myers pointed out how easy it was for landlords to do no work and yet reap immense profits. Tax laws allowed them to use "a largely fictitious depreciation expense to show a loss even though profit is realized," resulting in a windfall subsidized by the average taxpayer. More important were the huge unearned profits available from speculative buying and selling, paid for by renters. Myers cited the case of one four-unit complex in Santa Monica. It was purchased for $72,000 in 1974, sold for $100,000 in 1976, resold for $165,000 in 1977, and sold again for $195,000 in 1978. In four years, the rents soared 85 percent as each new owner sought to cover higher finance costs and raise rental income to increase the building's market value for the next sales go-round. Rent control was a way to enhance the tenants' control over their housing by limiting landlords' ability to reap unearned income.

A similar logic characterized other left economic perspectives in the city. Residents had little control over their neighborhoods and living environments because of nearly unrestricted development by corporations. The local left voiced support for development agreements that allowed neighborhood groups and city officials to regain control by making affordable housing, parks and recreation centers, jobs, daycare centers, social services, and other community amenities the price of doing business in Santa Monica. The price was not viewed as extortion in return for city permits, as developers claimed. Rather, it was perceived as a tax on unearned income that developers derived from locating in Santa Monica's near-ideal setting, drawing on the community's professional and consumer base, and using the city's economic infrastructure and services.[65] In some cases, the price was simply the rental fee for leasing city property. Referring to one leasing deal where public access was part of the price for a private club using beach property, James Conn stated, "What you're talking about is rich folks subsidizing something else that's happening; and what you've got rich folks subsidizing, in this situation, is the opportunity for poor people to have a beach club, to use a beach facility."[66]

The left's commitment to a one class society where earned affluence and economic independence coexist can be understood as a form of middle class unionism or consumer power. Residents mobilize and organize, combine their numbers, votes, and resources, and call on their agents in government to enhance their bargaining power in the marketplace. When successful, they generate enough leverage to force landlords, developers, and businesses to cut their unearned profits and to subsidize residents' economic independence. Santa Monica activists used consumer power to negotiate control over the production and disposal of toxic wastes, traffic and parking congestion, and other market byproducts that eroded residents' ability to control the quality of life in their community. Whereas economic democracy attracted some middle class support because it rhetorically promised to restore the prerogatives of professionals and extend them to workers, the struggle for one class society won considerable middle class support because it simultaneously validated the affluence of those who "earned" it and promised immediate reforms in line with new professionals' quality of life and social consciousness concerns.

While radical democracy is a convenient label for describing the Santa Monica left's attachment to values such as human scale community, participatory democracy, and one class society, it is not meant to imply that the left's core ideology was a coherent whole. It was not. The pieces did not always fit together. Indeed, there was considerable contradiction and ambiguity, as will become apparent in the discussions of leftist practice in Part 2. Also, activists plugged into the core ideology at different points, some drawing more on human scale community, for example, than on one class society. This partly reflects that fact that the Santa Monica left contained a significant number of people either still enamored of variants of New Deal liberalism or at least less than committed to new left visions and their offshoots.

The Ideological Periphery

"The New Deal has run as far as it can run," said James Conn, reflecting a general viewpoint among Santa Monica's new left graduates.[67] The struggles that gave rise to the New Deal and the legislation that issued from it were unquestionably an important stage in modern American history but were now dated. The New Deal was too programmatic and

issue-oriented, too much centered in the hands of elitist professionals
and too much involved in an imperial growth consciousness. To the
contrary, suggested Conn, "We are cutting against the consciousness of
empire; we are creating, I think, another way of looking at the world
and that way is one that's more concerned with our responsibility to the
earth, our connection to the earth, the kind of environment that we're
creating, the quality of life issues that are sort of nebulous and yet they
are felt."[68] Nonetheless, as Derek Shearer noted, SMRR was a "left
liberal coalition" instigated by former new leftists but one that "has been
open to and worked with real genuine liberals, people in the local Santa
Monica Democratic Club, or in the local trade unions who are not your
old sort of phony cold war, pro-Vietnam War liberals, but real authentic
New Deal, ADA, FDR liberals, the good folks."[69] Two of those "good
folks" were councilmembers Dolores Press and Kenneth Edwards.

Dolores Press identified with labor in personal and political terms.
"I'm only one generation from a working class family. My father was an
oil worker and worked in the refinery all his life."[70] Whom did she identify with in Santa Monica? "I certainly feel that my background and my
personal life can better relate to the [working class] people in the Pico
neighborhood than to the [affluent] people who live north of Montana
Avenue. I can't relate to them at all; I have no direct relationship with
rich people in my life." Press spoke with great facility about local labor
unions, their current activities, and their links to local and statewide
politics. And she functioned on the city council as a watchdog on municipal labor policies, sometimes with considerable frustration.

She disapproved of an old general services department policy of writing
contracts that deferred worker compensation payments until the third
day of illness. She was unhappy with the city's doing business with nonunion printers and the fact that the practice could not be stopped immediately because the city lacked a written policy favoring union shops.
She was dismayed that most of the bargaining units for the city workers
were "quote unquote associations" instead of AFL-CIO confrontational
unions. She was "appalled" at an attempt by the SMRR-appointed city
manager to contract out for cemetery workers to establish a cheap labor
force. "He had some figures that were very impressive about how much
money the city could save and I said I didn't care." On the other hand,
Press was pleased with the support that local unions had given to SMRR
and its candidates, rattling off a list of unions and the supporting services
they had provided.

She also had some concrete labor-related goals for the city. "I'm very
interested in having a social policy that says that we want to know if any
contractors we do business with have National Labor Relations Board
citations." Moreover, "I look forward to having some kind of meaningful
social policy guidelines in terms of not doing business with contractors
who do business in South Africa and not doing business with labor con-

tractors who discriminate and don't hire women and don't hire minorities." Press's feminism was less the theoretical sort that emerged from the new left than, again, a more programmatic, labor-oriented set of proposals. She wanted more women on the police force, women in the fire department, more women in positions of authority in city hall, particularly in upper-echelon bureaucratic posts. She also wanted to use city money to establish "comparable worth" practices whereby women assistant librarians would make as much money as male groundskeepers who worked for the city.

Press was aware that she was fighting an uphill battle within the Santa Monica left. SMRR people generally had different priorities; some simply did not show much interest in labor policies; and some even had a stake in opposing them. Press said, "I feel responsibility to keep the others informed about what is going on in those two areas"—labor and feminism—but she found it difficult to do so with a full-time job and family. She regretted that she could not be at city hall every day to follow through, talk with department heads, and create constant pressure on behalf of her priorities. "So I don't always have the strength of influence on the staff that other council people have; so therefore my issues may not be in the sunlight of attention." Fortunately, she added, Kenneth Edwards also had a "higher consciousness on labor issues."

Edwards identified himself not so closely with labor as with what he called "the real people" in the streets. "Many of my colleagues in SMRR come from quite well-to-do backgrounds. I'm probably the only legitimate poor person."[71] Edwards was concerned that SMRR colleagues too often engaged in "verbal gymnastics" or "bravado" or in talk about "municipal banks," which, he believed, had little meaning to less privileged people, who "see us as overly educated, using words they don't understand, involved in issues that they don't care about." In his notion of a progressive government, SMRR people would speak less to one another but rather "go out into the streets and have some uneducated people feel comfortable enough in their own words to tell us what they really want and listen to them." What Edwards had heard on the streets related little to new left quality of life issues and more to affordable housing, safeguarding and enhancing job opportunities, support for labor unions, efficient public services, and crime prevention. Edwards added that "the traditional victims of crime are the blacks, the browns, and the people that are the natural constituents of the Democratic party."

Edwards' version of New Deal liberalism differed from Press's outlook in three senses. First, Edwards talked about empowering people to be heard, participate, and share in decisionmaking but he also expressed great confidence in city bureaucrats. "I happen to like the city manager form of government," he stated. The city council should be viewed "much like a board of directors. You formulate policy. You delegate it to professionals and, if you're unhappy or it's not being carried out, you have the

option of removing them." Unlike Press, Edwards felt little need to pres- sure city staff because he had much faith in the professionals' good will
and ability to carry out directives efficiently. Second, Edwards was not
overly impressed with the no-growth or limited-growth consciousness of
many SMRR activists. He thought that his colleagues had been too
preoccupied with height limits, density limits, and green space, acting as
if "the world's going to rise and fall [on] every six-unit condominium
that is built." As a result, he stated, they "jacked" around developers at
the risk of imperiling the revenues and jobs that developers bring to the
city. Press, while interested in revenues and job creation, was by self-
admission likely to defer to other councilmembers on questions of "the
environment and stuff like that." Third, Edwards was very concerned
with facilitating interclass harmony. "It's a responsibility you have when
you take an oath of office to represent all of the people." He talked to the
opposition, sought common ground between the rich and poor or labor
and management or tenants and homeowners, and supported the appointments of developers, bankers, and downtown businessmen to city
commissions. In a sense, Press played Mother Jones to Edwards' Franklin Roosevelt.

Within the activist community, numbers likely supported Conn's core
belief that it was time to move beyond the New Deal; but key political
forces also supported Press's and Edwards' varieties of New Deal liberalism. Labor unions gave considerable support to SMRR, and Press
was their major voice in city politics. Many of the new professionals in
city hall, activists in community and neighborhood groups, and members of the Santa Monica Democratic Club were more comfortable with
Edwards' priorities and politics than with the younger generation of new
left graduates. Ultimately, the existence of such "good folks" ensured
that the interests of workers, minorities, low income groups, and women
(the so-called special interests of the Democratic coalition) were embedded in Santa Monica's ideological periphery despite the fact that
some of these groups had little clout at the ballot box.

The Santa Monica left was able to keep its coalition intact only by
negotiating its middle class appeal with the interests of more traditional
New Deal constituencies. The negotiation process was often difficult.
Major differences existed within the core, and between the core and the
periphery. Local activists had to make a concerted effort not to force
ideological coherence but to find some common ground on an issue-by-
issue basis. Thus, they talked about human scale community, participatory democracy, and some version of economic change in terms intended
to appeal to the less well-off, or they spoke about empowering the powerless but without sacrificing the quality of life concerns of the middle class.
But they had to discuss, bargain, and compromise constantly to locate a
lowest common denominator of agreement.

Perhaps the best symbol of that lowest common denominator was what Ruth Yannatta Goldway called "democracy with a small d," an invitation to keep the dialogue going between those discontented with the American Dream and those who still remained outside it.[72] For the most part, the Santa Monica activists were intent on avoiding the ideological rigidity that seduced some sections of the new left and on continuing an experimental attitude that kept goals and strategies flexible.

Democracy with a Small "d"

New left intellectuals, Tom Hayden and CED, and the Santa Monica left made a conscious choice to discard older ideologies that lacked an organic connection to the everyday lives of Americans and to situate their own values in an American historical context that shaped the everyday lives of citizens. Their general viewpoint was that American liberals had not gone far enough in promoting moral, political, and economic alternatives that effectively challenged the concentrated power of elites; and that American socialists, in their narrow economic focus, had ignored major moral and political problems, failed to mobilize large numbers of people to fight for solutions, and accomplished little in the way of gaining enough power to experiment with new directions, norms, institutions, and policies.[73] They believed that there could be a "third way" between the liberal reformism that too easily accommodated itself to hierarchical power and the socialist revolutionism that so often was a theoretical dialogue among isolated intellectuals. The source and inspiration for the third way is an historical strain of American thought that Isaac Kramnick identifies as "a bourgeois radicalism."[74]

Thomas Paine and Thomas Jefferson might be considered early bourgeois radicals. They were bourgeois in their defense of individualism, private property, marketplace competition, and limited government intervention. Nonetheless, they were radical to the extent that they envisioned an egalitarian society founded on nature, autonomy, and public virtue that justified protest and even revolution against the aristocratic, centralizing, and industrial impetus of national elites. Ralph Waldo Emerson and Henry David Thoreau have a place in radical chronicles because they exaggerated bourgeois individualism and placed it under nature's moral authority while standing against the growth of mass society, majoritarianism, and concentrated economic power. Radical histories also devote chapters to Susan B. Anthony and Frederick Douglass, who demanded bourgeois civil liberties, political rights, and property ownership for America's excluded and whose visions of equality ran up against the sexism and racism that predated capitalist America and would postdate socialist victories elsewhere. Late-nineteenth-century populists were bourgeois radicals too, seeking the survival of decentralized farming against the corporate domination of production, transportation, and financing.

These historical figures were bourgeois—which is to say only that they were Americans nurtured on some version of the American Dream, on its moral and political as well as material promises. Their radicalism was founded on a shared belief that the American Dream and its supporting social structures could be renegotiated to legitimate new possibilities for building an egalitarian society. They constructed moral visions to reconcile individual autonomy and community, not individual self-aggrandizement and instrumental relations. They developed political visions that combined democratic participation, intelligence, and public virtue, not mass resignation, intellectual hierarchy, and politics for special interests. They also designed economic visions; some questioned the goodness of industrial affluence, others were intent on redistributing that affluence, but virtually all contrived to redefine affluence as a means to moral and political goals rather than as an end in itself. Their many visions involved them in struggles to preserve aspects of the American past against marketplace erosion and to remake the future to dislodge the elitist foundations of power. In a sense, they wanted to save middle America, not as it was but as it might be, and salvage was possible only by restructuring society so that no one could dominate but everyone could share the Dream.

The Santa Monica left represented a bourgeois radicalism updated to twentieth-century standards. It wanted to save a middle America no longer located on imperiled family farms but on urban terrain where small businesses were dependent on the corporate economy and professionals' autonomy, intelligence, and service ethic were increasingly difficult to market. It wanted to restructure society to ensure that political and economic elites could not promote middle class subordination or prevent workers, minorities, women, and poor people from partaking of middle class independence. It focused mainly on the benign moral and political values that give meaning or quality to middle class affluence, not on the manichean capitalism versus socialism confrontation that was manufactured by media analysts of Santa Monica. In short, the Santa Monica left's version of bourgeois radicalism is appropriately labeled middle class radicalism.

Does this middle class focus make the Santa Monica activists less radical than the American socialists who claim ideologies of radical change as their own private property? Not necessarily. The middle class focus means that theirs will be a different sort of revolution if it succeeds.

Santa Monica's core ideology endorsed the morality of human scale community and the politics of participatory democracy, and thereby legitimated a middle class subculture subversive of instrumentalism, centrism, and economic domination, by extension, in both capitalist and socialist societies. Such a subculture, according to James C. Scott and other scholars of social change, can contribute to a defense of local traditions that mobilizes people to transform the social and power relations of their society.[75] The transformation process may include a struggle

against local representatives of national elites and then the national elites
themselves; and it may include a struggle for innovations that fortify the
subculture. In Santa Monica, for example, the transformation process
was manifested in opposition to the local growth machine, local notables,
and, at a broader level, what James Conn called "the consciousness of
empire" exhibited by political and economic elites,[76] and in support for
innovations such as E. F. Schumacher's "technology with a human face,"
which would drastically alter control, focus, practice, and application in
modern science and professionalism.[77] The transformation process was
also manifested in a fight for the decentralization and downward redistribution of political power in a post-World War II era when national
elites demand ever more concentrated political power to safeguard their
shaken hegemony in the world.[78] Santa Monica's core ideology "goes to
the root" of major problems that are not necessarily solved by economic
changes; the core ideology gave priority to moral and political matters
unlike the ideology of those American socialists who focused primarily
on economic relations and therefore might have a distorted vision of
dilemmas that threaten not only the desired economic future but the
future itself.

Of course, the Santa Monica activists did not ignore economic relations. They did experiment with values and strategies that put people
ahead of profits. CED members invited their audiences to rethink rather
than acquiesce in the received values of the marketplace; they legitimated
various forms of worker control and community control over production, investment, and distribution that, put into practice, would in fact
reshape the contours of American economic life. Local activists with an
affinity for some version of one class society promoted an economic
alternative that would require a major economic transformation and
likely result in far more economic equality than currently existed. While
Santa Monica activists did not explicitly think through a systematic
transformation to one class society, Philip Green can provide us with an
embryonic sense of such a transformation.[79]

Green says that an egalitarian economy can retain private property,
market relations, and wage labor if two crucial changes are made. One is
that citizens abolish the legal underpinnings of the limited-liability corporation, which would undermine the vast accumulations of capital that
make economic domination by the few possible. The other change is
that citizens use government to create public institutions that guarantee
all individuals the right to develop their skills without economic sacrifice
and the autonomy to hire themselves out, if they so wish, on their own
terms. In short, both the economic democrats and the one class levelers
legitimated a major redistribution of economic power. And there is no
reason to believe that their economic strategies, although vague to be
sure, were less fundamental steps toward Marx's "from each according
to his abilities, to each according to his needs" than overt socialized

ownership of the major means of production. Certainly, the mixed results of socialist experimentation around the world and the failure of
socialists to have much impact in the United States suggests that new
economic strategies merit consideration by radicals.

In one sense, Santa Monica activists could be considered more radical
than many American socialists. SMRR people self-consciously sacrificed
theoretical rigor and ideological coherence to facilitate communication
with mass audiences. Their ideas and terminologies were pliant enough
to capture the interest of Americans, who, according to Daniel Yankelovich, are now seeking the equally pliant goal of "self-fulfillment" that
could as easily lend itself to a communitarian ethic as to a narcissistic outlook.[80] Having captured popular interests, activists' ideas came through
with enough clarity and persuasion to give them a taste of political authority, which was then used to provide more public forums, media coverage, and experiments that facilitated more communication and dialogue.
The fact that activists' ideas were not frozen into a rigid ideological edifice
meant that real dialogue could take place because radicals had not pre-
determined all the answers.

By way of contrast, a good many American socialists have chosen
theoretical rigor over mass communication. They deal in highly technical
concepts and abstract terminologies that mean little to highly educated
people and almost nothing to less educated people.[81] They often claim
to represent working class interests but are prone to dissociate themselves from popular movements, including worker movements, because
real struggles "fail to conform to doctrinal prescriptions regarding constituencies, strategies, and demands."[82] And more than a few socialists
have been so enamored of their own theories that they want not dialogue
but mass compliance.[83] At the extreme, socialists have created the social
vacuum that makes them a threat to no one.

One might say that Thomas Paine wanted a declaration of independence and a revolution to promote democracy with a small d for America.
Though his ideas and pamphlets inspired both, the results were disap-
pointing. The elitist Federalists rather than the common people were the
main victors. One might also say that Santa Monica's radicals wanted a
declaration of independence and a revolution in power structures, this
time for the American middle class. But they were hesitant despite their
public optimism lest they fail to carry through radical change. They
wondered whether they could sustain everpresent tensions between individual autonomy and community, participation and leadership, grassroots politics and political office, or affluence and equality in both their
private and public lives. They were not certain that they could find the
common ground between the middle class and the New Deal constituencies to launch what Frances Fox Piven and Richard A. Cloward call
"a new class war" between the multiclass beneficiaries of the welfare
state and the upper class advocates of the warfare state.[84] And given the

history of radical politics in other cities and the constraints that come with governing, they had doubts if their reign would have much lasting impact. Like Thomas Paine, they dreamed radical American Dreams; unlike Thomas Paine, they inherited a heavy dose of middle class pragmatism that injects hope into doubt by validating compromises.

"You know," Maurice Zeitlin told me, "in the cocktail party circuit, you can make revolutions very easily."[85] When the Santa Monica radicals achieved power, they gave up the cocktail party circuit for the political laboratory. And their experiment in transforming middle class radicalism from theory to practice is a case study in both middle class radicalism in action and the barriers to radical change in the United States.

Part 2
The Practice

Sometimes it is said that man cannot be trusted with the government of himself. Can he be trusted with the government of others? Or have we found angels, in the form of kings, to govern him? Let history answer this question.

Thomas Jefferson

4
Of Principles and Politics

All matters of principle, program, and strategy require unanimity among the SMRR organizations. The result so far has been a radical-liberal coalition that works. Committed to full and free discussion and democratic decisionmaking, the coalition bends rather than breaks when differences arise.

This derives from a recognition that in today's America, splits among liberals, radicals, and socialists can benefit only the right and the status quo. SMRR also consciously abandoned the left's disdain for "practical politics" and works hard at translating abstract theory and political principles into effective action in the electoral arena.

Maurice Zeitlin [1]

"Winning," says Harry Boyte, "is the lifeblood of grassroots organizing,
danger to the principles that justify and catalyze grassroots movements
in the first place. Winning may mean a grassroots demobilization once
victories are institutionalized. Winning may pressure grassroots leaders
with political power to devalue principles in the name of political expedience. In matters of principles and politics, whether the setting is Santa
Monica or Mozambique, there are no secure marriages.

Rent Control Wars

In 1977, Tom Hayden and the Campaign for Economic Democracy
(CED) were not particularly interested in pursuing the principle of
human scale community through the politics of rent control. On the one
hand, Hayden's own version of "small is beautiful" focused mainly on
solar energy as a decentralized technology and an alternative to the concentrated power of oil cartels. On the other hand, Hayden's solution to
the housing crisis in California had little to do with human scale community or rent control. Hayden supported extensive building projects to
create new low cost housing and public housing.[3] Hayden and CED
were latecomers to the tenant activism that was emerging throughout
California that year.

The Coalition for Economic Survival took the lead in housing struggles in the Los Angeles area. It helped to organize tenant unions, demonstrations against inflated rents, and steady pressure on the Los Angeles
city council to enact some form of rent freeze, an antigouging ordinance,
and a rent control law. A group of Santa Monica seniors engaged in
similar activities but went the Los Angelinos one step better. The seniors
wrote, petitioned, and organized a rent control initiative that ultimately
became Proposition P on the June 1978 ballot. Their initiative was defeated by a 56 percent to 44 percent margin in the same election that
brought California its famous Proposition 13 tax reduction measure.
Apparently, many people voted against the rent control initiative based
on tenants' hopes and landlords' promises that lower property taxes would
be converted into lower rents.

Tenants' hopes were quickly shattered on the altar of landlords' profits.
An overheated real estate market combined with the confidence of electoral victory prompted landlords to raise rents, convert apartments to
condominiums, and sell out to speculators and big developers. More
than 70 percent of the population, Santa Monica tenants were incensed.
The battle lines were more clearly drawn than ever before and the growth
machine was the enemy.

The Santa Monica chapter of CED, approximately ten members at the time, had mixed views on the rent control struggle. Some activists, such as Dennis Zane, felt that rent control was Santa Monica's major organizing issue and that CED could and should direct it; but others, including Tom Hayden at the statewide level, opposed a major investment of activist energy in rent control.[4] In the face of possible intrachapter conflict, Zane pursued the rent control issue outside of CED. He and others helped to organize the Santa Monica Fair Housing Alliance (SMFHA) and to persuade people within the Democratic Club to join the rent control battle. As the grassroots movement gathered momentum, the local CED chapter exercised its autonomy and enrolled in the struggle despite Hayden's strategic opposition.

Soon after the June 1978 defeat, the growing tenant movement presented a rent rollback proposal to the Santa Monica city council. Tenants testified for the proposal in terms of renter rights, human needs, and the patent unfairness of speculative profits. A few mentioned the possibility of rent strikes, recall elections, and even riots should the city council fail to afford renters some form of relief.[5] The city council minority was willing to consider a modest gesture of relief but the majority, led by the city's bank officer mayor, refused even token action. Its refusal was consistent with a longstanding policy of stonewalling any citizen requests that seemed to interfere with the real estate market. According to Kenneth Edwards, "Seymour Cohen, who was on the council at the time, a realtor, said, 'We beat them once. We'll beat them again.'"[6]

Why didn't the conservative city council respond with some halfmeasure that might have taken the steam out of the rent control movement? First, the council leaders were part of the growth machine and shared the modern conservative belief that any restraints on market expansion are inherently unjust and economically foolish. Second, history seemed to be on their side. Stonewalling had worked in the past and the June 1978 rent control defeat implied that outright opposition would work in the future. Third, the opposition to rent control was too fragmented to strike a compromise on a modest half-measure. Christine Reed, a moderate councilmember, stated that the opposition forces in Santa Monica were "a diverse mish-mash of people" that included "Democrats" and "liberals" as well as "the old establishment—the Chamber, the downtown business interests, and the old line families, many of whom own rental properties."[7] In other words, professional managerial class liberals, growth machine conservatives, ambivalent small business people, and homeowner groups that opposed rent control had among themselves little common ground for talk much less for joint action.

The city council's response stimulated greater rent control activism with local CED members taking the initiative. The CED people midwifed Santa Monicans for Renters' Rights (SMRR), the rent control coalition consisting of themselves, SMFHA, and the Democratic Club. They could do so because they had developed a degree of mutual recognition and trust during the various struggles of the 1970s, because their overlapping memberships in the other organizations allowed them to argue the case for coalition as insiders, and because rent control had emerged as the crucial unifying issue on the left. The fact that CED's agenda was much broader than SMFHA's single-issue focus and significantly different from Democratic Club politics was no problem as long as the coalition was fighting to preserve the integrity of the community through rent control, in opposition to the growth machine. Thus, in late 1978, the SMRR coalition was born.

The SMRR people oversaw the drafting of a new rent control initiative that was to be placed on the municipal ballot in the April 1979 election. They sought out legal aid attorney Robert Myers to draft an initiative that would close the loopholes that undermined rent control laws across the nation and that would stand up in the courts. SMRR ran the petition campaign and the initiative became Proposition A, a city charter rent control amendment that Allan Heskin called "the toughest rent control amendment in the state."[8] The proposition called for the establishment of an independently elected and operated rent control board, with autonomous personnel and budgetary powers. The board would administer a rent control law with provisions for establishing base rent levels, regulating rent adjustments, banning the demolition or conversion of rental units, limiting just cause for evictions, excluding rent decontrol when units are vacated, defining the responsibility of landlords for building maintenance and service, and levying stiff penalties for landlord abuses. A key exemption was for "mom and pop" landlords with owner-occupied properties that had no more than three rental units. The overall object of Proposition A was "the preservation of the number and quality of rental units affordable to low and moderate income residents of Santa Monica," achieved through legal mechanisms that minimized the possibility of city council tampering.[9]

Because rent control could not be totally insulated from city hall, SMRR decided to run its own candidates for the city council. CED members were attuned to Tom Hayden's argument that the post-1960s was a time when leftist candidates could win public office; and the Democratic Club, affiliated with the Democratic party, took such electoral contests as normal politics. SMRR interviewed possible candidates pledged to support rent control and then endorsed the candidacies of Ruth Yannatta Goldway and William Jennings. Goldway was a consumer advocate who had narrowly lost the Democratic primary for a State Assembly nomination in 1977. Although not a member of CED, she had gained considerable support from CED in her State Assembly race and was associated with it on a broad range of issues. Jennings was a liberal lawyer, also a past president of the local Democratic Club. There was some talk about running a candidate for the third city council vacancy but some SMRR people thought it would be unwise to challenge the one incumbent standing for re-election and SMRR as a whole could not come up with a consensus third candidate.

If the April 1979 election was ever in doubt, the Santa Monica growth machine eradicated all uncertainties. Between 1977 and 1979, more than 2,000 Santa Monica rental units were demolished or converted to condominiums.[10] But just months before the April 1979 election, the city council and the city planning commission gave out tentative tract maps for the asking. This allowed landlords and developers the right to demolish or convert their units before Proposition A was submitted to the voters. What followed became known locally as "the demolition derby." Tenants were suddenly evicted en masse; buildings were torn down; new luxury developments were announced. One activist, who had served in Southeast Asia, put it this way: "I mean, there were parts of the city that looked like Vietnam."[11] Some 3,000 additional units were threatened by the city's largesse with permits. The darker side of the marketplace was illuminated and SMRR campaigners had the political savvy to organize in most of the affected buildings.

They accumulated enough voter support to win Proposition A by a 54 percent to 46 percent margin—a 20 percent turn around from the previous rent control initiative. SMRR also elected its two city council candidates by comfortable margins. And these victories were just the beginning. In July 1979, SMRR ran five candidates for the five seats on the new rent control board and won every single contest. That November, SMRR successfully ran a rent control candidate to fill a city council seat vacated by an ailing opposition member, giving the coalition control of three out of seven council seats; SMRR also engineered the defeat of a so-called fair rent initiative put up by landlords to gut rent control. In June 1980, SMRR activists were part of a winning statewide campaign to defeat an antirenter measure coming out of Sacramento. In short, the grassroots tenant movement had won, and rent control became an institutionalized part of Santa Monica life.

Although few people noticed or particularly cared at the time, SMRR's unbroken string of victories was purchased at a price. The actual struggle for rent control was a microcosmic form of human scale community. Organizing renters into tenant unions, volunteer groups, and political cadres stimulated interpersonal relationships and discussions among residents in the same buildings, blocks, and neighborhoods. People talked to each other about the nature of community, the local quality of life, and possible programs and strategies for preserving Santa Monica's small town virtues against the inroads of the regional marketplace. The losing battles of 1978, including the defeated rent control initiative and the city council stonewall, helped to mobilize citizens to demand greater control over their everyday lives and living conditions. And the struggle between SMRR, with few resources other than the appeal of rent control, and its well-heeled opposition was a David-versus-

Goliath confrontation that unified the underdogs. But victory worked against this mobilization and democratic activism.

The institutionalization of rent control through the charter amendment and the installation of the rent control board dramatically altered the nature of the issue. Tenants with complaints about their housing situations now appeared as individuals at hearings before the rent control board. Local talk focused less on community, the quality of life, and preservation strategies than on technical policies and rules, formulae, and procedures by which the rent control board was administering the law. Mobilizations for rent control lost some of their drawing power when they were converted into mobilizations in defense of rent control. Meanwhile, citizens' sense of empowerment was diminished as the political battlefield shifted from the local scene to various courtrooms, where rent control lawyers argued fine points of law and constitutionality, and to state government, where city lobbyists worked against efforts to deprive localities of rent control powers.

As the rent control board went about its business of upholding tenants' rights and depriving landlords of past privileges, sometimes with great speed and often with great rhetorical flourish, it made many enemies. The opposition claimed that it was becoming another bloated government bureaucracy, run by five "ayatollahs," that constituted a political Goliath intent on crushing the life out of the little guy who had invested his life savings in a modest six-unit apartment complex. And there was just enough truth in these claims, though they were vastly exaggerated and distorted, to dissuade many activists from investing their time and energy in an exhausting defense of the institution. Ironically, the price of victory was to channel momentum from human scale politics to greater individualism, administrative technicalities, professionalized debates, and a war of rhetoric that, like Vietnam, seemed unwinnable.

Leftwing Entrepreneurialism

The SMRR coalition's most important and decisive victory came in April 1981, when its four candidates for the city council won their races. Overall, the coalition candidates won by an impressive 57 percent to 43 percent margin, capturing more than two-thirds of the vote in heavy tenant precincts, 40 percent from middle income homeowners on the city's south side, and even 25 percent in the most affluent "north of Montana" neighborhood.[12] SMRR politicians now controlled the city council majority with five seats to the opposition's two seats and, for most purposes, all of city government. SMRR leaders attributed their string of increasingly remarkable victories, in large part, to their innovative campaign strategies. They had learned, said Derek Shearer, that "the trick is to combine modern electoral techniques with the grassroots

base of community organizing and to infuse the effort with a clear progressive theme." [13] What was SMRR's practical politics?

Shearer, who co-managed the 1981 campaign, stated that SMRR had
learned from the previous elections the importance of avoiding complicated theories and arguments in making one's case to the voters. Instead,
the coalition cultivated some expertise in simple, personal, and direct-
to-the-heart campaign appeals. In 1979, SMRR mailed out postcards
picturing an elderly couple with EVICTED stamped on their chests along
with a message from the couple's son, a one-time Goldwater Republican,
who was voting for rent control because of his parents' experience.
Another piece of direct-mail literature told of a terminally ill cancer victim who had suffered eviction and vowed to support rent control before
he died. Still another piece of literature asked, "Is Santa Monica for
sale?" and listed hundreds of realtors, developers, bankers, and landlords
as well as the amounts they had contributed to defeat the rent control
initiative. [14] Like *Mother Jones* magazine, these campaign publications
may have had too little content and too much gloss for many activists,
but most activists were convinced that the approach was politically effective: it won votes.

SMRR's card files on voters were soon streamlined by the computer
technology that was now accessible, due to the growth of the home computer market and to a few activists who specifically learned how to use
that technology for political purposes. Though they did not say it, "small
computers are beautiful" nicely captures the attitudes of some of the
radicals. Their floppy disks listed up to 18,000 households that had supported SMRR in the polls, some 5,000 addresses that had been the
source of campaign contributions to SMRR, another 1,000 individuals
who could be counted on as volunteers, and 50 to 60 activists who could
be set into motion at a moment's notice. [15] Meanwhile, SMRR experimented with a number of campaign techniques. Telephone canvassing
was organized and systematized so that SMRR leaders could get a quick
sense of residents' views on particular issues, voting preferences, and
funding potentials. Contacts with community groups and labor organizations were nurtured and sometimes formalized to give the coalition
access to more volunteers, money, meeting halls, phone banks, and endorsements. New campaigns brought new connections, for example,
with professional campaign consultants such as Bill Zimmerman and his
Loudspeaker organization. These connections, in turn, were a source of
new ideas on fundraisers, professional canvassing and polling, engineered
media events, and so forth.

Over a two-year period, SMRR grew from an informal coalition,
which could mobilize fifty to one hundred activists from its member
organizations and build a featherweight campaign chest that could not
begin to match an opposition able to outspend it twenty to one, into an
impressive political organization able to involve thousands of people in

its campaigns and, by 1981, narrow the financial gap—accumulating $80,000 to the opposition's $250,000, or a three to one ratio. Political growth created a need for greater organizational efficiency. SMRR met the need with "campaign management, field operations, fundraising, volunteer coordination, and press all handled by full-time but low-paid people."[16] SMRR campaigns, one might say, increasingly became professional and efficiently *managed* campaigns.

To William Jennings, SMRR's 1979 campaign co-manager and one of the coalition's city councilmembers, SMRR had become too managed. He felt that it had evolved into a political machine with a leadership that traded patronage for favors and practiced a "democratic centralism" whereby the organization claimed the authority to clear all public statements made by its members.[17] Several months before the April 1981 election, Jennings bolted the coalition and publicly denounced it. SMRR activists immediately disputed Jennings' reasoning, explaining his betrayal as a function of his personal ambitions. And SMRR leaders decided that they had better take more care in "picking trustworthy candidates."[18]

At approximately the same time, there were other rumblings within SMRR regarding the candidate selection process. The CED folks, who had originally organized SMRR, had an agenda that went far beyond rent control but, as yet, no member of their own group was on the city council. The other SMRR groups did not necessarily share the CED agenda and did not automatically support the candidates that it put up. Meanwhile, SMRR alliances with various community groups, single-issue organizations, and labor meant that keeping an eye out for their interests in the candidate selection process would be politically expedient. And since SMRR was now in the business of choosing candidates for a city council that made decisions on issues extending far beyond rent control, it became increasingly important for the coalition to regularize procedures for taking stands on issues that would inform candidate selection.

The result was that SMRR began to transform itself from a fairly informal coalition into a formal organization with rules, regular forums for deciding issues, and exhaustive and exhausting procedures for candidate selection. And SMRR did indeed come up with a politically wise slate of candidates. It chose Dennis Zane, a CED member also involved with SMFHA, the Democratic Club, community groups in the Ocean Park neighborhood, and SMRR itself. It chose Dolores Press, another CED person associated with the rent control board, the mid-city tenant district, labor unions, Democratic party politics, and feminism. It chose Kenneth Edwards, who worked with the Democratic Club, local social services, and the quality of life coalitions of the 1970s, and who also happened to live on the city's north side. Finally, it chose James Conn, the Ocean Park minister whose church had become a center for peace activism and other progressive causes for a range of Santa Monica and West Los Angeles groups. Together, these city council candidates represented the range of SMRR ideologies, the constituencies that SMRR hoped to attract, and the "trustworthy" people who were already known, tested by experience, and certain to be accountable to the SMRR grassroots base.

As an electoral organization identified most closely with rent control, SMRR's best hope for victory was to promote a large turnout at the polls among the city's tenant population. In 1981, SMRR orchestrated a last-minute blitz that pulled together the various components of its practical politics—slick literature, computerized technology, innovative experimentation, and efficient campaign management—to get out the vote. On small Statue of Liberty door hangers, SMRR computers printed out the polling places for 15,000 targeted households and, at 4:00 A.M. election day morning, one hundred SMRR volunteers distributed them throughout the city. SMRR electoral practices seemed validated that day. The coalition made a clean sweep of all contests and thus gained control of city hall. Who could argue with success?

Virtually no one in SMRR did. Activists were too busy celebrating and planning Santa Monica's future. But hindsight suggests that successful leftwing entrepreneurialism in the political marketplace would come with some attached costs, borne in particular by the principle of participatory democracy. The simple-but-slick approach to campaign literature, for example, aimed not at stimulating democratic dialogue among residents but at winning their votes through Madison Avenue tactics. The range of participants who might become movement leaders was constricted considerably when SMRR instituted the computer technology and sophisticated campaign techniques that lend themselves to special expertise. The ability of rank-and-file activists to have an impact on campaign decisions diminished as SMRR leaders incurred debts to various community groups who would have to be repaid, at the very least, in the coin of interest group influence. Overall, activist participation was cheapened by political growth as is almost always the case. Individual voices were diluted by numbers and activists' autonomy was limited by leadership coordination and management. There was an early tendency in SMRR for power to flow from the grassroots base to leftwing notables.

This tendency was reinforced with each election and each victory. The exhaustive nature of the candidate selection process and the great time demands on candidates discouraged many people from applying. The near obsession of some SMRR leaders to find fully trustworthy candidates encouraged them to invite their own reliable friends rather than to cast a broad net among rank-and-file activists. Newcomers to the movement had to prove their worth and mettle informally while oldtimers were privy to strategy discussions among key leaders. And the distance between the rank-and-file and the leadership increased when members of the leadership became elected city officials. At that point, activists mostly had the power to propose but the leftwing politicians had the insider information, multiple contacts, and public presence that gave them the power to dispose. Regardless of benign intentions, SMRR began to reproduce the differences in status, position, and power that mark the growth of political hierarchy.

On the outskirts of this emerging hierarchy loomed the figure of Tom Hayden. His role in the rent control and electoral contests was shadowy. By and large, he was a late and ambivalent supporter of SMRR politics, eventually helping out with some money and staff people. Still, he was on a lot of people's minds because the press and the opposition mistakenly portrayed him as the mastermind behind SMRR victories. Moreover, he was potentially important. He was the head of CED and had an influence on the local chapter despite its semiautonomy; his political organization had access to considerable financial resources, professional staff people and organizers, extensive media play, and statewide political connections (including California Governor Jerry Brown) that could be useful to the local coalition. Tom Hayden could not be treated as just another Santa Monica resident. His voice commanded more than equal interest. And given his history in Students for a Democratic Society (SDS), the new left, California politics, and CED, Hayden could be counted on to speak out in favor of participatory democracy but, at the same time, to play the role of powerbroker according to the demands of political expedience.[19]

Beyond Rent Control

The SMRR city council majority that assumed office in 1981 had a mandate but, beyond rent control, no one quite agreed on its content. The fact that SMRR activists had many different principles and priorities meant that councilmembers had few clear policy guidelines. The SMRR politicians were in a position where their every action or inaction threatened to alienate some activists and fragment the coalition that had put them into office. The city hall radicals could and did evoke "the need to defend rent control" or the specter of "the opposition returning to power" to forge some unity amid conflicts on particular policy issues. But they did more. They were able to develop some coherent policy directions and sustain coalition unity by practicing a leftwing version of conventional bourgeois politics.

C. Wright Mills's *The Power Elite* begins by identifying the major powers in American society as "a set of groups whose members know one another, see one another socially and at business, and so, in making decisions, take one another into account. . . . They form a more or less compact social and psychological unity; they have become self-conscious members of a social class."[20] Mills was writing about upper class participation in a shared culture that nourishes its sense of self, trust, and mutual concern, transforming it into a class-for-itself able to train and entrust authority to its own leaders. Grassroots groups also need to build a solid cultural foundation that cements mutual trust if they are to remain at all durable. Tom Hayden's 1976 senatorial campaign was premised on his belief that the new left had laid that foundation in the 1960s. And when Ruth Yannatta Goldway told me that activists "have three of four years of losing to do before they can finally win," she was reflecting back on the defeats of the 1970s that helped to build a self-conscious leftwing culture able to undergo the transition to political power in the 1980s.[21]

Santa Monica leftists had a poor batting average in the decade preceding their rise to power. They failed to stop the development of luxury condominiums that displaced elderly residents from affordable housing, to get the city council to act on quality of life proposals tendered by its own citizen advisory commission, to get Tom Hayden a U.S. Senate nomination and Ruth Yannatta Goldway a State Assembly nomination, and to win the 1978 rent control initiative and the ensuing rent rollback proposal. Nonetheless, the *process* of losing these political struggles enabled activists to build a common culture that would help to foster future cohesion.

The mobilizations of the 1970s forced activists to reach out to one another, work with an array of community groups, and thus locate an extended family of shared values. Leftists were challenged to articulate those values in a vernacular whereby terms like "human scale" or "participatory democracy" came to symbolize a subcultural sense of identity. At the same time, they became cognizant of available resources and resource bases, voluntary assistance and expertise, trustworthy allies, and the specific nature of their local opposition. Some overlapping memberships among groups and some new friendships between members strengthened emerging ties. Moreover, people learned who would commit time and energy, who could negotiate between groups, who could plan strategy, who could take some heat, and who in their own persons best represented various popular constituencies. "We have trust," said Dennis Zane, "because we have an organic relationship with the activist community." Constant interaction between activists and leaders, at formal meetings and informal parties, bred an atmosphere in which "they don't have to be fearful of talking or being critical of us," Zane continued. "These are our friends."[22] The Santa Monica left gradually developed a culture that predisposed people to emphasize points of consensus, to recognize differences of viewpoint as a matter of good will, and to air rather than to let fester their disagreements; it cultivated the sense of community necessary to experiment with a move beyond rent control, with an "organic" leadership pointing the way.

Such predispositions are a necessary but insufficient condition for developing goals in the face of diversity. Friendly disagreements can always change into enmity and polarization. According to G. William Domhoff, powerful elites in America avoid this by institutionalizing a process through which "the various special interests join together to forge general policies which will benefit all of them as a whole."[23] Private think tanks and public policy forums function to familiarize the various interests with important issues, provide opportunities for developing consensuses and compromises, hear experts on the topics at hand, and test new recruits for future leadership positions. The Santa Monica left developed a similar policy process by promoting the growth of private and public forums for raising, debating, and compromising issues that extended and transcended rent control.

The Santa Monica CED chapter and the Democratic Club, for example, were crucial miniforums that brought together a diversity of activists who eventually pinpointed rent control as a major political priority. They were augmented by SMRR, whose member groups debated and compromised issues as part of the process of coalescing, seeking endorsements, making candidate selections, and forging general principles of unity. In addition, Santa Monica's major neighborhood organizations— the Ocean Park Community Organization (OPCO) and the Pico Neighborhood Association (PNA), later to be joined by the Mid-City Neighbors (MCN)—held regular block meetings, neighborhood forums, and yearly congresses that brought together residents, activists, and leaders to chart some values, priorities, and strategies.

When the SMRR coalition won control of city hall, it enriched the policy formation process in two ways. First, the SMRR councilmembers themselves represented the range of core and peripheral ideologies and were forced to strike compromises in order to keep their council majority intact. After more than a year in power, Kenneth Edwards was able to say of the five-person majority, "I would question whether the five of us have ever broken on a real issue involving progressive politics."[24] Second, the SMRR-dominated council appointed a number of citizen task forces, commissions, and advisory groups with an eye out to filling them with activists representing the different interests within the coalition. These citizen committees provided leftists an additional opportunity to air differences, solicit expert advice, and work out enough of a consensus on policies regarding housing, land use, affirmative action, neighborhood power, crime control, and more to make recommendations to the city council. Derek Shearer suggested that they also served as a "kind of tryout" for individuals testing their own political commitments and for new recruits aspiring to leadership positions.[25]

The proliferation of forums did not necessarily highlight and reinforce differences within the Santa Monica left community. The reason is that leading activists had overlapping memberships in various political groups, much like the power elite's interlocking corporate directorships. The overlap prompted the leaders to look to overall goals and interests rather than to the special concerns of any particular group. Opposition councilmembers Christine Reed and William Jennings spoke of all the "overlap" that characterized the local left to suggest that totaling group memberships vastly inflated radicals' actual numbers.[26] Most activists owned up to the overlap, but as a basis for leftwing cohesion. It was common for CED members to be enrolled in the Democratic Club and several other organizations; for SMRR activists to spike their political affiliations with participation in various community and neighborhood groups; for OPCO and PNA people to work in tenant organizations or in city government. Overlapping memberships worked against an historical leftwing tendency to develop organizational loyalties reinforced by ideological rigidities that set group against group and fragmented leftwing politics as a whole.

In line with the conventional wisdom of political scientists, activists who were crosspressured by their various group affiliations tended to seek out a consensus, encourage mutual tolerance, and devalue outstanding differences to mute potential internal conflict. Still, no shared culture, general consensus, or predisposition toward tolerance can eliminate all differences within a movement or prevent them from becoming a source of fragmentation. The various interests within a movement still compete over policy priorities, financial resources, membership recruitment, and public support. And American left history is replete with instances when such competition has evolved into vindictiveness, hatred, and self-destructive sectarianism.

Ralph Miliband argues that the capitalist class, as a coalition of competing interests, deals with this dilemma through a system of "imperfect competition" in the political marketplace.[27] Each competing group has a stake in influencing government policies that can be advantageous or disadvantageous to them; and government policymakers have a stake in pleasing all competing groups to keep intact the class responsible for their political power. Both sets of needs are met when the groups engage in a "friendly competition" mediated by government authorities. No group achieves a decisive, permanent advantage or suffers permanent exclusion. Politicians negotiate compromises that provide partial victories for all groups; and those partial victories give all groups something worth defending, an incentive to strive for more, and an interest in forming alliances with other groups to enhance future leverage. The competition is "imperfect" only in the sense that anticapitalist or even noncapitalist groups have little chance to gain much influence over policymaking. To an extent, the Santa Monica radicals engineered a system of "imperfect competition in reverse": Santa Monica's grassroots groups competed for influence over the radicals in city hall; the radical politicians negotiated compromises that provided partial victories for the competing groups;

and, this time, the growth machine interests had little chance to gain much influence over policy.

Santa Monica's imperfect competition surfaced on many political fronts. A wide range of community groups competed for their slice of the city budget. Neighborhood groups vied for greater autonomy and authority that would potentially weaken other groups in the city. Tenant organizers confronted affordable housing people over the issue of limited equity cooperatives. City workers wanted more workplace autonomy and better salaries in competition with social services people, who wanted more say and funding for the needy. The list of intraleft policy disagreements could continue almost indefinitely. Meanwhile, both the SMRR leadership and the city councilmembers (mostly the same people) had a stake in pleasing everyone because they were committed to grassroots politics and because they had to make good on their commitment if they were to stay in power. Unable to make policies that magically resolved contradictory demands and lacking the unlimited resources needed to satisfy most demands, the city hall politicians had no choice other than to negotiate compromises that could be enforced with municipal authority.

The city hall radicals generally sought policies that provided partial victories to competing grassroots interests. If some groups were unhappy with particular bargains, they nonetheless knew that they had a chance to win better terms in the future and could most likely do so by striking alliances with other community groups. In any case, they knew that they were far better off with partial victories than with their no-win situations during the tenure of earlier city councils.

Fred Allingham, staff director of the Pico Neighborhood Association, which represented the minority, low income part of Santa Monica, was fairly free with his criticisms of the SMRR politicians. He believed that they did not adequately confront the needs of people in his part of town. Nonetheless, he quickly pointed out the importance of working with city hall, monitoring city policies, striving to influence them, and, ultimately, giving the SMRR politicians "credit" for how well they were doing in comparison to their predecessors.[28] Conversely, the conservative banking, real estate, and business interests of the growth machine wanted only to credit the SMRR politicians with bringing disaster to the city. A local business newsletter stated that "the long term intentions of Santa Monica's ruling radicals" was the establishment of "a permanent, publicly funded power base which will survive even electoral defeat."[29] Every dollar that the city spent on funding grassroots groups was seen by the opposition as a form of patronage intended to build a political machine rather than as a public policy process that the conservatives no longer dominated.

What then was SMRR's mandate when it emerged as the ruling force in city government? In part, it was the very general principles derived from the subculture, experiences, and discussions of the 1970s, the range of values that made up SMRR's core and peripheral ideologies. In part, the mandate was also a commitment to translate those values into policies through processes of self-conscious dialogue, the search for intraleft consensuses, the predisposition toward compromise and toleration of differences, and the imperfect competition among grassroots groups mediated by the SMRR officials in city hall. SMRR had indeed become a coalition that "bends rather than breaks when differences arise," as suggested by Maurice Zeitlin at the beginning of this chapter, but its ability to achieve general policy direction and to sustain movement unity was not inexpensive.

SMRR's leftist version of bourgeois politics worked against giving priority to the principles of economic democracy and one class society. The leftwing subculture that developed in the 1970s was a middle class subculture of relatively affluent white activists who generated their own sense of values, terminologies, networks, and leaders. Their subculture provided them an identity that, among other things, distinguished insiders from outsiders, the trustworthy from the untested, the tried and true from the neophytes. New people could enter into the subculture fairly easily if they had the required time and energy, sense of efficacy, education, and verbal facility that helped them contribute to grassroots groups and especially to dialogues at the left's numerous policy forums. But these were traits that favored people with middle class backgrounds and credentials, people who had known some success rather than people from the more powerless social classes who had the most to gain from economic democracy and one class society. As a result, the tendency of the Santa Monica left was to grow through middle class inbreeding rather than through integration with Santa Monica's most disadvantaged citizens.

Furthermore, the absence of clear ideological priorities combined with the presence of a self-conscious commitment to unity produced a political atmosphere where talk about abstract theories and principles was considered "bad politics" and talk about concrete policy compromises was taken as "good politics." This had some ironic consequences. One CED member told me that the economic democrats in the local chapter, with few exceptions, had little knowledge of or interest in the principles of political economy that inform the notion of economic democracy. And according to Allan Heskin, "the internal avoidance of ideological debate" in SMRR militated against the coalition's developing "coherent policies."[30] The Santa Monica left wanted to avoid the ideological wars that had consumed Berkeley's leftwing politics but did so only at the cost of giving little thought to the meaning and method of economic change in their own city. Thus, the SMRR radicals never developed an explicit set of economic goals, a systematic strategy for achieving them, or a coherent thread linking specific economic policies.

Relatedly, the compromises that emerged from discussions, overlapping memberships, and imperfect competition tended to yield "lowest common denominator" policies that favored the quality of life demands of insider, middle class groups over more systematic efforts to empower or meet the pressing material needs of the working class, minority, and low income people in the city. In terms of voter numbers and grassroots representation, the latter groups had little leverage in city hall and policy determinations. Consequently, neither economic democracy nor one class society as guidelines for policy were given very high priority. This is not too surprising. After all, middle class radicalism was founded on moral and political concerns far more than on traditional leftist emphases on the material realm.

city government. Initially, they did so by spending an inordinate amount of time working with city staff members to ensure that council policies were being administered properly. They also appointed new professionals to key city posts as a way of consolidating their authority. One of their most important appointments was putting John Alschuler in the city manager's office. A former advisor to Housing and Urban Development (HUD) during the Carter administration and the assistant city manager of a progressive government in Hartford, Connecticut, Alschuler brought to Santa Monica an extreme self-consciousness about securing local autonomy. He related his Hartford experience as a contrast:

> Hartford, unlike Santa Monica, is a city unable to control its own destiny in a significant way, given the enormous dependency of the city on both state and federal government in transfer payments. Also, Connecticut cities lack the kind of legal and regulatory autonomy that characterizes California cities. So many of the things that the Santa Monica city council has the power to do, in Connecticut, took an act of the legislature . . . because it in essence was a giant city council.[31]

Alschuler's job made him the executive officer of approximately 1,400 city employees; and one of his tasks was to see that the city staff, which he characterized as being "as talented a group of people as there is in the country in a government of this size," worked closely and smoothly with the city council to carry out council policies. His managerial approach was to mediate council–staff relations. He educated councilmembers to provide "clear direction," which is what the bureaucrats needed to do their jobs well; and he treated city bureaucrats, who he said "are among the more maligned" in American society, as dedicated professionals who "are in public service because they want in fact to provide service to the public."

Alschuler's approach bore fruit throughout city government. Assistant city planner Christopher Rudd, who worked under the old conservative councils as well as the new radical one, said that his division "really supports what the council's been doing" in terms of giving clear direction, facilitating planning, and actually implementing some of the quality of life proposals recommended but ignored in the 1970s.[32] Most impressive, the city council radicals were able to develop amiable relations with city police and firefighters. "We treat them decently as public employees," stated Derek Shearer.[33] The city council made an effort to improve police and firefighters' working conditions and salaries, facilitate dialogue with citizen groups concerned with public safety, and hire a city attorney who would respect them and work well with them. The results? Police Chief James Keane noted, "The Police Department has never had a better working relationship with the city attorney's office," and rank-and-file officers, who owned up to conservative political identities, nonetheless

spoke of "excellent rapport" with city officials; also, the city council won
plaudits from firefighters for having exercised the "intestinal fortitude" to enact strong but controversial fire safety rules.[34] Overall, the left-wing council did a remarkable job of securing support and cooperation throughout the city bureaucracy and, therefore, of securing the leverage and flexibility necessary for asserting city autonomy in the policymaking process.

When the city hall radicals enacted controversial laws and policies, they generally relied on three devices to ensure that their will would be done rather than "done in" by superior government agencies. First, they appointed the citizen task forces and commissions that provided popular support, procedural compliance, and democratic legitimacy for council actions. Anyone seeking to overturn their actions was consequently in the position of being accused of usurping local democratic authority. Second, they commissioned professional studies by progressive policy organizations that pinpointed historical and legal precedents for council decisions and provided clues to potential barriers to their enforcement. Thus the SMRR councilmembers were careful to shape their policies in ways that maximized the chances that no one would be able to overturn them on procedural or legal grounds. Third, the radical politicians relied on the professional expertise of the city manager and the city attorney to defend their policies before state agencies and the judicial system. These devices usually worked.

All three devices were employed when the city council majority decided to take control of development in Santa Monica. It appointed a commercial and industrial task force membered by citizens who produced a lengthy set of recommendations on zoning and controlled development. It paid the firm of Hamilton, Rabinowitz, and Szanton, Inc. to produce several hundred-page studies, entitled "Review of California Development Fee Policies" and "Review of Existing Santa Monica Development Fees," that provided professional legitimacy to council policies.[35] And it called on the city attorney to develop a defensible legal model for negotiating development agreements and on the city manager to put together a professional team to negotiate the agreements. Consequently, when the city council enacted Ordinance no. 1220 and later revisions intended "to ensure that development is consistent with public peace, health, and safety," it was able to implement its human scale approach to Santa Monica's future despite vociferous protests and legal actions taken by the opposition.[36]

The SMRR councilmembers also made a conscientious effort to extend their authority and impact beyond their limited tenure in political office. Their model was the structure of rent control, which was based on changing the city charter (which could not be easily undone) and creating a semiautonomous agency, the rent control board (which could function regardless of who runs city government). The radicals took advantage of their commitment and energy to rewrite the various elements that made up the city charter and thereby left their imprint on the legal framework for future city policies. They also created several quasi-governmental, nonprofit corporations that would provide institutional support for SMRR policies for the foreseeable future. And according to a source in the city attorney's office, "There are not a lot of old agreements that were entered into in the past that bind the city in the future; this city council has entered into a number of contracts that to some extent bind future city councils."[37] The SMRR-negotiated development agreements, in particular, were going to have a long-term effect on the local environment.

While all of the SMRR attempts to shape the future were potentially reversible, future politicians who try to undo SMRR policies will necessarily entangle themselves in a complex web of legal, political, and bureaucratic proceedings that may endanger their public support but offer little certainty of success. Dennis Zane made this point graphically: "Once we institutionalize some of the programs that are in place, it will be a significant political peril for anybody to try to fuck with them."[38]

In theory, the greatest threat to the radicals' power was the ability of local business people to put pressure on them as has happened in many other cities where grassroots movements came to power. Such pressure usually takes the form of offering the carrot of new investment if politicians cooperate to provide a healthy business climate or the stick of disinvestment if people in government act contrary to what business elites consider the community's best interests.[39] Aubrey Austin, Jr., chairman of the Santa Monica Bank, was quoted shortly after the April 1981 election as saying, "Being a businessman in that council chamber makes you feel like a bastard at a family reunion. These people don't realize that you can't run a city like a gas station."[40] Santa Monica's local newspaper constantly quoted local business leaders to the effect that SMRR's policies were economic disasters; that firms were preparing their departures from the city; and that banks were becoming reluctant to lend money for business ventures in Santa Monica. Nevertheless, it was clear early on that the theoretical threat of disinvestment had little factual basis.

Barry Rosengrant, a developer who negotiated a project with the new city council, saw little evidence of a "capital boycott" by businessmen or a "refusal" by banks to lend money to new ventures. He stated in late 1981, "We're not leery about working here. We can work with the council, and on our next project we'll know what we're up against and we'll be able to tally up the costs to see if the project is feasible."[41] A large local corporation such as Welton Becket Associates, which did business in the People's Republic of China, was quite willing to do business in Santa Monica as long as the company could foresee profits. This view, largely shared by investors, explains how John Alschuler could say of the "capital flight" threat, "It's preposterous. . . . The list of people who walk into this office wanting to invest here is lengthy. . . . This is some of the most valuable real estate in the world."[42] As if to eradicate any doubts regarding Alschuler's accuracy, Barry Rubens—who recently opened both a bank and a savings and loan in Santa Monica—said that he chose the city because it "has a lot of new firms coming in. It is incredible how many people have approached us."[43] A handful of business people tried to use economic pressure to restrain council policies but their efforts were undermined by the steady stream of investors hoping to get a piece of the Santa Monica action.

The main economic restraint on city council policy was a projected revenue–expenditure gap. California's middle class taxpayers distrusted government authority and certainly did not want to pay into general revenue coffers that allowed governors a blank check. Thus they passed the Proposition 13 tax reduction measure that made it extremely difficult for municipalities to raise local tax revenues. But the SMRR politicians were committed to expenditures that would maintain and expand social services, upgrade the salaries and benefits of city employees, facilitate affordable housing for all city residents, fund neighborhood projects, enhance the local environment, and so forth. The radicals who took power were not certain that they could sustain current expenditure levels much less increase them to subsidize desired policies. Their approach to this fiscal dilemma was to find ways to enhance revenues without raising property taxes while changing expenditure priorities.

For the most part, the SMRR councilmembers looked to their appointed professionals to find ways to enhance revenues, and the professionals went to work with considerable zest. City staff people unearthed $330,000 that had been on deposit with the state at only 6 percent interest. Staff investigated city business license fees, development fees, lease agreements, and contract arrangements to discover that Santa Monica charged much less for its services than nearby cities of comparable size. Staff also did cost-benefit analyses that show that the city would have more disposable revenues if it stopped contracting out legal work and increased the city's legal personnel. Staff proposed ways to generate more income from city-owned enterprises, from the local tourist industry, from limited partnerships with the private sector, from municipal airport property, and from hidden pockets of money in county, state, and federal governments. From the left's viewpoint, fiscal responsibility, efficiency, and creativity meant more disposable revenue for worthwhile projects.

The council majority also made some decisions on spending priorities. James Conn mentioned how the SMRR politicians brought to city government "a new consciousness of the financial and economic impact of decisions that are made by the city and how they affect people in the city as a whole, in contrast to how they merely affect the business community."[44] Part of that new consciousness was manifested in early budget decisions. "The first budget we received," Conn noted, "was an equipment budget; and we cut out all the equipment and put programs in." The program priorities shifted expenditures, for example, from subsidies to the Chamber of Commerce to support for neighborhood projects. As a result of the SMRR council's efforts to close the revenue–expenditure gap, Santa Monica was one of the few California cities in the early 1980s that upgraded social services; almost every other city in the state was forced to make cutbacks.

The SMRR politicians, in short, practiced what is conventionally considered to be "good government." They ran city government like a business, making sure that the ledgers balanced. But "good government" and SMRR's core principles did not always complement one another. Human scale community and a finely tuned government bureaucracy do not necessarily mix, the one being founded on interpersonal relationships and the other on impersonal procedures, laws, and accountant reports. Participatory democracy may be more symbolic than tangible when politicians rely too heavily on professional experts in public administration, law, and policy. And one class society does not fare particularly well when fiscal responsibility means cutting deals with developers or enhancing revenues by leasing city land to the highest bidder rather than investing in the economic independence of all citizens. The tendency of Santa Monica activists, SMRR leaders, and city hall radicals was to practice political pragmatism without giving serious thought as to whether it works in behalf of basic principles.

Does Political Pragmatism Work?

Christine Reed, an opposition councilmember, had mixed views on the SMRR people who shared the council chambers with her. In one sense, she was quite unhappy with their expressed principles and rhetoric. She saw the council radicals as "repressive on property rights" and adding "a whole layer of emotionalism and anger and vituperativeness" to Santa Monica politics. In another sense, she was not particularly upset with the radicals' brand of pragmatic politics. "When you get down to what they're actually doing," she said, "they haven't done anything terribly earth-shattering, yet."[45] Was the Santa Monica left mostly a coalition that expressed radical principles compromised by the politics-as-usual pragmatism that changes very little? Or, as Reed's "yet" implies, was it more a matter of activists seeking a way to put political pragmatism to work in the service of leftwing ideals?

Carl Boggs argues that radical ideals and pragmatic politics do not mix. Those who try usually sacrifice their egalitarian values to the politics of power and expedience. Grassroots movements lose their oppositional nature when they are subordinated to electoral competition and electoral machinery. Political mandates founded on diffuse values, coalition compromises, and interest group competition invite integration with dominant elites rather than systematic attempts to dislodge dominant elites from power and restructure the distribution of influence and wealth in America. Radicals who assume political positions within the American political economy are forced to bow to the bureaucratic and legal constraints that reinforce the nation's class-divided society. The result of "power-defined success" that lies at the heart of political pragmatism is, according to Boggs, "the abandonment of collective decisionmaking, a decline of rank-and-file vitality, and the emergence of an insular elite stratum." [46] By the standards of radical change, political pragmatism does not work.

Boggs is not necessarily wrong. In the following chapters, we will see specific instances when activists compromised, sacrificed, and abandoned their radical principles in the pursuit of pragmatic political power. We will witness moments when human scale community, participatory democracy, and one class society took a backseat to movement elitism and professionalism. But Boggs is not necessarily right. Some of the more thoughtful people in SMRR offered a somewhat different construction of their political reality.

Conceivably, SMRR's radical rhetoric could help to legitimate a set of egalitarian ideals and, say Martin Carnoy and Derek Shearer, "redefine what is possible." [47] Were more people to become familiar with and supportive of such values, then political pragmatists would have greater flexibility in experimenting with public policies founded on such values. The consequence would be a gradual shift to the left in both political talk and action. "What I've learned from this experience," stated Ruth Yannatta Goldway, reflecting on her four years as a councilmember and two years as mayor, "is that social change, needed social change, does not come easily." But it does come, evidenced by the leftward drift of SMRR's opposition by 1983. "Everyone who ran for city council this time supported rent control. Every one of the [opposition] candidates who was elected believes in rational zoning, in a human scale city, lower rise buildings, believes in environmental and toxic controls, believes in social service programs, in citizen participation, in programs that were simply not even discussed four years ago." [48] In short, the principles and politics of middle class radicalism, from the point of view of these activists, point to a slow revolution where changes in people's values eventually make possible new social and political relationships.

To ensure constant movement to the left, a few SMRR activists argued the importance of sustaining what Maurice Zeitlin called "a healthy tension" between radical principles and political pragmatism. [49] Grassroots movements need continuous mass mobilizations that force their leaders and politicians not to sacrifice leftwing ideals to the demands of power. But such mobilizations in themselves cannot bring change. People's values, needs, and desires must be systematically articulated, translated into concrete strategies and policies, adjusted to actual limits and potentials in the political environment, and, ultimately, administered with a degree of efficiency. In other words, leftwing movements need to beware of their leaders and yet recognize that they need some form of democratic authority structure to convert theory into practice.[50] We will also see in the following chapters incidents that highlight the extent to which pressure from below forced the SMRR politicians to adhere to movement principles even when political pragmatism dictated otherwise.

Perhaps the best way to understand the practice of middle class radicalism as manifested in Santa Monica is to examine what actually took place when the SMRR radicals won power and began to legislate policies. To what extent did "winning" mean a sacrifice of principles? To what extent did "winning" lay the groundwork for implementing principles? And to what extent did the SMRR coalition's first defeat in 1983 alter the relationship between principles and politics?

5

Revising the Ends

Needless to say, wealth, education, research, and many other things are needed for any civilization, but what is needed most today is a revision of the ends which these means are meant to serve. And this implies, above all else, the development of a lifestyle which accords to material things their proper, legitimate place which is secondary and not primary.

E. F. Schumacher[1]

A human scale city, says Kirkpatrick Sale, is one where individuals "can
feel a degree of *control* over the processes of life."[2] That control mostly
concerns culture and lifestyles. Individuals can cultivate a better quality
of life, one that stresses warm interpersonal relationships instead of instrumental material relationships. They can construct a social life where
harmony, mutual fulfillment, and human meaning take precedence over
the marketplace. The Santa Monica radicals who came to power in 1981
were committed to fostering a human scale city through public policies
that would strengthen residents' sense of community, control over their
neighborhoods, and the small business economy that upgrades human
sensitivity and downgrades the profit motive. Their intention was to
implement the idea that people come first, nothing short of revising the
ends of human interaction in the city of Santa Monica.

Human scale policies seemed like a natural link between Santa Monica's middle class residents and its middle class radicals. In theory, small
business operators would support restraints on growth that would both
affirm their commitment to community and enhance their survivability.
The city's professionals would favor the "small is beautiful" reforms that
promised to keep Santa Monica as the quality of life alternative to the
megalopolises that they had left. The politicians of Santa Monicans for
Renters' Rights (SMRR) supported human scale values both as virtues
in themselves and as levers for shifting public consciousness and local
politics toward leftwing egalitarianism: if people experienced greater control over the quality of their lives, then they would be more prone to
question and contest the control once exercised by the growth machine
elites. At least that was what the city hall radicals expected when they
gave top priority to legislating a human scale agenda.

The Politics of the Pier

Ruth Yannatta Goldway viewed the Santa Monica municipal pier as "the
symbol and soul of our city. It gives us a sense of history and tradition
that a city needs for its stability and sense of place."[3] The pier was a
cultural link to Santa Monica's small town past when railroad magnates
and politicians nearly destroyed the city and when the beachfront tourist
trade saved it. The pier stood for community pride, a rallying point of
local consensus that bound neighborhood to neighborhood as well as
residents to the small businesses that operated on the pier. Santa Monicans united in the early 1970s to save the pier from a proposed high rise
condominium development; and the leftwing council mobilized citizens
in the 1980s to upgrade pier facilities to ensure the structure's perpetual
health. Shortly after assuming office, the SMRR council appointed the
pier task force to make appropriate policy recommendations.

The pier task force met for six months, held public hearings, and
consulted with experts and politicians before issuing its report. It then

recommended that "the existing open, low cost, friendly atmosphere" be retained and enriched by a $7.9 million rehabilitation project.[4] The blending of old and new was to include support for the world-famous carousel then undergoing repairs, an amusement area, a children's play area, family-style arcades, an adjacent park, expanded fishing facilities, an historical and marine museum, and a pavillion for community events. Many of the pier's older buildings were to be fixed up, repainted, and landscaped; and at least one large structure was to be refurbished to house a theater and restaurant. Congestion would be avoided by closing the pier to automobile traffic, providing public access by a modern tramway tied to distant parking facilities.

Ideally, Santa Monicans from all walks of life could congregate there in communal solidarity. Tourists from around the world would be drawn there to boost the small business economy. And everyone would experience the symbolic sense of Santa Monica as a small town with a distinct personality of its own.

At a time when other city policies were generating controversy, the pier task force recommendations stimulated peaceful and constructive discussion. Santa Monicans generally liked the idea of upgrading the pier regardless of the price tag. They simply had to work out the details of the kinds of changes that were desirable. The local Santa Monica newspaper was generous in its coverage of pier discussions and consequently drew more residents into the dialogue. But talk was cut short by the powerful winter storms of 1982-83, which turned the pier's wooden support beams into matchsticks, causing the collapse of one-third of the decking and several buildings on it. A large crane, deployed by the city government to prevent further structural damage, fell into the Pacific Ocean when a new storm destroyed more pier supports. Early estimates of the damage approached $15 million.

Without pause for second thoughts, the radical politicians promised to do everything in their power to restore the pier regardless of cost. Mayor Goldway and state assemblyman Tom Hayden took a well-publicized helicopter tour to assess the damage; SMRR councilmembers and candidates for the April 1983 municipal elections unanimously resolved to rebuild the pier; and city professionals set out on a systematic search for funding to underwrite the reconstruction. The importance of the pier was manifested in the time that city officials spent on it. City manager John Alschuler reported that 50 percent of his workday went to pier matters; a deputy city manager gave 50 percent of her time; and the head of the community and economic development department devoted 70 to 80 percent of his workload to the symbol of community.[5] Pier politics, always important in Santa Monica, was the city's number one concern for several months.

The major political question was not whether millions of dollars in revenues and official city work time should be devoted to the pier, but

how the pier restoration should be managed. The city staff recommended
that the council create a nonprofit public corporation to repair and operate the pier along the lines of early task force suggestions. The Chamber
of Commerce, however, wanted the pier leased to a private management
firm that would not constitute another layer of local government bureaucracy but would operate the pier according to sound business practices
and marketplace pressures. A major confrontation was avoided because
a consensus quickly emerged in favor of the staff recommendation.

The SMRR council majority supported the idea of a nonprofit public
corporation to ensure that the pier remained a human scale community
center rather than became, in Dennis Zane's words, "a Disneyland-by-
the-sea."[6] Moreover, the nonprofit corporation could be operated efficiently, even generate some additional revenue for the city, if the council
appointed to its board people with expertise in "development finance,
commercial leasing and development, coastal issues, recreation facility
management, urban architectural design, and landmarks."[7] Pier task
force members also wanted the nonprofit corporation; their chairman
Ernie Powell put it this way, "I don't want a management firm running
the pier, saying the bottom line is getting dollars and cents out of the
public for profit. What I want are concerned citizens managing the pier."[8]
The small business operators who leased pier space agreed. They wanted
"a people's pier" free of high rents, high-priced concessions, and the fancy
promotional schemes that are business as usual for private management
firms. Pier concessionaire Maynard Ostrow stated, "Any private developer is going to want to make a lot of money. The only way I see you
making tremendous amounts of money on the pier is to put a very high-
scale development there."[9] And high-scale development would mean
clearing out the marginal small businesses currently plying pier trade.
Given a broad citywide consensus, save the Chamber of Commerce, the
city council created a nonprofit public corporation called the Pier Restoration Corporation.

In the midst of this sequence of events, SMRR politicians perceived
pier policy as a model marriage between principles and pragmatism.
The radicals were able to plow major resources into the symbol of community, cooperate with people from all city neighborhoods, and win
support from a highly visible segment of the small business economy.
The prognosis for a leftist future was bright. Residents spanning the
ideological spectrum had shown a willingness to affirm human scale
principles against the logic of the marketplace. Thus, it was conceivable
that Santa Monicans were developing a cultural consciousness that put
the interpersonal relationships of people above the drive for profits, and
that SMRR was transforming itself from a single-issue coalition founded
on rent control and a tenant base into a quality of life movement with
broadbased public support. Self-confidence in city hall, however, was
premature.

The radicals' pier patriotism may actually have undermined their principles and exaggerated their public support. Pier policies fed a sense of community pride that bordered on local chauvinism and gave rise to cultural insularity: Santa Monica was special, even superior to other cities such as Los Angeles. This insularity devolved down to particular groups in the city that felt special, even superior to other groups. The result sometimes was to generate intramovement conflicts that invited elitist powerbrokering instead of decentralized human scale control. The tendency toward insularity also promoted a partial blindness. The radicals were so "proud" of their pier politics that they failed to notice that most Santa Monicans supported their policies for reasons having little to do with human scale principles or even politics.[10] Residents supported SMRR pier policies in the same way that U.S. citizens support federal upkeep of the Washington and Lincoln Monuments: "That's nice but what have you done for me lately?" As we will see below, where politicians saw principled political victories, rank-and-file activists and residents noticed significant problems.

Which Human Scale Community?

In 1982, Santa Monica city hall came out with a newsletter called *Seascape*. The title symbolized the city's oceanfront culture, and the design of the logo aptly represented the city's low rise skyline as well as its pier and beaches in an artist's rendering of Santa Monica's near-ideal environment. Here was a "community" with a distinct identity, or so thought the SMRR politicians, who often mistook one neighborhood subculture for all of Santa Monica.

Atop the radicals' agenda was concern for community-building. They wanted Santa Monica to be a place where people identified with one another, worked together to enhance the local quality of life, and shared in everyday enjoyments. The kind of emotional fulfillment that they imagined was premised on the very ancient notion that only small scale or interpersonal settings can promote an affective sense of community. To this end, they acted to stop the overdevelopment that caused growth, congestion, and psychological distance if not confrontations between neighbors. They declared a moratorium on new developments, set strict height limits to keep out the high rises, and did some downzoning to ensure that residential areas did not suffer commercial and industrial invasions. Santa Monica was to be a friendly, small town community with open-air pedestrian malls and bicycle paths marked by warm greenery; it was not to be a claustrophobic concrete jungle inhabited by a lonely crowd.[11]

Furthermore, Santa Monica was to be a beautiful community that nourished the human spirit. What residents called the Lincoln Properties deal was a settlement between the SMRR council and a developer in the Ocean Park neighborhood that was to bring the city $15 million in amenities, revenues, and new taxes. The SMRR council slated one-third of the bonanza for beautifying and improving the Ocean Park beach. Several city officials told me that such expenditures were necessary for winning state coastal commission approval of the settlement, but they also justified spending the money on beautification on its own merits. City manager John Alschuler, for example, stated,

> That beach is one of the primary visitor serving facilities in the whole country and it's not a rich people's playground down there. That's for working people and low income people. I see families in the parking lot spreading out their blankets because there's not enough room on the grass. If we could put a little more grass, a little more shade down there and that costs a few bucks, I can't see the money as wasted.[12]

Many Santa Monica radicals viewed city beaches and parks as epitomes of human scale space. Residents identified with them; people from all social classes and races mingled in them; and tourists were attracted to them and therefore patronized the small businesses that border them. Like the pier, green space was what Santa Monica was all about.

Inland beauty was also a SMRR council priority and the arts were a privileged part of city hall talk and action. The council appointed a city arts commission to study policies ranging from public funding for the arts to specific guidelines for city-funded or permitted murals. Arts commissioner Sarah Tamor saw the group's mandate in this way: "One of the things public art can lend to an urban environment is the sense of the human scale; through a handmade object is achieved a more personal spirit."[13] The city council also invited communitywide discussion of the arts by sponsoring public forums that Kenneth Edwards portrayed in this light: "Forums such as this are the first step in developing a public arts program in the city which I believe is especially important in the city of Santa Monica where citizens and businessmen alike take pleasure in the visual attractiveness of the city." Edwards then added, "Also, the more attractive and diverse the look of the city, the better the place it is to live, to work, and to invest in."[14] And Dennis Zane pointed out to me that "among the poorest in our society are artists," implying that public support for the arts is also public support for poor people.[15] Again, SMRR's politics of the arts seemed to combine commitment to core principles and the pragmatic effort to win interclass popularity.

Talk led to some action. The city council funded a $30,000 survey to ferret out historical sites to "get a handle on the architectural resources of the city"; the council also demonstrated a willingness in dealings with developers to trade off zoning variances for architectural aesthetics.[16] The council kicked in money to support public art fairs that gave a boost to local artists and artisans in addition to subsidizing public mural projects that provided low income youth a simultaneous source of neighborhood pride and needed wages. The council and city staff also entertained a $100,000 proposal for a public arts project intended to make Wilshire Boulevard look like "the Champs Élysées in Paris."[17] And city officials considered various plans to convert the Santa Monica Mall into a public arts complex. These were its longer-term artistic visions.

Finally, the city hall radicals wanted Santa Monica to be a healthy community. They quickly got involved in making a broad range of environmental policies. They enacted a toxic chemical disclosure law. They sought strict safeguards for underground oil pipes beneath the city. They passed a smoke-detector ordinance. They endowed a model curbside recycling program. They engineered a first-of-a-kind municipal energy-savings program and invested in a clean-air hydroelectric generator expected to pay for itself in seven years. They also founded a municipal solar-energy utility to facilitate solar power leasing and energy tax savings in the city. In terms of time and energy, these policies were especially high on the council agenda. Not only were they considered crucial to building a human scale community; they were also a reflection of political reality. According to a city survey, "A clean natural environment is the No. 1 priority for Santa Monica residents, who are also concerned about threats to the environment."[18] Another marriage between principles and pragmatism?

That was especially the view of SMRR leaders and councilmembers Dennis Zane, James Conn, and Ruth Yannatta Goldway. Zane favored "that kind of bonding and the kind of greater sense of social harmony" that would come with community pride.[19] Conn hoped to create "another way of looking at the world and that way of looking at the world is one that's much more concerned with our responsibility to the earth, the kind of environment that we're creating, the quality of life issues that are sort of nebulous and yet they're felt."[20] Goldway's desire was to "provide a good deal of activity for the community to come together and enjoy itself and to enhance the cultural life of the whole city."[21] The three SMRR politicians agreed that building a community identity based on low density neighborhoods, beautiful beaches and parks, thriving public arts, and a robust environment was central to their electoral mandate. What they failed to grasp, however, was the extent to which their particular version of community suffered the insularity of tunnel vision.

Zane, Conn, and Goldway each had deep personal, residential, and political roots in Santa Monica's Ocean Park neighborhood, which was like no other neighborhood in the city. It was a community unto itself. Ocean Park occupies the southwest quadrant of Santa Monica and is separated from the rest of the city by the freeway and a major commercial thoroughfare. Located on a hill gently sloping into the Pacific Ocean, it is an older neighborhood populated by retired people, artists and arti-

sans, counterculture types, and young professionals who live in rented
bungalows and apartments and who often center their lives around the beaches. Ocean Park is the kind of neighborhood that boasts an active street life, highly unusual for Southern California, and a disproportionate number of alternative-style small businesses.

When the SMRR majority came to power, Ocean Park residents were effectively organized under the umbrella of the Ocean Park Community Organization (OPCO), whose constitutional goal "is to protect the unique identity of Ocean Park"; it did so, in part, by working for "energy conservation through development of recycling centers, bike routes, and solar technology; improving telephone service; controlling the dumping of toxic wastes into our air and water, and much more!"[22] The Ocean Park neighborhood was and still is an artsy-craftsy kind of place where environmental consciousness runs deep. It was also the kind of neighborhood, according to scholars, that was most likely to give rise to successful grassroots movements. It had "the leisured and sophisticated middle class" that Harvey Molotch identifies as the core of modern antigrowth machine movements.[23] It hosted the kind of lifestyle that made it ripe for a more general trend described by William Tabb and Larry Sawers:

> Artists and other creative people locate in a poor area of town where rents are low. Soon their needs are met by coffee houses, art galleries, organic food instead of processed chemicals, and handi-crafted products instead of plastic ones. As a market is developed, corporate capitalism and the consumer society move in. Chain stores drive up rents, and coffee houses where one could sit playing chess over a cup of coffee are driven out. High-rise structures are built in place of the small buildings of the previous century, which had stonework, intricately inlaid woodwork, and handmade glass. What happens to the way space is consumed is essentially the same as what happens in other areas of the economy: production is dominated by profit-seeking firms.[24]

The gentrification of Santa Monica in the 1970s hit especially hard in the Ocean Park neighborhood, where antigrowth activism was not only a matter of residential stability but also a test of cultural survival. Ocean Park activism fit Harlan Hahn and Charles Levine's description of urban movements that are "more oriented toward maintaining the neighborhood lifestyle by protecting the status quo" than toward unifying all neighborhoods in behalf of a better city for everyone.[25]

Ocean Park provided the core rank-and-file and leadership of the emerging Santa Monica left. Its activists spearheaded the quality of life and rent control movements of the 1970s; its cadre founded, served in, and held leadership posts in CED and SMRR; and its political leaders —Zane, Conn, and Goldway—were the majority of the SMRR city council majority. Further, Ocean Park activists had the history, experience, recognition, interpersonal ties, and organizational support that made them the prime candidates for public appointments when their leaders took control of city hall and opened the doors of municipal government to citizen participation. As a result, the Ocean Park left was ready and able to imprint its own version of human scale community on city council policies without really understanding that other leftists and other neighborhoods had different views on community.

SMRR's two councilmembers from outside Ocean Park certainly supported their colleagues' community-building policies but with less intensity and more skepticism. Dolores Press told me of one incident in which "diehard feminists" from Ocean Park "jumped all over" her when she suggested that $1 million from the Lincoln Properties deal should go not to Ocean Park but to finance comparable worth for the city's women employees.[26] Kenneth Edwards joked with me about the Ocean Park obsession with "green space" and its narrowness, capsulized in the words of one Ocean Park person at a public hearing: "Hey man, we can't put that housing on the beach because it's messing with my view of the ocean."[27] Press and Edwards were not particularly interested in projecting Ocean Park lifestyles on the entire Santa Monica community; they were more interested in building a community marked by gender equality, adequate housing for all residents, and full employment. And at least some local radicals were alienated by what they saw as the "elitism" of the Ocean Park "clique" that was thoroughly organized to ensure that its quality of life agenda was SMRR's agenda and thus the city council's agenda too. This meant, among other things, that representation for seniors in positions of influence would wait quite a while.[28]

One person working with OPCO characterized the group as "passionate white activists who are middle class" and have "very little experience with minorities."[29] This was also the view of Fred Allingham of the Pico Neighborhood Association (PNA), who said that the Ocean Park activists "are concerned with aesthetic things like art centers and access to the beach and new concepts in green space. . . . My neighborhood, at least the people who are with us in the Association, are appalled that they would even contemplate putting $5.8 million [from the Lincoln Properties deal] on new concepts in green space when we see people moving out of this neighborhood because they can't afford the rent."[30] Several of the Ocean Park councilmembers told me that Allingham's assessment of city priorities was inaccurate, pointing out numerous actions that the council had taken in behalf of the low income, minority Pico neighborhood. But a city-commissioned study, issued two years after the radicals came to power, gave substance to Allingham's views. The study reported that Santa Monica Latinos, mostly from the Pico area, were "alienated" from city government for not taking action "to resolve problems raised by Latino residents."[31] In the eyes of some Santa Monica radicals, the

Ocean Park activists cultivated their quality of life policies first and only then took a serious interest in matters of economic and racial justice.

Did the SMRR councilmembers have any other choice? Several activists did not think so. After all, they told me, the majority of Santa Monicans were of the affluent middle class. They had come to the city because of its quality of life and would lend support to leftwing politicians only if they safeguarded the pier, the beaches and parks, and so forth. This line of thought led to the conclusion that the SMRR-dominated council had to give priority to their own version of community if only to secure enough power and time to do some good for low income and minority people. There are some flaws in this reasoning.

First, there was so great a consensus among affluent Santa Monicans regarding the need to protect the environment that few people looked on it as a *political* issue. They simply expected their government to maintain the quality of life just as they expected their government to maintain the streets, stop lights, and sewers. Second, it was by no means obvious that affluent Santa Monicans were happy with the way that SMRR politicians packaged their quality of life policies. Why clothe them in so much ideological rhetoric? And why try to impose the Ocean Park alternative lifestyle on neighborhoods that were less artsy-craftsy and far more suburban? I suspect that more than a few Santa Monicans who liked suburban lifestyles and took their children to Disneyland each year gave a knowing smirk when they read that local businessman David O'Malley did not want a nonprofit pier corporation if it meant giving authority to "some wacko from Ocean Park." [32] Largely insulated in their own circle of Ocean Park friends, some SMRR councilmembers consistently failed to hear such remarks or investigate their symbolic meaning.

To an extent, the narrowminded insularity evidenced in Ocean Park was reproduced elsewhere in the city. The representatives of homeowner groups spoke as if they were the city. Some members of the local CED chapter had a tendency to confuse their own agenda with the official city agenda. Within the Santa Monica left, the result was latent and patent conflict, which was usually contained within the SMRR coalition. SMRR developed a sense of movement "solidarity," which meant that one disagreed and griped and argued in private but always went along with SMRR councilmembers in public. According to Maurice Zeitlin, "We get pissed as hell at each other; but we realize that we get pissed as hell at each other who are members of the same family and on the same side." [33] And that family unity was certainly reinforced by the knowledge that there was an opposition out there, always ready to take advantage of cracks in coalition unity.

Nonetheless, even internal family conflicts can breed a degree of mistrust that makes members wonder about each other's intentions. Such mistrust gives rise to increased testing of newcomers and allied outsiders while the veterans of past struggles close their ranks for mutual security.

One way to evade the threat of fragmentation—the human scale way—
would be to empower people in the various neighborhoods to determine
for themselves precisely what kind of community they desire.

Neighborhood Power(lessness)

By Kirkpatrick Sale's reckoning, the optimal size for a human scale
neighborhood is 400 to 1,000 residents: small enough for people to get
to know each other but large enough for people to pool adequate resources for shaping their shared lives.[34] Milton Kotler, founder of the
Alliance for Neighborhood Government and then the National Association of Neighborhoods, argues that the virtue of neighborhood power is
that "people see that they have to assume responsibility for their own
social life" and in the process "discover the common good together."[35]
Neighborhood power transforms geographical proximity into cultural
sharing and control.

Santa Monica's seven neighborhoods average nearly 13,000 residents
apiece. Each one is not only larger than Sale's 1,000-resident optimum
for neighborhoods but also larger than Sale's 10,000 optimum for human
scale cities. The SMRR councilmembers, following this logic, should
have done their best to empower the neighborhoods or even subsections
within neighborhoods. They set off in that direction early on when they
appointed a citizen task force to make policy recommendations on development permit processes and neighborhood planning.

The task force began working on development permit processes first
and issued its report in August 1981. It pointed out the need to stream-
line development permit processes by having the city staff issue guide-
books "formulated with input from local homeowners' associations,
neighborhood organizations, local architects, engineers, developers, city
departments and commissions."[36] The original version of the report
included a recommendation that "it is desirable to have some type of
representation of neighborhoods being affected" on the city's environmental quality review committee but this statement was deleted because
the staff argued that putting a public member on a staff committee "is in
conflict with the city manager form of government."[37] In short, the first
set of task force recommendations included little more than a nod toward
neighborhood "input." But the task force was hurried at that point because of other events in the city's development dealings; it was able to
correct itself when it went on to study the possibilities for neighborhood
planning at a less hurried pace.

From early September 1981 to late March 1982, the task force held
twenty-three meetings, toured city neighborhoods, ran public forums,
solicited advice from neighborhood organizations and business groups,
reviewed the appropriate professional literature, and surveyed neighbor-

hood planning projects around the country. It then submitted a report
that began by affirming the principle of neighborhood power.[38] The task force wrote, "We unanimously endorse the concept of grassroots neighborhood organizations—independent entities charged with increasing participation of Santa Monica residents in decisions that affect their lives." These organizations would "organize, educate, and empower those who have not previously been involved in local government" as well as "provide a sense of community for residents of the neighborhood." Along these lines, the task force recommended that "the city delegate as much power as a neighborhood organization is prepared to accept." The principle was clear but the task force recommended policies that meant virtually *no* delegation of power to neighborhood organizations.

A "legitimate" neighborhood organization, the report noted, is "democratic and participatory," making its decisions through the "membership, not the leadership." This stipulation may have been a de facto exclusion of homeowner associations that relied mostly on leadership for initiative and decisionmaking; but it also could be used as an exclusionary threat against organizations like OPCO and PNA that were mostly run by staff directors under the guidance of small executive boards. Even if an organization was deemed legitimate, the report did not offer it much to do. The neighborhood organization could give the city "advice" on neighborhood matters as could any other group, but "policy development and implementation still rest entirely with the city." The organization should "feel free to urge its point of view on any issue before any governmental or nongovernmental body," but city officials should feel free to employ "compelling arguments and evidence" for rejecting the neighborhood point of view. The organization might seek appointments on "city task forces and commissions," but it was left to the city council to decide how "neighborhoods are broadly represented on such bodies." The neighborhood organization could assess and propose "the service needs" of its area, but "actual responsibility should remain with the city staff." Finally, the organization might serve as "parent body for entrepreneurial activities" such as community development corporations or cooperatives, but it would have to rely on the city government for "the collection and dissemination of relevant information" and funding. Put differently, the task force took six months to affirm the principle of neighborhood power and to recommend the practice of centralized city hall power.

The gap between principle and practice in the report was an accurate representation of the views of SMRR politicians. Several months after the report was issued, I asked community liaison officer Vivian Rothstein about the kinds of power that had actually been delegated to neighborhoods. She mentioned a program to establish neighborhood councils with decisionmaking power over activities at local parks; but nothing else was being planned.[39] Shortly thereafter, the PNA's board of directors chairman published a letter to the editor in the local newspaper that concluded on this note: "Sadly, our observation of the new progressive city council's appointments leads us to conclude that while they may support some PNA projects, they have no intentions of sharing political power with our community in a real way or opening up the process of government to our residents."[40] As if to test city officials' intentions, the PNA put together a neighborhood plan that proposed that the PNA, as a legitimate neighborhood organization, should be delegated veto power over commercial and industrial developments in its part of the city. SMRR councilmembers and city staff, predictably, opposed such a delegation of power.

Dennis Zane stated, "The council has the responsibility to the whole city, not just to a single neighborhood. I don't believe it would be appropriate to grant any neighborhood that level of authority." Kenneth Edwards added, "Duly elected public officials of the city as established in the city charter have those responsibilities." And city staff member Mark Tigan concluded, "We support maximum citizen neighborhood involvement in the process, but we would never recommend releasing the decisionmaking part to the neighborhood or providing them with veto control."[41] Many leftwing activists agreed. How could SMRR politicians fulfill their electoral mandate if they needed the consent of neighborhood organizations? And, given that city hall was now so accessible to people in the neighborhoods, was any further decentralization of power really necessary?

Why the gap between principle and practice? OPCO was the one neighborhood organization with enough leverage to politicize the issue of neighborhood power but it did not do so for two reasons. First, OPCO people felt that they were already empowered. They were the Ocean Park people who filled SMRR's ranks and offices, sat on the city council, and held appointments throughout city government. A push for neighborhood power would have weakened OPCO by removing decisions that it could control through city hall to "outsider" neighborhoods where people's priorities might be quite different. James Conn told me, "I've been in Ocean Park now ten years . . . and we've got leadership coming out of our ears in this community but you look at the minority [Pico] community, they don't; that's because their leadership development process is only a couple of years old now."[42] The implicit message was that the Pico neighborhood was not yet ready to be delegated power because its leadership was not properly seasoned—not quite trustworthy. And Kenneth Edwards told me that some of his Ocean Park colleagues on the council "go crazy" at the mere idea that all neighborhoods should be organized and empowered because that would mean giving decisions over to non-SMRR people and homeowners' groups in Santa Monica's more affluent neighborhoods.[43]

Second, the overlap among people from Ocean Park, OPCO members, SMRR, the city council, and city appointees made it extremely

difficult for OPCO leaders to focus exclusively on their own neighborhood concerns. They were constantly crosspressured to do what was
right for the movement or what the council considered right for the city
as a whole. In at least two instances, OPCO activists opposed new developments in their neighborhood only to have their own organizational
leaders, SMRR people, and SMRR councilmembers broker compromises that allowed developments to proceed. In one case, writes Allan
Heskin, "OPCO eventually capitulated and publicly favored the proposed settlement, earning the undying hostility of a portion of its constituency."[44] PNA leaders, on the other hand, were not crosspressured.
They wanted neighborhood power but simply could not get it from the
city hall radicals.

Ultimately, SMRR councilmembers felt "responsible" for deciding
what was good for individual neighborhoods and for the city as a whole.[45]
In their view, their responsibility was a function of their legal duties as
popularly elected city officials. And as tensions within the SMRR coalition emerged, the councilmembers also felt responsible for mediating
conflicting demands and forging compromises that would keep the coalition intact. This meant, however, that the councilmembers needed to
consolidate their political authority rather than delegate it to smaller,
more human scale units.

For example, the Lincoln Properties deal looked like a $15 million
windfall to every leftwing group and social organization in Santa Monica.
Similarly, when SMRR councilmembers voted to close down the Santa
Monica Airport and open up its land for possible development, people
in the movement and on the fringes had an empty canvas upon which
they painted their heart's political desires. Some people wanted to invest
the money and land in green space and the arts; others imagined a huge
tract for affordable housing; a few conceived a complex of alternative
small businesses and community development corporations; several envisioned the growth of light industries that would enhance local employment opportunities for the poor and unskilled. Were the council to delegate authority over revenues or city land to those neighborhoods most
directly affected, it would invite a war of each against all and, in the
process, destroy its own organizational and electoral base. Were the council to consolidate authority—as it did—it would be nicely positioned to
grant favors, strike bargains, and broker its own survival.

The SMRR councilmembers also felt responsible as middle class radicals to do a professional job of governing, albeit along new professional
lines. Whereas OPCO originally opposed the Lincoln Properties deal,
the council radicals persuaded the organizations' members otherwise,
relating the advice of the city attorney that rescinding an earlier contract
with the developer would likely have put the city on the losing side of a
threatened $23 million lawsuit. When people in the affected neighbor-
hoods supported closure of the Santa Monica Airport, they encountered

a city council that turned to the talents of the city manager to negotiate some sort of compromise with the Federal Aviation Administration, which had a long-term contract demanding the continuation of airport activities. A number of local activists wanted to stop the Lincoln Properties deal and close down the airport regardless of inherited contracts and then let the aggrieved parties test the law of contracts in the courtroom. The city hall radicals were sympathetic but ultimately chose otherwise. Mayor Goldway stated why: "I think it's much easier for people on the *outside* to say that and ask their government to test the law than it is once you're in government and you're responsible in so many areas where you have to make a decision about where your resources are best spent."[46] Now the decentralized, human scale, grassroots groups and organizations were on the "outside." What counted most was the cost-benefit analyses of inside professionals. Thus, the SMRR councilmembers did invite neighborhood groups to speak their piece, but the politicians protected the higher ground of legitimate authority and professional expertise.

An ambiguous relationship developed between Santa Monica's neighborhood organizations and city government that was dramatized in a 1983 incident. After a year of laying groundwork, some residents of the heavily tenanted Wilshire neighborhood with the help of city officials founded the Mid-City Neighbors (MCN). The residents organized to address neighborhood quality of life issues, and the city council seeded them with $35,000 and then another $74,000 for the coming fiscal year. MCN was soon involved in giving advice to the city, which was negotiating an ongoing development in the Wilshire area. According to some MCN members, their advice was ignored in the final compromise between city hall and the developer. The unhappy residents published in their newsletter an article highly critical of city officials, only to incur the wrath of city hall. City manager John Alschuler vehemently disputed MCN claims that it had been ignored and, more important, the city council voted "to review the overall performance of such organizations each quarter."[47] This not-so-veiled threat to MCN funding suggested that harmonious relations between neighborhoods and the city hall radicals might be enforced by governors willing to give money to the friendly but take it away from critics. So much for neighborhood power.

The Small Business Booster(ism)

SMRR's "Principles of Unity" stated that "the council should establish a mechanism to encourage small business in Santa Monica."[48] This mechanism would give a boost to the small business economy where neighborliness held greater esteem than net worth. But like "community" or "neighborhood power," the idea of small business was often used as an abstraction begging a definition.

By "small business," the Ocean Park folks often meant alternative businesses that served and supported particular neighborhoods. The pro-

gram for one of OPCO's yearly congresses included advertisements for
Building Women contractors, Co-Opportunity food cooperative, Oak-
wood Gallery, Colors of the Wind kite shop, Anne's Tiques, Hang
Gliders of California, Ambrosia Epicurean Catering, and other such
small neighborhood businesses. One ad announced that the local owner
was "proud to be a part of the Ocean Park community," while most ads
suggested a conscious sensitivity to the alternative lifestyles that distinguished the Ocean Park neighborhood.[49]

Even the notion of alternative businesses was ambiguous. An article
in the OPCO newsletter read as follows:

> Broadway plays have backers called "angels." For as long as we can
> remember, OPCO has had an angel called Irv Siegel. You may not
> know Irv by name, but you surely know the pizza place he brought
> to Main Street called Wildflour. Over the years, Irv has donated a
> multitude of foods to a variety of OPCO events and fundraisers,
> including our annual congress.[50]

Reading on, one learns that Irv owned not only Wildflour but its several
franchises as well. Does his still count as a small business because he
contributes to OPCO? If so, do the two large banks and the Pioneer
Chicken and McDonald's restaurant outlets that also bought ads in the
OPCO program count as small businesses? After all, even giant corporations understand that it is good for business to establish friendly relations in local arenas of operations.

City planning commissioner Derek Shearer tossed human scale quality
and human contact into the definitional hopper. He told me of one Ocean
Park restaurant that served good food at a fair price until the owner got
"greedy," expanded into a new shopping mall, and "quality went down."
Shearer also related the story of a small bakery run by a friendly husband
and wife team that was "really great" until the couple expanded into the
catering business and then "a lot of people stopped going because the
quality and the human contact weren't there" anymore.[51] Shearer's message seemed to be that "real" small business is not only a matter of size
but of values, in particular, of the human scale over the marketplace.

The SMRR council's first effort to boost small business did not encounter any definitional problems. The council subsidized the creation of
a weekly farmers market just off the Santa Monica Mall. It was all
things to all people. The farmers market was an opportunity for small,
sometimes hippie-like farmers in the region to sell fresh produce directly
to the public and thereby avoid the costs of dealing with corporate mid-
dlemen and packing houses. The venture served nearby seniors by providing quality produce at below-market prices within walking distance
of their homes. It also helped the Mall's family businesses by luring
potential customers to their location. "Hey, give them credit," said one
Mall merchant. "No one fought harder against their election than I did.

But the market is the first positive action to help us in several years."[52] Also, the farmers market functioned as a weekly community gathering place where local residents met and chatted. Buoyed by its success on this project, the council underwrote a second farmers market in the Pico neighborhood.

But ambiguity caught up with the council when it sought to enrich the local tourist trade. The council created the Santa Monica Convention and Visitors Bureau, a nonprofit public corporation financed by a 2 percent increase in the city's transient occupancy (hotel and motel) tax. With a first-year budget of nearly $200,000, the bureau's job was to promote the tourism that supported Santa Monica's small business past and would guarantee the city's small business future. The prospective beneficiaries would include Ocean Park's alternative businesses, the pier's small operators, the family businesses of the Santa Monica Mall, and so forth.

However, the SMRR council did not look to small business people to run the Santa Monica Convention and Visitors Bureau. "Mom and pop" stores were poorly organized outside of the Chamber of Commerce; their owners lacked the professional business expertise necessary for long-term economic planning; and they gave little indication of interest in participating in the planning process. The council looked to the Chamber of Commerce and some local high rollers who were organized, professionally qualified, and interested. As a result, the council put the human scale future of small businesses into the hands of big business managers connected with the hotel industry: Richard Messer, assistant manager of the Beverly Hillcrest Hotel; Beverly Moore, a marketing vice president of Manor Park Management, which operated one of Santa Monica's largest hotels; and David O'Malley, president of the Santa Monica–based Welton Becket Associates, which was involved in worldwide hotel construction.

The bureau managers commissioned a study on the impact of tourism on Santa Monica. It showed that more than $200 million annually was pumped into the city economy by tourists. It also said that Santa Monica needed more "first class hotels," with the qualification that "these should fit into the overall scale of the city."[53] In effect, it presented a trickle-down theory of tourism, calling for maximum usage of the Santa Monica Airport, major hotel developments, and major chain-store operations like automobile rental firms that cater to affluent visitors. Once tourists arrived, got their accommodations and a car, then they would spend some of their travelers checks at small business establishments.

This trickle-down perspective was consistent with the council's dealings with the pier and the farmers markets. The human scale pier with its small business operators was to be preserved, but it was also to be managed efficiently by the Pier Restoration Corporation run by a board of business professionals and a highly paid executive director who had once worked for the New York City Ports and Terminal Department.[54] The

farmers markets did not somehow emerge from the grassroots demands
of citizens or small business people; they were initiated and planned by
city hall professionals and by consultants such as Larry Larson, who
held a master's degree in agriculture.[55] Small businesses were certainly
to benefit from these policies, and their advice, along with that of all
citizens, was solicited, but the SMRR councilmembers felt responsible
for doing a professional job and thus turned mostly to the professionals
for policy recommendations and implementation.

The turn toward professionals brought the SMRR council and the
Santa Monica Area Chamber of Commerce closer and closer together.
Originally, the SMRR politicians expressed considerable disdain for the
Chamber. Mayor Goldway regularly traded barbs with the Chamber
people; and her husband Derek Shearer explained that "the Chamber
tends to be dominated, as I think all Chambers are, not by the small
shopkeeper but by real estate, the banks, the insurance companies." He
estimated that only one-eighth of Santa Monica's 8,000 small businesses
were Chamber members.[56] Councilmembers could write off the Chamber
of Commerce as essentially a representative of larger, growth machine
businesses that were insensitive to the needs of the little guy, and they
sometimes did. Nonetheless, the Chamber was the only major business
group that could claim to represent small business; it had the expertise to
do so; and its constant attacks on SMRR were increasingly considered
a political liability in the eyes of some councilmembers. In time, the
SMRR people began to seek a more professional relationship with the
Chamber of Commerce.

For its part, the Chamber people were somewhat divided. Its older
and more ideologically rightwing members had an especial dislike for
mayor Goldway as well as for the council in general. Some of the Chamber leadership, said Kenneth Edwards, "literally hate Ruth." But, according to Derek Shearer, some of the Chamber's "younger people want
to work with us."[57] Included in the latter group was thirty-five-year-old
store owner Joe Miko Jr., who became Chamber president in 1983.
Miko's incoming message to the Chamber reaffirmed disagreements with
the SMRR people in city hall but concluded on a conciliatory note, "I
believe in America and the free election system it offers by which our
own city council has been elected. Therefore, I am committed to working
with the city council because doing anything else I feel would make me a
hypocrite. . . . Nothing has ever been resolved to a mutual satisfaction
without open dialogue."[58] Miko's offer of detente was gladly accepted by
Kenneth Edwards, who replaced Goldway as mayor in early 1983.

While some rhetorical antagonism and distrust continued, the council
and the Chamber were able to broker a series of policy compromises.
They worked together to create a nonprofit public corporation called the
Third Street Development Corporation, budgeted at nearly $1 million,
as a first step toward revitalizing the Santa Monica Mall. The council
chose eleven directors for the corporation: four people from architectural

firms, two in real estate, two lawyers, one banker, and one social service executive. The city council and the Chamber of Commerce also worked together to revise Santa Monica's business license tax rates, which were 50 to 80 percent lower than those in adjacent cities. After a brief conflict during which Dennis Zane assured residents that the SMRR people did not have an "antibusiness attitude," the councilmembers and Chamber representatives worked out a package that meant lower fees for small businesses, higher fees for large businesses, and some key exemptions.[59] Here again, the council worked in behalf of small businesses but it did so by working through the Chamber of Commerce professionals.

The city hall radicals became increasingly insulated from small businesses as they became more comfortable with professional brokering. When a number of small businesses faced eviction because of rent increases by commercial landlords and then petitioned the council to consider commercial rent control, SMRR officials responded that they doubted they could do anything.[60] When the leases of small beachfront vendors expired, the city invited them to submit new bids with the understanding that their rents were going up dramatically and that the city would give preference to a single vendor planning to operate all five stands. City attorney Robert Myers was quoted, "If we can get people to bid, why shouldn't the city get $8,100?"—as opposed to the $2,300 per month it had been getting. "It's their problem, not ours," Myers concluded. City parks and recreation director Don Arnett put it simply, "We're looking to get a solid business in." What appeared to be a plain cost-benefit analysis to city professionals looked like an eviction notice to the small-time beach operators, who predicted that the city would probably strike a bargain with "the American image down there, and that image is something like McDonald's."[61] Sure enough, within a month, the city council awarded the vending contract to McDonald's restaurants, which had been approached by the city and came in with by far the highest bid.

SMRR broke ranks on the McDonald's contract. James Conn abstained on the vote after failing to persuade his colleagues to postpone the decision until NAACP charges of racial discrimination against the hamburger corporation were investigated. Dennis Zane voted against the contract, arguing that different vendors should be chosen for each of the stands. But city attorney Robert Myers' argument that the council should not "jeopardize the integrity of the competitive bidding process" won the day when the other SMRR councilmembers joined with the opposition to grant the contract to McDonald's. Outside the council chambers, ten picketers marched, claiming that public hearings should have been held prior to the vote; and they chanted, "City council give us slack / we don't want no more Big Macs."[62] It was not a particularly good day either for the principle of small scale businesses or for the pragmatic need for coalition unity.

McDonald's immediately began a $1 million renovation project on
the beachfront stands in order to be able to open shop before the 1984
Olympics brought hordes of tourists as well as media people to Santa
Monica. Working with city architects, the corporation designed McDonald's outlets without the gaudy golden arches and more in tune with the
beach. There was a short delay in construction when nearby residents
complained that the corporation had nearly doubled the height of the
structures, thereby obstructing both their ocean view and beachfront
aesthetics. City professionals had approved the new height but quickly
backpedaled to work out a compromise once the issue was publicized.
At approximately the same time, the Pier Restoration Corporation held
public hearings on whether to build a fifteen-foot-high breakwater to
protect the pier from future structural damage. The discussion gravitated
to aesthetics, with former mayor Ruth Yannatta Goldway asking breakwater advocates if they had really considered "the visual impact" of a
fifteen-foot-high stone wall in the middle of the ocean.[63]

To an extent, the SMRR councilmembers replicated the traditional
Chamber of Commerce attitude toward small business. On the one hand,
the SMRR politicians sang the praises of small business and human scale
virtues. On the other hand, they did not particularly like to deal directly
with small business people, who, in their view, acted somewhat errati-
cally. For example, the SMRR council came to power by supporting
tenant rights and yet found themselves in the position of evicting a pier
restaurant that was more than $70,000 behind in its rent. City staff person
Mark Tigan expressed the councilmembers' feelings well:

> This is certainly not a pleasant position to be in. The city encour-
> ages and supports small businesses, especially the types that are
> family run. But . . . it's our responsibility and requirement that we
> protect the public interest. We can't justify giving away free space
> in a public-owned piece of real estate.[64]

In an odd way, councilmembers were far more comfortable dealing with
Chamber of Commerce professionals, who, despite their ideological opposition, shared concerns such as maximizing city revenues or guarding
the city's architectural integrity. The result, over all, was more small
business boosterism but not more small business control over the city's
economic fortunes. And more than a few small business people, who
were otherwise prone to support SMRR, became disenchanted with
what some of them considered the brokering away of their interests.

Human Scale Values and Middle Class Virtues

Human scale values such as community, neighborhood power, and small
business sensitivities are abstractions that nearly everyone can support

in principle. Like peace on earth and good will to men, these values were popular among middle class Santa Monicans, who could afford to be concerned with the cultural quality of their lives. The Santa Monica radicals gave top priority to these human scale values in the hope of preserving Santa Monica's small town virtues and simultaneously winning political support for the idea of putting people ahead of profits. Conceivably, Santa Monicans would begin to see the virtue of revising the ends of social life by making materialism secondary.

The radicals, however, were relatively insulated. The Ocean Park base of SMRR support tried to imprint its alternative lifestyles on working definitions of community only to distance itself from other radicals and other residents. The SMRR council liked the idea of empowering neighborhoods but only when the organized groups gave voice to local concerns in ways consistent with SMRR priorities. The council radicals were not interested in actually delegating decisionmaking power to neighborhood organizations that might have different priorities, making some people sense a heavy-handedness in city hall. The SMRR politicians were enamored of small businesses but adopted a macroeconomic perspective that favored close relations with the Chamber of Commerce and professional planners. At best, small business people felt that the council provided them indirect assistance.

The results of SMRR's human scale policies were mixed. On the one hand, Santa Monicans had little reason to believe that the radicals had enhanced their "*control* over the processes of life." The contours of local culture were still being shaped in city hall despite the rhetoric of empowerment. On the other hand, residents who had been ignored or slighted in the past did gain a greater degree of *representation* in city policymaking. The Ocean Park neighborhood concerns came out high on the city agenda. The Pico neighborhood, though unhappy with city priorities, was now represented by an organization that at least gave voice to the concerns of the city's low income and minority population. And the small business community, still disorganized and dominated in the Chamber of Commerce, could no longer be ignored in planning and development policies.

Control and representation are very different phenomena. Control, according to human scale logic, requires small scale units with relatively autonomous decisionmaking on local matters. Decentralization and autonomy invite individuals to develop their political personae and skills, forge some common bonds in the process of defining and deciding their shared culture, and enjoy the human relationships that militate against the sovereignty of individual self-aggrandizement in the marketplace. Such control would allow people to choose for themselves whether green space or full employment should be given higher priority, or whether small business amateurs instead of business professionals should engage in local planning. Ultimately, human scale control in a city as large as

Santa Monica tests whether residents can tolerate a plurality of sub-cultures—some revising the ends of social life but others humanizing more conventional, materialistic ends. Representation, however, suggests the continuation of centralized decisionmaking. Citizens remain dependent on elected and appointed officials who may be benign but nonetheless have a tendency to impose their own cultural preferences across neighborhoods. And when they legitimate that imposition by invoking their electoral mandate or professional expertise, they implicitly foster public quiescence instead of the self-reliance at the heart of human scale values.

Why would radicals, sincere in their advocacy of human scale values, make policies that worked against decentralization of power and citizen autonomy? Why would they try to consolidate their own cultural control and justify it by conventional doctrines of representation? Why the gap between principles and politics?

First, few American radicals are willing to take community control very far. "Decentralism and injustice," writes David Moberg, "have hardly been incompatible."[65] Delegating authority to some neighborhoods where materialism still reigns supreme, for example, could mean empowering people who are less concerned with ecology and more interested in closing off their borders to minorities who they believe will lower their property values. Until people have already revised the ends, radicals do not trust them. Further, middle class radicals are ambivalent about how much they want the ends revised and how long the process will take. Middle class people do not want major corporations to set up oil wells and refineries in their neighborhoods but they are not ready to give up the conveniences of their automobiles for the foreseeable future; they do not want big industries or commercial developments built across the street from their homes but they like the taxes that large firms generate for city services. Middle class radicals are no different. They question size but do not want to give up the benefits that come with it. Thus, the crucial question facing middle class radicals is: who will negotiate the trade-offs?

Santa Monica's middle class radicals were similar to an earlier generation of middle class professionals who, with the self-confidence born of success and education, believed in their own problem-solving capacities. They did not consider themselves mere instruments for converting democratic demands into public policies. They were missionaries, albeit left-wing ones, spreading the gospel of the human scale and engineering a model that others would emulate. They alone could decide which trade-offs worked, though they were usually willing to listen to others' advice. James Conn put *their* need for control in psychological terms: "We're all a bunch of obsessive-compulsives. . . . I think obsessive-compulsives have a very difficult time letting go of running things."[66]

Second, whereas grassroots movements usually support some version of human scale control against political representation, the demands of political governance inside of city hall work in the opposite direction. Most grassroots movements in U.S. history have been what Frances Fox Piven and Richard A. Cloward call "poor people's movements" through which the powerless defy the powerful.[67] The excluded begin to question the legitimacy of dominant elites, assert what they consider their rights to self-government, and develop a sense of efficacy that makes changing the rules of political life seem possible. The powerless temporarily become insurgents who use daring rhetoric made meaningful through collective action, generate relatively spontaneous mobilizations, and create an atmosphere of uncertainty and unpredictability in the relations between themselves and elites. Above all else, poor people's movements threaten to disrupt the prevailing attitudes and practices that define political normality.

Political governance assumes a contradictory culture. Politicians and bureaucrats need unambiguous priorities rather than daring rhetoric to frame policy issues. They may support popular collective action but they cannot tolerate spontaneous outbursts of mass protest that undermine the policy planning process. Governors must rely a great deal on professional experts who know how to follow established procedures and rules that align policies with legal requirements. Most important, city officials must eliminate unpredictability lest policies administered one day have unintended effects the next day. In sum, grassroots movements thrive on the threat of disruption whereas political governance survives on order.

According to Piven and Cloward, the key turning point for poor people's movements is when middle class radicals "organize" them. The organizers try to coordinate movement resources, adjust them to movement ends, and plan for the long-term growth and effectiveness of the movement. Their attempts to enhance political efficiency is their peculiar form of public service. But the flaw in their management is that they undermine the movement's most potent weapon: the threat of disruption. The organizers bring discipline to the movement; they create procedures for legitimate decisionmaking; and they found an identifiable leadership able to tame rank-and-file activism in return for concessions from elites. The relations between movement people and elites becomes regularized, even bureaucratized. "Organizations endure, in short, by abandoning their oppositional politics."[68]

Santa Monica obviously did not have a poor people's movement. It had a middle class tenant movement that was being transformed into a middle class political movement. When outside of city power, the movement did cultivate some defiance, spontaneous activism, and threats of disruption, but only to a very limited extent. That was because the city's middle class radicals also generated a lot of "organized" groups such as CED, OPCO, and SMRR. Movement discipline, procedural regularity, leadership, and intergroup brokering existed from the start, and the threat

that the movement would disrupt political governance was never more
than minimal. As such, the SMRR politicians came to power in a city where they could assume, with considerable accuracy, that grassroots insurgency would not be turned against their political governance. They were free to meet the demands of political governance and consolidate their "representative" authority with little resistance. And their middle class sense of efficacy and professionalism virtually guaranteed that they would be a force for political order. Thus, it is not particularly surprising, for example, that the SMRR politicians regularized relations with the Chamber of Commerce.

Third, the SMRR politicians generally believed that their human scale policies were working well for the first few years of city hall power. They were taking distinct steps toward preserving and promoting a human scale city. Their environmental policies, the new neighborhood organizations, and greater concern for small businesses could be considered a foundation upon which they would build stronger public support and quality of life reforms in the near future. They had politicized human scale issues, tamed growth, and intended to do more to cultivate the human spirit.

Some SMRR councilmembers did admit privately that they had made mistakes: They might have done more to develop a more pluralistic view of community that included the views of seniors, minorities, and home-owners. They could have experimented more with delegating power to neighborhood groups. And they should have been more cognizant of small business interests. But they were new to the internal workings of government. They were learning through on-the-job training about what was or was not possible. Given more time, they would do more to close the gap between their human scale ideal and political reality.

But their time in office was contingent on their ability to maintain and enhance public support. Most SMRR politicians believed that their human scale policies had enhanced their electoral base, but, as noted earlier, this was questionable. Still, they did not plan to rest on human scale laurels. Part of their effort to wed principles to pragmatism involved promoting the participatory democracy that would involve citizens in government and also provide them a stake in supporting the middle class radicals.

6
Who Will Make a Difference?

Politicians—women or men—will make a difference, will create the changes that result in greater equity and dignity . . . when those politicians believe change is needed, and owe their election victories to citizens groups working for real social change, . . . social justice, democratic principles, and feminism.

Ruth Yannatta Goldway[1]

Citizens will make the difference in political life. That is the main premise
of participatory democracy. People's participation in shaping, deciding, and administering public policies will foster both the psychological sense of efficacy and the political skills necessary for popular self-government. Conversely, "the movement for participatory democracy," writes Isaac Balbus, "has shown that representative and bureaucratic political forms perforce imply the domination of representatives and bureaucrats over the very people they are ostensibly obliged to serve."[2] When politicians make the major difference in political life, they reinforce citizens' sense of impotence and dependence, preparing them to suffer the vicissitudes of elitist rule.

The Santa Monica left accepted the main premise of participatory democracy. Nevertheless, as the opening quotation suggests, Santa Monica's middle class radicals also felt that they were the ones who would determine the fate of the political experiment. This feeling was an accurate reflection of the radicals' experiences in the SMRR coalition, in city hall, and, most important, in middle class America. When this feeling was reduced to public policy, the result was something far short of the ideal of participatory democracy.

Consensus and Conflict

Santa Monica radicals had two views of the Santa Monicans for Renters' Rights (SMRR) coalition. One was that SMRR was a microcosm of participatory democracy. It nurtured among its members a social consciousness that stressed decisionmaking through unanimous group consensus in the hopes of producing an exemplary organization. The other view was that SMRR was an electoral instrument for bringing to power politicians who would facilitate the growth of participatory democracy in the city of Santa Monica. The winners' mandate was to share political authority in opposition to elitist adversaries. In fact, both views of SMRR were partly misleading.

"Decisionmaking in SMRR is by and large by consensus," according to SMRR staff member Roger Thornton. "It must be unanimous" when candidate selections or public positions on issues are at stake.[3] Activists from SMRR's constituent groups—the Santa Monica chapter of Campaign for Economic Democracy (CED), the Democratic Club, and the Santa Monica Fair Housing Alliance (SMFHA)—would congregate at open forums to discuss important coalition matters. The discussion would continue when activists returned to their separate groups to formulate official constituent positions. Each group then sent two representatives to the SMRR steering committee where differences were worked through and consensus was hammered out. Once each constituent group authorized its steering committee representatives to affirm the consensus, the coalition had its decision. At that point, it was expected that all group members would see the wisdom of the consensus and that those who disagreed would voluntarily accept the decision because it had been produced by democratic processes and movement solidarity.

Chief among SMRR decisions was the selection and election of political candidates who would support the democratization of city government. Naturally, Santa Monica activists disagreed among themselves about who was most committed to participatory democracy and who was most likely to win in a municipal election but they showed a remarkable willingness to air strategic differences and find generally acceptable solutions. Dennis Zane told me, "One of the virtues of SMRR is that it has been phenomenally successful in making those kinds of compromises, and having heated, difficult, and disputed questions that people get angry about and yell about but always come around to create a consensus."[4] Candidate selection battles were resolved through discussion and diplomacy, and the SMRR process did indeed produce a consistent lot of candidates who agreed on the goal of participatory democracy and were also able to win elections.

To the extent that SMRR was a microcosm of participatory democracy founded on consensus, it was so because it contained a relatively small and selective membership composed of activists predisposed to trying out political equality in the organization. Neither SMRR nor its constituent groups were exactly mass-based organizations. In 1981, CED, the Democratic Club, and SMFHA were joined by the Ocean Park Electoral Network (OPEN)—a spin-off of the Ocean Park Community Organization (OPCO), which had to avoid direct political participation lest it endanger its tax-exempt status and eligibility for government funding—to make SMRR a confederation of four modest community groups. Both CED and OPEN were small groups that held private meetings attended by few individuals. The Democratic Club and SMFHA were open to mass membership but never attracted more than a scattering of active members. Multiple memberships in the four groups, symbolized at one point by a CED member's also being president of the Democratic Club, suggest that the actual number of people under SMRR's organizational umbrella was very small. Allan Heskin's estimate of SMRR's *active* membership is probably accurate: "SMRR has been in reality a coalition of cadre, not groups. This cadre consists of about fifteen people at its core and about a hundred at its periphery."[5] If SMRR was a participatory democracy, it was a participatory democracy for the few.

There is some reason to believe that SMRR's version of participatory democracy was compromised by a strong dose of elitism. SMRR was largely inactive between elections, with a handful of people working in their homes to keep the organization's files intact and updated. When SMRR was reactivated just prior to elections, it operated at a forced pace that favored elitism. Haste meant that the Ocean Park regulars were overrepresented in the rank and file and the leadership, that CED was more than equal given the organizational energy of its members and its access to Tom Hayden's electoral resources, and that Ruth Yannatta Goldway and Derek Shearer were a special force by dint of their powerful personalities and intellects as well as their outside connections. Time pressure meant that it was nearly impossible to challenge SMRR's hierarchy of power even when activists recognized it and complained about it. The older generation of activists concentrated in the Democratic Club and SMFHA, for example, were pressured to follow the lead of the younger people, which often meant that the seniors would do coalition legwork and paperwork rather than assume important positions in electoral campaigns or city government. The older activists were reticent to make an issue of inequality lest they be accused of undermining coalition unity in the midst of an electoral campaign.[6]

Moreover, important SMRR business reportedly took place on the telephone and in private conversations. SMRR leaders might work out particular strategies and then, as in the earlier-cited case of Tom Hayden at Columbia University, form a compact minority able to impose its will on a relatively disorganized coalition majority.[7] This practice was abetted by several factors. SMRR leaders were positioned within city government and could use their unique positions, access to information, and sheer energy to command a consensus. Also, SMRR decisionmaking, often a last-minute affair, provided little opportunity for sustained disagreement, the development of systematic alternatives, the growth of a cohesive internal opposition, or the use of the democratic but cumbersome formal procedures to contest the leadership. In some instances, the SMRR consensus was less the offspring of democratic discourse than the child of leadership initiative and political expedience.

Elitism within SMRR reared its head more openly as each election day approached. As noted earlier, SMRR increasingly became a hierarchical organization that expected discipline from the troops and professionalism from the generals. To the extent that middle class activists accepted as necessary the use of campaign professionals, they were not likely to object to their diminished role. And SMRR leaders had less incentive to mount a democratically derived campaign as they came to rely more heavily on the expertise of campaign managers and consultants. Nearing election day, SMRR elitism was overt but not particularly noticeable because activists' attention was focused on beating the adversaries.

Accusations and lawsuits were often lodged against SMRR and its candidates at the electoral eleventh hour; and the coalition depended on its professional campaign staff to deal with these irritants. On the eve of the April 1983 municipal election, for example, the opposition accused SMRR members of complicity in the theft of a Rolodex file that potentially would affect the outcome of a ballot measure; also, a major financial supporter of the opposition brought a $117 million defamation suit against SMRR for invading his privacy during the electoral campaign. Someone had to speak for SMRR and professional campaign manager Parke Skelton took it upon himself to do so:

> I just want to say to Mr. De Santis that if he is accusing me or any individual or SMRR of playing any role in allegedly stealing a Rolodex from Larry Kates, he himself had better be prepared to defend himself from a multimillion dollar defamation suit because it is absolutely and unequivocally untrue and we will not tolerate being accused of criminal acts by Paul De Santis or any of his big real estate backers.[8]

Elections throughout the American political system generate a de facto state of emergency that empowers campaign leaders and professionals to speak for those with whom they have not had time to consult. In most instances, a goal such as participatory democracy is put on the back burner, at least until after the election is completed.

SMRR was less than an ideal microcosm of participatory democracy and at least some members were unhappy with the informal elitism that emerged within the coalition. Still, they avoided contesting the consensus and engaging in open conflict with the leadership, in part, because they believed the coalition was effective at electing politicians who would foster participatory democracy in the city as a whole. The means did not necessarily determine the ends. Nonetheless, SMRR's leftwing politicians got their feet wet in the SMRR electoral campaigns, took for granted the political entrepreneurship and professionalism that pervaded the campaigns, and, once in office, continued to act as if a permanent state of emergency was the framework for making public policy.

The Issue That Would Not Die

The SMRR council came to power committed to expanding democratic participation in Santa Monica politics. They fulfilled this commitment, in part, by politicizing the crucial issues of the day. The city hall radicals appointed citizen task forces and commissions that held public hearings, solicited expert advice, and stimulated discussion on the status of women in America, the dangers of the nuclear arms race and the desirability of a nuclear freeze, and other domestic and foreign policy issues. The council itself fostered political dialogue by passing resolutions protesting the presence of a nuclear reactor at nearby UCLA, cuts in county health programs, proposed cuts in social security benefits, Immigration and Naturalization Service raids, U.S. intervention in El Salvador, possible Soviet intervention in Poland, and so forth, with the object of generating informed public exchanges and giving voice to grassroots public opinion.

Such council actions, stated Dennis Zane, "provide an opportunity for people to delve into issues, to study issues and develop expertise as well as an opportunity to take issues out into the community. . . . They provide additional mechanisms for expanding the body of public participation."[9] The SMRR politicians succeeded to the extent that Santa Monica became marked by a highly charged political atmosphere.

That atmosphere, however, was not necessarily conducive either to councilmembers' popularity or their ability to make public policy. In some instances, the radical politicians felt that they were forced to choose between extending participatory democracy or exercising political authority, and the SMRR council often chose the latter. This is illustrated in the case of the issue that would not die.

In the early summer of 1982, Tom Hayden was gearing up for his campaign to represent the Santa Monica area in the State Assembly. Hayden and Jane Fonda took a highly publicized trip to the Middle East during which the couple voiced support for Israel despite its recent invasion of Lebanon. Their statements to the press prompted some American leftists to accuse Hayden of having sold out his principles in order to woo Santa Monica's considerable Jewish vote. Santa Monica CED people were in some cases less upset with Hayden's position on the Middle East, which they claimed was sincere rather than opportunistic, than with Hayden's propensity to take positions on issues with neither discussion with nor advice from the CED grassroots.

At first, the episode affected Santa Monica municipal politics in two minor ways. On the one hand, SMRR's opposition consistently claimed that Tom Hayden controlled not only the Santa Monica CED but SMRR and city hall too. Anything Hayden said or did reflected on the SMRR council, whose members were forced to defend or distance themselves from Hayden's views. On the other hand, SMRR politicians certainly did support Hayden in his race for the State Assembly. Hayden's values were similar to their own; Hayden had lent verbal and financial support to the coalition; and Hayden could be extremely useful to the SMRR council were he elected to the State Assembly. As such, those councilmembers who did not want to defend Hayden's views nonetheless did not feel that they were in a position to distance themselves from them. Overall, Hayden's remarks caused a minor dilemma for SMRR politicians, but they certainly were not a major factor in city politics.

Hayden's remarks did become a major factor when SMRR's opposition put a last-minute resolution on the city council's consent calendar favoring Israel and its invasion of Lebanon. If SMRR councilmembers supported the resolution, they would stir up dissension within their own coalition, reinforce the notion that they were pawns of Tom Hayden, and politicize an issue as controversial in Santa Monica as abortion is in national politics. If the SMRR councilmembers rejected the resolution, they would still stir up dissension and politicize the issue, and possibly undermine Hayden's campaign by inviting his opponents to argue that Hayden's own people were anti-Israel and, by extension, so was Hayden. Off the record, several activists told me that the SMRR politicians got wind of the resolution just hours before the council meeting, placed a call to Hayden, who met them at city hall, and quickly composed their own alternative resolution minutes before the council meeting convened.

SMRR's alternative resolution was an attempt to please everyone and thereby defuse a potentially explosive issue. It affirmed the right of Israel to exist as a nation and to protect itself against Palestinian Liberation Organization (PLO) terrorism; it expressed hope for an independent, sovereign Lebanon with the speedy removal of all foreign troops; it supported the Camp David process as the only viable way to resolve Palestinian autonomy; and then it criticized the Reagan administration for drifting away from the Camp David approach to peace in the Middle East.[10] The alternative resolution was an exercise in ambiguity because it skirted the key issue of the justifiability of Israel's invasion of Lebanon. Apparently the SMRR councilmembers hoped that support for Israeli statehood would calm Jewish residents; the mention of Palestinian autonomy would quiet leftist activists; and skirting the invasion issue would dissociate SMRR from Hayden without undermining Hayden's position. Kenneth Edwards was the only SMRR politician who refused to support the alternative resolution on the argument that it was placed hastily on the council agenda and the public had not yet had the opportunity to discuss it. The other four SMRR councilmembers voted for the alternative resolution which passed by a 4–3 margin.

Rather than defuse the issue, the council's vote stirred up a hornet's nest of controversy in a city where SMRR had contributed to creating a concerned, vocal citizenry. For more than a month, the council chambers were filled to overflowing as people demanded a right to speak out on the Israel resolution, thereby prolonging Tuesday evening council meetings into Wednesday morning marathons. Anti-council and anti-SMRR harangues competed with pro-Israel and pro-Arab verbal clashes. SMRR councilmembers had difficulty carrying on with normal city business and grew tired of the insults and name-calling aimed at them. At one point, the city hall radicals considered shutting down public discussion of the Israel resolution during the council meetings; but they decided that such action would only exacerbate tensions. The SMRR politicians finally did meet with activist groups to discuss strategy, heard arguments for and against rescinding their resolution, and finally decided to tough it out until the furor died down.

The furor did not die down. Unhappy with the council's refusal to rescind their resolution, some twenty-six members of the leftist rent control board staff signed a letter announcing their opposition to the council's action, and they had the letter read publicly during one of the council's marathon meetings. The SMRR politicians were especially upset with this fracture in coalition unity and with the public airing of an intraleft dispute during what was a moment of particularly great political tension. Councilmember Dolores Press took it upon herself to respond to leftist critics only to have her letter appear in the local newspaper and radio to cause more furor in the city.

Press wrote to the rent control board staff critics, "Your letter was entered into testimony along with people who called us fascists, murderers, nazis, warmongers, baby killers, widowmakers, agents of a foreign government, totally ignorant fools who have no knowledge of the Middle East."[11] She criticized the staff people for not having communicated with SMRR councilmembers on earlier resolutions but only now when the tension peaked, and then asked, "Is it justice that during an entire year in which we took stands which support the agenda of both the local and national left that, without consultation with any of us or the groups that elected us, you have written a letter of condemnation of our actions?" This injustice was apparently compounded by the staff members' failure to recall what SMRR and its leaders had done for them. "Need I remind you that the success of an electoral politics strategy is responsible for the source of your livelihood and the fact that you have the very best labor contract in this (and probably any other) city hall? We have supported your right to autonomy, your right to strike (the ONLY city agency that has that provision) and your right to have a more modernized, comfortable space in which to work. In return, don't you think that we deserve the courtesy of a phone call by ONE of you before attacking us in public before the radio, newspapers, and the amusement of the landlords present?" Dolores Press concluded, "There is no doubt that our decision was hasty and ill-advised. Unless the Mexican army attacks San Diego, I plan never again to take a position on foreign policy. However, in my opinion, your response has given aid and comfort to the enemy."

The staff reply to Dolores Press's letter touched on both substance and process. One staff critic reiterated opposition to the Israel resolution and added, "It is clear that the council in this matter has succumbed to expedience of political opportunism and disregarded principles of non-violence, non-aggression, and self-determination." Another staff critic stated that public opposition "was the exercise of the democratic right to speak against the action of a political body. You, above all, should have defended that right."[12] Meanwhile, SMRR's opposition thoroughly enjoyed themselves. They wrote letters to the editor that claimed that SMRR had finally shown its true colors by opposing the constitutional right of free speech and by revealing its strict "Marxist-Socialist" party line. Opposition councilmember Christine Reed put it somewhat differently:

> I think what we have here are my fellow councilmembers, the radicals, who are so taken with being in a position of "power and authority." It's sort of like kids being in charge of the junior high

school or the United Nations for a day. Like, gosharoonies, folks, we can do this.[13]

It was several more months before the charges of unprincipled, antidemocratic, antiliberal, and infantile behavior by the SMRR councilmembers began to abate.

The episode itself was not forgotten either by activists who opposed the council resolution only to be treated as if they had committed treason or by the opposition who noted the cracks in SMRR unity. The ironic footnote to the issue that would not die was a statement by State Assembly candidate Tom Hayden at a luncheon meeting of a nearby Rotary Club: "I don't think the city of Santa Monica ought to have a foreign policy."[14] If the SMRR politicians had been unwilling to dissociate themselves from Hayden, Hayden himself had no such scruples.

The SMRR councilmembers might have deferred the Israel resolution until it could be discussed within the coalition, subjected to study by a citizen task force, or opened to general public discussion in the name of participatory democracy. That was more or less what Kenneth Edwards had suggested and, in retrospect, what some city hall radicals admitted should have been done. But their hasty action was indicative of their prior campaign experiences. They had learned to avoid dealing with potentially divisive issues to keep the coalition together and to win elections; they had made tough decisions with the underlying assumption that they spoke for the coalition, which somehow represented the city majority; and they had taken it upon themselves to overcome the accusations and dirty tricks of the opposition during the heat of campaigns. Taking the initiative came naturally to the SMRR politicians. Thus, they took the initiative away from their opposition by drafting and passing their alternative resolution on Israel.

When the resolution generated conflict within the coalition and the city, the SMRR councilmembers again drew on their campaign experience. This was another state of emergency that required decisive leadership to maintain SMRR unity in the face of possible fragmentation, to maintain support among the city electorate while dealing with a touchy issue, to broker with Tom Hayden, and to ensure that the leftwing experiment continued, since the 1983 municipal elections were only months away. Public participation was put on the back burner, manifest in the fact that the SMRR politicians consulted with SMRR activists *after* they passed the resolution and in the councilmembers' resentment toward the staff critics who voiced their opposition *before* consulting with their political leaders. That the SMRR councilmembers even considered shutting down debate on a public issue reveals at best a mixed commitment to participatory democracy. Kenneth Edwards put it quite simply, "We tend to be paternalistic."[15]

The Israel episode was unique but the SMRR politicians' sense of political entrepreneurship was part of a pattern set during their first weeks in office. That was when they assumed the responsibility to take policy initiatives with the expectation that activists and citizens would consent after the fact. They immediately declared a moratorium on new and ongoing developments. Former SMRR councilmember Cheryl Rhoden commented, "I thought the moratorium happened too quickly. I would like to see changes occur that involve a lot of discussion."[16] In some cases, the SMRR council evidenced little interest in facilitating discussion, especially when it was predictable that talk would go against council initiatives. For example, the SMRR politicians did not move one of the council meetings from their small council chambers to the large Civic Auditorium next door when it was clear to them that a large number of people were coming to speak out against their housing policies. The local newspaper editorialized, "Their talk about seeking public input, wanting to hear citizen views and the like is pretty shallow if not out and out false if it develops that what they really mean is that they like to hear praise, but not disagreements with their positions."[17] In other instances, the SMRR politicians did stimulate a great deal of public discussion but only after having taken the crucial actions that set and thereby restricted the terms of public debate.

Another early SMRR council decision was to bypass conventional recruitment processes and public hearings to appoint Robert Myers as city attorney in a closed council session that was boycotted by the two opposition councilmembers. The SMRR council was facing a host of lawsuits against the rent control law and expected more suits to follow from the moratorium on development; thus the radicals perceived an urgent need to protect their legal flank and took on the responsibility of making a hasty appointment of a trusted friend and SMRR ally. When I asked a source in the city attorney's office about the short-circuited path to Myers' appointment, he responded, "It was certainly the prerogative of the city council to choose a city attorney with which they would feel comfortable because our office is very important to accomplishing the objectives of the city council. . . . They didn't do a formal recruitment process and they weren't required to and they wouldn't have found anyone better qualified."[18] In short, the appointment was legal, expedient, and effective in putting a highly qualified professional in an important post; but whether activists and citizens agreed would have to be decided after the fact.

From the vantagepoint of participatory democracy, the SMRR politicians had an exaggerated sense of their own responsibility.[19] They felt themselves responsible to the movement, to their perceived leftwing mandate, in fiscal matters, as managers of city employees, in running the day-to-day operations of government, in overseeing the administration of their policies, and more. Perhaps James Conn put it best when he said,

> When a city bus runs over an old lady, we all feel guilty like we were all somehow complicitous with the bus running over an old

person. Sure we shouldn't feel that way but we do, we want to. Why can't they drive the buses right? How come we're hitting people? This shouldn't happen.[20]

The radical politicians' enthusiasm, energy, and compulsion to do things "right" may have been admirable but resulted in a tendency for them to do things themselves—and then await reactions. This tendency was reinforced by the institutional pressures that existed within the corridors of city hall.

For Fear of Amateurs and Experts

Business entrepreneurs who enlarge their holdings through shrewd and innovative successes in the marketplace are often torn in two directions. On one side, they claim responsibility for their successes and are loathe to share managerial responsibilities with others. On the other side, their businesses may have grown too big and complex for them to manage alone. Still, they fear turning operations over to "amateurs" who take past successes for granted and whose miscalculations could undo years of entrepreneurial effort; and they fear ceding control to managerial experts lest the bureaucrats sacrifice entrepreneurial drive for professional slavery to the ledger sheets. Often, such entrepreneurs hold on to the reins as long as possible but eventually face the choice of either molding amateurs in their own image or hiring professionals to keep their firms going. Santa Monica's radicals could be considered political entrepreneurs who had experienced the dilemmas of political success. On entering city hall, their first impulse was to consolidate their own power but they soon faced the choice of molding amateur participants to help carry on city business or relying on professional bureaucrats to keep the wheels of city government humming.

In line with their principles, the SMRR council initially chose to foster amateur participation. And they began with what they considered the most promising material. They solicited the largest possible pool of applicants for council appointments to task forces and commissions, and then selected those individuals most qualified by SMRR reckoning. The de facto qualifications included activist backgrounds, overt commitments to SMRR principles, and the appropriate educational and occupational credentials for the job at hand. The recruitment process did open up city government to an extent, but to a narrowly defined population.

Invitations to apply for unpaid political positions, even more so than invitations to register to vote, draw a predictable response in the United States.[21] People who are already politically organized and active, highly educated and verbally articulate, economically well off, in jobs with flexible hours and leisure time, and members of the white majority are far

more likely to apply than the unorganized, the less educated, the low income groups, the nine-to-fivers, and minorities. The former can afford to
participate, have the self-confidence and skills to do so, and have the developed motivations for political joining whereas the latter are less able,
less skilled, and less interested in enrolling in civic activism.[22] Even when
special efforts are made to augment predictable applicants by soliciting
participation from traditionally excluded groups, the results are usually
meager. Government experiments in "maximum feasible participation"
for poor people, for example, usually did not overcome the excluded's
keen sense of political distrust and then failed to provide adequate resources for making participation worthwhile and effective for those who
did get involved.[23] Overall, when the Santa Monica left and the SMRR
politicians opened up new avenues of public participation in city government, they mainly provided more mechanisms for affluent middle
class political influence.

Neighborhood groups such as OPCO and PNA solicited participation
but the most active joiners did not accurately represent Santa Monica's
two lowest income areas. Among the nominees for OPCO's 1981 board
who listed their occupations were a college professor, a psychologist, a
theater manager, an executive director of a nonprofit women's organization, two attorneys, two writers, and two graduate students.[24] PNA,
representing the city's major low income and minority neighborhood,
had a white director with advanced college degrees and board of director volunteers who listed their occupations as environmental consultant,
attorney, teacher, plant manager, rent control board investigator, trans-
mission equipment installer, and teletype operator.[25] When the SMRR
council solicited public participation in task forces and commissions,
encouraging applications from low income and minority people, councilmembers reported that they had few applicants outside of the conventional affluent middle class occupations.

Whom did the council end up selecting? The roster of the important
commercial and industrial task force provides a good indication. First,
care was taken to ensure that the task force majority would be "trustworthy," which meant that most of its chosen members had roots in the
Santa Monica left and in SMRR's constituent organizations. This freed
the council to select a few developers as well, but not nearly as many potential opponents as on another task force chaired by Kenneth Edwards,
who argued "that as long as I have an 8–7 vote, winning by one vote is the
same as winning 15–0."[26] Second, *everyone* selected for the commercial
and industrial task force was a part of the professional and managerial
class. Members included a writer, a civil engineer, a lawyer, a law student, a sociologist, an energy consultant, and four business professionals.
Mayor Goldway chaired the group and a city planning commissioner
acted as staff liaison.[27] From the beginning, it was clear that this task
force would make recommendations consistent with the development

initiatives already taken by the city council, and the recommendations would be framed with clear insight into the technical and legal complications of city zoning policy.

Christopher Rudd, a city planner who served as staff support for the task force, said it met about twice a week for several evening hours over a six-week period. Tensions did emerge between the activist majority and the token businessmen, and it "got to the point where we were starting to have minority reports. . . . It got sticky at times." Usually, however, "compromises were worked out" because the group was highly professional. According to Rudd, the staff "presented them with a lot of materials and fortunately they were all very bright people. They did their homework and they picked up these concepts really quickly. . . . It was just a matter of presenting them with the material." In no time, they could deal with "floor-air ratios" and "density requirements." Only occasionally did the staff have to remind task force members that "they were merely an advisory-type group and the people who made the decisions of course are ultimately the city council." [28] In fact, such reminders were overkill, given that that task force's report had to go through city planning commission review before being forwarded to the council.

Like task force members, city planning commissioners were appointed by the council. The selection qualifications were similar but more emphasis was placed on professional experience and expertise in planning, given the technical matters that commissioners handled. Among the most controversial SMRR appointments to the planning commission was that of Derek Shearer, who, as mayor Ruth Yannatta Goldway's husband, was vulnerable to charges of appointment through nepotism. Goldway abstained on the appointment vote but later defended it in these terms:

> I think it's really just a coincidence that he happens to be my husband. He was the manager of the [1981] campaign, he has a national reputation in planning issues, and he is probably the most competent person that our community could appoint to a planning commission. . . . There is no conflict of interest and no nepotism involved. [29]

Upon receiving the commercial and industrial task force recommendations, the planning commissioners felt that the process had been too rushed and they hesitated to endorse the amateurs' ideas. The planning commission reviewed the recommendations and eventually transmitted the task force report to the city council with addenda such as "the commission feels that these recommendations have merit warranting further study" or "the commission recommends a careful analysis of the legal questions related to withholding a demolition permit pending approval of the replacement project" or "it is inappropriate to adopt these recommendations at this time since they would predetermine programs implementing policies that have not been adopted in the city's housing element."[30] In effect, the city planning commission was both an institutional corrective for the amateurism of the task force and a city bureaucracy that could either legitimate or delegitimate citizen recommendations on the basis of professional criteria.

In this instance, the council-appointed task force issued a report that was overall deemed to have "merit" by the council-appointed planning commission, which transmitted the final recommendations to the council itself. Nevertheless, the council did not turn the recommendations into public policy. Instead, the SMRR councilmembers passed Resolution no. 6385 and Ordinance no. 1251, which declared city government's intention to amend the comprehensive land use element of the city charter and, in the meanwhile, adopt interim development guidelines.[31] This strategy meant that the council would have to consolidate its authority in order to orchestrate current development policies, debates over the fiscal, environmental, and legal impacts of those policies and proposed new ones, commissioned studies by public policy professionals, and various bureaucratic negotiations necessary for amending the city charter. And the citizen amateurs on the task force would have to wait years to learn if their recommendations were to be adopted, revised, rejected, replaced, or simply ignored. Also, this strategy meant that the council's success in imprinting its own development policies on the city charter would hamstring future city councils whose participation and recommendations might point in other directions. Overall, amateur participation played a very minor role in public policy as the SMRR council began to concentrate on keeping the complex wheels of city bureaucracy turning toward concrete results that would be durable; and the wheels turned slowly.

As the SMRR politicians gained more experience in city hall, they simultaneously improved their amateur recruitment record and increased their dependence on professional expertise. Whereas early council appointees were mostly white and male, the later appointees on the city arts commission included a black and a Latino as well as a relatively equal mix of women and men. But it too was filled with affluent experts: several professional artists, an art dealer, four educators, and a few businessmen.[32] Indeed, the "amateur" nature of public participation diminished to nearly nothing by the time that the council appointed directors for the Pier Restoration Corporation and the Santa Monica Convention and Visitors Bureau. When the council got around to appointing people for the Third Street Development Corporation, it named a redevelopment executive to the $50,000-a-year staff directorship and chose for the board a commercial property owner, an architect, a banker, and an attorney.[33] The earlier enthusiasm for amateur participation in city government had all but disappeared.

Why did enthusiasm ebb? Part of the reason was that few activists were pushing it. Those who were members of a neighborhood organization, a political group, and perhaps a city task force found that they had little time left over for things like family and friends, much less careers. Those with strong political commitments began to worry that SMRR's activist and leadership ranks were being decimated by city appointments, leaving few people with the energy and skills necessary for carrying out grassroots organizing or electioneering. Meanwhile, the first burst of enthusiasm for being part of a leftwing experiment in government gave way to second thoughts when the relationship between participation and policy proved to be indirect at best and when interesting issues were transformed into mundane technicalities. Activists who had proposed more participatory democracy earlier in many cases simply had had more than enough participation, enough meetings, enough homework, enough discussions, and enough politics by mid-1982. They certainly were not about to push for even more.

At the same time, pressure mounted in favor of bureaucratic expertise. The SMRR council came to power at a time when Santa Monica's city manager position was vacant. Having no trustworthy friend to appoint immediately, councilmembers took on the responsibility not only of making policy but also of spending hours and hours at city hall to ensure that the carryover staff implemented it properly. After several months and a nationwide search that split the SMRR majority between two candidates, the council hired John Alschuler as city manager. With Alschuler, they had a highly qualified new professional who basically supported council goals and could educate the council on how to convert their goals into realities. Dennis Zane commented that there was "a lot of initiative" from Alschuler's office "and that's good because [our action] has to stand the legal muster; we have to know in fact whether or not it's going to have a positive or negative fiscal impact and those kinds of things. Otherwise, a left government fails."[34] Dolores Press had a somewhat different construction of bureaucratic reality: "We do have a kind of Ivy League, you know, sort of highly professional person who's running the city manager's office. I think that a green council doesn't have any insight in depth of how much power a city manager has till you really are doing it, you know, so he has considerable power in making those decisions."[35] The power calculus was not complicated. Councilmembers who held full-time jobs outside of government and had no more than on-the-job training in government had little leverage over a full-time city manager with expert knowledge about what could be done, how, at what cost, and with what likelihood of success.

Between 1981 and 1983, the council and the city manager coexisted with a relative balance of power. Ruth Yannatta Goldway was voluntarily unemployed during this period and was able to turn being mayor into a full-time job. She not only developed the political expertise to serve as a counterweight to Alschuler's bureaucratic expertise; she also had a galvanizing effect on the other SMRR councilmembers, which helped them to give clear direction to Alschuler. However, when Goldway left city government in early 1983, the remaining SMRR politicians did not have the time, the expertise, or the clear priorities necessary for constructing policy directions for Alschuler's office to administer. Within this partial vacuum, Alschuler's brand of new professional expertise increasingly became city government's main source of initiative.

Alschuler was an unusually bright and competent administrator. He was concerned with enhancing public participation in government but he was also keenly aware of the complexities of running city government, the significance of the bureaucracy in overseeing the process, and especially the importance of keeping a keen eye on the city's budget. When asked what he considered the most serious challenges in city government, he did not hesitate to outline his own priorities: "I think the first is the overall lack of support for government today and the resulting lack of financial resources and that very deeply hurts Santa Monica. It hurts us in a hesitancy to raise additional revenues here."[36] Alschuler devoted himself to educating the council on a projected $5-million-a-year budget gap if the city were simply to maintain the current level of services. He continued: "I think the second most serious obstacle is the identification of clear priorities which balance questions of fiscal stability, development priorities, and environmental concerns." One aspect of Alschuler's job became educating the council on how to strike rational and legal balances, particularly between fiscal needs and social services for the needy. "The third problem," he concluded, "is capacity-building and I put capacity-building at the level of neighborhoods and interest groups developing the capacity to identify their agenda and then communicate it, . . . capacity at the level of the council to digest an enormously complex and changing environment." Alschuler worked hard to educate citizens and councilmembers to improve their ability to be politically articulate in the terms of public administration but that process takes time: "One of the greatest challenges I see, and it's a task that I'm in awe of, is people who come into very important and powerful positions and are asked to take on enormous responsibilities with very little support and very little technical background, and local officials really need time to develop."

Alschuler was quite effective at helping councilmembers develop a professional respect for fiscal matters and technical complexities in city government. Some activists thought that the city manager was so effective that he had mesmerized councilmembers, who had lost their commitment to nurturing amateur participation in the city. Whether or not mesmerized, the councilmembers had great faith in Alschuler's new professionalism as demonstrated by their support for a complex bargain that Alschuler negotiated with Santa Monica's Sand and Sea Club.

The Sand and Sea Club is an expensive private beach club that leased public land administered by the city of Santa Monica though owned by the state of California. In 1981, the Sand and Sea Club's ten-year lease

expired and the club's directors as well as several other businesses put in
bids to rent the beachfront property. After nearly a year, the city department of recreation and parks recommended that the Sand and Sea Club
be granted a new twenty-year lease. Opposition councilmembers Christine Reed and William Jennings opposed the renewal, charging that the
arrangement "maintains the same use for the same wealthy people" and
that the Sand and Sea Club was a "venture which will largely serve an
exclusive clientele."[37] A local contingent of the Gray Panther organization also objected, particularly because the city was going to loan the
Sand and Sea Club $2 million to upgrade its facilities when both the
money and the facilities could have been used for a needed senior citizens center. It certainly seemed anomalous that a leftwing city council
majority would approve a lease and a loan to subsidize a private beach
club for the rich. But that is what the SMRR politicians did.

The city hall radicals defended their action in terms of enhanced public
access. The leasing arrangement provided open admission to club facilities at a daily rate of seven dollars for adults and five dollars for children
who are nonmembers; it included a lottery system to allow five hundred
Santa Monica families to buy club memberships at the drastically reduced price of five hundred dollars a year plus twenty-two dollars per
month; it opened up a percentage of club beach cabanas to anyone
willing to pay thirty dollars a day or four thousand dollars for the whole
year; and it provided that up to five hundred low and moderate income
people would be admitted free each week on a group reservation basis.[38]
The SMRR politicians also supported the arrangement as a way to preserve a unique historical structure. The club operated out of an estate
originally built by William Randolph Hearst and occupied by actress
Marion Davies; and the Sand and Sea Club operators promised to
maintain and upgrade the facility on the basis of a good management
track record. Further, some councilmembers pointed out that the Sand
and Sea Club was the most progressive private beach club in town.
Unlike its three main competitors, it was nondiscriminatory, with many
Jews and some blacks and Hispanics holding memberships. These arguments were extraordinarily weak given that public access, preservation,
and nondiscrimination could have been guaranteed far better if the city
simply took over the facility.

I asked James Conn, the city council liaison person on this deal,
about the anomaly between SMRR principles and council practices. He
responded:

> It is always astonishing to me the number of things you look at
> from the outside and say "That?" and you get into the position
> where you have to make some decisions about it and realize that
> there are many vectors of power and so many people have some
> interest at stake in it that in fact you just can't go pfft! It's more
> complicated than that.[39]

The complexities and the stronger motivations behind the Sand and Sea Club lease were fiscal, and John Alschuler was the one sorting them all out. According to Conn, Alschuler was unhappy with the meager $90,000 a year that the city was getting from the beachfront property; furthermore, he was unhappy that the lease money had to be plowed back into beach amenities because of Santa Monica's existing arrangement with the state of California. And so,

> John said, "That's not enough money but how are we going to get more money?" The way we get more money is we buy into the deal and we buy into the deal without putting up any of the city's money. . . . He's cutting a business deal on behalf of providing a whole pot of money that can go back into beach amenities . . . or that goes into the general fund and provides some other kinds of services to the city.[40]

Alschuler's deal seemed brilliant, a real lesson in creative fiscal management for the city council radicals. However, it required the cloak of secrecy, which excluded public participation or discussion prior to the final city decision.

In the year between the expiration of the Sand and Sea Club's old lease and the council approval of the new lease, Alschuler quietly worked out a bargain that he could sell to the club's operators, the city department of recreation and parks, the city council, and the state of California. The club would get a new long-term lease and a $2 million loan for upgrading facilities. The loan would carry with it the same low interest rate that it would cost the city to procure a $2 million loan for itself. For its part, the city would not simply rent out the property; it would become a limited partner in two new restaurants slated to be built on the property. According to expert estimates, the city would collect a minimum of $150,000 annually or 3 to 4 percent of the club's gross receipts for property rental *and* the city would perpetually collect 10 percent of the gross receipts from the restaurants even after the $2 million loan was paid off, an additional yield of $750,000 in the third year of operation and $1.2 million by the sixth year. And since the restaurant revenues would fall outside of the property lease, they would go into the city's general fund to make a fairly sizable dent in Alschuler's projected budget gap. Meanwhile, the additional leasing revenues and the new forms of public access would please both the city department of recreation and parks and the state of California.[41]

The bargaining process was obviously complex and touchy. Conn said that Alschuler did not tell the club operators that they had to accept the city partnership or lose their lease, but, "What John basically said to the Sand and Sea Club was we want to be happier than you're making us . . . and they were willing to deal."[42] Meanwhile, Alschuler had to educate the council on the budget crunch as well as work out the technicalities of the $2 million loan necessary for swinging the deal. The arguments and terms of public access and historical preservation as well as the legalities of financial arrangements had to be fine-tuned to assure that a strong case could be made to state agencies. To have introduced various forms of public participation into this calculus would have certainly made it even more complex and would have threatened the tenuous balance necessary for arriving at a fiscally sound resolution. In this instance, the public was not invited to participate; rather, it was to be served by its representatives and bureaucrats.

The leasing deal entered into limbo when, after several public hearings, the state Parks and Recreation Commission unanimously rejected the lease because it did not adequately provide for public access in the eyes of state officials. Alschuler went back to the bureaucratic drawing board. He proposed a land swap with the state that would result in the transfer of ownership of the club site to the city and thereby "allow Santa Monica as a community to determine within a local regulatory framework the use of the property."[43] This would require approval of the state legislature and thus an intensive lobbying effort over an extended time period. But whether or not the plan is eventually approved, it was made clear that the financial dealings of Santa Monica municipal government were being handled not with the advice and consent of Santa Monica amateurs but by city professionals concerned with the bottom line. Certainly, this was the pattern followed, as noted in the last chapter, when the city negotiated a contract with the McDonald's Corporation to take over Santa Monica's beachfront vending concessions.

The contrasting rhetoric of participatory democracy and the reality of closed business dealings again became an issue when the bylaws of the Pier Restoration Corporation were debated. Nearly everyone agreed that the corporation's meetings should be open to all citizens but no one was quite sure whether the corporation could negotiate individual pier leases in closed sessions. Mayor Kenneth Edwards sought a legal opinion from the city attorney. Robert Myers promised to investigate but stated that regardless of his findings, the Pier Restoration Corporation professionals would be able to negotiate the leases in private as long as they ratified them in public.[44] Relatedly, a threatened suit against the rent control board and the city resulted in the scheduling of a closed council session to discuss the legality of hiring outside lobbyists. In response to complaints that the issue should be aired in a public forum, Robert Myers stated, "It's not standard city practice to discuss lawsuits in public session."[45] The invocation of SOP (standard operating procedure) is the bureaucrat's way of saying that such matters had best be left to the experts.

In summary, the SMRR political entrepreneurs could not run city hall alone. They initially favored a select group of amateur participants to assume roles in city government but gradually turned more and more to staff expertise to sort out the complexities and strike the balances involving what the professionals called "fiscal stability" or "capacity building." The city hall radicals mostly adapted their politics to the city bureaucracy instead of using participatory norms as guidelines for restructuring city government. The adaptation process was in part an outgrowth of the radicals' middle class predisposition favoring professionalism. But then maybe the new professionalism was different from the old?

163 Who Will Make a Difference?

Turf Wars

Ruth Yannatta Goldway described her early days in office in these terms:

> When my critics first began calling me "Ruthless Ruth, a hardball player," I was shocked and hurt. I see myself as a caring, dedicated public servant. I have a soft voice, a pleasant smile, and, regrettably, I have never played competitive sports—I swim or bike with my family to keep in shape.[46]

Goldway knew that she was perceived as something of a dragonlady by the press, the local opposition, and even some activists. She said that such perceptions and labeling resulted from men's discomfort with women in positions of power; and she cited similar encounters suffered by other women politicians to support her assertion. Within this context, it seemed that the SMRR council would have some difficulty translating its principled support for feminism and women's participation in government into actual policies.

One omen of the difficulty was manifested when the city council created the commission on the status of women and then appointed only women to it. The city was immediately sued for having discriminated against men by disallowing their right to participate on the citizens commission. The council was forced to revise its selection criterion. Nevertheless, the SMRR politicians were able to increase women's participation in city government because they took a "professional" approach to affirmative action that could be sold to Santa Monica's professional population. But the selling of professional feminism was not the same as enhancing women's power in city government.

Aside from seeking an appropriate mix of men and women on SMRR candidate slates and appointments to city task forces and commissions, the city hall radicals' main effort to enhance women's political participation was to survey, set, and implement affirmative action guidelines within the city bureaucracy. The council mostly worked through the city personnel department and Susan McCarthy, a woman who had worked her way up through the ranks to become department head. A top priority was to get more women into decisionmaking positions in a city government that had long been an all-male bastion, save the head librarian position. Here, the council succeeded admirably.

In 1974, Santa Monica city government had one top female administrator and twenty-two women in professional positions; by the fall of 1982, it had eleven top female administrators and sixty-seven women in professional positions. In part, this change represented a nationwide phenomenon. In part, the city's "aggressive affirmative action stance has probably helped to lure women into professional positions."[47] The council also made some effort to retain women professionals by instituting a fairly liberal maternity leave policy and an innovative job-sharing program.

The council made an additional effort to train more women for professional posts. In particular, it brought together the city's fire chief, the fire fighters union, the city manager's office, and the personnel people to work out a comprehensive plan to integrate women into the fire department. The result was a special two-year training program aimed at qualifying women (and minorities) to pass the rigorous physical and written tests for employment. The goal was for women to become 42 percent of the fire-fighter force, the same percentage as the ratio of women to men in the Greater Los Angeles labor force.[48] The city's male fire chief helped to draft the plan and the city's male fire fighters union unanimously approved it because, they stated, it ensured that professional standards would be maintained.[49]

Finally, the city council sought to facilitate the upward mobility of experienced women into professional positions. The SMRR council directed the personnel department to audit the bureaucracy's job classifications and to recommend changes likely to foster women's movement up the ranks. A six-month audit and then city council action resulted in a major reclassification that changed the titles of secretaries and clerks to Staff Assistants I–IV. The title changes meant that secretaries and clerks who once had no channel into professional administrative and supervisory roles now had a direct route to positions with greater autonomy, challenge, and public service capacity. The changes also meant that secretaries and clerks who were already doing professional tasks would receive appropriate recognition and remuneration for their work. And skilled and experienced minority women without the "appropriate" educational backgrounds, credentials, or degrees would now have a chance to move up the bureaucratic ladder on their own merit.

The SMRR politicians received considerable praise for their approach to affirmative action. The new professional idea of opening up the professions to the excluded was consistent with the radicals' middle class backgrounds that validated both expertise and popular access to it. And it was noncontroversial because it was implemented with overt assurances that women's qualifications would measure up to standards that were acceptable to Santa Monica's largely professional and managerial citizenry. The councilmembers did feel pride in their accomplishment because, unquestionably, more women were participating more in responsible city positions.

However, the response of city staff women to the reclassification of job titles hinted at a problem. Some liked the changes but others were quite unhappy. Jean Stanley, for example, was a senior secretary supervising seven clerical workers. She was reclassified as Staff Assistant IV, but two of the people working under her received the same classification. She commented, "That puts us on the same level, which undermines my supervisory job." Another secretary, who said that her work was mostly unsupervised and that she generated many of her own projects, was dismayed with her classification to Staff Assistant III, which potentially meant that her work would become more constrained.[50] This discontent was not simply a matter of fear of the unknown, or of petty jealousies, vain egos, or individual greed in the face of change. It was more a matter of paraprofessionals and professionals who feared that their autonomy was going to be compromised. And their fears had some foundation.

Santa Monica had no gender wars per se, but it did have bureaucratic turf wars. When women moved into the upper echelons of the city bureaucracy, they found themselves amidst a group of highly competitive males who did play hardball to defend their own autonomy even at others' expense. City manager John Alschuler, city attorney Robert Myers, and city community and economic development department head Mark Tigan were at the center of many conflicts. At various moments, rent control board officials such as Michael Heumann, David Finkel, Wayne Bauer, and Gerald Goldman entered into the bureaucratic fray as did city planning commissioners Derek Shearer and Robert Kleffel.[51] In all the confrontations that surfaced publicly and those I was able to unearth through interviews, the major actors in the turf wars were all men. And how these men settled issues concerning who had appropriate professional credentials, authority, and legal claim to various aspects of the decisionmaking process determined the significance of women's participation at all levels of the city bureaucracy.

The male turf wars meant that women were participating more but with little control over the effects of their participation. Of course, this was consistent with Santa Monicans having more voice or better representation in government but little authority over policy and with amateur participants on task forces and commissions playing a more vocal role in the policy process but nonetheless having at best a minor and indirect impact on actual decisions. More important, this "participation without power" accurately reflected an historical ambivalence inherent in middle class professionalism and manifested in Santa Monica's version of feminist participation.

As noted in Part 1, professionalism in the United States combined a dedication to autonomy, intelligence, and public service with a tendency toward managerial control over nonprofessionals. The new professionalism of the 1970s was an effort by radicals to resolve this ambivalence by reconstructing professional norms in a way that exorcised managerialism. The new professionals pledged themselves to defend everyone's autonomy, break down the barriers between experts and amateurs, and democratize decisionmaking in their organizations. The unspoken dilemma was that somebody had to decide how universal autonomy could be defended without fostering fragmentation; someone had to figure out how experts and amateurs could cooperate without sacrificing skills and experience; and someone had to decide at what pace decisionmaking could be shared without empowering new professional elites. In other words, who would *manage* the transition from the old professionalism to the new professionalism?

Unquestionably, the new professionals felt that they themselves were the most dedicated and qualified to manage the transition, which is precisely what happened to affirmative action in Santa Monica. The city hall radicals' approach epitomized the limits of the new professionalism. The council took it upon itself to determine the ways in which women employees could enhance their access to more challenging jobs; and the council took it for granted that the best methods for breaking down the barriers between experts and amateurs was to recruit, train, and make experts out of amateurs; and, largely by default, the council left it to highly competitive male bureaucrats to fight the battles that determined the pace at which women in city government would actually be empowered. The meaning of the new professionalism once set to practice was that representatives and bureaucrats continued to dominate decisionmaking but now in the name of managing the transition to greater participatory democracy.

Ex Post Facto Participation

The SMRR council did heed the advice of citizen participants on numerous occasions. For example, it followed the recommendation of its commission on the status of women to pass a resolution protesting against "Custer's Last Stand," a video game premised on the sexual abuse of Native American women. And the council did take some initiatives based on the knowledge that they would easily win popular consent. Thus, it drafted an ordinance prohibiting discrimination against gay people after the governor of California vetoed related state legislation; and it did so knowing that there would be support in a liberal city such as Santa Monica. But there were also many occasions during which the city hall radicals took initiatives without having prepared the groundwork by inviting public participation or having surveyed likely public reaction. The Israel resolution and the Sand and Sea Club lease were two such instances but not the only ones.

A mundane but revealing instance occurred in October 1982. In an effort to increase revenues to the tune of $310,000 per year, city department of general services director Stan Scholl recommended installing 1,100 new parking meters, most of which would be placed in Santa Monica's industrial corridor. Scholl said that he sent out eight hundred notices to the affected businesses, inviting their representatives to a breakfast meeting. Only eight people showed up. The council then authorized the new parking meters as routine business and the meters were soon installed. People who worked in the industrial corridor were outraged. They said that they had never been notified, that the parking meters would cause them undue expenses of thirty-seven dollars each month, and that the logistics of feeding coins into the meters throughout their workday would interfere with their job schedules. The workers quickly circulated protest petitions, contacted the media, and publicly made a case that the meters should be removed. At that point, the SMRR council had the meters dismantled and directed city officials to meet with the workers to find a mutually satisfying alternative.[52]

Two factors stand out in this episode. First, the principles of participatory democracy were taken seriously enough that the general services director did go through the notification process for a public meeting. That he did not get much response was partly because city agencies called so many public meetings that it was difficult for people to sort out which ones were of consequence to them, a case of participatory overkill. Relatedly, the lack of response may have resulted from the fact that the city officials notified the affected businesses instead of the affected workers at those businesses. In this and other cases, communication between city representatives, bureaucrats, and business owners did not filter down to the general public until after action had been taken. People's only option for participation was to react rather than to initiate or shape policy.

Second, the principles of participatory democracy were taken seriously enough that the SMRR council demonstrated a willingness to reconsider past decisions in light of public protests. In this instance, the council did have the parking meters removed. And while the council did not rescind its Israel resolution in response to a storm of protest, it did reconsider the resolution and it did decide not to make unilateral foreign policy statements in the future. Thus, rather than declare Santa Monica to be a nuclear-free zone by legislative fiat, the city hall radicals appointed a citizens task force, heard its report, and then supported putting a referendum on the municipal ballot to allow city residents to decide the issue themselves.

The SMRR politicians unquestionably fell short of putting into practice the norms of participatory democracy. They often solicited public voice and even a public role in shaping issues. But their selectivity regarding whom they heard and whom they appointed, their willingness to devalue public involvement to the status of a minor factor, their increasing reliance on bureaucratic expertise, and especially their inconsistent record of seeking out public participation meant that "outsiders" entered into the policymaking process only at the pleasure of insiders. The representatives and the bureaucrats continued to rule. Especially after 1983, some local activists came to suspect that the councilmembers' own participation was being manipulated by the shrewd, efficiency-minded city manager and city attorney.[53] Certainly these bureaucrats made a major difference.

So too did Santa Monica citizens, but in an after-the-fact manner. The city hall radicals often acted on their own but were then sensitive to whatever public and private criticisms followed their actions. Unlike former city councils that ignored protest, the SMRR council did make an effort to hear out dissent, respond to criticism, and even accommodate the backlash. While this did put people in a reactive mode of participation, it also afforded people a channel of participation that could affect government policies. Such *ex post facto participation* actually helped to politicize people, if only out of anger, and sometimes motivated them to demand a right to participate in policymaking prior to decisions. In the long haul, ex post facto participation may prove to be a step toward participatory democracy.

At best, however, it is a very faltering step. It puts politicians and city professionals in the position of being crisis managers who regularly confront problems raised by antagonistic citizens. Enough confrontations with city hall, even when protests get positive results, are likely to undermine the authority of people in city hall. And a crisis in political authority could drive politicians to centralize their power more to meet an overload of public demands and drive citizens away from politics out of distrust and frustration.[54] Either way, a movement toward participatory democracy suffers. Furthermore, ex post facto participation forces city officials to give priority to the concerns of those organized, educated, and affluent groups that are most likely to mount a protest or stage a demonstration. In other words, it almost guarantees that city politics will center on middle class concerns instead of on movement toward the one class society that is most beneficial to low income people.

7

The Hassles of Materialism

I can't stand the hassles of materialism. Things bring trouble. I can't stand the clutter of things.

Tom Hayden[1]

I have money, I have businesses, [but] I try to watch myself very closely to make sure I'm being honest with myself about why I do what I do.

Jane Fonda[2]

Tom Hayden cannot stand the hassles of materialism. Since his Port Huron–SDS days, he has emphasized cultural and political principles far more than the redistributive notions of justice associated with the old left. Even his mid-1970s version of "economic" democracy stressed individual autonomy and political control as primary, a more equitable distribution of wealth being derivative. In 1980, Hayden closely identified himself with Henry David Thoreau, who sought to free himself from dependence on things rather than to remake capitalist society.

Hayden of course is no Thoreau. His antimaterialist simplicity is strictly a middle class version. His voluminous writings, numerous speaking engagements, occasional teaching stints, and current work as a state assemblyman have certainly provided him enough income to ensure that he and his family can meet basic housing, food, clothing, health care, and educational needs. Ironically, Hayden's case is one in which the pursuit of Thoreauvian principles has been quite profitable. Furthermore, Hayden is part of a complex middle class economy that allows individuals to disdain materialism because they have their own informal social safety net. Should the need for money arise, members of the middle class economy can draw on their background and experience, education and savvy, and a lifetime of social connections to gain access to the requisite resources.

Hayden also departs from Thoreau in his politics. Hayden believes that a human scale environment and a participatory polity can emerge only if people organize to challenge the rapacious individualism, mass consumerism, and corporate concentrations of wealth that dominate American social life. He locates that challenge in grassroots and electoral politics, the leftwing of the Democratic party, and winning political office himself. He understands that the challenge is a costly affair. Fortunately for Tom Hayden, he can afford to mount the challenge because he is bankrolled by the critical mass of capital provided by his wife.

Jane Fonda thrives on the entrepreneurial pursuit of profit. She has used her personal wealth, talents, fame, and shrewdness to build numerous businesses that include her own film production company, numerous health studios, a clothing line, publications, and more. She runs a multi-million-dollar corporate domain—something far grander than any "mom and pop" small business but certainly less grandiose than the Fortune 500 multinationals. At least part of Fonda's drive to make money is her belief that wealth is needed to underwrite leftwing principles. She invests her profits in the American conscience, people's physical and psychological health, and even citizens' employment—her clothing line is union-made in the U.S.A. She also invests in Tom Hayden's Campaign for Economic Democracy (CED) and his lavish political races. Hayden's 1982 race for the State Assembly cost a record-setting $1.7 million.

Can a Thoreauvian preacher opposed to materialism be trusted to foster radical economic change when he takes for granted the economic prerogatives of the American middle class and depends on his wife's corporate financing for his politics? If Hayden's biography raises this question, the economic policies of Santa Monica's city hall radicals answers it on a more general level.

A Dream Deferred

Dolores Press told me that the politicians of Santa Monicans for Renters' Rights (SMRR) had to make great personal sacrifices in order to serve Santa Monica citizens. Dennis Zane worked at a part-time job so that he could devote more time to city hall and progressive politics. And, "Ruth Yannatta Goldway is a highly capable woman who is educated, probably could earn a substantial salary at management level in private industry, but nevertheless works there [at city hall] every day from nine to five for $150 a month. I consider that to be a financial sacrifice."[3] The SMRR politicians certainly did make personal and financial sacrifices in the pursuit of their principles. But their sacrifices must be understood within a middle class context. For example, Goldway could be a full-time mayor receiving a token salary because she could count on her husband's income as a college administrator and professor as well as successful author. Furthermore, whether or not intended, her years in city government could be seen as a career investment. She gained experience in managing a $90-million-a-year public corporation and she gained important nationwide contacts that made her a highly salable commodity in the management marketplace. In the meantime, her family did not lack the basic necessities of life.

For the most part, Santa Monica's middle class radicals took for granted their own ability to satisfy basic needs. What they considered material simplicity might mean choosing to travel to a political conference instead of buying a new home stereo system. What they thought of as financial sacrifice could easily be perceived as a privileged choice to forego, perhaps temporarily, a few luxuries: they drove Toyotas instead of Volvos. They had experienced enough material success in their parents' homes and their own to highlight the struggle for a better quality of life as the major economic challenge; their vantagepoint dimmed others' continuing struggle for the basic necessities of material life. Living amid Santa Monica's general affluence, it was almost natural for the middle class radicals to see environmental degradation as an immediate concrete problem calling for action now and poverty as a more distant abstract dilemma calling mostly for discussion.

Economist Lester Thurow captures this perspective in his reading of environmentalism as a middle class movement:

> Environmentalism is a natural product of a rising real standard of living. We have simply reached the point where, for many Ameri-

cans, the next item on their acquisitive agenda is a cleaner environment. . . . Lower income groups simply have not reached income
levels where a cleaner environment is high on their list of demands,
and it often threatens their income-earning opportunities.[4]

Santa Monica's radical politicians did *not* view their own environmentalism as something purchased at the expense of lower income groups.
Their efforts to upgrade beach and park facilities or to endow public arts,
in their eyes, created a better environment for all income groups to enjoy.
And the council's toxic waste disclosure law aimed at guaranteeing a safe
and healthier environment for both residents and working class people
exposed to chemicals on the shopfloor. Nonetheless, the SMRR politicians could not avoid the choice of trade-offs between middle class quality
of life policies and lower class bread-and-butter issues, a lesson that they
were to learn during their first month in control of city government.

The SMRR council's moratorium on new and ongoing developments
in Santa Monica had two goals. One was to enact a stopgap measure to
ease congestion, pollution, speculation, and other harmful effects of unrestrained growth. The other goal was to buy enough time to hammer
out new development guidelines aimed at limited, controlled, and balanced growth for the city's future. The immediate result of the moratorium was to halt some construction projects, delay others, and cast
serious doubt on those in the early planning stages. Naturally, developers,
bankers, building contractors, and the lawyers representing growth interests were upset but no more so than Santa Monica's local construction
workers. The construction workers had gone through an industrywide
recession that caused mass layoffs and unemployment; now they suffered
a moratorium that made their economic prospects even bleaker. The
local building trades joined with their employers in bringing a lawsuit
against the city of Santa Monica to void the moratorium.

Had the SMRR councilmembers opted for a human scale environment at the price of limiting the economic opportunities of construction
workers who were having difficulty fulfilling their basic needs? Had self-
identified economic democrats, two of whom were on the council, supported a policy that further disempowered one segment of American
labor? Almost no one connected with SMRR was willing to give an affirmative answer because virtually everyone had a mitigating explanation.

Several activists explained that the SMRR council had no other
choice. SMRR's electoral base was solidly middle class and political expedience dictated that quality of life reforms take precedence. This familiar explanation was augmented with the idea that, were Santa Monica
an industrial city with a working class base of support, the council would
have had more options and perhaps other policy possibilities. In any
case, if the SMRR council could maintain its middle class base of support, it would be in a position to do far more for people in labor than
any previous city government. Maurice Zeitlin put it this way, "This will

be a government that will always bend over backwards to give the best deal that it possibly can to working people but that doesn't mean that it will always necessarily be a good deal. It means that someone else in power would have given them a hell of a lot worse deal."[5] The problem with this thinking, at least in the case of the moratorium, is that the city hall radicals had just taken power and they did not have a concrete sense of what they could or could not do without alienating their electoral base. Conceivably, the council could have combined a moratorium with some sort of public works project to provide employment for construction workers, selling the entire package to Santa Monica's middle class in a New Deal wrapper.

Another mitigating explanation was that policies harmful to construction workers did not count as policies harmful to "real" labor groups. Construction workers are notorious for being among the most conservative, racist, pro-management, and now pro-Reagan fractions of the American workforce. Dolores Press stated:

> Sensible people in labor appreciate that there is no foresight and that there is no particular broad understanding on the part of the building trades. They have one focus and this is more and more buildings; and they'd build a twenty-story apartment building on the Santa Monica beach if they could, and everyone else be damned.[6]

Whether or not it is true that construction workers especially lack class consciousness, it does not deny the fact that the SMRR council gave precedence to their human scale values and thereby forced working class people to pay the direct cost in the coin of unemployment and underemployment.

The most revealing explanation was the public one. The councilmembers believed that they had bought the time necessary for working out development guidelines that, in the long run, would simultaneously protect the local environment and speak to the economic needs of workers. Rapid, uncontrolled development would create temporary and unsteady employment and only to the point where every inch of Santa Monica was utilized. That point was not far away. However, "balanced" development would create steady work for an indefinite time period. Councilmembers invited dialogue with people in the building trades and offered them the opportunity to participate in drawing up the new development guidelines. But the building trades people preferred legal action against the council. Why? The councilmembers did not quite understand that concern for the long run was a middle class luxury or that workers, living paycheck to paycheck, must give priority to the present.[7] Legal action promised quicker results.

Overall, Santa Monica's middle class radicals showed little sensitivity to different class perspectives on time. They took almost as axiomatic

that people can defer material gratification today as an investment in
tomorrow without giving serious thought to the fact that one must have
a steady source of income or access to substantial resources before being
able to budget for the future. Working class and lower class Americans,
faced with the recessions of the 1970s and the disintegration of the federal social safety net in the 1980s, confronted increasing uncertainty
regarding their incomes. And their access to the key resource of credit
diminished as interest rates soared. Their economic reality was figuring
out how to pay last month's rent rather than imagining how to ensure
employment several years hence. The middle class radicals' lack of sensitivity appeared not only during the debates following the moratorium
but also in the rhetoric of economic democracy.

When asked by a "60 Minutes" reporter what economic democracy
meant to him, Derek Shearer stated, "Well, it's really a matter of control."[8] People must organize to take control of government. They must
participate in government to extend political control over the marketplace. At that point, workers, consumers, and public representatives will
have democratic control over economic planning mechanisms. "Now that
doesn't redistribute the wealth automatically," Shearer noted. The reporter asked if the net result of economic democracy would be a redistribution of wealth, and Shearer replied, "I would hope so. My own
personal bias is that America is a profoundly unequal country." In other
words, the immediate challenge *is* control and the derivative result *may
be* a redistribution of wealth; and the derivative result is articulated not
as a matter of justice but as a reflection of personal bias, as if to say the
issue is still debatable.

Shearer, who was not a member of CED, was far more concerned
with the redistribution of wealth than were the people within CED.
Consequently, it was not surprising that neither California CED nor the
Santa Monica chapter of CED, which emphasized quality of life concerns and political control, failed to win much working class or lower
class support. What CED may be offering people outside of the middle
class, at the extreme, is the odd combination of empowerment and unemployment for the time being—another American Dream deferred to
the uncertain future.

After Control Comes Ownership

The Santa Monica left understood that rent control did not address the
most basic housing needs of Santa Monica's low income groups. Some
residents were too poor to pay either controlled rents or the very modest
increases allowed each year by the rent control board. Moreover, thousands of Santa Monicans were too close to the economic margins to
rehabilitate deteriorating units suffering a combination of age and land-

lords who pleaded that rent control made repairs impossible. Meanwhile, former residents who had been forced out of Santa Monica by the rent gouging and condominium conversions of the 1970s could not get back into the city in the 1980s. Santa Monica had one of the lowest apartment vacancy rates in the country for reasons that included the desirability of the area, the rent control that kept people settled there, and some large landlords who kept units off the market as a form of protest. The handful of available rentals were going to affluent professionals who could invest the time, energy, and resources necessary to campaign for vacancies; who sometimes shelled out up to $1,000 to former tenants, landlords, or agencies in black market efforts to crack the housing market; who were deemed more responsible and reliable than low income tenants in the view of landlords; and who were in the best position to purchase their units if the landlords were able to push through a referendum allowing for conversions.[9] I know one professional woman who tried to get a Santa Monica apartment for more than a year without success, but she broke into the city, finally, by marrying someone who already had an apartment there.

The SMRR politicians made a principled commitment to augment rent control with a policy of providing affordable housing for low income people. Shortly after taking office, the city hall radicals entertained a series of proposals aimed at providing affordable housing by raising density limits. A citizen advisory commission recommended revising the city code to allow for the rental of mobile homes on residential lots, the letting out of bedrooms in residential areas, and the construction of low and moderate income housing in residential neighborhoods. These recommendations were summarily rejected by the leftwing council. The rapid rejection, allowing for little public discussion, raised questions about the radicals' commitment to participatory democracy as well as their commitment to meeting the housing needs of the city's low income people.

One of the questioners was local economist and activist David Shulman, who published an article in the local paper entitled "SM City Council: Conservatives Posing as Radicals."[10] Shulman did not believe that the SMRR council majority was serious about meeting the housing needs of low income people. He argued that the only way to provide significant amounts of affordable housing in an already-developed city was to increase residential densities but, he noted, that "runs counter to the desire for low density" inherent in the councilmembers' attachment to a human scale environment. While some leftwing critics felt that the SMRR council had caved in to homeowner protests against the prospect of higher densities, Shulman hinted at a deeper political reality:

> Middle income renters living in rent-controlled apartments will respond to low and moderate income housing in their neighborhood the same way as their homeowner counterparts, with opposition. . . . The young, professional, middle income renter has more

in common with the typical Santa Monica homeowner than with many of the residents of the [low income] Pico Corridor.

The SMRR councilmembers had already shown a willingness to withstand the protests of homeowners but they would continue to shy away from policies likely to alienate any significant portion of their middle class, tenant base of electoral support.

Dennis Zane, the council's liaison person on housing issues, responded to Shulman's charges: "We are committed to developing such housing. I simply do not agree with David over the ways to achieve it."[11] Over the next three years, the SMRR council opened several fronts in the struggle for affordable housing. Each strategy assumed that maintaining low densities was unquestionable; and each strategy ultimately did limit densities but failed to do much to meet the housing needs of Santa Monica's low income groups.

The centerpiece of SMRR's affordable housing policy was the formation of the Santa Monica Community Corporation, a community development corporation seeded with a $50,000 city council grant. The money was intended to pay for a professional study of the possible purchase or construction of affordable housing that would take the form of limited equity cooperatives. The advantage of limited equity cooperatives is that they allow low income people to buy into their housing at submarket prices and to exercise control over their housing in cooperation with their neighbors. However, the low income owners cannot accrue much equity and therefore have to sell out at submarket prices if they desire to move. According to Allan Heskin, who was hired as a Community Corporation expert, the idea of limited equity housing is a "great idea" for people who fear losing their apartments but provides no persuasive answers to "white upwardly mobile people" who want to know, "What's in it for us?"[12]

The Community Corporation's quest for economic democracy in housing moved forward at a snail's pace. Many tenant activists opposed the idea of limited equity cooperatives. They feared that the corporation would mostly buy up and convert apartments, and thereby erode the city's already inadequate rental stock. They also argued that the conversion process would mostly benefit not low income but middle income people. Poorer people could not afford to buy into a $30,000 or $40,000 cooperative even if its market value was nearly $200,000, but middle income people would more likely jump at the opportunity. The issue of preserving the rental stock versus fostering limited equity cooperatives became a source of tension within SMRR.

In addition, the Community Corporation faced the complex question of whether the conversion of rental units to any other form of housing was legal under the city's rent control charter amendment. Its ability to get a clear ruling was hamstrung both by the numerous court cases that were determining the meaning and constitutionality of various sections of the rent control law and by the discussions, studies, and proposals aimed at producing a new housing element in the city charter that would legally frame the city's housing policy for the future. Other problems in moving forward included overcoming the mutual distrust between leaders in the Ocean Park and Pico neighborhoods, who were to cooperate in building the community development corporation, foraging for funding sources to underwrite purchases or construction, and dealing with the conservative opposition that was willing to support limited equity housing if only city officials would also sanction full equity condominium conversions.

The SMRR council was in control for more than two-and-a-half years before it began to allocate the capital needed to get the Santa Monica Community Corporation into the affordable housing business. In late 1983 and early 1984, it approved programs that would provide $580,000 for the purchase and rehabilitation of fifty-eight units in the Pico neighborhood; another $804,000 to buy and rehabilitate two buildings with a total of twenty-seven housing units; some $300,000 to upgrade thirty houses to provide low cost housing for people working in the downtown area; and then $600,000 to construct a nineteen-unit townhouse for low and moderate income residents.[13] The funding mainly took the form of low interest loans rather than outright grants and came from a combination of private and public institutions. For example, the Bank of America and the Ford Foundation's Local Initiative Support Corporation kicked in large chunks of money, as did the U.S. Department of Housing and Urban Development (HUD). Given the intricacies of funding, it was not clear how many of these units would be administered as public housing or become limited equity cooperatives.

The council opened a second front on affordable housing by supporting inclusionary zoning or a variant of it as part of its development agreement negotiations. The radical politicians demanded that on-site or adjacent-site affordable housing be subsidized and built by the developers of multifamily, commercial, and industrial projects in order to win city approval for zoning variances. The model was a development agreement negotiated between the city and Welton Becket Associates. The city allowed Welton Becket to build a 900,000-square-foot, multipurpose commercial complex; and Welton Becket contracted to build one hundred units of affordable housing with the assistance of a $2.2 million state grant administered by the Los Angeles County Housing Authority.[14] Other development agreements assumed a smaller scale but most included some provision for affordable housing. Activists feared that this model would be scuttled when a local judge enjoined the city from imposing fees for development permits that have "no rational relationship" to defraying the costs of added burdens to the community and then specified, "It's not reasonable to demand low cost housing or a new park as a condition for building a five-story building."[15] But city officials argued successfully that large developments put serious pressure on the city's housing stock by attracting workers who compete for already scarce low and moderate income housing. Consequently, imposing demands for affordable housing does have a rational relationship to defraying community costs.

In theory, inclusionary zoning written into development agreements could have increased densities in residential neighborhoods but it virtually never did so in the city's affluent homeowner and tenant areas. On the one hand, the SMRR council did not readily approve large developments. That would have run counter to the council's human scale commitments. On the other hand, those large developments that were approved were concentrated either downtown, where relatively few people lived, or in areas adjacent to low income neighborhoods, where the demand for affordable housing was greatest and resistance to it minimal. As a result, neither affluent homeowners nor tenants had reason to fear that low income people would be adding congestion to their neighborhoods or eroding their quality of life.

The SMRR council's affordable housing policies seemed firmly set when, after two years of effort, the SMRR politicians adopted a new housing element for the city charter. This new element rejected raising density limits, and supported limited equity cooperatives and inclusionary zoning as the official means toward the affordable housing goal. However, just as the new housing element was being finalized, SMRR's conservative opposition mounted a successful drive to place what would be called the HOME (Home Ownership Made Easy) Initiative on the April 1983 ballot. If passed by voters, the measure would have allowed apartment owners to convert their buildings into full equity, market rate "cooperatives" with the consent of 60 percent of the building's current tenants. SMRR leaders immediately denounced the HOME Initiative as a "condo initiative." [16] The radicals saw it as an attempt to split the tenant movement by luring away middle and upper income renters who could conceivably buy into condominiums. Such a split would have simultaneously undermined popular support for rent control and for the SMRR politicians associated with rent control.

Large amounts of money were poured into the referendum campaign; and several court struggles took place over the HOME initiative's wording and the epithets hurled by both sides. Ralph Nader came to Santa Monica to support the SMRR position and to denounce the HOME Initiative as "a dubious proposition giving real estate speculators every incentive to harass tenants." [17] The battle was fairly intense, in part because tenant and landlord groups around the nation viewed the HOME Initiative as a prototype for gutting rent control legislation. The outcome? In an election in which the SMRR candidates for the rent control board won overwhelming victories, SMRR just barely defeated the HOME Initiative by a 13,860 to 13,053 margin.

Some activists interpreted the election results to mean that Santa

Monicans still supported rent control but a good many tenants were also interested in having the opportunity to become owners. The election nearly coincided with the publication of Allan Heskin's study of the Santa Monica renter movement, which revealed a strong relationship between "tenant consciousness" and "the desire to buy a home."[18] Middle class tenants often supported rent control because they could not amass enough capital to buy a home but SMRR's political opposition now offered them a possible instrument for purchasing their piece of the American Dream in the form of a condominium. Could SMRR maintain the support of affluent tenants while standing in the way of the realization of that Dream?

Key people in SMRR thought not. Despite considerable controversy within SMRR's ranks, SMRR leaders and councilmembers met with the conservative opposition behind the HOME Initiative to draft a compromise proposal—one that would protect rent control and yet allow tenants to have the opportunity to become owners. After several months of negotiations, a bargain was struck. The ad hoc group announced its bipartisan support for a ballot proposition that would allow landlords to convert apartments to fully equity cooperatives if two-thirds of a building's tenants approved the idea and if one-half of the tenants signed a statement that they intended to buy their units. The proposition included provision for maintaining rent control and eviction protections for tenants who decided not to buy their units; and the proposition called for a conversion tax that the city could use to subsidize low and moderate income tenants who wanted to buy and renovate their apartments. The measure became Proposition X, which, according to Dennis Zane, had two virtues. First, the conversions most likely to result would be in luxury apartments, bringing tax dollars from the rich that would be used to provide affordable housing opportunities for the poor. Second, Zane stated, "I believe if we didn't adopt a measure now, we would be faced with a much worse one in the future, one more hostile to renters."[19] With bipartisan support, Proposition X appeared on the June 1984 ballot and passed by a remarkable 70 percent to 30 percent landslide, consummating the marriage between rent control and private ownership.

What was the result of more than three years of policymaking aimed at providing affordable housing for low income people who had gained little from rent control? The immediate benefits went to Santa Monica's middle class residents. The council's decision to give high priority to low density meant that the city's affluent homeowners and tenants would face no influx of low income people. In addition, the passage of Proposition X virtually guaranteed that landlords in the wealthier parts of town would rent almost exclusively to upscale professionals who, in turn, were in a position to purchase their units. Put differently, those who had invested in Santa Monica's quality of life and the city's real estate could feel confident that their investments were protected by the city hall radicals.

The long-range benefits, which were rather meager, were reserved for

low income people. By refusing to tamper with densities, the council
guaranteed that minimal affordable housing would be provided in the city regardless of other policies. Quite simply, Santa Monica had little open space left for affordable housing, save some airport land that was tied up in complex legalities and negotiations with the federal government. The several millions of dollars channeled through the Santa Monica Community Corporation to provide a few hundred new units was a significant accomplishment but also a limited one. Neither these units nor the ones expected to emerge from development agreements had much impact on the overall housing crisis faced by thousands of current and former city residents who continued to find Santa Monica's 47,000 housing units inaccessible. Also, the units were slated for low *and* moderate income people, which, according to HUD guidelines, meant that many of them would be occupied by families with incomes above $20,000 a year. Whether the city would be able to find enough money to subsidize more than a few low income families hoping to buy into limited equity cooperatives was questionable. In fact, the only certainty was that it would be years before a substantial portion of Santa Monica's low income people knew if any of the slated housing would be available for them. Get your name on a waiting list.

Housing policy was *the* major thrust of the radical politician's commitment to empower lower class people; and councilmembers' limited success in providing affordable housing far outstripped any other efforts, for example, to empower the unemployed, marginalized workers, seniors living on fixed incomes, and other low income people. The city hall radicals had no systematic policy of job creation. Or consider the SMRR council's approach to health care for the needy. The council sponsored a professional policy study on the state of local health care. The study revealed that poor people were all but shut out of citywide services despite the presence of two major hospitals in Santa Monica. The study recommended that "the city consider operating its own medical clinic to serve its poor whose needs aren't being met by the county, the state, or private facilities."[20] But the SMRR councilmembers, who were quite willing to go into the pier business and the tourist business, did not want to go into the health care business. They preferred instead the conventional social services strategy of channeling government monies into private clinics; and they preferred the conventional politics of pressuring private hospitals to provide care for Santa Monica's 6,400 Medi-Cal patients. These strategies were often couched in the language of empowering the needy but actually reflected a version of "government *for* the people."

Government for the People

In his 1978 State of the Union address, President Jimmy Carter said, "We must have what Abraham Lincoln sought—a government for the people." Critics pointed out that Carter had neglected Lincoln's "of the people" and "by the people" as if to imply that government rules and citizens obey. No talk of democratic empowerment here.[21] Santa Monica's city hall radicals did not see themselves practicing conventional government for the people. Their goal was government by the people. But their actions did very little to enhance the opportunities of low income people to become economically independent and thus to be self-governing in their everyday lives.

In late 1982, the SMRR council approved a social services commission recommendation on city guidelines to help people to "take more effective control over their own lives and actively participate in a community . . . to define their own needs, determine their own priorities, and have those priorities met." The guidelines suggested that the city develop a "human services plan" that would "insure every citizen the opportunity to obtain a decent place in which to live, a proper diet, the protection and care needed in childhood, quality schooling, fulfilling employment, dignity and security in senior years, a healthy and safe environment, ample cultural and recreational facilities, and an atmosphere that encourages peaceful diversity in thought and action."[22] Ideally, the council would guide the city toward a one class society of independent people secure in the fulfillment of their basic needs and able to enjoy the environmental, cultural, and intellectual amenities of local life.

The council had an opportunity to take a small step toward this ideal when the last major supermarket in the Pico neighborhood closed its doors. There was much talk among city officials regarding the facilitation of a community-owned food cooperative. This would allow the area's low income residents to control both food quality and prices; it would also serve as a center of community pride, cooperation, and collective action. The vacated site could be purchased with Community Development Block Grant (CDBG) money slated for needy neighborhoods; and technical assistance for training residents in food management could be underwritten by low interest loans from the National Consumer Cooperative Bank. Fred Allingham of the Pico Neighborhood Association (PNA) stated, "I'd really like to see us get into co-ops and some kind of community-owned store."[23] In this instance, talk led to study rather than action.

The SMRR council set aside some CDBG money for the PNA to hire a professional consultant to investigate the closing of the neighborhood supermarket and the more general problem of disinvestment in the Pico neighborhood. Eight months later, the consultant suggested that the neighborhood needed some sort of subsidy in order to attract a developer willing to build a new supermarket; the terms of the subsidy should be set in the context of possible zoning changes that could enhance neighborhood-serving businesses; and the zoning changes would be a function of current council efforts to rewrite the land use element of the city charter.[24] In other words, the talk about a community-owned store mediated by a professional consultant shifted to discussion about subsidizing a private developer once zoning and land use issues were decided, several years down the line. Pico residents were not to assume control over basic food necessities but, if patient, the council would eventually encourage a major chain to open shop in their neighborhood. The issue was dropped pending the outcome of other decisions.

On most policy questions, the SMRR council did not even talk about helping low income people gain direct control over basic resources. Instead, it did an admirable job of funding social services agencies that distributed resources to needy people. The council allocated money to public agencies and private nonprofit organizations that provided food for the hungry and temporary housing for the homeless, prenatal care for pregnant women who could not afford the medical costs, transportation for seniors and the disabled, door and window locks for people needing crime protection, legal aid for people who could not afford to pay attorney fees, and information on jobs for youth. The council also invested money in programs aimed at helping alcoholics, victims of rape and other abuses, mentally ill people unable to pay for their own therapy, and more. Nancy McFarland, the city's CDBG coordinator, made continuous efforts to inform residents of available social services, solicit their comments on city-sponsored programs, and keep the council informed of residents' opinions on outstanding needs.[25]

The council was quite effective in expanding social services programs at a time when tax cuts had forced almost every other California city to reduce social services expenditures. The city hall radicals deferred some infrastructure and equipment expenditures to keep up social services and directed city bureaucrats to conjure up more money for programs. Remarkably, the city was able to nurture a good working relationship with the extremely conservative Los Angeles County Board of Supervisors and receive a "larger than average" allocation from it, including $2 million for mental health programs and $50,000 for summer youth employment.[26] Fiscal creativity allowed the SMRR council to create a new office for disabled people, for example, that assessed the needs of disabled people, put them in contact with various agencies, coordinated services among agencies, educated the council and residents on disabled people, and proposed projects to serve them. Among the more immediate impacts were a council-declared "Disability Awareness Day" and council-financed construction projects involving curbcuts for wheelchairs and improved access to public buildings and restrooms.[27] Unquestionably, the SMRR council's commitment to funding such social services was valuable to a broad range of recipients.

Nevertheless, Santa Monica's social services posture had the immediate effect of reinforcing the authority of politicians, city staff, and agency professionals but, at best, only a distant promise of fostering independence for people on the lower rungs of the social ladder. Derek Shearer provided some insights into the social services dynamics in Santa Monica:

> One of the things the city does is fund social service projects. We obviously do that because we think it's the right thing to do. And there's been cutbacks in this area and it's necessary. Also, it's cheaper for the city. It's probably more efficient to have a private nonprofit group do a lot of these projects than to have to set up a permanent city agency to carry them out. So there are public hearings . . . in which we decide which groups are efficient, competent, which ones we fund, which ones we go with, how much we give them.[28]

The SMRR council shied away from creating city-controlled agencies. It was busy with other priorities. And it felt that funding existing agencies would be more cost-effective. This meant that the city hall radicals would not build public institutions that could be run by the recipients themselves but would instead rely on private groups run by social services professionals. The council implicitly reinforced professionals' control over decisionmaking by linking its funding priorities to city staff reports on the relative efficiency of agencies under review and to agency professionals' ability to demonstrate a track record of administrative competence. In effect, the council also enhanced its own influence by playing the role of arbiter among public and private sector professionals, leaving virtually no authoritative role for potential recipients. Thus, Santa Monica's needy may have become less dependent on the economic marketplace but they became more dependent on city government.

The council did not fare much better when it came to fostering independence among working class people in Santa Monica. The SMRR radicals did make policies that improved the wages and bargaining power of people who worked in city hall but these were mostly professionals. Moreover, several councilmembers told me of their close relations with organized labor in the city, mentioning among other unions the United Auto Workers, the Communications Workers of America, the Retail Clerks Union, the American Federation of State, County, and Municipal Employees, the Coalition of Labor Union Women, the Service Employees International Union, the AFL-CIO, and more; but the council's support for what James Conn called "progressive legislation in behalf of labor" was quite limited.[29] The legislation referred to banning machine pricing in city supermarkets augmented by lobbying efforts in support of item pricing at the state level. More often, legislation was not involved at all, for example, when some SMRR politicians lent moral support to striking cable television workers by walking the picketline with them.[30] Overall, SMRR council relations with organized labor never went beyond this conventional give-and-take for two reasons.

First, neither the SMRR rank and file nor its leaders had a systematic idea of what kinds of municipal policies were needed to enhance the independence of organized labor or working class residents in Santa Monica. SMRR's "Principles of Unity" were completely silent on labor issues. Santa Monica's CED chapter did discuss "extending some basic constitutional democratic principles to the workplace, minimally, things like you cannot be fired in the city of Santa Monica for political reasons." But according to Maurice Zeitlin, the movement had been able to work out no consensus on such issues, in part, "because that requires time and commitment when you have a thousand other pressing things." [31] Add to these factors a local sense that there is not much that a municipal government can do for labor, a lack of information regarding the overlap between Santa Monica residents and workers, some fragmentation among organized labor groups in the city, a reticence of undocumented workers to have any kind of public presence, and then the low percentage of working class voters in the city; and the result is that almost no one wanted to put in the "time and commitment" to forge a systematic labor policy. In the main, working class independence was not an issue in Santa Monica.

Second, the SMRR politicians had good reason to avoid formulating clear goals or guidelines for labor policy. They were caught between their own rhetorical commitment to extending the rights of working people and their institutional positions as managers of city employees. Former councilmember Cheryl Rhoden was involved in both SMRR and organized labor, and could wholeheartedly support city policies to enhance workers' independence. For example, she wanted the city to stop contracting out work on the basis of the lowest bids submitted by private firms but to start taking into account the labor practices of the firms in awarding contracts. In many cases, the lowest bid comes from companies that pay the lowest wages, provide the fewest benefits, and fight the hardest against union organizing in their shops. "Union busting," Rhoden argued, "is exactly what contracting out often accomplishes." [32] However, Dolores Press, who also was involved in SMRR and organized labor and agreed with Rhoden's analysis, was far more sensitive to the crosspressures that existed inside of city hall. After her workday at the Retail Clerks Union, Press stated, "I go over to city hall and put on a management hat; and so there I have to worry about fiscal responsibility." [33] What was fiscal responsibility? For some councilmembers and most city professionals, it meant taking advantage of competitive bidding to cut city costs and enhance city revenues; it meant contracting out work (for example, printing or cemetery maintenance) to the lowest bidder; it meant leasing city land and concessions to the highest bidder. In other words, it meant ignoring the labor practices of the businesses in the competition.

The SMRR politicians did not reconcile their roles as friends of labor and city managers. Instead, they dealt with the crosspressures on an issue-by-issue basis. They tried to help out labor without raising city costs but they still kept a close eye to the bottom line. After all, they did not want to incur the wrath of the city's middle class taxpayers by appearing to waste city funds but they did want to maximize disposable dollars to maintain and upgrade city social services. One might say, overall, that low income and working class Santa Monicans figured more in the balances struck at city hall during the SMRR reign of power than previously but these classes of people certainly did not gain greater independent control over the decisions and resources that go into fulfilling basic human needs.

The city hall radicals, in short, did not practice Fred Harris' "Up with those who are down." But they might have moved toward a one class society by experimenting with "Down with those who are up." That is, they could have enhanced the opportunities of people on the bottom rungs of the socioeconomic ladder by asserting the legitimacy of public control over the corporate economy and by proposing or experimenting with embryonic extensions of public power into the corporate marketplace. This was part of the SMRR rhetoric rooted in the core ideology, but was it a pragmatic basis for public policy?

Playing the Market

Many SMRR activists believed that the fundamental dispute in Santa Monica involved the "collision of personal rights and property rights."[34] Tenants, workers, seniors, disabled people, women, minorities, and the poor have rights; people have rights. Unfortunately, people's rights are abused and denied by those using the shield of private property rights and the marketplace to foster huge concentrations of wealth and capitalist control of American society. Those who operated large corporations were considered the worst offenders. And, according to Dennis Zane, part of SMRR's electoral mandate was to defend people's rights on the basis of "egalitarian principles" by demonstrating "a desire and willingness to do political combat with big money."[35] Obviously, no local movement or municipal government could make a major dent in the armor of big business. But radicals could hope to undermine the legitimacy of large corporations and make some inroads into their power over local affairs. The council essentially did this when it took on Shell Oil Company in a dispute over people's right to control the subsurface of their community versus the corporation's right to run a pipeline under the city; or when the council took on General Telephone Company, supporting residents' right to an efficient utility system against the corporation's right to hike its rates.

Yet one had to wonder about the depth of SMRR's anticorporatism when scanning the July 20, 1982, issue of the Santa Monica *Outlook*. On an inside page, one might notice a photograph of a smiling mayor Ruth

Yannatta Goldway, surrounded by three smiling corporate executives, about to cut the ceremonial ribbon to celebrate the opening of a local branch of Merrill Lynch, Pierce, Fenner, and Smith Incorporated—the noted brokers that are "bullish" on U.S. corporate capitalism. Kenneth Edwards' reaction to the photograph was, "Good, it came a year too late!"[36] In Edwards' view, SMRR leaders had overindulged in anticorporate rhetoric. Such talk was foolhardy in light of the fact that the SMRR council was working with corporations and not against them.

The SMRR politicians' anticorporate stance was actually shortlived. Their moratorium on development prolonged much of the anticorporate rhetoric because the radicals used the people's rights versus property rights argument to justify the policy and defend it against developers' criticisms. And the criticisms were fairly harsh. Corporations with ongoing projects sometimes won exemption from the moratorium by promising to provide community amenities such as affordable housing, daycare facilities, or greenspace, and then argued that they had been victimized by city council extortion. Other executives claimed, for example, that "the delays have caused our company to suffer $1.8 million in losses" resulting in bankruptcy proceedings.[37] Still other big businessmen felt that the anticorporate council was promoting an unhealthy atmosphere that meant, in one case, "We wouldn't touch anything in Santa Monica."[38] When the city government published its "Guide to Property Development" aimed at clarifying the development permit process, one local property owner suggested that the booklet be renamed, "Why You Should Not Develop Property in Santa Monica."[39] At first, city hall radicals reacted to critics by claiming to represent the public interest against the greed of speculators, or as Ruth Yannatta Goldway stated on one occasion, "If we scare some developers away who hope to make a fast buck, we're doing the city justice."[40] Soon, however, city hall rhetoric began to accommodate political reality.

The political reality was that SMRR politicians were working hard to normalize relations with corporations. In effect, their moratorium on development was an announcement that the municipal government was using its public authority as a resource for entering into the local marketplace. Its entrance, like that of any new actor, caused considerable uncertainty. For its part, the council was not quite sure about the nature of its own participation. And representatives of local corporate outlets were somewhat perplexed at how to factor city council influence into their calculations. This uncertainty was gradually diminished in the next few years.

Initially, no one was quite sure what role affected neighborhoods would play in negotiations between the city and corporate developers. When city officials and developers worked out the first agreements alone, affected neighborhoods felt that they were not properly represented, venting their frustration both at the council's failure to make good on the promise of participatory democracy and on the corporations' concerns for profits over people. But the vectors of public opinion became more predictable once the council made an effort to include neighborhood people in the negotiations.

For example, the Pico Neighborhood Association became involved in working out the terms of a 540,000-square-foot office complex slated for its neighborhood. PNA, the city, and the developer worked out a "Memorandum of Understanding." The neighborhood organization and the city would support the project; in turn, the developer would build low and moderate income housing for area residents, pay fees for community and social services, provide training and relocation for workers affected by the development, and allow PNA a 2 percent limited partnership in the office complex. CeCe Bradley, chair of PNA's board, commented, "It's a good agreement; anything that comes out of this project will be for the betterment of the community, and that's what we're pleased about." [41] Relatedly, Ocean Park residents were overwhelmingly opposed to a major hotel expansion in their neighborhood until they were invited into the bargaining. Ultimately, they helped to strike some compromises that resulted in neighborhood satisfaction and city approval. Dennis Zane explained his vote for approval this way: "I didn't believe there would ever be an occasion on which I'd support a 10-story project anywhere in Santa Monica . . . but far be it for me to stand in the way of the democratic process." [42] Bringing the neighborhoods into the process functioned to stabilize relations between city hall radicals and corporate developers.

Another uncertainty came from within city hall. City professionals, always wary about neighborhood groups threatening to invade bureaucratic turf as well as about inefficient expenditure of their time, soon tired of all the effort that went into negotiating development agreement after development agreement. They instituted an informal freeze on negotiations, claiming that they did not have adequate staff to process the avalanche of applications, that the process was too controversial and irregular, and that the staff should be devoting more time "to projects backed by the largest segment of the public, such as the pier." [43] At that point, the city attorney announced that the freeze was illegal and the professionals in the city manager's office backtracked, saying there was no freeze per se but only a slowdown due to inadequate staff. [44] This wrangling reflected an internal disagreement about city development policy. People in the city manager's office questioned whether city planning commissioners were doing their job professionally; the planning commissioners felt that their authority was being circumvented by the city manager's office. One resigning planning commissioner said, "I was concerned about the changing role of the commission, that it was becoming more reactive than initiative." [45] More so than the council's early rhetoric or its later invitation of neighbors into negotiations, bureaucratic turf wars disturbed business investors.

For example, a huge Cadillac dealership proposed to build a 300,000-square-foot development in Santa Monica. The city council and the city manager's office favored the development because it would bring more than $500,000 in tax revenues into city coffers each year. The planning commission, however, delayed the permit process. It protested that nearby residents had not been adequately consulted and that the proposed project did not meet the development guidelines being worked out as part of the city's new land use element. The planning commission eventually refused its approval. The city council then overturned its own planning commission and approved the project, with Kenneth Edwards arguing that it is bad government never to deviate from guidelines when the public interest is at stake.[46] The conclusion of this sequence came when the Cadillac dealership canceled its project despite city approval, laying the blame on "conditions, restrictions, and financial burdens" imposed by prolonged city decisionmaking.[47]

The SMRR councilmembers made a two-pronged effort to eliminate the factors that interfered with their corporate dealings. One was to tone down and sometimes even reverse their anticorporate rhetoric. This explains why mayor Goldway was photographed cutting the ribbon at the new Merrill Lynch office and why SMRR councilmembers sometimes went out of their way to convince people that they were not antibusiness. In part, this also explains why the SMRR council majority chose Kenneth Edwards to replace Goldway as mayor after the April 1983 election. Edwards considered SMRR's anticorporate rhetoric bad public relations that interfered, for example, with council efforts to negotiate with Systems Development Corporation, which had threatened to move out of Santa Monica and take three hundred jobs with it.[48] Under Edwards' leadership, the SMRR council would quite openly court friendship with the Chamber of Commerce and local corporate developers.

The other strategy for normalizing relations with the corporate world was for the SMRR council to change the key presumption underlying its development policy. In 1981, the council, the planning commission, and the commercial and industrial task force presumed that their job was to figure out how to *limit* growth in the city. The ultimate product of their calculations was to be a new land use element in the city charter. The council poured a quarter-million dollars into consultant fees and, two years later, the consultants reported on "the enormous ability of the city to grow."[49] The consultants' main presumption was that *controlled* growth was where Santa Monica's future lay. And controlled growth meant balancing six considerations: adequate city revenues, employment opportunities, a mixture of businesses, preservation of the housing stock, improvement of the city's physical environment, and consideration for unemployed and underemployed residents.[50] Among other things, the consultants recommended more office growth, the development of neighborhood shopping centers, the conversion of the downtown into a hotel and entertainment district, and special height exemptions for commercial areas. The city staff, which worked closely with the consultants, were quite happy with what they believed was a fiscally responsible plan that would maintain a healthy economic environment and provide revenues to meet social services responsibilities.

These recommendations became the fulcrum for land use discussions. Local developers thought that the recommendations were too restrictive and labeled them a "no growth" plan. City manager John Alschuler arranged to meet with conservative business groups in the hope of winning bipartisan support for the plan. As a result of some private brokering, Alschuler won the support of business interests for a compromised version of the plan. The Chamber of Commerce representative involved in the talks put it this way: "Alschuler is a real professional. He . . . did a commendable job of negotiating some of the most sticky points. I don't say we buy everything in the plan, but the key issues have been negotiated."[51] The SMRR councilmembers showed their indirect support for Alschuler's compromise when, upon his announced resignation (for personal reasons), the councilmembers decided to retain him as a private consultant to see through the ratification of the new land use element. They then showed their direct support by giving Alschuler's plan the tentative approval needed for moving to the next stage of adoption.

At the same time, several community groups were unhappy with the city manager's actions as well as the growth patterns written into both the consultants' recommendations and Alschuler's compromise plan. Ken Genser reflected their feelings when he told the council, "The city manager has negotiated with developers in closed sessions and this doesn't look good for government. I urge you to reaffirm that you care about the quality of life."[52] Meanwhile, several city planning commissioners were upset that the council gutted their own compromise plan that put greater emphasis on growth limits. Their views were described by a local reporter in these terms:

> The Santa Monica city council is giving in to Darth Vader's sinister call to "come over to the dark side"—literally and figuratively—with its easing of tight development restrictions, several planning commissioners say. Although they didn't put it quite like that Monday night, commissioners criticized the city council for changing the commission's proposed land use plan. They said that changes could result in higher, darker buildings that might one day loom over the city, much like Darth Vader, the black-clad, black-helmeted "Star Wars" villain.[53]

The city council eventually compromised a few points of concern to neighborhood groups and planning commissioners and then approved what was essentially Alschuler's plan, which, parenthetically, included important density bonuses for automobile dealerships.

Perhaps more striking than the council's self-censorship of anticorporate rhetoric and its self-conscious effort to smooth over corporate relations was its active linking of community interest and corporate interest in at least one instance. When the second phase of Welton Becket's 900,000-square-foot complex was stalled due to a shortfall in private financing, the city council went to bat for the corporation.[54] It directed city bureaucrats to apply to HUD for a $10 million Urban Development Action Grant (UDAG). The city would then take that money and make a low interest loan to Welton Becket so that the corporation could proceed with phase two of its project. The argument was that the community would benefit in terms of both finances and the jobs expected to materialize out of phase two, and Welton Becket would benefit by inexpensive financing and profits expected from the completed development. Symbolically, this line of economic policy did not mean that the SMRR politicians had become team players in the corporate marketplace but it did indicate that they became predictable players who would deal rather than contest the legitimacy of corporate control over vast accumulations of wealth.

Muddle Through Economics

The Port Huron Statement of the early 1960s had student radicals criticizing their parents' generation for tolerating the "muddle through" approach of their politicians and "the pervading feeling that there are simply no alternatives." Santa Monica's middle class radicals of the early 1980s were clearly more comfortable dealing with moral and political issues than with confronting systematically the leveling of class differences. At best, the SMRR politicians muddled through their economic policies, doing what they could to ensure that life did not become materially worse for low income residents. But they were not sure that there were other alternatives.

The economic configuration of Santa Monica did not change much as a result of the radicals' experiment with political power. Perhaps the major change was in the nature of municipal government. In the past, city councilmembers represented the interests of the growth machine. Now the politicians were mediators who negotiated interclass relations between broadly conceived community interests and private business investments. They provided additional environmental safeguards for middle class residents, social services for lower class residents, and controlled development guidelines for investors to lubricate class relations. In the short run, they enhanced their own power by consolidating their authority to negotiate the bargains that would keep everyone partially happy.

In the long run, however, the mediator's role points to the erosion of municipal autonomy. The SMRR politicians needed resources to keep everyone partially happy. They fine-tuned city efforts to secure funding from county, state, and federal agencies as well as from private corporations and foundations. The process of grantsmanship requires the professionalization of city government. On the one hand, city business must be run on an efficient cost-benefit basis to persuade potential funders that they should invest in Santa Monica programs. On the other hand, the technical and legal aspects of securing grants, loans, and other revenues demand that people with professional expertise oversee the process, and their oversight is almost certain to affect the nature of the policies in question. The more that local politicians venture into grantsmanship, the less they can afford to engage in controversial political experiments that put off city professionals or funding agencies.

Furthermore, outside funding almost always comes with strings attached. Even the need to meet agency deadlines may require politicians to compromise their values as the Santa Monica city council learned in at least one incident.[55] That was when the council was discussing a particular city housing program and prepared to hear public debate on it. The city manager informed the council that it must act immediately lest it miss a HUD deadline and thereby miss out on millions of federal dollars. The council immediately enacted the housing program to the dismay of some citizens who wanted more public discussion and participation. In other instances, the SMRR council adjusted its own policies to align with the priorities and specifications of funding agencies. This form of local politics pointed toward an increasing dependency on outside guidelines that were certain to exclude any impetus toward economic democracy or one class society.

When Dennis Zane told me of SMRR's desire and willingness to do combat with big money, he added the qualification that "we are constrained by the nature of real possibilities."[56] This meant that the SMRR council had to maintain the support of Santa Monica's middle class electorate in order to promote the shift leftward that would *eventually* help to empower the powerless in the poor neighborhoods. The nature of real possibilities also depended on the broader political context. According to Derek Shearer, "What happens six years from now in Santa Monica depends, not entirely but in large part, on what happens nationwide."[57] The SMRR experiment would be helped or hindered by the prevailing political attitudes of American citizens and their politicians. From this vantagepoint, the council's economic policies might be considered impressive. They helped to stabilize the position of low income residents at an historical moment when conservative county supervisors, a conservative state governor, and a conservative president systematically eroded the opportunities of low income Americans. Conceivably, the possible range of economic policies in Santa Monica will expand once the nation's political climate becomes more liberal.

The Santa Monica radicals were not especially concerned with abstract criticisms of their economic policies. Whether their housing policies, for example, amounted to some sort of "reformism" that helped accommodate low income people to an inegalitarian economic system or whether their negotiations with corporations implicitly "legitimated" corporate capitalism were academic questions that rarely touched on the immediacy of everyday politics. Ruth Yannatta Goldway suggested:

> I think that it's incredibly counterproductive for people on various parts of the left to argue among themselves and then also to spend this enormous amount of time deciding what the *correct* line is and what the *proper* strategy is for running the government when anyone who is in politics knows there is no such thing. You can't make a formula a priori. You have to be there. You have to be in power, in the specific situation with your specific constituencies and develop the program as you go. . . . The council may not be doing things exactly the way I'd like them to be done but they're sure moving a hell of a lot better than any council before them.[58]

Goldway and other SMRR leaders were political pragmatists. They experimented with what worked better than in the past and with what promised to work better in the future. And they did so with considerable caution. For example, they would not allow themselves to be redbaited out of office. When SMRR's opposition claimed that the coalition intended to promote municipal ownership of rental property, a kind of housing socialism, the SMRR leaders quickly denied harboring any such intention.[59] Some of the city hall radicals knew that they were compromising their principles and falling short of their ideals, but they planned to stay in power long enough to learn from their experiences and to approximate principles through new policies.

What they neglected to consider was that political pragmatism does not always work. That is, it does not guarantee re-election. Approaching the April 1983 municipal elections, the SMRR politicians were confident that their policies would be validated at the polls. After all, they had won every electoral contest they had entered in the past four years, and Tom Hayden's November 1982 election to the State Assembly seemed to indicate that the coalition's popular support was still solid. Despite some conflicts within the SMRR coalition, most activists believed that grassroots support was still strong and that the opposition remained "a group of buffoons," as one councilmember told me off the record. The stage was set for still another SMRR victory. The only problem was that the Santa Monica electorate was poised to stage the defeat of every SMRR city council candidate.

8

In the Shadow of Defeat

The majority of people in the city identify closely with
our ideas and programs and people. That's why we win
—because we represent the city.

Ruth Yannatta Goldway[1]

When you're dealing with grassroots politics, you can't
forget to water the grass.

Cheryl Rhoden[2]

Santa Monicans for Renters' Rights

The Santa Monicans for Renters' Rights (SMRR) coalition kicked off another political campaign on February 13, 1983, amid pervasive optimism. Dennis Zane served as master of ceremonies and told the activist audience that the coming April election would be "the *coup de grâce* that will assure our rent control and our progressive city council for the remainder of the decade."³ Only one of five SMRR council incumbents faced re-election and even the opposition agreed that Ruth Yannatta Goldway was unbeatable. Meanwhile, SMRR had high hopes that feminist KerryAnn Lobel and senior activist the Reverend Alvin Smith would defeat both opposition council incumbents who were trying to save their seats. If all went according to plan, the coalition would emerge from the election with a 7–0 majority on the city council, and SMRR would only have to retain one seat in 1985 to assure its majority through 1987. The radicals were virtually certain that they would win the time necessary to continue to build and improve their model of leftwing municipal government.

After a two-month campaign during which SMRR's professional staff worked efficiently and the coalition amassed its largest-ever campaign war chest, local activists reconvened on April 12, 1983, to listen and cheer as the vote count was announced. Early returns were mixed and some confusion in the counting made it difficult to determine the trends in various parts of the city. When asked about his reading of the early totals, Tom Hayden responded, "I think that our coalition will probably win. Being Irish, I always have a sense of foreboding until every last vote is counted."⁴ Hayden's caution was justified during the evening as it became clear that the desired SMRR landslide was not going to materialize. Several council races were quite close and activists began to doubt whether the two opposition councilmembers would be unseated. Kenneth Edwards told a reporter, "It will really mean the same thing whether it's a 7–0 or 5–2 city council and that is that democracy has worked in Santa Monica."⁵ By the time that people went to bed, it looked like it was going to be a 5–2 city council.

Shock set in the next day when absentee ballots were counted and included in the final tally. Not only had opposition councilmembers Christine Reed and William Jennings retained their seats by comfortable margins, but a little-known conservative named David Epstein had defeated Ruth Yannatta Goldway by a 13,038 to 12,769 margin. SMRR's mayor and most formidable public figure had lost. The SMRR council majority was now reduced to a precarious 4–3 edge. Moreover, it would have to re-elect all four of its remaining council incumbents in 1985 if it was to retain control of city government for the last half of the decade.

Activists had little time to recover from electoral shock when a second blow struck. Shortly after the April 1983 election, state courts handed down a series of decisions that voided significant aspects of Santa Monica's rent control law. Most important, the city's "independent" rent control board lost most of its autonomy to the city council at the very moment that the radicals saw the council slipping into the opposition's grasp. The specter of yesterday's rent control victories being reversed by tomorrow's rightwing city council became far more salient than any vision of leftwing model building.

If winning is the lifeblood of grassroots movements, then what is losing? Santa Monica's activists were acculturated to middle class optimism and efficacy; they did not allow a few setbacks to serve as excuses for defeatism, resignation, or withdrawal from the political fray. Their sense of political competence was strong enough for them to view losing very much as scientists view experiments gone awry: one learns from failure and does better the next time. What did Santa Monica's middle class radicals learn from defeat?

The Professional Approach

The voting data from the April 1983 municipal elections revealed two patterns. First, shifts in voter turnout favored SMRR's opposition. SMRR suffered a slight drop in turnout in renter neighborhoods whereas the opposition engineered a significant increase of voter turnout in the city's most affluent homeowner areas. For example, Ocean Park voting declined by 1 percent but the wealthy "north of Montana" enclave registered 8 percent more people voting than in 1981. Second, Santa Monica voters from all city neighborhoods supported SMRR candidates in smaller percentages than previously. In 1981, SMRR council candidates won Ocean Park by a 72.3 to 21.8 percent margin; in 1983, the margin was reduced to 64.2 to 27.2 percent—roughly a 14 percent turnaround favoring the opposition. SMRR's declining voter support was much steeper in other neighborhoods.[6] How were the data interpreted?

Local election analyses focused mainly on the first trend, the shift in voter turnout. SMRR had failed to get its supporters to the polls while the opposition succeeded in getting its people to cast the decisive ballots. How did this happen? According to Ruth Yannatta Goldway, "We did what we could but you have to remember that all our energy was going into running government—I was working 60 hours a week for little pay while they were out organizing homeowners."[7] The unstated message was that the SMRR coalition was quite dependent on the SMRR councilmembers for campaign leadership but the opposition had a campaign leadership distinct from its council candidates. As a result, the SMRR campaign started late, moved slowly because SMRR councilmembers were deeply involved in efforts to rebuild the storm-damaged Santa Monica pier, and ceded the political initiative to the opposition. The more overt message was that SMRR had been outsmarted. The opposition provided the margin for defeating all three SMRR council candidates by putting together an extremely efficient and successful absentee voter drive in selected areas of the city.

Some activists felt that SMRR had not put enough energy into communicating to residents the SMRR council's many accomplishments over the prior two-year period. Since 1979, SMRR had consistently received negative coverage in the city's only newspaper, a fairly typical rightwing outlet allied with growth machine interests, that hammered away at the council's shortcomings. The SMRR council came back with a monthly city newsletter in mid-1982 but it was a matter of too little, too late. Moreover, the opposition criticized SMRR politicians for using taxpayers' money to subsidize what is considered to be a political propaganda effort. Several SMRR leaders believed that negative media coverage could be neutralized during city council meetings that were broadcast weekly over a local radio station, and they went out of their way to communicate their accomplishments to the radio audience. But the council meetings were well attended by people who hated SMRR and used air time to criticize and condemn the SMRR council. This forced the city hall radicals to defend themselves and make counteraccusations, lending credibility to the opposition's argument that SMRR's main accomplishment was to polarize city politics. Overall, SMRR's campaign literature was not effective enough to overcome negative media images or to focus voters' attention on the council's environmental legislation, citizen participation efforts, and social services programs.

Activists also felt somewhat outsmarted by the opposition's campaign. The anti-SMRR people continually pressed forward the idea that the SMRR council alienated people, polarizing the city by attacking anyone who disagreed with the council majority. For example, opposition leader Thomas Laramore told a reporter, "When people tried to speak at city council meetings, you were continually insulted and if you didn't agree with Ruth Goldway on everything, you were treated as a rightwing extremist."[8] The opposition's alternative to polarized politics was represented symbolically in its new name: the All Santa Monica Coalition (ASMC). The ASMC promised to take the high ground by ensuring that all segments of the Santa Monica community would be heard and influential in city politics. SMRR leaders were unwilling to take the lion's share of blame for polarization but they agreed that it was a problem that hurt them on election day. Ruth Yannatta Goldway's farewell speech to the council included the statement that "I am particularly hopeful that . . . the next two years will not have the rancor or anxiety or personal criticism that were so prevalent during the past two years," and Kenneth Edwards' acceptance speech as new city mayor pointed out the importance "of creating peace and tranquility in this community," which begins by political competitors "treating each other with respect and dignity."[9] According to some activists, SMRR supporters did not vote partly because they were upset with the "rancor" of local politics and they perceived that SMRR leaders had been fueling it.

Relatedly, some local analysts looked back on the campaign and wondered whether the coalition had been wise in running three candidates for the three contested council seats. SMRR had created the possibility of a 7-0 council majority for itself without reserving a single seat for an opposition voice. Moreover, analysts asked if SMRR should have endorsed delegate slates for the city's two school boards, suggesting the intrusion of politics into the sphere of educational administration. These decisions invited the opposition to come down hard on SMRR as a "political machine" wanting total control of the city and cementing that control by distributing political patronage to allies such as the Ocean Park Community Organization people. One local editorial read:

> There are undoubtedly those who will quickly deny that the present majority at Santa Monica city hall comprises a political machine, but it is our contention that former Chicago Mayor Richard Daley, the late Tom Pendergast of Kansas City and others of that type would be proud of what is going on here. Obviously, we do not feel such should be the case.[10]

Opposition councilmember William Jennings, who had bolted SMRR years earlier because he considered it an elitist, democratic centralist organization, commented to the press, "The only issue in this election is whether one group of 30 or 40 people should control all seven seats."[11] Jennings and other ASMC people also decried SMRR school board endorsements as an extension of machine-style politics into an enterprise where professional expertise should reign.

The SMRR leaders were on the defensive. KerryAnn Lobel emphasized SMRR's record of "bringing together people who until four years ago did not have a voice in the community."[12] Ruth Yannatta Goldway argued for the necessity of having "seven strong voices" on the council to defend rent control against juridical and legislative attempts to gut it.[13] And Kenneth Edwards tried to redefine the issue in terms of "democracy":

> If we really look at what the meaning of democracy is, it's victory by a majority and that's the case in all elections; and when we attribute any other motives or any other definition to what a 7-0 or a 5-2 council may mean, we are really defaming the integrity of this entire city and all its residents. When people go to the polls, they exercise their democratic right to vote and they choose those people who they want to represent them.[14]

At the same time, the SMRR-endorsed school board candidates argued that their slates were functions of the exigencies of campaign financing as well as a strategy for ensuring broad communitywide representation. In one case, a school board candidate found herself in the position of having to deny that she was an agent of Tom Hayden's political machine: "I have never been trained by CED, I have never been to a CED meeting and have no contact with CED members to my knowledge, at least on the level of their CED interests." [15] Despite these attempts at denial and redefinition, the combination of SMRR campaign decisions and defensiveness lent enough credibility to ASMC charges to keep some of SMRR's supporters from voting.

The most widespread explanation for the 1983 voter turnout pattern was that SMRR did not convince its supporters that rent control was still a "political" issue. SMRR took its rent control base for granted. It did not put enough energy into persuading tenants that the future of Santa Monica rent control depended on having a supportive city council. The ASMC people deftly sidestepped rent control by coming out in support of it, or as Christine Reed put it, "We're all for rent control now. It's a motherhood issue in Santa Monica. No one who is against rent control is going to get elected in the foreseeable future." [16] The ASMC candidates did suggest, however, that there were problems with how rent control was being administered, reinforcing the notion that rent control had largely become a technical matter. And if it was a technical matter, then it was a concern best left to the experts rather than an issue that would draw tenants to the polls. The main lesson of this election, according to SMRR campaign manager Parke Skelton, was that SMRR must repoliticize rent control: "The way you get renters to vote is to convince them that the other side is a serious threat to rent control." [17]

In an important sense, the SMRR leadership had a vested interest in explaining the election losses as a function of voter turnout brought on by poor campaign tactics. Such explanations allowed the leaders to avoid a reassessment of their principles or policy priorities. SMRR politicians could continue to assume that they did represent the city majority rather than raise conceivably relevant questions about coalition goals that would most certainly cause fractures in activist ranks. Also, the advantage of focusing on voter turnout and campaign tactics was that they could be viewed as "problems" that were amenable to the familiar problem-solving techniques of professionals. SMRR could hire a year-round organizer rather than wait until just before elections to gear up its campaigns; it could investigate and utilize systematic techniques for improving its public image, communicating its achievements, and broadcasting its openness to diverse viewpoints; and it could employ some of its city hall leverage to ensure that the adverse judicial decisions that weakened the rent control board remained an important political issue in the city. In sum, the SMRR leadership mostly learned from defeat that it had a pragmatic need to become even more professional.

The Back to Basics Approach

Some rank-and-file activists approached their analysis of the election by looking mainly at the second trend, which showed that SMRR candidates had lost support in all parts of Santa Monica. This approach made sense to them because their own growing ambivalence toward SMRR politics made it understandable that others would begin to withdraw support. They had originally joined or worked with SMRR groups to be part of a movement that stood for what they considered important principles. But between 1981 and 1983, they witnessed those principles being compromised and sometimes ignored by the city hall radicals. For these activists, the election losses served as an opportunity to get back to basics, that is, to reconsider the meaning and direction of grassroots politics in Santa Monica.

Was SMRR really a grassroots organization? The making of its 1983 campaign did not afford a positive answer. The coalition was more or less moribund until just before the election. It did not serve as a forum for open discussions about which issues should be highlighted in the campaign, nor did it involve the general activist population in the process of sifting and winnowing a pool of potential candidates. The basic decisions came from the top.

SMRR was slow in revving up its campaign machinery, in part, due to sheer cockiness. Kenneth Edwards told me that his SMRR colleagues were in no hurry to put together the campaign because their attitude was, "We beat them once and we'll beat them again"—the same attitude the old growth machine city council had had just prior to its defeat by SMRR candidates.[18] There may have been some justification for this attitude in 1983. After all, SMRR was an acronym that stood for Santa Monicans for Renters' Rights and renters were still the vast majority of the local population. Meanwhile, SMRR's activist base was in no position to assume campaign initiative. Many people were working at ongoing projects in community organizations, citizen advisory councils, city government, Tom Hayden's State Assembly campaign, other CED matters, Democratic party politics, single-issue politics, and more. They simply did not have enough time to work through SMRR's organizational procedures to get things moving. Further, they had largely come to depend on SMRR leaders to take the initiative. In retrospect, it was clear to activists that the campaign was not launched until SMRR's city council leadership decided to press the button.

When the decision was made, two months before the election, time was a scarce commodity. The coalition leadership took it upon itself to find the most suitable candidates. The Ocean Park "clique," working under the assumption that everyone would support Ruth Yannatta Goldway's candidacy for re-election, offered up two more young and "trustworthy" Ocean Park people for the two remaining slots on the city council slate: long-time Ocean Park activist KerryAnn Lobel and former rent control board chairman William Allen. However, Goldway favored a "senior citizen for one of the positions" and the Santa Monica CED chapter wanted someone from outside of Ocean Park on the slate.[19] The leadership brokering process resulted in the Reverend Alvin Smith replacing William Allen as the coalition's third council candidate. Allen bowed out gracefully, commending the coalition for "trying to expand from our original activists to reach out to other areas of town and to a diversified group of people."[20] The Goldway-Lobel-Smith slate was then presented to the Democratic Club, whose choice was either to okay it or stand accused of upsetting the coalition applecart with the election just around the corner. "We were intimidated," a Democratic Club member told me.[21] And thus the Democratic Club and other coalition members went along with the slate. SMRR's formal confirmation of the candidates was mere ritual.

With no time left for broad-gauged discussion on SMRR's campaign platform and no apparent desire by the SMRR leadership to encourage such discussion, the candidates mostly rehearsed earlier campaigns. Yesterday's rent control achievements were replayed; individual candidates expressed a more or less predictable set of priorities; and coalition leaders drew on past experience and professional advice to cue candidates on voter preferences. Those rank-and-file activists concerned about issues other than rent control had little opportunity to be heard; those who opposed running three candidates had difficulty finding listeners. One might make a case that the absence of serious grassroots discussion all but eliminated the arguments that would have been a counterweight to the campaign decisions that helped produce election failures. While some activists hinted at such a case, several were quite explicit in saying that they were in the uncomfortable position of agreeing with the ASMC opposition that SMRR had indeed become a top-heavy political machine.

The April 1983 election also raised the question about where the coalition was going. Several months before the election, the opposition publicized a tape recording of a talk that Derek Shearer had delivered at a 1981 conference on local elections; several weeks prior to the election, the ASMC leadership mailed a seven-minute version of the tape to 15,000 Santa Monica voters. In both instances, Shearer's talk received considerable play in the local newspaper.

Shearer was heard telling an amused audience, "You have to understand that political campaigns are not educational vehicles. . . . What you do is play on [voters'] feelings and sentiments about what's going on in society," which could mean producing campaign literature that shows an elderly tenant couple looking "a little bit like an Auschwitz picture" or perhaps a cancer victim saying, "Before I die, I'm voting for Ruth Yannatta and rent control."[22] The tape also had Shearer saying, "While we cannot use the 'S' word [socialism] too effectively . . . we found the word 'economic democracy' sells. You can take it door to door like Fuller brushes."[23] SMRR campaign manager Parke Skelton immediately denounced the opposition's mailing of "what is obviously a doctored, slickly edited tape."[24] But many activists recognized in the tape a familiar strain of SMRR *realpolitik* that had informed earlier elections. Now, however, it struck them differently. In 1981, such political entrepreneurship was seen as an effective means for winning the power necessary to realizing SMRR's core principles; in 1983, when two years of city hall power had yielded little principled change and considerable compromise, political toughness was viewed as a questionable technique for maintaining the power of politicians whose pragmatism often betrayed core values.

While Santa Monica radicals might disagree on whether such naked political pragmatism was an embarrassment or a necessity, they were reminded that the meaning of electioneering and the goals of the coalition were rarely discussed anymore. SMRR had been so consumed by running the city that its various goals had somehow been submerged. After SMRR forged its "Principles of Unity" in early 1981, the most common mode of coalition talk and action had been interest group bargaining. For example, neighborhood groups made demands, the SMRR councilmembers weighed them against competing demands, and temporary bargains were made. This process did not address questions of principle, much less identify or reduce disagreements over values. Rather, it silenced debate over basic principles. But many activists were concerned about principles. Some were upset with city council decisions that denied core principles, and some wanted to voice their discontent publicly. The storm that raged over the council's Israel resolution made this clear but quieter storms brewed throughout SMRR's first two years in power. One of them broke weeks before the April 1983 election and raged for a short time afterwards.

Since SMRR councilmembers had come to power, the Ocean Park Community Organization (OPCO) and the Pico Neighborhood Association (PNA) had engaged in a series of mild conflicts with city officials. Some of the neighborhood activists felt that their own organizations should have been more independent in pressing their political demands and that the city hall radicals should have been less heavy-handed in forging and enforcing compromises. These concerns became especially salient just before the April 1983 election. That was when opposition councilmember Christine Reed sent a letter to the Department of Housing and Urban Development (HUD) claiming that OPCO and PNA had violated their funding contracts by engaging in politics: both neighborhood organizations had publicized their views on an upcoming ballot proposition. Because city government was responsible for administering the HUD grants, Reed also asked city manager John Alschuler to cut off funding to both neighborhood groups. HUD referred Reed's letter to Alschuler and Alschuler responded that he was launching an investigation into the matter, making it clear that infractions of contract prohibitions against political activities would indeed result in funding cutbacks.[25] The unmistakable message from city hall was that OPCO and PNA had virtually no "human scale" autonomy because they were the city's financial dependents.

Alschuler's message was reinforced by two post-election events. First, Alschuler issued the results of his investigation. He found that both In the neighborhood organizations had violated their contracts and warned Shadow of them, "Repeated violations will result in either a reduction of funding or Defeat a denial of program eligibility."[26] OPCO and PNA were reduced simply to denying the violations. The warning combined with a similar one to Mid-City Neighbors (MCN) dispelled any residual illusions that the neighborhood groups had been empowered in a serious way. Second, OPCO's city funding was suddenly cut from $117,598 per year to $25,000 per year in the June 1983 city budget hearings. In essence, city attorney Robert Myers disqualified councilmember James Conn from voting on the OPCO allocation because of a conflict of interest: Conn's church rented space to OPCO. Without Conn's vote, SMRR's 4–3 majority was reduced to a 3–3 faceoff, which allowed the ASMC opposition to eliminate nearly 80 percent of OPCO funding.[27] There was also some question whether Kenneth Edwards' vote should be counted because Edwards served on the board of two social services agencies tied to Conn's church, which rented space to OPCO. Conceivably, the interlocking network of leftwing friends and neighbors that had sustained SMRR unity would mean the undoing of SMRR power despite its city council majority. Ultimately, some legal wrangling supported Conn's and Edwards' right to vote and OPCO's full funding was restored, but activists in all of the city's neighborhood groups learned that their very survival was contingent on a tenuous city council majority.

Relatedly, some SMRR activists had spent nearly two years building up resentment about the limits of participatory democracy and the growth of professional influence in city government. They lamented the shortage of blacks, Hispanics, women, seniors, and low income people in key city hall posts as well as the ease with which the council allocated high salaries and fat consultant fees to affluent white professionals. They were sensitive to how little the council had done to empower low income people, and they were not overly surprised at the extraordinarily low voter turnout in the Pico neighborhood—as low as 32 percent in some precincts. Their explanation did not focus on mistaken campaign techniques or historical nonvoting among low income groups. Instead, they felt that the SMRR city council did not take the needs of these people seriously enough and therefore did not win their support. The bitter contrast was with how seriously the council took matters concerning the pier and harmonious relations with the business community.

Grassroots disenchantment with the gap between principled rhetoric and actual policy was fairly diffuse until Allan Heskin wrote an essay called "After the Battle Is Won: Political Contradictions in Santa Monica."[28] The essay was an insider's critique of SMRR, one that articulated publicly what many radicals had felt privately. Heskin argued that SMRR had failed to develop a coherent vision beyond rent control.

He pointed out, for example, that coalition members had at least nine different positions on housing policy that ranged from "no growth" to "encouraging and exploiting nearly all forms of development to raise money to do some undescribed progressive housing policy in the future." On the other hand, SMRR people had no distinctive positions on many policy issues because they avoided the discussion of sensitive topics that could cause coalition fragmentation. Furthermore, the avoidance of discussion was enforced through the practice of democratic centralism, pressure being put on people who articulated problems after council decisions had already been made. The coalition, Heskin continued, showed no real interest in fostering the mass involvement that might open up leftwing dialogue and even be the basis for a democratically derived vision. The SMRR cadre felt that people outside of their immediate circle did not have the political consciousness or the professional competence to make important judgments. And the SMRR councilmembers preferred to consolidate their own power, implicitly in the name of their own political consciousness and their appointees' professional competence. This leftwing elitism militated against grassroots mobilizations by neighborhood organizations, belied the rhetoric of participatory democracy, and displaced socioeconomic justice with efficiency as the heart of government policymaking.

Lacking vision, the coalition leadership could not excite the "passion" of activists; practicing elitism, the SMRR leaders did incite leftwing antipathy. After the April 1983 election and the widespread circulation of Heskin's essay, the silent concerns of disenchanted activists came pouring out.[29] Some people felt that their leaders had sold out. Many were unhappy and confused. Almost everyone admitted that the passionate commitments of the early days had disappeared. And quite a few, like Heskin, felt that the election losses pointed to a pressing need for SMRR to reassess the relationship between its principles and practices lest the grassroots continue to wilt.

Good Energy?

Two months after the April 1983 election losses, SMRR staff director Thom Poffenberger stated, "There's a lot of good energy. The complacency's been shaken out of people."[30] The immediate aftermath of electoral shock was talk. People from all segments of the Santa Monica left began to reconsider the significance of early rent control battles, SMRR, city politics, and the future. Both the pragmatics of campaign politics and the principles behind grassroots mobilizations were informally scrutinized as people aired their hopes and vented their fears. It was even possible to believe that a rebirth of activist passion was in the offing. "The central question," Dennis Zane suggested, "is keeping people's energy high. What losing does is it shakes out a lot of overconfidence that builds up when you win regularly."[31] As it turned out, the idea of keeping people's energy high was itself a product of middle class overconfidence.

Local talk quickly focused on the need to broaden SMRR's base of support, to revitalize the coalition, and to make it work better. But such talk forked into two directions. Some people understood it in terms of reaching beyond tenants to a larger middle class audience. They wanted to extend a peace offering to more small business people, affluent homeowners, and even the landlords who stood with the ASMC opposition. The SMRR coalition would then be able to demonstrate that it truly represented all segments of the Santa Monica community, enhance the electability of its candidates, and secure the political power necessary for protecting past gains and promoting future reforms. For other activists, broadening SMRR's base of support suggested rebuilding and reinvigorating the grassroots movement that had given birth to the coalition. Membership invitations should be extended to friendly individuals and leftwing or progressive groups in the city; the new members would raise issues of principles, enrich activist participation, and perhaps recapture some of yesteryear's passion. For a brief moment, it looked like SMRR was going to open up debate about the relationship between its principles and politics.

That moment was shortlived. SMRR's constituent groups got into an argument over how to restructure the organization. Should SMRR admit new individual members or new group members or both? Should the coalition switch to majority decisionmaking or should it retain the unanimity requirement? These procedural questions were especially important to the Democratic Club. Its members already experienced second-class citizenship in the coalition, and both organizational growth and majority rule threatened to erode the Democratic Club's influence even more. Further, members feared that organizational growth might mean the admission of ideologically oriented groups that could fragment the coalition and increase political polarization in the city. Kenneth Edwards stated, "There are quite a few groups that want to get into SMRR. The Democratic Club has to have some concern. Some of them may have principles contrary to the Democratic party."[32] Rather than reassess SMRR principles and then decide what kind of net to cast, SMRR activists tried to strike a procedural compromise and, failing that, simply maintained the organization's original structure.

In the midst of this internal bargaining, the Ocean Park Electoral Network (OPEN) decided to disband. OPEN chairwoman Marianne Boretz denied that the disbanding was a product of SMRR's internal wrangling; but it is reasonable to believe that the election losses combined with the failure of the coalition to agree on a coherent direction motivated the withdrawal of some OPEN activists. Boretz explained that "some people [in OPEN] felt like they could accomplish more by working inside of other organizations in SMRR" and then added that "some people were dissatisfied with the way city government works with community organizations."[33] This same mixture of pragmatic and principled reasoning explained why the Santa Monica Fair Housing Alliance (SMFHA) would disband within the year. Meanwhile, the local CED chapter was about to enter into a period of inertia when it became difficult to get together enough chapter members to hold a meeting. The "good energy" dissipated rather quickly. And even some "bad energy" on the city council became apparent. I can recall one city council meeting on restoring OPCO's funding when Dennis Zane made a motion and no one among his SMRR colleagues was willing to second it.

With grassroots enthusiasm dwindling, SMRR's organizational future in doubt, and its councilmembers uncertain of their direction, political initiative shifted to city hall professionals. More power accrued to city manager John Alschuler, whose values were apparent in his praise for one new city appointee: "He's a very talented young man and will be known as someone who is fair, impartial, and professional."[34] City attorney Robert Myers also played a larger role. His approach was demonstrated in his endorsement of the election of an incumbent judge who carried out his "judicial duties in a fair and impartial manner"—despite the fact that SMRR had endorsed the judge's leftwing challenger. Myers added, "I just think, from a personal perspective, I find it somewhat unfortunate that we have to have judges running for election."[35] The professionals' deep belief in fairness, impartiality, and expertise undergirded their tendency to depoliticize city government affairs in Santa Monica. They brought under close scrutiny the *political* activities of neighborhood organizations and rent control board employees, and they circumvented some of the radical political impulses of several city planning commissioners. They also employed *administrative* exigencies of fiscal responsibility to justify making deals with McDonald's and other corporate enterprises. Many activists' discontents were magnified when they witnessed the SMRR city council majority going along with the bureaucrats' efforts to compromise core principles.

In fact, the SMRR councilmembers did not seriously address activists' discontents when they more or less decided to take the professional approach to the next election. SMRR hired Thom Poffenberger as a full-time professional organizer who would prepare the coalition for the next election well in advance of the actual voting. Poffenberger's job was made easier by the fact that there would be no serious debate over principles and policies during candidate selection processes because everyone expected SMRR's four city council incumbents to run for re-election. Poffenberger could therefore concentrate his energies on year-round fundraising and campaign strategy. Meanwhile, the SMRR council majority, following Kenneth Edwards and city professionals, was changing its public image to demonstrate that it could deal fairly with homeowners and the business community. The SMRR council supported bipartisan efforts to facilitate tenant homebuying; and it cooperated with the Chamber of Commerce on the new business tax structure, development of the pier, revitalization of the Santa Monica Mall, stimulating the tourist industry, and the rewriting of the city's land use element. By the time the next municipal election rolled around, the ASMC opposition would have difficulty persuading the public that the SMRR politicians were a divisive element in the city.

The SMRR leaders addressed the problem of voter turnout in two specific ways. First, they sponsored a ballot proposition that would change Santa Monica's elections from April of odd-numbered years when only local issues were at stake to November of even-numbered years to coincide with the national, state, and county races that historically attract a larger turnout. Kenneth Edwards led the fight for what became Proposition Y on the June 1984 ballot, arguing that any reform that enhanced voter participation deserved community support. He estimated that "as many as 15,000 new voters" would be drawn into local elections.[36] Given Santa Monica's demography, nearly 12,000 of the new voters would be tenants likely to support SMRR candidates. Councilmember Christine Reed led the fight against changing election dates, calling the proposition SMRR's "last ditch stand, a desperate attempt to stay in power."[37] The proposition passed by a 53.3 to 46.7 percent margin, which meant that SMRR's four council incumbents would face re-election in November 1984 rather than April 1985.

Second, the SMRR leadership took steps to ensure that the new tenant voters understood that rent control was still an important political issue and that a city council friendly to rent control was needed to defend it. The court decisions that whittled away at the powers of the rent control board kept the issue alive in the city. So did the city attorney's attempts to win reversals on appeal to higher courts. Meanwhile, the rent control board and the SMRR councilmembers engineered a ballot proposition that would clarify the original 1979 rent control charter amendment and reword it in ways that would reestablish greater rent board autonomy. The proposition would appear on the November 1984 ballot, making rent control an issue that coincided with the city council elections. If this strategy worked, rent control in Santa Monica would be strengthened and the four SMRR candidates associated with it would be re-elected; if the proposition passed but SMRR did not retain its council majority, at least rent board autonomy would be guaranteed and thereby insulated from the brunt of a predictable attack by an ASMC majority on the council.

The wisdom of SMRR's electoral strategy became somewhat doubtful as the November 1984 election approached. On the one hand, the strategy all but ignored grassroots disenchantment and thereby invited the competition of non-SMRR candidates who hoped to win away support within the activist community. Gerald Goldman, a labor lawyer who had served as a SMRR member of the rent control board and later represented rent control board employees, announced his candidacy for the city council. He pointed to SMRR's shortcomings as his reason for running. The coalition, he said, operated in an "undemocratic" and "fascistic" manner. Indeed, "SMRR is a danger to society." SMRR councilmembers were duplicitous, he continued. "When I saw the SMRR council, who professed to care about workers' rights, and I saw the way they treated the rent board employees, I thought they were dishonest and untrustworthy." Goldman characterized his candidacy as an attempt to establish a "progressive but more open-minded" presence on the city council, an appeal to radicals who felt that the coalition had become an elitist organization that was more opportunistic than principled.[38] Furthermore, M. Douglas Willis, a liberal black professional involved in family services and also the local chapter of the NAACP, announced his candidacy. Willis voiced his agreement with much of SMRR's policymaking but based his campaign on the coalition's failure to provide adequate representation of the Pico neighborhood, minorities, and low income people.[39] Implicitly, both Goldman and Willis appealed to principles that SMRR activists voiced but that the SMRR council had given low priority.

On the other hand, the ASMC opposition dusted off and refined its successful 1983 strategy for the November 1984 campaign. ASMC endorsed only two candidates for the four open seats, demonstrating that its intent was not to dominate the whole city council as SMRR had tried to do in the past. Furthermore, ASMC's endorsees were two moderate Democrats: Herb Katz, a professional architect who promised to take politics out of city government, and Irene Zivi, a community organizer who identified herself as a feminist. Both ASMC candidates supported rent control and decried SMRR attempts to make it the central campaign issue all over again and thereby polarize the city. Katz put it this way:

> Let's get off the oneness of rent control and get on to other things. We've dwelled on it and dwelled on it. If the council weakens rent control, the people will rise up either through the initiative process, or by voting the councilmembers out of office. But the feeling that they [SMRR] must be protectors of rent control and that no one else can do it is a denunciation of democracy.[40]

Zivi especially emphasized the gap between SMRR's spoken commitment to democracy and its performance in city government:

> The thing that irritates me to no end is that the majority says they are democratic, but they stack the boards and commissions with people who agree with them, and they've effectively shut out many segments of our community. My main motive for running is that I

don't feel our current council majority operates in a democratic
fashion, and I'd like to see the council be a place where everyone
feels welcome and is treated in a fair fashion.[41]

The ASMC candidates, working under the assumption that they would
carry the more conservative vote in the city, concentrated their efforts on
portraying SMRR, once again, as a political machine. They did not talk
much about disagreeing with SMRR candidates on substantive political
issues. Overall, their appeal was to affluent tenants who, in the past, had
supported SMRR for lack of a liberal alternative or had not voted at all.

Squeezed between left liberal candidates who threatened to erode the
activist base and moderate Democrats who hoped to be the liberal alternative for affluent tenants, SMRR candidates' electoral chances were
complicated by two last-minute imponderables. As a result of poor planning if not plain foolishness, Dolores Press filed a nominating petition
with just over the one-hundred-signature minimum. When several of the
signatures were disqualified, Press was three signatures short and therefore ineligible to have her name placed on the ballot. Various court
appeals failed and Press was forced to run as a write-in candidate, significantly reducing her chances for re-election and therefore SMRR's
chances for maintaining its city council majority. Then, one month before
the November election, a three-judge state appeals court unanimously
overturned the lower court ruling that had deprived the rent control
board of its autonomy. At any other time, SMRR leaders would have
celebrated the new ruling but now it was a mixed blessing. Why should
Santa Monica voters support a proposition aimed at ensuring rent control board autonomy if the state court had already reestablished board
autonomy? Moreover, why should residents support a SMRR slate
pledged to defend rent control when the state court had already recognized its legitimacy? No one was quite sure how Press's write-in campaign or the court ruling would affect the election outcome; but everyone
more or less knew that the "good energy" following the April 1983 electoral losses had pretty much dissipated before the specter of SMRR's
loss of municipal power in 1984.

For Want of Principles?

SMRR's four city council incumbents ran as incumbents—that is, there
was no real talk about goals like empowerment or building models of
leftwing governments, about new experiments in participatory democracy, or about contesting corporate hegemony and creating economic
democracy. Rather, the SMRR councilmembers ran on their records of
being good governors.

Dennis Zane linked his future to the rent control base. "I think it's
correct to say," he told a reporter, "that I'm the councilmember who

focuses the most attention and leadership on protecting renters and rental housing." Regarding the contention that rent control was no longer a serious political issue, Zane stated, "Rent control will always be an issue in the community as long as the landlord association supports anti-rent control candidates and anti-rent control measures."[42] James Conn put his campaign emphasis on his record of facilitating the arts and helping to settle the airport dispute. "I think the arts have the capacity for altering the way in which we understand ourselves in the urban environment. They remind us of our own humanity." Conn added his pride at developing plans "to build a new airport, make it quieter for the neighbors, make it safe and generate money."[43] The SMRR council, through the mediation of John Alschuler, had worked out a compromise with the Federal Aviation Administration over the disposition of the Santa Monica airport to end a twenty-year struggle and Conn had helped broker the compromise.

Neither Zane nor Conn was nonplussed by the fact that these issues did not distinguish them from their opposition, who also supported rent control, the arts, redoing the airport, and some of the SMRR council's other accomplishments. They simply wanted recognition for past accomplishments and another four years in office to protect and extend them. In Conn's words, "Now the question is, can we see them through?"[44]

Dolores Press and Kenneth Edwards mostly replayed the same themes that they ran on in 1981, this time citing a record of achievements. Press talked about support for labor and feminism but now with a somewhat greater focus on social services, where the SMRR council had committed considerable energy: "The first responsibility of government is the concern for human needs, particularly when these areas have been so decimated on a federal and state level. It's very important that local government have the political will to take up the slack."[45] And while Press again expressed her populist distrust of slick professionals and lawyers in government, Kenneth Edwards again expressed his liberal faith in professional governance: "This city is in the most financially solid shape in its history. We have increased citizen participation and have a new working relationship with the business community."[46] Like their Ocean Park colleagues, Press and Edwards simply wanted to communicate all of the good things that they had done; as Edwards said, "The main issue the city will be facing is whether or not people will recognize the achievements of the council majority the past 3½ years."[47]

The "hottest" substantive issue in the November 1984 election was Proposition TT, an initiative intended to make the city of Santa Monica into a nuclear-free zone. Since 1981, some sixty American cities had prohibited nuclear weapons work within their jurisdictions; but these prohibitions were symbolic because none of those cities had ongoing nuclear weapons work in their jurisdictions. In Santa Monica, however, the proposition threatened the research and development activities of five corporations: Rand Corporation, Puroflow Corporation, G. & H. Technology, Systems Development Corporation, and Lear Siegler. The passage and implementation of Proposition TT would force these companies either to abrogate some of their defense contracts or at least relocate some of their facilities outside of Santa Monica. Kelly Hayes-Raitt, who directed the campaign for a grassroots group called Citizens for a Nuclear-Free Santa Monica, said, "The powerful statement Santa Monica would make to our federal government would reinforce the ongoing grassroots and national efforts for arms control."[48] What did the SMRR city council candidates have to say about a ballot proposition that lent itself to principles such as the affirmation of human life over profits or community control over centralized decisionmaking in Washington, D.C.? Very little.

The SMRR politicians initially supported the proposition to the extent that they voted to put it on the municipal ballot. But they made no effort to make it a major campaign issue. They did not want to be on the receiving end of accusations that they supported a ballot proposition that was antibusiness, could cause corporate flight and the loss of jobs and tax revenues, and was probably unconstitutional according to their own city attorney. Furthermore, the SMRR politicians did not agree among themselves on the wisdom of the proposition. James Conn gave it some public support but Kenneth Edwards came out against it, while Dennis Zane and Dolores Press generally avoided addressing it. Proposition TT did not become a SMRR campaign issue. And when the Santa Monica *Outlook* editorially condemned the proposition as a measure that "would put the city in the 'Big Brother' mode of watching over research and development agencies in Santa Monica," it did not mention the SMRR councilmembers who, in turn, did not contest the newspaper's definition of the issue.[49] Some activists felt that the SMRR politicians had missed an opportunity to restate their commitment to core principles because they had become captives of political pragmatism.

With one important exception, SMRR's "good government" campaign brought in the votes. SMRR's campaign operations ran smoothly and Dolores Press's write-in effort stirred even SMRR skeptics to participate in her "underdog" race. The SMRR council's record since April 1983 had been one of moderation; its campaign focused on re-electing responsible incumbents and not winning complete political control; and charges that the coalition was an ideological machine that polarized city politics were not very persuasive this time around. Most important, switching the election date from April of odd-numbered years to November of even-numbered years produced approximately 12,000 more voters, most of whom were tenants prone to support SMRR candidates. The overall result was victory for nine of the ten candidates that the coalition endorsed for city council, the rent control board, and city school boards; SMRR also won the several proposition races that the coalition had endorsed. "SMRR Is Still Strong" read the bold print Santa Monica *Outlook* headline when election results were announced.

The important exception was that Dolores Press lost her city council seat. She amassed 12,652 votes, which put her seventh in a contest where only the top four vote-getters won city council seats. ASMC opposition candidate Herb Katz outpolled her by nearly 5,000 votes for a fourth-place finish that assured the ASMC opposition of its own 4–3 majority on the new city council. Whether or not Press would have won had her name been printed on the ballot was moot. For all of its electoral successes, SMRR's lone defeat in November 1984 meant that it lost control of the city council and therefore of Santa Monica municipal government. Overnight, SMRR's agenda shifted to minimizing the damage that the ASMC opposition could do before the next election.

Even if Press had won and SMRR had retained its political control, the November 1984 election would still have raised serious questions about SMRR's ability to adhere to its core principles while practicing political pragmatism. More than anyone else, Kenneth Edwards ran a campaign that spoke not to radical principles but to his record of moderation, professionalism, and accommodation to business interests. Edwards' pragmatism worked in that he outpaced all other candidates by a considerable margin, receiving 25,780 votes to second-place finisher James Conn's 20,073 votes. Similarly, the same election had Tom Hayden run an extraordinarily pragmatist campaign for re-election to his Santa Monica area State Assembly seat. Hayden stressed his record as a responsible state legislator and a representative of all of his constituents while attacking his opponent, viciously some said, for a twenty-year-old drug bust. Hayden largely avoided discussion of substantive principles or issues, in part, by refusing to debate his conservative opponent in a public forum. Like Edwards, Hayden won re-election by a substantial margin.

Meanwhile, James Conn and Dennis Zane (who placed third with 19,954 votes) ran with somewhat greater emphasis on issues such as the environment and rent control that at least evoked memories of SMRR's core principles. Yet that emphasis combined with their incumbency gave them little more than a 2,000-vote victory over fourth-place Herb Katz, who received 17,424 votes. Furthermore, the ballot proposition intended to ensure the autonomy of the rent control board passed by a slender thread, 53 percent of the voters supporting it and 47 percent opposing it. That was SMRR's narrowest victory on any rent control issue since the coalition's founding. One possible explanation for these narrow margins was that SMRR's base of popular support on principles and issues had not grown but may even have diminished. And part of the reason was that residents were having a hard time distinguishing SMRR's positions from those of the opposition.

What some activists considered SMRR's want of principles was ap-

parent in the fight for a nuclear-free Santa Monica. SMRR had become
the main center for leftwing fundraising in Santa Monica and its leaders' decision to steer clear of the antinuke issue essentially condemned Citizens for a Nuclear-Free Santa Monica to nickel-and-dime fundraising. The grassroots group was able to raise $17,000 in small contributions but the proposition's opposition easily doubled this figure by direct appeals to the Rand Corporation, Lear Siegler, and the other affected corporations.[50] Furthermore, SMRR's distance from the issue meant that Proposition TT supporters could not rely on the city's well-known public figures to help define the issue, legitimate it, and defend it against some fairly outrageous criticisms; the opposition, however, could rely on numerous local notables and candidates to make unanswered criticisms of the measure. Proposition TT was decisively defeated with 61.4 percent of the voters against it, though Santa Monicans had as decisively supported a statewide nuclear freeze initiative a few years earlier. Also, Gerald Goldman and M. Douglas Willis, who entered the council race because they felt that SMRR politicians were wanting in principles, received, respectively, 6,369 and 4,310 votes. One can make a case that a significant minority of voters supported these candidates' shoestring campaigns because they were interested in principles concerning worker rights, minority representation, and social justice; they apparently wanted more than "good government" from their politicians.

Philosophers and Politicians

Stephen Rivers, who served as Tom Hayden's press aide during the November 1984 election, was asked by a local reporter to assess SMRR's electoral performance. Rivers replied:

> We won everything on the ballot. It's quite clear SMRR has a very strong base in the city, and if it weren't for the snafu with Dolores Press and the ballot, we would have had four [council seats] instead of three. It's clear that SMRR is the majority voice in the city. I don't think that can be disputed.[51]

If election results are indicative of general public opinion, then SMRR could rightfully claim to be "the majority voice" in Santa Monica despite having lost control of city government. It was, however, a majority voice that spoke quite softly on matters of radical principles and that supported very modest reforms in the city.

One might make the case that the SMRR leaders had sacrificed radical principles for conventional liberal pragmatism between 1979 and 1984. Grassroots activists did not become coparticipants in an expanding movement so much as the object of their leaders' top-down decision-making in an increasingly bureaucratic political coalition. Neighborhood

groups were not empowered but better represented. Participatory democracy in the city was mostly symbolic while professional authority thrived.
And issues related to economic justice for low income groups were given
very low priority. In the span of five years, the expression of radical principles was progressively muted and the sweeping changes envisioned
were systematically compromised as SMRR politicians consolidated
their power in city hall and worked to enhance their own re-election
chances. In light of these trends, it is not surprising that the SMRR
leaders learned from their 1983 election losses to become better political
pragmatists and thus run a 1984 campaign that all but ignored radical
principles.

What did it mean to be "the majority voice" in Santa Monica in 1984?
SMRR's majority included many residents who normally did not vote
in local elections, much less participate in local politics in more direct
ways. They voted this time because the local elections coincided with
county, state, and national elections. There was little reason to believe
that the new voters' support for SMRR candidates meant more than
that middle class liberals who sent liberal congressman Mel Levine back
to Washington and chose Walter Mondale over Ronald Reagan also
supported SMRR people who were considered more liberal than the
opposition candidates. And there was little reason to believe that voters'
support for SMRR politicians had any real relationship to SMRR's core
principles because the principles barely surfaced during the campaign.

One might extrapolate this line of thought to argue that SMRR was
evolving into an institutional microcosm of the national Democratic
party. A few discontented activists would serve the function of Jesse
Jackson's Rainbow Coalition, keeping alive basic principles and some
grassroots momentum on the political fringes. The major movement
decisions regarding candidate selection, campaign strategy, and policy
direction would be brokered between the Ocean Park version of Gary
Hart's yuppie liberalism and the Democratic Club rendering of Walter
Mondale's New Deal liberalism and the city bureaucrats' brand of liberal
new professionalism. Like so many other radical movements in American history, SMRR would have followed the pragmatist road to assimilation to the liberal mainstream.[52]

The problem with this scenario or interpretation is that it neglects
the fundamental tensions between philosophical principles and everyday
politics in the United States. Political theorist Michael Walzer poses the
problem this way:

> What is the standing of the philosopher in a democratic society?
> This is an old question; there are old tensions at work here; be-
> tween truth and opinion, reason and will, value and preference, the
> one and the many. These antipodal pairs differ from one another,
> and none of them quite matches the pair "philosophy and democ-
> racy." But they do hang together; they point to a central problem.

The philosopher claims a certain sort of authority for his conclusions; the people claim a different sort of authority for their decisions. What is the relation between the two?[53]

The philosopher, the person of principles and perhaps radical values, detaches himself or herself from the political community in order to assess its virtues and shortcomings. According to Walzer, the philosopher is an authoritarian figure with a set of abstract standards to impose on the political community. The political activist, politician, or citizen in a democratic society, however, is engaged within the political community and can never ignore the vectors of power or the directions and misdirections of public opinion that shape the political community. If the political person is a democrat, he or she must consider supporting the power of public opinion even when it seems misguided. At the very least, the politically engaged person must be willing to compromise with public opinion to remain a member of the political community.

What happens when people of principles become involved in a political community where the structures of public opinion and political power demand that they compromise? There is no obvious answer. Instead, there are persistent tensions and these tensions were manifested in the Santa Monica experiment. Neighborhood groups, leftist citizen groups, and committed radicals in and out of city government continued to demonstrate some support for SMRR's core principles against the SMRR politicians' pragmatism. One Mid-City Neighbors activist told me that his group was poised to increase demands for neighborhood power regardless of who controlled city hall after 1984.[54] Citizens for a Nuclear-Free Santa Monica planned to continue their struggle for community control over research and development in the city, and members of the city's Latino task force formulated ways to enhance Hispanic participation in Santa Monica civic life.[55] At the same time, politicized people on the rent control board and the city planning commission were in some degree still struggling against the professionalization of city hall; and non-SMRR political activists such as Gerald Goldman and M. Douglas Willis were still pressing issues such as worker rights and economic justice for the less affluent. Radical principles were not the centerpiece of SMRR's 1984 campaign strategy but they had become a legitimate part of political dialogue in the city—no small accomplishment.

In addition, the SMRR leadership and even Santa Monica's city professionals had not altogether abandoned the core principles despite the fact that they chose to compromise and broker those principles. Between 1979 and 1983, when they had known only electoral victory, SMRR politicians and bureaucrats took some conscientious risks to test what was politically possible. They supported human scale policies that promised more voice for the voiceless and potentially prefigured more decentralized control of city life. They invited more participation among more groups in the city than their predecessors could have imagined and these groups came close enough to power that they conceivably will strive for more. The city hall radicals also took some important steps toward transferring chunks of the private marketplace into the public domain, particularly on housing and development issues, perhaps setting precedents for more extensive reforms in the future.

When the SMRR politicians suffered the shocking electoral defeats and courtroom setbacks of 1983, they retrenched. They took fewer risks in the hope of consolidating past gains and protecting future political power. Certainly they compromised, ignored, and even contradicted core principles but this was not wholly a matter of political pragmatism. The SMRR people were committed to the overall principle of democracy, which was a matter of respecting public opinion even when they believed it was mistaken. In 1983, the message from the electorate seemed to be that people were not especially enthusiastic about the principles that pushed SMRR beyond rent control and that SMRR had lost some citizen support for its policies and initiatives. SMRR's successes in the November 1984 elections, the new voters notwithstanding, suggest that retrenchment may have been what the demos was demanding.

Moreover, the tensions between principles and pragmatism did not wholly disappear during that November 1984 election. Dolores Press's underdog write-in campaign demonstrated the continuing possibility of grassroots mobilizations despite SMRR's hierarchical tendencies. Many activists enthusiastically worked for Press's re-election even though they were somewhat disenchanted with SMRR and the city council. They were part of the four hundred-plus volunteers who spent hours and hours discussing the uncertainties of a write-in campaign and the coalition's future, did door-to-door canvassing, distributed campaign literature, educated people on how to do a write-in vote, and spent election day passing out pencils with which to write in their candidate's name.[56] Even SMRR's opposition was impressed by the surge of grassroots support that resulted in nearly 13,000 write-in ballots for Dolores Press.

Perhaps the main reason that tensions between mass mobilizations and hierarchy, decentralism and city hall control, amateur participation and professionalism, and radical economic rhetoric and conventionally modest economic policies persisted is that these tensions are deeply rooted in the American middle class. Both the Santa Monica radicals and their affluent constituents represent an evolving class that prides itself on ideas and ideals. They believe in autonomy and shared intelligence and service to both their communities and humanity. They are often self-conscious carriers of the more radical aspects of middle class morality and strive for its perpetuation in the face of adverse cultural, political, and economic trends in American society. Yet neither the Santa Monica radicals nor their constituents are Jeffersonian angels. They cannot govern themselves in philosophical detachment from public opinion and structural realities. They also represent an evolving middle class pragmatism that honors efficacy, expertise, and achievement, that links individual effort to reward, knowledge to authority, and public influence to success in the marketplace. They are realists who at some level believe that America's lower social strata will not be able to assume their full share of the American Dream until they develop middle class culture, skills, and influence. Thus, their more benign tendency is to help lower class people develop the necessary tools for empowerment but to defer actual empowerment to a later date. In their eyes, the price of not compromising their principles would be isolation from the political community and thus impotence.

Did the Santa Monica radicals sacrifice principles to pragmatism? Of course they did, and so too has every bona fide reformist and revolutionary who has become engaged in actual struggle for social change. More important is that Santa Monica's activists were able to sustain the tensions between principles and pragmatism to explore the political possibilities for egalitarian change in the United States. Herein lies the basis for assessing the future promise of middle class radicalism.

Part 3
The Promise

If you have built castles in the air, your work need
not be lost; that is where they should be. Now put
the foundations under them.

Henry David Thoreau

9

The Democratic Idea of America

Ideas have a power that can free untapped hope and
energy in a people. The democratic idea of America
has been and can again be a powerful weapon.

Martin Carnoy and Derek Shearer [1]

At what point does adaptation to the "American
heritage" become a synonym for adaptation to
bourgeois hegemony?

Carl Boggs [2]

The promise of middle class radicalism is that it can attract widespread popular support for egalitarian change in the United States. It can draw on America's democratic heritage, emphasize the unity of people and power rooted in the Jeffersonian past, and build a movement in favor of equal respect for people, equal protection of their interests, equal opportunity for personal growth, and, ultimately, equal power. The Santa Monica left explored the democratic idea of America, advocating a version of radical democracy that did garner considerable support among the city's affluent residents. But when they assumed municipal power, the radicals' ideals proved consistent with fairly conventional forms of elitism.

Why did SMRR's principles lose their egalitarian spark when situated in city hall? An important part of the reason involves middle class ambivalence. The middle class radicals sincerely believed in their core ideology and wanted to implement it, but they also felt justified in consolidating their own authority, professionalizing it, and adapting it to the prevailing marketplace. This tendency was reinforced by their middle class constituents, who were drawn in by radical democratic values and yet simultaneously consented to contrary norms of leadership, efficiency, and competition. The ambivalent loyalties of middle class activists and residents resulted in a propensity for political talk to focus on potentially radical notions such as empowering the powerless while everyday practice gravitated toward the rituals of mainstream "bourgeois" politics.

Still, the Santa Monica radicals can be considered pioneers in middle class ambivalence. They emerged from the tensions that define middle class life in the United States; they experimented with ways to extract some radical meanings from those tensions; and they maintained those tensions in their principles and politics in the hope of building more public support for greater equality. Their successes and failures provide us with a measure for gauging the extent to which middle class radicalism can draw on America's democratic heritage without simply adapting to elitist hegemony.

Middle Class Ambivalence

Grassroots or movement organizations are usually founded on some variant of radical democratic ideology. They are alternative organizations that honor maximum commitment and participation among members who play a direct role in dialogue, decisionmaking, and implementation. They prefigure greater democracy at the same time that they attempt to challenge elitist power structures in society. Public interest groups and political parties, on the other hand, are conventional organizations. Membership mostly involves providing financial support, usually in the form of yearly dues, to the organization. And the organizational leaders themselves manage the lobbying or political campaigns. In 1985, both the

California Campaign for Economic Democracy (CED) and the Santa
Monicans for Renters' Rights (SMRR) became hybrid organizations
that structurally reproduced the tension between alternative and conventional formats.

CED augmented its decentralized system of local chapters and intense
participation with an open membership drive. In a mass mailing portraying CED as the major barrier in California to the domination of "the
Far Right," CED executive director Jack Nicholl invited the membership of anyone who was willing to remit twenty dollars in yearly dues.
As a bonus, new members would receive free of charge the organization's
monthly newsletter, *The Economic Democrat*.[3] Almost simultaneously,
SMRR announced that it was adding to its constituent groups the opportunity for any individual to join the coalition, also for twenty dollars
a year in dues. The announcement came in the direct mailing of a new
publication called *Year Seven* (as SMRR was in its seventh year of
existence), self-described as "a journal about our quality of life—rent
control, housing, community safety, land uses, and the vitality of our city
and its government."[4] Torn between the ideal of practicing radical democracy and the pragmatism of securing a solid financial base, CED
and SMRR sought to do both.

The choice made sense for two reasons. First, it made sense in terms
of the evolution of alternative organizations from the 1960s to the 1980s.
Many of those organizations were founded in the crisis atmosphere of
the Vietnam war. But as the crisis atmosphere abated, those who had
created alternative schools, newspapers, and law collectives, for example,
could not sustain their organizations on the basis of individuals' exhaustive time, energy, and commitment; they tired of movement wages, the
impoverished conditions that eroded their own quality of life, and the
constant uncertainty of their groups' fiscal stability. Indeed, many alternative organizations did not survive "for want of any reliable flow of
income."[5] Others converted their alternative organizations into conventional ones premised on lower member expectations, higher salaries, and
steady though politically compromised sources of income. Paul Starr
writes, "Public interest organizations seem to have held up rather well.
Some have put themselves on a relatively firm foundation by mastering
sophisticated direct-mail techniques that enable them to appeal to thousands of small contributors."[6] The public interest organizations, such as
Common Cause, are not embryonic democracies but highly professionalized groups that have a proven ability to survive beyond moments of
mass political unrest and excitement stemming from a crisis atmosphere.

Neither CED nor SMRR wanted to give up their internal experiments with radical democracy, but both groups planned to survive an
era of conservativism in American politics. They compromised by becoming two-tiered organizations. CED local chapters and SMRR constituent organizations would continue to serve as settings for activists

wishing to play a direct role in organizational politics. And the individual mass memberships of twenty-dollar-a-year contributors would provide an avenue of passive support for citizens with the interest and wherewithal to ensure financial survival of the organization. Whether or not the two-tiered membership will exacerbate tensions between the idealists and the realists remains to be seen.

Second, the choice to become hybrid organizations made sense because the hybrid accurately reflects the tension between idealism and realism manifest among middle class Americans. Middle class Americans, suggests Jennifer Hochschild, "are torn between what ought to be and what apparently must be."[7] They comprise a class that inherits, mediates, and transmits democratic traditions of community and autonomy, participation and political equity, general welfare and the pursuit of happiness. They are moral idealists. At the same time, middle class Americans also constitute a class that contributes to human dependence, social control, and economic hegemony by lending their intellectual skills to the highest bidders in the marketplace. They are political realists too, compromising their morality for materialism. This middle class ambivalence explains both the fickle politics of affluent Americans and the challenge that middle class radicals face when they attempt to develop an alternative vision and strategy for the future.

Middle class ambivalence can be traced back to the American revolution. That was when relatively affluent colonists were caught in the "middle" of contending political forces. The urban and rural lower classes were struggling to increase their own social leverage by demanding a direct voice in making public policy. The British aristocrats, who ruled the colonies, were making a sustained effort to enhance their own authority and taxing power over the Americans. Both radical democracy from below and aristocratic rule from above threatened to erode the power, wealth, and status of colonial notables.

The notables had mixed feelings about the contenders. They partly identified with lower class aspirations for radical democracy that justified resistance to the British aristocrats; but they distanced themselves from lower class demands lest the ignorant and unruly mobs displace the notables. Relatedly, the affluent colonists saw some virtue in the British authority that could tame the mob though they also feared that authority as potentially tyrannical. Significantly, the notables' ambivalence did not result in political paralysis but in intellectual and political creativity: the affluent Americans lent credence to popular demands for radical democracy and at the same time set themselves up as authorities able to tame mass discontent and channel it against the British. Their efforts, according to historian Howard Zinn, "showed future generations of leaders the advantages of combining paternalism with command."[8]

The notables documented their support for radical democracy in the Declaration of Independence, which proposed a vision of the democratic citizen who "would not just participate in politics but would join in the actual creating of a political identity."[9] The idea of unifying the people and power to create a new order spread throughout the colonies, inspiring some radical experiments in constitution-making and generating broad support for the revolution. The democratic idea also informed generations of nineteenth- and twentieth-century political activists whose version of the American Dream defined political morality in terms of community, intellectual progress for all, and the leveling of political and economic opportunities.[10] This heritage persists today, manifested in grassroots citizen movements that invoke selected ideals from Paine and Jefferson to justify opposition to the established authority of powerful elites.

Never quite trusting the people, however, the colonial notables also documented their desire to tame the masses and to exercise paternalistic authority, most dramatically in the U.S. Constitution. They created a complex political system that largely reduced democratic citizenship to an occasional vote for representatives and virtually guaranteed that "the right sort of men" would rise to public office; and they thereby dissipated the popular energy that might have been mobilized in behalf of direct citizen control over public policy or over the emerging capitalist marketplace.[11] Soon, citizen passivity was wed to the capitalist ethic of individual self-aggrandizement to give rise to the American Dream of privatized success: individuals with enough savvy to outperform the competition in the marketplace deserve a more than equal share of power, wealth, and status. The older notion of paternalism with command was translated into its modern incarnation of individual consent to the authority of successful competitors, that is, modern elites.[12] Today, the conjuncture of consent and capitalism legitimates huge concentrations of private power.

Affluent middle class Americans today are heirs of the colonial notables. They have inherited both the radical democratic values antagonistic to elite power and the notion of privatized success combined with consent to elite authority. They lend credence to the idea of unifying the people and power but they also practice the political passivity and economic competition that empowers elites. They search for community in suburbs and satellite cities but "still dream of individual success and 'getting ahead' (meaning nearly anything other than falling behind)."[13] They advocate more equality but also contribute to inequality. The two poles of the middle class American Dream are symbolically represented by the two poles of the modern women's movements.

The feminist movement and the antifeminist movement are polar middle class responses to what Barbara Ehrenreich calls "the age-old insecurity of the family-wage system" wherein men are expected to provide financial support for the family.[14] On one side, feminists stand up for radical democratic values such as equal respect, more equality in parenting, greater political equality, and enhanced economic independence and equality for women—at an historical moment when men are beginning to shed the responsibility of supporting a family. On the other side, antifeminists consent to play a passive role in the patriarchal family as a means of taming errant males and forcing them to be family providers. Ehrenreich suggests, "Women chose opposite strategies: either to get out (figuratively speaking) and fight for equality of income and opportunity, or to stay home and attempt to bind men more tightly to them."[15] An increasing number of young middle class women today want both feminist independence and patriarchal security, a career and a male provider, only to discover that the two dreams do not easily mesh: career mobility requires an individual assertiveness that militates against passive acquiescence to one's spouse. The temptation to sacrifice career to family or family to career remains quite strong.

Middle class ambivalence is also manifest among small businessmen. They often do strive to enhance their communities and the local quality of life for everyone in them; thus, they participate in service organizations such as the Community Chest or the Boys' Club that promise to help those people on the lowest rungs of the social ladder. Yet they also sense that their efforts are at best remedial, wondering whether lower class folks have the entrepreneurial drive and skill necessary for full membership in the community. Similarly, middle class professionals generally want to be good democratic citizens. They want to help people to help themselves, to "empower" as well as serve their clients, neighbors, and humanity. But they fear that people may not be smart enough to take advantage of their expertise and thus are not up to snuff as their peers. If middle class ideals ally them to egalitarian norms, middle class doubts and fears contribute to their willingness to believe that inequality is "what apparently must be."

This dual legacy is at the foundation of the middle class's fickle politics. Small businessmen may join in mobilizations against the local growth machine but they may also cast their individual lots with the growth machine. Professionals may cede local politics to the people but they can also stand behind the expert planners who shape the people's options. Middle class Americans who seek community, a healthy environment, more personal and political autonomy, and perhaps more equality sometimes enlist in leftwing backyard revolutions that put people ahead of profits, but they oftentimes invest their hope and energy in greater individual success in the marketplace, perhaps validating their choice in ways that get their names placed on one of Richard Viguerie's new right mailing lists.[16] Frequently, they do political flipflops like the neoconservatives who once flirted with a vision of egalitarian socialism but now reconcile themselves to the inevitable persistence of virtually all forms of inequality. Middle class Americans have divided political loyalties and their inconsistent political behavior reflects that fact.

This is the soil in which middle class radicalism has germinated. The new left, new business people, and new professionals who gave life to the new politics of the 1970s and 1980s evidence a disjunction between their radical democratic values and their consent to established authority. Many new leftists who fought against the powers of centralized government to wage an undeclared war in Vietnam, for example, eventually consented to centralized government authority when it seemed that people such as Robert Kennedy, Eugene McCarthy, and George McGovern would be in a position to exercise it.[17] The new business people who set up shop to serve their neighbors also kept a close eye on the bottom line, sometimes sacrificing community service for higher salaries and business survival. And the new professionals who worked to empower their clients continued to find ways to lay claim to the special expertise and prerogatives that gave them leverage over less-educated staff members and clients. The persistence of ambivalence among middle class radicals was and is especially manifest in the politics of leftwing citizen movements.

Leftwing citizen movements usually built a base of support by advocating and sometimes implementing radical democratic values. They often succeeded in terms of enhancing community power against local elites; gaining recognition and rights for women, minorities, gays, and so forth; and testing policies that gave precedence to shared human needs rather than marketplace profits. The movements often overcame political passivity to get people directly involved in an effort to shape a new political identity and recreate the social order. But success itself built up pressure to reduce activism to passive consent to leftwing versions of paternalism with command.

Community organizers, movement intellectuals, and progressive politicians claimed leadership authority, and then reinforced their claim by getting networked into prestigious leftwing institutions such as the Midwest Academy, the Institute for Policy Studies, and the Conference on Alternative State and Local Policies. Moreover, movement successes created a demand for leftwing experts who claimed the professional authority that is instrumental to electioneering, lobbying, city management and administration, urban planning, legal proceedings, policy research, and so forth. Like the middle class in general, middle class radicals in particular wanted to empower people, sometimes doubted whether people were really up to the task (at least for the time being), and therefore felt justified in assuming the authority to guide social change. Because the shift in loyalties from radical democratic values to leadership or professional authority usually was uneven, intramovement conflict almost always surfaced.

In many instances, the conflict pitted neighborhood organizations against leftwing leaders. This happened, for example, in Hartford, Connecticut, where a grassroots coalition became estranged from progressive mayor Nicholas Carbone, creating a rift that may have cost Carbone his

office in 1979. Similarly, local activists in Cleveland, Ohio, found themselves at odds with populist mayor Dennis Kucinich, reproducing the
tension between radical democracy from below and leftwing authority
from above that contributed to Kucinich's 1979 electoral defeat.[18] The
same tension appeared in Santa Monica but in multiple combinations:
between the local CED chapter and Tom Hayden; between CED and
the Democratic Club; between non-SMRR radicals and SMRR; between neighborhood organizations and city hall; between the planning
commission and the city manager; between the rent control board staff
and the city council. The tension within the left certainly played a part
in mayor Ruth Yannatta Goldway's forced retirement in 1983. And these
shifting loyalties and alliances within the left were middle class radicals'
own version of fickle politics.

The political ambivalence typical of middle class Americans and middle class radicals has produced the impression of political paralysis,
making both populations seem ripe for recruitment by others. American
socialists have generated "new class" theories that partly amalgamate
middle class and working class interests, and thereby justify efforts to
recruit middle class people and activists to some variant of working class
socialism. Still, socialists doubt "whether the professional managerial
class will be a reliable ally of the working class movement" and only
tentatively seek its support.[19] Liberal politicians such as Jerry Brown
and Gary Hart have sought support from middle class audiences and
radicals on a range of issues and campaigns. Recognizing that they are
in a political arena marked by diminishing Democratic party identification, the liberals hope to rebuild their constituencies by linking up with
grassroots movements and harnessing the organizing talents of grassroots activists. But they have as yet to figure out how to win the consistent loyalty of these people.[20] Conservatives such as Michael Novak
divide the "new class" into potential friends who are "defenders of our
basic institutions" and dangerous adversaries who believe that "what's
bad for business is good for the country and vice versa."[21] They strive to
win over the defenders and to isolate the adversaries.

These ideological contenders believe that today's middle class and its
radical offspring have no political path of their own. Socialists, liberals,
and conservatives all work hard to persuade middle America to resolve
its ambivalence in favor of their particular version of conventional ideology. But the main problem with this competition is that neither middle
class Americans nor middle class radicals are likely to resolve their ambivalence in the foreseeable future. Instead, they are apt to continue their
divided allegiance to radical democratic ideals and established modes of
authority because it is deeply embedded in their historical heritage and
ongoing culture. Their ambivalence is both reflected and reinforced in
American political structures that are founded on the premise of popular
sovereignty but administered on the basis of elite hegemony. And their

dual loyalty is reproduced daily in an American economy that is legitimated by small business morality even as it undergoes monopolization and conglomeration, and that is sustained by professional norms of autonomy even as the knowledge industry is subjected to managerial controls. Middle class people will occasionally line up behind liberals and conservatives, and even socialists, but as long as middle class ambivalence persists, the lines will be uneven, shifting, and unpredictable.

In the struggle for the hearts and minds of the American middle class, middle class radicals have a decided advantage. Middle class radicals cannot promise to resolve middle class ambivalence because they share it. The challenge is whether middle class radicals can root their own vision of egalitarian change in that ambivalence. Conceivably, they can use their class ambivalence as a springboard for intellectual and political creativity as did the colonial notables two centuries ago. The new organizational hybrid being tested by CED and SMRR may be an example of such creativity, providing one tier for radical democratic experimentation and yet another tier for more conventional forms of political support. Furthermore, the Santa Monica experience suggests that a two-tiered system of dissent and consent may be able to attract and sustain middle class support for egalitarian change.

Dissent and Consent

The Santa Monica left's rapid rise to prominence in the late 1970s was possible because it coalesced into an organization that simultaneously appealed to middle class idealism and realism. SMRR was a new forum for discussing community life and for experimenting with radical democratic principles. Above all else, it was a center for dissent against growth machine interests and their city hall cronies. SMRR also demonstrated that it could be an effective political organization, able to win elections and orchestrate political reforms. The coalition understood the political marketplace and could exercise leadership in it. However, the radical coalition could not long sustain the compatibility of ideals and effectiveness, especially after assuming municipal power in 1981. Activists became increasingly concerned that their leaders were bartering away core values and many residents felt that the SMRR politicians were polarizing the city rather than leading it toward a new consensus. It appeared that SMRR was not very principled or pragmatic by the time all three SMRR council candidates lost their races in April 1983.

How did this happen? One explanation is that it is relatively easy to sustain a commitment to radical values when operating outside of and against the prevailing power structure. Opposition movements can be sanctimonious critics because they have no record of their own to defend. But it is almost impossible to sustain the commitment once inside government. Ralph Miliband and Nora Hamilton, among others, have documented several historical instances during which radical movements propelled their leaders into lofty government positions hoping to use newfound power to implement principles. However, the leaders compromised and even disavowed the principles when confronted with the legalities, bureaucratic pressures, and economic constraints that exist within what marxists sometimes call "the capitalist state."[22] Ultimately, the leaders alienated many of their supporters, suffered political isolation, and were soon removed from office. The combination of principles and pragmatism inside of government, according to this logic, is self-destructive.

Katherine Coit invokes this logic of self-destruction to argue that "local action organized at the grassroots level with *no* official ties offers *more* possibility for meaningful social change."[23] She believes that grassroots movements should keep their distance from local governments and remain oppositional forces against local power structures. That way, activists can make radical demands or take militant actions without fear of being sold out by their leaders. Also, activists can disseminate their values, practice them, and present people with an alternative that challenges popular consent to the political economic system of dominant elites. Overall, Coit's argument is that grassroots opposition to local government rather than leftwing complicity in it is more pragmatic.

It is certainly true that SMRR leaders experienced great pressure to compromise core principles once they moved into city hall. And to the extent that they gave in to that pressure, they did alienate some of their supporters, isolate themselves from their base, and nearly find themselves removed from power in 1983. But it does not necessarily follow that the radicals would have been better able to disseminate radical values, make change, and win popular support had they remained members of an oppositional movement against local government. As Frances Fox Piven and Richard A. Cloward have shown, grassroots movements uncompromised by official government ties also generate leaders who broker away radical principles in the name of efficiency only to catalyze movement self-destruction.[24]

The more fundamental tension, manifested outside and inside the power structure, is between egalitarian values and the drive toward effective change. Michael Walzer puts it this way:

> Equality literally understood is an ideal ripe for betrayal. Committed men and women betray it, or seem to do so, as soon as they organize a movement for equality and distribute power, positions, and influence among themselves. Here is an executive secretary who remembers the first names of all members; here is a press attaché who handles reporters with remarkable skill; here is a popular and inexhaustible speaker who tours the local branches and "builds the base." Such people are both necessary and unavoidable, and certainly they are something more than the equals of their comrades.[25]

Most American radicals have wrestled with the tension between building an egalitarian movement and benefitting from the special skills of experienced leaders. But they have as yet to come up with an adequate resolution.[26]

American populists and marxists, for example, have flirted with variations on the concept of "organic intellectuals" who would mediate relations between the rank-and-file membership and the skilled leadership.[27] Ordinary members would receive the theoretical education and the practical training that would qualify them for leadership positions. Then, in their own persons, they would provide the harmonic link between movement soldiers and generals. There are numerous problems with this concept once set into practice. For example, not all members are created equal. Some do not want to become leaders. Others lack the background necessary for learning leadership skills. Many do not have the time or the commitment. Perhaps more important, established leaders are usually reticent to cede their authority and they can always find arguments to demonstrate why it is not yet time to change the palace guard. American feminists and the founders of alternative institutions have tried to resolve the tension between membership and leadership by rotating members in and out of leadership posts.[28] In theory, everyone would have access to leadership authority but no one would wield it long enough to consolidate it. In practice, however, rotation does not necessarily foster greater appreciation for radical democratic values or greater political effectiveness (the opposite is more likely) but it does make activists feel as if they are interchangeable cogs in an organizational machine. It may simply be the case that the tension between the membership and the leadership has *no* resolution: the tension persists just as long as grassroots movements striving for more equality persist.

I broached this topic with several Santa Monica activists by asking them whether a grassroots movement committed to more equality could afford to have a few media stars who assume the authority to speak for the movement. In particular, did the rank-and-file resent the fact that Tom Hayden, Jane Fonda, Ruth Yannatta Goldway, and Derek Shearer were the media-chosen representatives of the Santa Monica left? I received ambivalent answers. The activists were unhappy that a few individuals, sometimes given to self-promotion, became SMRR's public advocates. At the same time, the activists were pleased that the movement had a few bright personalities able to attract media attention and spread the word about Santa Monica's model politics. SMRR councilmember James Conn gave a representative response: "No. I don't think that a people's movement can afford to have stars. On the other hand, the stars are helpful. It depends upon whether or not the stars can get out of the way when it's time for them to get out of the way."[29] Conn's statement mirrors middle class radicals' ambivalence about equality and effectiveness; and it also pinpoints the challenge faced by activists who want both.

Do stars or leaders get out of the way when it is time for them to get
out of the way? Not in Santa Monica. In theory, the consent of members was what authorized the SMRR leaders to speak for the movement and to take political initiatives. When the members became discontented with their leaders, they expressed their dissent in ways that should have shifted debate and decisions on key issues from the leaders back to the rank and file. But it did not work out that way. The SMRR leaders invoked the need for movement unity in a time of crisis to quiet dissent. They also used their superior command of intellectual skills, verbal facility, resources and connections, and experiences to degrade and ridicule dissent as unfounded. In short, the SMRR leaders almost always found compelling reasons to consolidate their authority and refused to admit that it was time for them "to get out of the way."

Nonetheless, the Santa Monica experiment is instructive because it provides some pragmatic reasons the SMRR leaders should have invited open dissent to enhance their effectivness. Briefly recall the April 1983 election, when all three SMRR city council candidates were defeated. Part of the reason for their loss was that rank-and-file activists were unhappy with the consolidation of authority in city hall and did not put out the grassroots effort needed to mobilize electoral support for even more SMRR domination in city hall. To the extent that the SMRR leadership was aware of discontent, it invoked the need for unity to silence open debate. Still, the discontent grew and finally spilled into the public realm, in the aftermath of the Israel resolution, in a way that communicated the leaders' fortress mentality. The SMRR leaders treated dissent as a form of treason only to fuel opposition charges that SMRR was an antidemocratic political machine; and these charges were persuasive enough to keep many would-be SMRR supporters from the polls.

It is easy to second-guess what might have been but that is the advantage of retrospective vision. Suppose that the SMRR leaders had reacted to activists' discontent differently. They could have invoked radical democratic principles to open up debate within the movement and to legitimate members' right to public dissent. Three pragmatic consequences might have followed. First, open debate within the left would have been public testimony to the coalition's commitment to democratic principles and the interplay of different viewpoints. Second, public dissent may have routinized disagreements and therefore minimized the impact of any single disagreement (for example, over the Israel resolution) as well as served as an early-warning system that some leadership initiatives were simply unacceptable to rank-and-file members. Third, open debate and dissent in the public arena would have made it extremely difficult for the opposition to persuade voters that the SMRR coalition was an antidemocratic political machine. Conceivably, then, the SMRR leaders would have been able to take the high road to more democracy and at the same time enhance their own election chances.

Another feature of SMRR's April 1983 defeat was the ability of the opposition to persuade voters that the city hall radicals polarized Santa Monica politics rather than exercised effective leadership for the whole community. The SMRR politicians invited this criticism. They originally came to power as part of a grassroots movement that mobilized middle class residents' sense of autonomy and distrust of political authority against city hall. Once in power, however, they did not do much to respect that sense of autonomy or build on that distrust. For example, they were less than gracious to people who were unhappy with city policies and they did little to channel people's distrust of political authority toward higher government bodies. Instead, they practiced "good government." That meant that the city hall radicals had to quiet intraleft debates that might inhibit the policymaking process and that they had to consolidate and build city hall authority to ensure the efficient administration of their policies. These tendencies set the stage for the conservative opposition to assume the role of primary defenders of citizens' autonomy against city hall authority. Because intraleft dissent against city hall was mostly submerged, the conservative opposition had a public monopoly on criticisms of centralized power, bloated bureaucracy, and free spending in city hall. Because SMRR's "good government" practices did in fact require centralized power, an efficient bureaucracy, and additional expenditures, the opposition's criticisms made sense to both discontented activists and many middle class residents.[30] As a result, the opposition was able to engineer a political climate where it was possible to argue effectively that the SMRR politicians were not leaders but usurpers who threatened people's autonomy and thereby polarized the city. The argument worked well enough to keep some of SMRR's supporters at home and to bring out new voters opposed to the city hall radicals.

Again, suppose that the SMRR leaders had invited activists' dissent as well as residents' dissent against their own authority instead of calling for movement unity and ridiculing citizen critics. Such open dissent might have allowed discontented activists rather than the conservative opposition to play the role of primary defenders of citizens' autonomy against city hall. Activists who publicly questioned city hall authority could have shifted citywide debate away from conservatives' championship of marketplace individualism and toward grassroots concern for the rights of people to control their neighborhoods and to participate more directly in city hall decisionmaking. That would have simultaneously allowed the activists to build bridges to residents also discontented with city hall and to put pressure on SMRR politicians to make good on their own values of human scale community and participatory democracy. Conceivably, the city's bipolar politics would have been replaced by a more genuine public pluralism and the SMRR politicians would have been better placed to act as mediators of community differences instead of as partisans representing a small portion of the community. And this would have been a political climate more likely to bring out old SMRR supporters and win some new ones on election day.

One problem with second-guessing, as several activists reminded me, is that it is easy to ignore the pressures that existed at the time. In particular, many activists believed that open dissent within the movement, whatever else it may have accomplished, was simply too dangerous between 1981 and 1983. It would have produced the ideological arguments and sectarianism that fragmented and ultimately destroyed many new left organizations such as Students for a Democratic Society (SDS).[31] While this possibility was a real one, it was nonetheless invoked with little justification.

Santa Monica's rank-and-file activists were not student idealists or working class revolutionaries. They were middle class radicals who were predisposed to restrain their own differences because of their ambivalence. They wanted radical democracy within the movement and thus felt that open dialogue and dissent were justified; but they also respected their leaders, who had a proven capacity for initiative, intelligence, and effectiveness. If anything, Santa Monica activists demonstrated too much deference to their leaders and thereby allowed their disagreements to become festering discontents. And it is hardly imaginable that Santa Monica's leftwing leadership would tolerate so much dissent that it would produce serious fragmentation problems. The SMRR leaders harbored enough distrust for people outside of their immediate circle and an exaggerated sense of their own responsibilities that they were too quick rather than too slow to smooth over disagreements. Within this particular context, one can reasonably argue that far more dissent would have enhanced SMRR's commitment to radical democratic principles and its leadership's electoral effectiveness without causing the coalition to self-destruct.

To a limited extent, the Santa Monica left learned this in the aftermath of the April 1983 election defeats. More of SMRR's internal differences were aired in the local media and many SMRR activists were willing to vent their criticisms of the SMRR council majority in public forums. This public dissent did not produce a hundred flowers of ideological sectarianism but it did produce a budding interest in examining whether the coalition had strayed from its core principles and whether coalition leaders had taken too much initiative and responsibility. Dissent went far enough to generate some leftist political candidates running against the SMRR slate but it did not fragment the coalition or hurt SMRR politicians' electoral chances. To the contrary, SMRR's November 1984 campaign was one of its most effective. The opposition was unable to persuade voters that SMRR was an antidemocratic political machine or that it polarized city politics; and SMRR incumbents were able to demonstrate to voters that their coalition represented a plurality of viewpoints and the leadership ability to mediate and compromise different interests in the community as a whole.

One can draw three lessons from this analysis. First, a two-tiered system of dissent and consent may be the best way to sustain the tension between membership and leadership. Members' freedom to dissent is simultaneously a counterweight to leaders who take too much initiative (and thereby undermine equality) and, in some circumstances, a means of enhancing leaders' effectiveness in the political marketplace. Furthermore, leaders need to command consent if they are able to put their skills and experiences to good use. But they are unlikely to command consent for long if they attempt to silence discontent instead of air it and respond to it by mediating differences. The Santa Monica experience suggests that the tension between members' freedom to dissent and leaders' need for consent may be the best guarantor of both equality and effectiveness.

Second, a grassroots movement that publicizes this tension is more likely to sustain and build popular middle class support than one that keeps it within the family. Members' demand for more equality against leaders, whether or not they are in city hall, demonstrates activists' commitment to the radical democratic ideals that do appeal to middle class Americans. And leaders' ability to command consent and mediate people's differences testifies to the sense of realism and effectiveness that also appeals to middle class Americans. The Santa Monica case thus provides some evidence that middle class radicals can sustain some compatibility between principles and pragmatism and win the support of Americans with divided loyalties.

Third, however, the tension between dissent and consent will almost certainly make it very difficult for city hall radicals to consolidate their authority and practice "good government." Dissent implies disorder whereas good government is founded on predictability. As we will see below, this difficulty may in fact enhance commitment to democratic values by limiting political authority.

Democracy and Authority

Political movements founded on values such as human scale community, participatory democracy, and one class society engage in two relatively distinct projects. One, they strive to subvert the popular authority and power of established elites who deny these values. Two, they seek to legitimate their own democratic alternative to elite hegemony. In many instances, political movements accomplish the first project but not the second one. A movement such as SMRR can win people's support for removing growth machine elites from political power without winning people's support for alternative democratic values. People can still opt for more growth; they can persist in the political passivity that invites new elites to assume power; and they can continue to honor the marketplace that gives rise to economic inequalities and corporate domination. In short, the same values that promise to liberate people from established elitism can justify empowering people who consent to implicitly elitist values and practices.

Middle class radicals must face this question: Can a "liberated" people be trusted to follow voluntarily the path toward the democratic promised land? If the answer is no, even with qualifications, then middle class radicals must consider playing the role of democratic visionaries or vanguards who assume the authority to lead people through the political desert. Better than most radicals, Eugene V. Debs understood the problem with playing Moses: "Too long have the workers of the world waited for some Moses to lead them out of bondage. He has not come; he will never come. I would not lead you out if I could; for if you could be led out, you could be led back in again."[32] Debs did not consider this a major problem. He adhered to a marxist historical theory that virtually guaranteed that people would choose the right path on their own. But it is a major problem for middle class radicals. They have no historical guarantees that people will opt for human scale community, participatory democracy, and one class society; and middle class radicals' own ambivalence alerts them to the fact that affluent Americans are as likely to consent to some variant of elite hegemony.

SMRR's core values were ambiguous enough in their appeal to middle class residents to leave them the necessary latitude to consent to some variant of elitism. Consider human scale community, environmentalism, and other quality of life values that justify empowering people to assume relatively equal control over their everyday lives and surroundings. In one sense, these values call for liberation from elites who support unrestrained high growth, high technology, and high consumption, which, in the long run, exact great physiological, psychological, and social costs that are potentially catastrophic to all human beings.[33] In another sense, these values justify movement toward some vision of ecological sanity, however defined. Affluent citizens may have a stake in liberation from elites who authorize projects that have immediate negative impacts on citizens' lives. But the same affluent people may have little or no interest in achieving the alternative vision. They may have internalized a degree of passive resignation to modern quality of life problems or lack the political consciousness necessary for making sound ecologic choices on matters that only indirectly affect them. Except in cases of immediate self-interest, they might not recognize the costs of growth or be particularly interested in them. In some cases, they may be able to escape those costs and even profit by having other people pay them. For example, wealthy neighborhoods can and do often achieve low density housing made possible by poorer neighborhoods' absorbing high residential density. Do radicals seriously want to empower affluent people who might voluntarily pass on costs to other residents or do radicals devalue neighborhood power until citizens are "properly educated"?

Participatory democracy justifies direct citizen control of political discourse, decisionmaking, and administration: everyone should have an equal share in defining and shaping the political order. But some people may distrust politics and avoid it while other people may simply have no interest in it. Perhaps most people have no more than a partial commitment to civic life and prefer to leave most of the everyday work to others. Furthermore, most avenues of participation in complex organizations are more symbolic than tangible. Some five hundred American corporations have "quality-of-work-life" programs in which the powerless "acquire therapeutic benefits from participation but remain subjugated as before to the will of others."[34] Do radicals really want to open up political participation when only a select few will join in and then experience more the illusion than the reality of political power? Or do radicals consolidate their own authority to buy enough time and leverage for spreading the virtues of participation among the community?

One class society comprehends a family of values that justifies an alternative economy marked by small egalitarian businesses, greater worker and consumer control, and degrees of public planning, regulation, and ownership. Reforms aimed at achieving the alternative promise to shift to the people some of the economic power that is now concentrated in the hands of corporate owners and managers. However, many people see small businesses not as economic ends in themselves but as the means for accumulating enough capital to become big businesses; and marketing patterns (for example, distributors who give price breaks to larger customers) favor business growth. Some people see worker or consumer control as a way of gaining a more advantageous position in the marketplace. A lot of people see public intervention in the economy as a mechanism for protecting and subsidizing their own investment and accumulation opportunities. Do radicals still want to empower people who "fail to challenge bourgeois hegemony or even push the limits of corporate control" or do they stall on economic priorities until such time as people are ready to opt for a more egalitarian economy?[35]

These questions were relevant in Santa Monica and the middle class radicals had no self-conscious answers to them. They did not have their own equivalent to Marx's theory of historical development, class contradictions, and praxis that might have provided them some insight into the relation between their radical democratic values and public consciousness. They did not even have a systematic understanding of how their core values could be reconciled with one another much less of how their moral ensemble could legitimate a strategy and vision of egalitarian change. Lacking such a theory and understanding, Santa Monica's middle class radicalism was largely an ad hoc mixture of values that invited residents to read their own meanings into them, and that stranded city hall radicals between the rock of empowering untrustworthy people and the hard place of assuming the authority of being civic educators. The obvious gap between the rhetoric of empowerment and the reality of centralized power made it increasingly easy for discontented activists and residents to see the SMRR politicians as the city's latest political elite.

A more self-conscious middle class radicalism might have developed
a theory and understanding that linked democratic core values to political authority. But remember, middle class radicalism is a fairly recent
phenomenon. It only emerged after World War II, took shape in the
early days of the new left, and became relatively coherent in the mid-
1970s. It has had little time to mature. As Sandy Carter suggests,
"'Middle class radicalism' does not yet set itself historically. It remains
only vaguely aware of its roots, its interests, its relationship to other
classes. And it retains only the dimmest awareness of how it is perceived
by those outside of its insular subculture."[36] This is a slight exaggeration.
A few self-conscious Santa Monica activists did have some sense of the
tension between democratic values and the consolidation of political authority in city hall, and they hinted at a two-tiered system of empowerment and civic education as a way of sustaining that tension.

"I'm willing to have a new ethic," Derek Shearer told me, "if it doesn't
destroy my daily life."[37] Shearer said that he probably would not save
bottles and newspapers if he had to put them into his car, drive them
down to the recycling center, unload them, and then drive home again.
But he was willing to do his ecological bit because the city hall radicals
had made it easy to do so. All that he had to do was to put his re-
cyclables on the curb in front of his house where city trucks collected
them weekly. He added, "You've got to make it so most people who live
their daily lives fit in; so what we've done is make it pretty easy and
people love it because they can live the environmental ethic without too
much hassle." People with only a minimal environmental consciousness
could be trusted to do the right thing if little was asked of them; and
political authority would remain quite modest if its only role were to
facilitate citizen ease in doing the right thing. However, the Santa Monica
left was not certain that minimal consciousness was enough to make the
people trustworthy and consequently looked to their city hall politicians
to shape people's options.

The Santa Monica left emerged from an insular subculture. The
Ocean Park activist base created a human scale identity shared mainly
by young, white, educated, and affluent people committed to the neighborhood counterculture. That identity was reinforced by friendships, networks, and alliances coming out of the politics of the 1960s and 1970s,
and institutionalized in the leadership of the Ocean Park Community
Organization (OPCO), CED, and SMRR by the 1980s. It was marked
by overarching concern for beaches, green space, environmentalism, the
arts, and the geographical integrity of the Ocean Park neighborhood, a
kind of "true consciousness" that distinguished activists from other Santa
Monicans. And the view from Ocean Park was that outsiders simply
were not committed enough to either human scale living or the struggle
to protect and nurture it. Other residents, in a sense, suffered "false
consciousness."

Consequently, the Santa Monica radicals quieted most talk about neighborhood power and allowed their city hall leaders to consolidate city hall authority. The silence even continued after November 1984, when the SMRR politicians lost their city council majority. In 1985, SMRR distributed a neighborhood organizations questionnaire asking members about the appropriate activities for neighborhood organizations and their relationship to city government; but the questionnaire did not offer choices beyond giving advice to city hall politicians.[38] Apparently, SMRR leaders had less trust in people in the neighborhoods and more trust in their city council minority to broker human scale reforms.

The radicals did have an alternative. They could have applied Derek Shearer's reasoning to empower neighborhood groups with minimal human scale consciousness and thereby give citizens the opportunity to live the human scale ethic "without too much hassle." Different neighborhood groups would have been free to determine for themselves what counted as human scale in their part of town. People in homeowner areas tended to prefer a more suburban lifestyle than Ocean Park activists; they put more emphasis on backyard privacy and chain-store convenience than on community gatherings and "mom and pop" store personalism. They might be willing to trade off some "inhuman scale" growth such as the development of a new modern shopping center in return for consumer convenience; but then they might hesitate if the shopping center were to bring more congestion and density to their own neighborhoods. Low income and minority residents were not particularly impressed with the Ocean Park "greens" but they were concerned with paying their rents, finding steady employment, getting affordable health care, and moving up the economic ladder. They might be more interested in using public land in their areas for labor-intensive commercial and industrial developments rather than for parks; but then they too desired parks for themselves and their children. Empowering neighborhood groups would have made it easier for residents to discuss, decide, and experiment with their own human scale trade-offs than to petition city hall politicians and bureaucrats on a case-by-case basis. In fact, the petitioning process favors the interests of the more affluent and educated, who are more skilled at organizing and carrying through a lobbying effort.

Ocean Park fears of the false consciousness of outsiders notwithstanding, it is not certain that residents from other neighborhoods would have made decisions antagonistic to human scale values. Homeowners and low income minorities might have enriched Ocean Park's insular definition with a greater plurality of legitimate viewpoints and perhaps a greater sensitivity to the possible relationship between quality of life reforms and people's material needs. However, two consequences are fairly certain. First, decentralizing decisionmaking on development agreements, zoning guidelines, and budget expenditures would have brought more people into the dialogue over human scale community and enhanced their control over the public policies that most directly affected their everyday lives. Second, the disorder that attends freewheeling discussion, experimentation, and diversity as well as the power ceded to neighborhood organizations would have significantly curtailed the political authority of city hall politicians and bureaucrats. Their ability to impose their own priorities across the city would have been diminished. Instead, they would have had to depend more and more on building up the moral authority necessary for arbitrating conflicts between the neighborhoods and educating residents to appreciate the communitywide or civic impact of their choices.

In fact, the SMRR politicians had to face the tension between the diversity of citizen priorities and their own version of human scale priorities anyway. SMRR's Ocean Park councilmembers were committed to greening issues but the coalition's other councilmembers were more at home with New Deal liberalism and the interests of its various constituencies. The councilmembers bargained among themselves, trading off some human scale priorities for some social services, in order to keep peace within the SMRR family. Moreover, the city hall radicals were located at the center of municipal politics where they were forced to compromise Ocean Park issues with homeowner, minority, and business demands as well as with political, legal, and bureaucratic pressures. Like it or not, they brokered compromises among competing neighborhood interests. But because the SMRR politicians assumed the authority to broker among themselves, they were the ones who were blamed by discontented activists and residents. And that public blame undermined their potential moral authority as leaders in the cause of building a human scale environment. Had people in the neighborhoods been empowered to make their own trade-offs, the SMRR politicians would have appeared less as powerbrokers and more as city statesmen and women acting on a moral plane.

Appearances are important if building public support for radical values is the issue. But more than appearances were involved. Vivian Rothstein of the city manager's office told me that "pressure from below" is the best way to prevent city officials from becoming mere "functionaries."[39] That pressure could take the form of relatively autonomous neighborhood associations or participatory democracy within city government. Citizen amateurs must openly express their views, participate as critics and decisionmakers, and hold their politicians closely accountable if the reemergence of elitism is to be prevented. But, Rothstein continued, "there are some decisions that the council was elected to fulfill" and they needed to have the public authority necessary to take the initiative in those areas. Rothstein hinted that a sustained tension between amateur participation and city officialdom was the best hope for balancing democracy and authority.

An open invitation for citizen participation in government, even when some groups of people do not accept it out of disinterest or distrust, can begin to reshape the moral foundations of local politics. As people project their "private" concerns into "public" life, they extend the boundaries of democratic debate and actions. The limited extent to which Santa Monica amateurs became involved in local development policy, for example, signified growing recognition of the need for popular control mechanisms that would constrain the maneuverability of landlords, bankers, realtors, and developers in the local marketplace. Also, legitimating new avenues of citizen participation increases both the likelihood and the ability of citizens to challenge the reproduction of elitism in city hall, whether the seats of power are occupied by leftwing officials and their appointees or by conventional politicians. This phenomenon was manifested in Santa Monica when activists and residents protested against the SMRR council's Israel resolution and the city bureaucracy's leasing deals with the Sand and Sea Club and the McDonald's Corporation. I suspect that the legitimacy of protest against city hall, more so than the establishment of citizen task forces and advisory commissions, is one of the strongest checks on the tendency of politicians and professionals to exercise paternalism with command.

Moreover, both citizen disinterest and distrust play an important role in participatory democracy. Disinterested citizens tend to avoid political participation. They may be apathetic, committed to other priorities such as family life and individual careers, uncomfortable with political conflict, or simply uninformed about local political events—at least until local politics has a direct negative effect on their private lives. They are people who tend to "stay away from meetings . . . and only then discover that something outrageous has been perpetrated that must be mocked or protested."[40] Their mocking and protesting can be taken as indicators that perhaps some "private" concerns should be insulated from "public" authority, a point that radicals all too often ignore. Distrustful citizens tend to be alienated from politics. They are sensitive to the historical gap between politicians' promises and political performances. They are skeptics whose very existence is a standing challenge to advocates of participatory democracy who so often find excuses for circumventing their own ideals. In Santa Monica, for example, the lack of Hispanic participation in city politics challenged the SMRR politicians to take some affirmative action, setting up a Latino task force and funding groups such as the Pico Neighborhood Association and the Latino Resource Organization. Once funded, these groups partly functioned as critics who constantly alerted the city hall radicals to the gap between their principles and practices.

By itself, however, mass political participation does not necessarily empower people. The many voices of people in the community are no more than a din unless they are somehow translated into specific values and priorities that can inform coherent public policies. Those values and priorities are a mere wish list unless juxtaposed to a strategic understanding of available support and resources for implementing them as well as contextual potentials and risks that shape the likelihood of success. Finally, implementation requires some degree of efficiency and expertise if the democratically inspired policies are to have the desired effect in the community. People's movements and activism may be the foundation for participatory democracy but they require some authoritative mechanism for articulating the public will, converting it to policy, and administering it.[41] In short, people's movements need a system of political authority —for example, radical politicians and professionals who can translate democratic voices into effective public action.

The danger of political authority, of course, is that it can be used in ways that demobilize amateur participants and exaggerate institutional powers. This happened in Santa Monica for several reasons. Activists invested too much trust in their politicians and the politicians exaggerated their own sense of responsibility. Yet the Santa Monica left was able to sustain a tension between democratic demands and city hall authority until April 1983. At that point, Ruth Yannatta Goldway was dismissed from office and Santa Monica's city professionals were given fairly free reign; and their version of new professionalism proved to be quite consistent with an emerging concentration of power in the hands of the experts.

For the most part, Santa Monica's new professionalism turned out to be a one-way street. The city's leftwing experts did hope to share power with city amateurs but they also believed in the importance of conventional training, qualifications, and experience. The amateurs, however, proved to be slow learners and needed time for "capacity building" in order to measure up to professional standards.[42] Thus, the new professionals were able to lay claim not only to policy and administrative authority but also to pedagogical authority for the indeterminable future, and the new civic educators guarded rather than distributed their power. Had Santa Monica's middle class radicals been more self-conscious from the start, they might have provided two checks on professional authority.

First, the city hall radicals might have heeded more closely Dolores Press's warning about "how much power a city manager has."[43] Political newcomers all, the SMRR politicians tended to treat city bureaucrats as neutral instruments for administering SMRR policies rather than as people with discretionary powers that could be used to shape both options and consequences. The city hall radicals could have exercised more skepticism and oversight of the bureaucracy. Second, the SMRR people might have been more clear about what they wanted from city professionals. There is a post-new professionalism literature that suggests that leftwing movements need professionals who "become experts about their clients" as well as administrators.[44] Larry Hirschhorn puts it this way:

> Professionals must become experts in the *process* of role definition, life-course planning, and the collective definition of mutual re-

sponsibilities. They must learn how to establish the necessary and sufficient *conditions* for client learning. Professionals design the environment within which clients develop their own conceptions of satisfactory roles. To design such settings, professionals must become experts in how clients learn, clarify, plan, and decide.[45]

This post-new professionalism is premised on a tension between official expertise and the self-definitions of citizen amateurs who have direct experience in confronting daily needs, interacting with neighbors, and striving toward a plurality of goals. Ideally, the limits of professional authority could be established at the boundaries of democratic community life. But the SMRR politicians would have had to be conscious of the need to establish those boundaries in order to check professional authority.

The most serious ideological failure of the Santa Monica left was that it never articulated a clear understanding of the relationship between democratic politics and the economic marketplace. The radicals valued varying degrees of political intervention in the local economy. Ruth Yannatta Goldway, for example, wanted to make "people feel that they are . . . really making decisions about the economy of their neighborhoods or actually participating in enterprises that have some level of employee and neighborhood participation in them."[46] But the SMRR people did remarkably little to explain, justify, or experiment with democratic control of the marketplace. They sometimes felt that Santa Monica residents were not interested in radical economic policies and, further, that anything beyond fairly conventional regulation would be construed (or misconstrued) as socialism. They were also more concerned with moral and political values than economic ones, and ultimately made peace with the marketplace rather than risk alienating their middle class base of support.

Making peace with the marketplace meant two things. It meant that Santa Monica activists concentrated on getting traditionally noncompetitive groups of people more leverage in the marketplace. They lent support to organizing renters and city workers and securing the health of the small business sector of the economy. It also meant that the SMRR activists demanded some community responsibility from actors in the marketplace. Thus, SMRR officials negotiated amenities from developers and they founded nonprofit public corporations that served community interests. Neither economic democracy nor one class society was at the core of their actual economic policies.

Nevertheless, the Santa Monica experience provides a hint for how one can make peace with the marketplace and, at the same time, legitimate an egalitarian alternative to the economy's current configuration. Rent control reforms enhanced people's interest in tenant ownership and cooperatives as well as in public housing—hinting at the possibility that *particular* spheres of community life may be appropriately located in the political realm and outside the economic marketplace. A self-conscious effort to name and defend those spheres can conceivably be the basis for a radical approach to economic change that is consistent with middle class ambivalence.

"It is a great mistake," argues Michael Walzer, "when people worried about the tyranny of the market seek its entire abolition. It is one thing to clear the Temple of traders, quite another to clear the streets."[47] While people usually look down on the buying and selling of religious offices, for example, they often have good reasons for supporting the free exchange of material goods and services. Buying and selling, owning and investing, negotiating contracts, and so forth validate the initiative, enterprise, and innovation of autonomous human beings *when restricted to their proper sphere.* Market relations breed antidemocratic domination and elitism, Walzer suggests, only when they invade other spheres of human life and especially when they invade the democratic polity.

On the one hand, market relations foster domination when they become the basis for determining political membership in a community. Citizenship should not be bought and sold but should be subjected to the standards of the polity. In cities, residence is the foundation for political membership; one cannot vote in municipal elections without establishing it. If the real estate market determines who may or may not reside, forcing current residents to emigrate due to inflated housing costs and opening in-migration only to a wealthy few, then the real estate market has usurped the right of the democratic polity to develop the standards for political membership. Further, depending on how the democratic polity defines membership, one might argue that job opportunities and low cost health care as well as housing are public matters that do not belong in the market sphere.

On the other hand, market relations that produce huge accumulations of private wealth do not necessarily foster domination, says Walzer. Extraordinarily rich people who buy huge estates or take Caribbean cruises each month pose no particular political problem. "However, when money carries with it the control, not of things only but of people, too, it ceases to be a private resource."[48] Wealth that is used to peddle political influence, bribe officials, control elections, or manipulate people's lives and options should be subjected to democratic controls. Again, depending on how the democratic polity defines the conversion of wealth into political power, one might argue that community members, consumers, workers, women, minorities, and other social groups have democratic rights against large-scale investors and corporations who practice elitism by dominating choices in the neighborhood, workplace, and government.

Walzer's approach to political economic relations makes sense for middle class radicals for two reasons. First, it taps into middle class ambivalence. By stating that there is a proper sphere for market relations, this approach validates both the middle class desire for autonomy and its historical consent to the marketplace; by affirming the integrity of the democratic political system, it provides a basis for discussing and experimenting with reforms that extend democratic control mechanisms in ways that speak to the middle class sense of community and public service. One can imagine both a fairly wide-ranging public dialogue over boundary questions and a more solid moral basis for radical politicians to test the boundaries. Second, Walzer's spherical perspective might prompt middle class radicals to treat economic policy as seriously as human scale morality and participatory democracy. Neighborhood power and amateur participation in government are subspheres of the democratic polity whose integrity must be protected against a marketplace that tends to overspill its legitimate boundaries. I suspect that a leftwing dialogue over boundary questions would help Santa Monica's middle class radicals develop a more coherent understanding of the relationship between their core values and greater self-consciousness about policy priorities and directions.

Economic democracy, on the other hand, does not capture middle class attention or provide coherent direction for middle class radicals. Economic democracy projects political concepts such as popular sovereignty, consent of the governed, citizen participation, and so forth into the sphere of production and distribution. Ultimately, it implies that the democratic polity has *unlimited* authority over the marketplace and thus the implicit right to destroy the autonomy that middle class Americans associate with free exchange. In my opinion, Derek Shearer is wrong to believe that you can take economic democracy door to door like Fuller brushes; the middle class is not buying. And, as we have seen, economic democracy gives temporal priority to citizen control of the polity, which means that moral and political struggles are likely to take precedence over economic change, requiring lower class people to defer their hopes and thereby alienating lower class people from middle class radicals.

One class society comes closer to recognizing and redrawing the boundaries between politics and economics. But Santa Monica's radicals were not very self-conscious about articulating or nurturing such a debate. They wanted to ensure the economic independence of individuals by enhancing popular control over basic human needs but they did not see a connection between independence and political membership. They wanted to justify rewards measured by merit in the marketplace but they had little notion of how or where to limit market relations. Thus they failed to communicate a coherent economic message that articulated egalitarian principles in a way that could build popular middle class support for radical change. Conceivably, Walzer's approach or some variant of it could be the basis for developing a coherent, communicable message.

Overall, the main lesson as I see it is that self-conscious middle class radicals must situate their core values in ways that address middle class ambivalence and yet orient it toward radical change. That means toler- ating, nurturing, and sustaining tensions between popular democratic demands and limited radical authority. Democracy requires that people with minimal environmental consciousness, limited commitment to participation, and attachment to the marketplace have a legitimate tier of power, however disorderly, that justifies public actions to limit the authority of city hall radicals, professionals, and policymakers. But if it is to be effective, democracy also requires a legitimate tier for political authority. Political leaders are needed to translate the public will into community action; professionals are vital for shaping an environment in which all citizens can define their own priorities; and civic educators are essential for promoting the dialogues and sensitivities that build support for equal respect and equal power. The tensions that lie between democracy and authority name the intersection of middle class Americans' dual legacy and potentially direct middle class Americans to take a more egalitarian path to the future.

Middle Class Counterhegemony

Can middle class radicals draw on America's indigenous democratic heritage to generate widespread support for more equality? The Santa Monica experiment has yet to provide a positive example. But then the Santa Monica left is a relatively new political movement that is only beginning to become self-conscious about its historical roots and its relationship to its middle class constituents and its own potential. What I have tried to do in this chapter is to draw on the Santa Monica experience to extract some lessons about what a middle class counterhegemony might be like.

"Dissent implies consent," writes Hannah Arendt, "and is the hallmark of free government."[49] American radicals have rarely understood this. For the most part, they have advocated dissent against bourgeois norms, political practices, and economic institutions that support elite hegemony only to put themselves at odds with the norms, practices, and institutions that a majority of Americans value to some degree. Meanwhile, the radicals have also advocated virtually unqualified consent to their own organizations and leaders, treating dissidents more as traitors than as friendly critics. They have therefore produced their own leftwing elites who simultaneously estrange those activists who want to experiment with more democracy and potential public supporters who do not trust the radicals' democratic pronouncements. This pattern certainly appeared in Santa Monica. But the Santa Monica left did not self-destruct either through internal fragmentation or public isolation. The SMRR coalition weathered both victory and defeat to maintain a continued moral and political presence in the city. It was able to do so because the middle class radicals were themselves ambivalent. They qualified their dissent against mainstream values and were therefore able to keep the lines open to Santa Monica's affluent middle class public; and they qualified their consent to their own leaders in enough instances to keep alive the hope for building and publicizing a democratic mass movement. Haphazardly to be sure, the SMRR coalition sustained the tension between dissent and consent, in the city and in the movement, and thereby remains in a position to continue the experiment in middle class radicalism.

"Connecting authority and disorder is not arcane," suggests Richard Sennett. "It is simply taking seriously the ideal of democracy."[50] Radical ideologies have usually justified an alternative political order premised on more equality in all spheres of life. But these ideologies have only rarely supported the free spaces for the disorders that inevitably accompany cultural debate, mass participation and decisionmaking, and a plurality of economic interests. Consequently, Americans have had good reason to fear that radicals in power would consolidate their authority and use it to impose their own version of order on a recalcitrant population. Again, this pattern was manifested in Santa Monica among discontented activists, the political opposition, and many residents who viewed SMRR as a political machine. The city hall radicals' willingness to impose their preferred order on the city, however, was never more than partial. Homeowners and minorities were able to protest and win some remedial action; activists and residents did fight back at times and limited the consolidation of authority in city hall; and talk against making peace with the marketplace continued. If the Santa Monica radicals did not succeed in conveying a clear vision of an alternative order that pointed middle class residents in the direction of more equality, they have not yet failed to tolerate and even promote some of the disorders that force them to continue their pioneering efforts to tap into middle class ambivalence and explore the possibilities for a middle class counterhegemony.

Even if middle class radicals were able to use the democratic idea of America as a basis for winning popular support for egalitarian change, they would have only begun to fulfill their promise. Popular support is not the same thing as reordering political life. A majority of Americans, for example, supported the Equal Rights Amendment but it still failed to overcome all of the barriers in the way of passage. To investigate more fully the promise of middle class radicalism, we must consider whether small-scaled experiments in cities such as Santa Monica contribute to changing the structures that reinforce inequality, domination, and elitism in the United States.

10

A City on a Hill

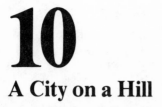

What happens here will set a national example. It will surely be watched attentively by other cities and by major investors not immediately affected by this small city's affairs.

Maurice Zeitlin[1]

The theology of The City on a Hill contains a demonology and a thirst for immortality that are inherently, inevitably destructive.

William Appleman Williams[2]

Can modest political experiments change the world? The Puritans who
settled the New England area thought so. They planned to build a model city on a hill destined to transform the wilderness. The Founding Fathers believed that their exercise in political architecture would blueprint progress for the Western world. President John Quincy Adams and his successors sermonized on America's mission to spread its brand of political civility across the entire globe. American idealism was meant to be infectious.

Santa Monica, California, is literally a city on a hill overlooking the Pacific Ocean and its middle class radicals were infected by missionary zeal. They intended to build a model of radical government that would be emulated up and down America's Main Streets. Grassroots organizing and electoral successes in cities would then be the basis for a widespread national movement. Tom Hayden argued that local movements for economic democracy would ultimately produce a "majority coalition" able to capture power at the state and then the federal level of government.[3] In his book with Martin Carnoy, Derek Shearer argued that community activism could quickly grow into a national contest for control of the White House, which, in turn, would be instrumental to radical democratic change in both domestic and foreign policy.[4] The middle class radicals' faith is that localism will outgrow its own boundaries to ignite the second American Revolution.

Middle class radicals, however, are not the first to invest their hopes in the grassrooting of America. Between 1910 and 1920, American socialists and labor radicals won impressive victories in their struggle for municipal power. They led many grassroots mobilizations, published scores of community newspapers and periodicals, and elected hundreds of officials to city government posts.[5] But their victories neither prefigured nor promoted radical change in the national arena. The activists paved the road to municipal power at the same time that national leftwing organizations such as the Socialist Party of America and the Industrial Workers of the World were declining in popularity and influence. And their municipal experiments in radical governance did not tame the power of the nation's dominant elites. To the contrary, post-World War I America saw a decline in the power of local citizens and governments and ever more concentrated power in the hands of national elites. A modest inference from this episode is that radicals' access to local power has no necessary relationship to egalitarian change in the larger nation-state.

Is middle class radicals' faith in localism warranted? Is it founded on an understanding of the structural barriers that stand in the way of radical change in the United States? Or is their faith blind, more an exaggerated sense of middle class efficacy than a consequence of self-conscious analysis? The Santa Monica experience provides us a basis for gauging whether middle class radicals promise to build their cities on hills overlooking the American future or on islands distant from the main configurations of American power.

Localism: The Theology and Demonology

Middle class radicals have a vested interest in putting localism at the center of their strategies for radical change in the United States. Decentralized politics is consistent with middle class desires for autonomy and self-reliance; it is congruent with radicals' core values of human scale community and participatory democracy; and it fits nicely with the activists' idea that democratic change must come from the bottom up. Further, community politics is where middle class radicals have had their organizational and electoral successes. They have a demonstrated ability to ignite some backyard revolutions and thus an incentive to build on what works.

More important, middle class radicals see local politics as the classroom where citizens will learn the lessons of civic virtue, the skills necessary for political effectiveness, and the potential power that comes from cooperation that can then be applied on a nationwide scale. Ruth Yannatta Goldway told me, "I don't think people are going to care about or significantly change national politics until they have some real impact on local life; then politics becomes meaningful."[6] With the collapse of complacency, citizens will be ready to play their role in a national movement for democratic change.

Harry Boyte is more explicit about the dynamics that link grassroots activism to national change.[7] First, he argues that localism is founded on a loyalty to the organic institutions that emerge from people's everyday social life: "churches, synagogues, neighborhood associations, union locals, civic and ethnic groups, Parent-Teacher Associations, farm organizations, and the like." These homegrown institutions have not been wholly integrated into America's market-oriented society. They still nurture a moral sense of "commonwealth" that frees and encourages members to practice compassion and cooperation. And they are the primary source of grassroots movements that provide "schooling in the skills and values of citizenship" and serve as "the building blocks of a national political movement."

Second, Boyte believes that community politics can be the basis for renegotiating the relationship between local autonomy and national elites. Local activists discover the limits of their sovereignty at the point where municipal jurisdictions are subordinated to the federal bureaucracy. In many cases, they question the legitimacy of that subordination. "Local initiatives across the country have revived the idea that government should provide the necessary tools and resources so that particular communities can revitalize themselves and become self-reliant." On a widespread basis, this revival could build significant public support for reversing the twentieth century flow of political power from localities to the central government.

At the same time, local politics provides a means for a new generation

of progressive politicians to enter into national politics. The new generation promises to put empowering the powerless at the top of national
priorities. According to Boyte, the clearest manifestation of this phenomenon involves the growth of feminism, first in communities and then
in Congress. "Many of the most prominent female politicians today,
including Representatives Barbara Mikulski and Geraldine Ferraro, got
their start in community organizations that sprang up in the 1960s and
1970s." Conceivably, local politics will be the most important classroom
for educating and electing feminists, economic democrats, and other
leftists to national office.

Finally, Boyte believes that grassroots politics can change America's
political agenda, for example, by building public support for themes of
"community and commonwealth" central to the economic alternatives
offered by progressive politicians and policy institutions. People who
appreciate local community, environmentalism, decentralism, and civic
good are less likely to accept the "imperatives of technological innovation and traditionally defined progress" that pervade national economic
policy; they are more likely to put their political weight behind "the
proposals for community-based planning put forth by Representative
John Conyers Jr. or by the Project for Industrial Policy and Democracy." Relatedly, people schooled in grassroots politics develop the civic-
mindedness that gives preference to human rights and human needs
over private profits and violence; thus they potentially form a critical
mass of opposition and resistance to the domination of corporate and
military elites. In short, local grassroots politics is both the alternative to
current configurations of national power and a source of opposition to
national elites.

Once middle class radicals accept the localist faith, as so many do, the
one remaining question is that of tactics: how do radicals organize local
institutions, grassroots groups, progressive politicians, and policy alternatives on a regional and national basis? Harry Boyte opts for a new
version of the old Committees of Correspondence to coordinate local
actions. Tom Hayden and Derek Shearer want to use the established
mechanisms of the Democratic party. Other activists follow the third-
party route, hoping to found an American version of Europe's "Green"
parties. However, the question of tactics is premature because the localist
faith is flawed.

Radicals enamored of localism betray what George Shulman calls a
"pastoral tendency" that converts localism into a blunt leftwing theology.[8]
Middle class radicals in particular are prone to associate the grassroots
with abstract virtues like nature, goodness, simplicity, and truth—the
theoretical virtues of an earlier age. They tend to treat modernity as the
enemy. It is the source of urban growth and human decay, wrenching
conflicts between classes, races, and genders, technocratic and bureaucratic authority, and the political and economic domination of powerful

elites. The pastoral tendency was evident in Santa Monica among activists whose romance with the city's small town past found its complement in a repulsion for neighboring Los Angeles and its megalopolitan sprawl. The demonology of localism is that it can be destructive to democratic change whereas modernity can be instrumental to it. The growth of localist loyalties is a mixed blessing.

Consider the organic institutions that give rise to grassroots movements. In Santa Monica, the city's more progressive churches did preach compassion and cooperation; and they did play an important role in the founding of neighborhood organizations and the Santa Monicans for Renters' Rights (SMRR) coalition. But other homegrown institutions were problematic. Should the SMRR activists have allied themselves with local fundamentalist churches that reserve equality for the next world, preaching either political complacency or rightwing moralism in this world? Did the localist faith demand that the radicals pay homage to the landlord associations that opposed rent control, the construction union locals that favored unrestrained growth, or civic groups like the Chamber of Commerce that often made a virtue out of material selfishness and competition? An historically ambivalent middle class population will cultivate both democratic institutions and market institutions. And people's membership in them is as likely to provide schooling in the skills and values of political apathy and reaction as in the practice of democratic citizenship. The localist faith provides no criteria for distinguishing among local groups.[9]

The radicals often skirt this issue by creating what Paul Starr calls "the phantom community," which he describes as follows:

> By "the community" radicals often had in mind blacks, Hispanics, or low-income white ethnics — the groups they wanted their organizations to serve. But who actually represented "the community" and what were its true interests? Many of the people the radicals wanted to see represented had no communal consciousness or organization. Their representatives often had to be invented; their interests often had to be imputed. The community — so palpable in its misfortune — became elusive whenever its presence was sought.[10]

Santa Monica's radicals constantly invoked "the community" to justify values and policies. But their version of community, although it did more or less represent the cooperative ethic of the Ocean Park neighborhood, bore little relation to the interests of low income residents, minorities, homeowners, and many business people in the city. In many cases, the rhetoric of community and cooperation masked the fact that there were serious, longstanding antagonisms rooted in class and race that continued to generate conflict, competition, and intolerance in the city. Part of the civic lesson here is that "the community" is often an imposition intended to deny the reality of antagonisms.

Still, local participation can build a degree of community cooperation,
more incentive for demanding local autonomy, and a base from which left politicians can gain entry to higher government arenas. Santa Monica's participation strengthened the link between environmentalism and community good, the desire for local autonomy against state attempts to gut rent control, and the prospects for Tom Hayden to win state office. But local participation and parochialism often come wrapped in a single package, producing a sense of community selfishness that militates against regional or national cooperation on radical issues.

Local participation and community-mindedness invite cities with limited resources to accomplish their goals at the expense of other cities and citizens. A community can cheaply protect its environment by requiring taller smokestacks that lift pollutants into the upper atmosphere where winds carry them, alas, to other cities. Or a community can outlaw toxic waste dumping and oil drilling in its jurisdiction only to have these activities foisted on outside residents who are less ecologically oriented, poorly organized, or more in need of employment opportunities. Also, a city's best chance for enhancing its revenues is not to engage in a power struggle with federal bureaucrats but to romance federal bureaucrats to win funding from them. This puts communities into competition with one another, increases their dependence on high-level policymakers and administrators, and empowers central political elites to broker the differences. Within this context, a grassroots movement that sends one of its own to the state capital or to Washington, D.C., is actually sending a lobbyist whose re-election is contingent on his or her ability to feed constituents' hunger for a quick environmental fix or to broker some porkbarrel revenues for the folks back home. Thus, the relationship between local dependence and federal power may be reinforced rather than reversed.

These patterns all surfaced in Santa Monica. Local radicals certainly fueled community selfishness in a number of instances. Their rent control initiative, for example, all but eliminated the vacancies that might have allowed former residents and outsiders to move into the city. At one point, the radicals worked to keep General Telephone, one of the city's largest employers, from moving its corporate headquarters to another Southern California city without the slightest concern for the outsiders who would gain new job opportunities as a result of the move. David Vogel comments on Santa Monica's limited growth initiatives:

> I can certainly appreciate the desire of the residents of Santa
> Monica to preserve the character of their community in which they
> reside, but what of the interests of those who would like to move to
> Santa Monica, or to work in a new factory or office building there?
> How does bringing economic democracy into Santa Monica
> improve their ability to control the economic decisions that affect

their futures? Their political impotence is fundamentally no different from that of the autoworkers in Fremont whose plant GM recently closed.[11]

SMRR policies did more than close Santa Monica to outsiders. They also took resources away from outsiders. The SMRR politicians were seemingly unaware that their success at grantsmanship and thus their record of fiscal responsibility was premised on attracting county, state, and federal funds away from competing communities. And while the city hall radicals did recognize that winning outside funding meant toeing the bureaucratic line set down by higher-level government officials, they usually did not mind trading off some local autonomy for political bucks.

Santa Monica residents and activists sent Tom Hayden to the State Assembly, where he went out of his way to fit the image of a responsible state legislator. Hayden did his homework on narrow policy issues and worked in close, harmonious relationship to other Democratic party liberals. He represented Santa Monica area interests, for example, by searching out funding with which to restore Santa Monica's storm-damaged pier and by working against anti-rent control state legislation. He focused much of his time on educational and environmental issues certain to be popular among his affluent constituents. What he did *not* do, however, was to make demands for economic democracy in California, for empowering the powerless at the expense of dominant corporate elites in the state. Hayden's legislative moderation was reflected in the evolution of his Campaign for Economic Democracy (CED) statewide organization.

When Hayden went to the state legislature in Sacramento, CED followed suit by becoming an increasingly conventional electoral organization that raises money and runs campaigns rather than radicalizes state politics. CED director Jack Nicholl explains the change in these terms:

> We saw economic democracy in the old days as an umbrella concept that allowed us to talk about economic power. It became an attack on major corporations. . . . Now we're moving into a more traditional economic struggle. We're trying to be the political voice of the disenfranchised and needy in the state. To do that, we have to address issues that they're concerned about. Frankly, they're not concerned about putting John Doe on a corporate board.[12]

Neither Hayden's election to state office nor CED's evolution as a power in state electoral politics did much to put citizen empowerment or resistance to corporate power on the California agenda. Instead, both events reinforced the conventional liberal practice of having white, middle class politicians and activists "represent" the interests of the powerless and regulate the corporations.

Do the lessons citizens learn in local arenas automatically transfer to national politics? Sometimes they do. On some of the SMRR council's foreign policy resolutions, for example, local activists traced the path from renters' rights to human rights to people's rights to self-determination in El Salvador and Afghanistan. But sometimes, local civics work against democratic change on a broader scale. For example, citizens may simultaneously support limited growth and amateur participation in their own community and yet vote for "the imperatives of technological innovation and traditionally defined progress" for the nation. That is essentially what Santa Monicans did in the June 1984 Democratic party primary for the presidency, when they gave an overwhelming victory to Colorado Senator Gary Hart and his high tech, high growth liberalism. Jesse Jackson put human rights and needs at the heart of his campaign; and he placed a distant third among Santa Monica voters. SMRR's city hall radicals were not immune to a brand of civic-mindedness that set them apart from national efforts at democratic change. In November 1984, they chose to secure their own community power and experiment by keeping their distance from the controversial nuclear-free Santa Monica initiative that was part of a national campaign to put people's health ahead of violence and profits. Building a local model may in fact preclude doing national missionary work.

If localism does not necessarily contribute to democratic change, modernity does not necessarily inhibit it. Large urban centers often provide far more free space for minorities and gays, for example, than do small towns. The heterogeneous populations of big cities do not lend themselves to the rhetoric of the phantom community, sometimes allowing historical conflicts to surface so that they can be faced and even resolved. While radicals have good reasons for fearing the authority of technocrats and bureaucrats who manage important segments of society, the fact remains that these folks have a far better record on civil liberties issues, for instance, than most localities. Small is not always beautiful; and big is sometimes better.

The alternative to middle class radicals' pastoral tendency is not reliance on top-down change. Those who hope that sympathetic politicians in the White House, Congress, and the courts will initiate radical democratic change often forget that grassroots mobilizations are what prompt federal officials to take such initiatives. William Appleman Williams explains: "It is simply absurd to argue that the central government gave freedom to the blacks. Having been in the South as long ago as 1945–46, I know that local and then regional blacks organized the power to force the rest of the country to recognize their humanity."[13] Localism is a flawed strategy but there is no democratic substitute for it. Localism must be demystified, however, if middle class radicals are to become self-conscious about how grassroots politics can contribute to democratic change in the nation. And the beginning of self-consciousness is regard for the historical relationship between local radicalism and the national power structure.

In 1981, the Santa Monica radicals could easily believe that their local experiment would have a broad national impact. Television, radio, newspaper, and magazine coverage was extensive, suggesting that the whole world was watching this small city. SMRR leaders were being sought out for advice by grassroots activists elsewhere who hoped to learn from and even repeat the Santa Monica phenomenon. The prospect of seeing "Santa Monicas coast to coast," Ruth Yannatta Goldway told a reporter, was not unthinkable.[14] In retrospect, this leftwing optimism represented an exaggerated sense of middle class efficacy, the "can do" spirit that says small changes can mushroom into major movements if only people try hard enough. By 1983, the dreams of being a model to the nation had worn thin. SMRR activists were more concerned with local survival than with spreading word of their successes. To date, their experiment remains a relatively isolated one.

Historically, local isolation has been the normal plight of municipal radicals. Philadelphia in the eighteenth century played host to one of the most radical democratic experiments in U.S. history. The next century saw radical Henry George nearly win control of New York City. Even twentieth-century Los Angeles, an entrepreneurial mecca, harbored the radicalism that planted Job Harriman's socialist utopia on the city's border and Upton Sinclair's End Poverty In California (EPIC) campaign in the city's neighborhoods.[15] But America's wealth of local reform movements was always matched by America's poverty of enduring national mobilizations.

The contrast between local activism and national complacency is structured into the American political system. The Founding Fathers reserved the politics of civic virtue and citizen participation for the localities. That choice was consistent with two thousand years of republican thought and that is where untrustworthy citizens could spend their democratic energies without endangering the larger political order or the interests of private property. Local radicals had little chance of influencing national matters because of the complexity of federal checks and balances. They would have to fight their way through a staggered electoral system dominated by two relatively conservative political parties only to confront the three branches of federal government, its overlapping bureaucracies and agencies, and its multiple enforcement mechanisms. Were the radicals to survive this gauntlet, their demands would be so compromised as to pose little threat to national elites.

The distance between local politics and national politics was so great that municipal radicalism could be rather easily tolerated by elites. Radicals could compete for power in Chicago and even win it in Milwaukee at the turn of our century but, Manuel Castells explains, "real representation at the level of local government of social interests contradictory to the structurally dominant ones does *not* trigger a general crisis of the system."[16] An isolated experiment in radical governance in this city or that city made little difference to emerging corporate elites and their political allies concerned with macroeconomic issues involving federal regulation and guarantees, foreign policy, international trade, and so forth.

In some ways, municipal radicalism actually served the interests of America's dominant elites. The rise and fall of local reform movements served as a safe barometer of public discontent, prompting national elites to call for more enforcement or more concessions to reinforce the national consensus that underwrote their power. The threat and sometime reality of radical victories in urban America also drove small businessmen into the corner of big business, giving rise to the system of local notables and regional alliances that simultaneously contained local radicalism and legitimated national elites. Thus it was possible for grassroots movements to fight city hall and even win control of it only to strengthen the forces that would isolate radicalism.

When the press came to Santa Monica in 1981, its members were struck by the "irony" that local radicals came to power at the same time that conservatives were colonizing the federal government. In fact, there was no irony because the relationship between local radicalism and national politics is indirect if not inverse. CED activists hoped that SMRR's local victories would set off a statewide wave of radical democratic change; instead, Californians replaced liberal Governor Jerry Brown with conservative Governor George Deukmejian. Soon thereafter, Harold Washington became Chicago's first black mayor while blacks and other minorities were being all but ignored in Washington, D.C. The same November 1984 election that gave radicals control of Berkeley's city hall gave Ronald Reagan a landslide victory and four more years in the White House. For most of U.S. history, radicals have built their model cities on political islands far away from the architects of national destiny.

Still, there are signs that the relationship between local and national politics is becoming more interdependent. Since the turn of the century, local politics has suffered a significant loss of political autonomy and vitality.[17] Decentralized political parties have become less important as primaries replaced caucuses, the civil service took away patronage, and television and direct-mail campaigns replaced door-to-door canvassing. Local governments have become less powerful as many of their responsibilities have been transferred to higher levels of government. Major policies and programs as well as the funding for them have shifted to the nation's capital. Major local issues have been depoliticized and professionalized, administered by experts whose main job is to meet standards set down by higher-level policymakers. With some qualification, local politicians have become lobbyists who, for example, go begging to the county for welfare funds, the state for educational subsidies, or perhaps

the federal government for small business and housing loans. The consequence, manifested in extraordinarily low voter turnouts in most municipal elections, is that citizens have less incentive to participate in local
politics because they have little chance to influence local policy priorities,
which are determined elsewhere.

As the federal government has assumed greater responsibility and
control over people's lives, it has come to depend on local governments
as its administrative outposts on the urban frontier. City governments
are now "the main organizations charged with the management of public services and collective goods."[18] The federal government mandates
policies, programs, and guidelines; but local political officials interpret
them, determine recipients' eligibility for them, adjust them to fit actual
circumstances and peculiarities, and report on their impact. In a significant sense, local officials are ambassadors of the federal government and
they make the on-the-spot decisions necessary for implementing federal
mandates.

Federal mandates are in part blueprints for social control. National
elites decide how to manage social crises in ways that tame popular
discontents. They may take the velvet glove approach, legislating social
welfare programs that cushion the impact of economic change. Or they
may take the iron fist approach, providing guidelines, training, and technology to police forces.[19] In both cases, the success of their plans is
contingent on the actions of their local ambassadors, who have the administrative discretion to make frontline decisions. The locals can adhere
to the spirit of federal policies and the letter of federal laws; but they also
have some potential to undermine and even oppose the spirit of policies,
do some creative administrative composition with the letter of the laws,
and thereby work against mass compliance.

For the most part, the growing interdependence of local and national
politics has involved American citizens in a trade-off: citizens must accept less self-government at home in return for social benefits doled out
of Washington, D.C. Further, this interdependence forces local political
officials and professionals into a trade-off: they must accept less autonomy within their jurisdictions in return for administrative access to
federal funds and connections with the federal bureaucracy that could
have future career payoffs. Both trade-offs, however, have proven fragile
in recent years.

Citizens have had less reason to spend their democratic energies in
local arenas when important decisions affecting their lives have been
made in the distant reaches of the American political system. The erosion
of local participation could have undermined consent of the governed
and public faith in the political system; but consent was sustained as
long as the federal government and its local ambassadors made good on
the provision of public services and collective goods, social welfare and
entitlements. By the 1960s, however, there were indications that citizen

expectations were beginning to outrun national performance. Neither Kennedy's New Frontier programs nor Johnson's Great Society policies restored the balance.

Public discontent took two discernible routes. First, more and more groups within the American public began to demand their piece of the federal pie. Blacks' demands for civil rights, social programs, and even reparations for past injustices helped pave the way for Hispanics, American Indians, Asian Americans, feminists, environmentalists, seniors, gays, and others to make similar demands on the federal government. Second, public opinion polls began to show that citizens' distrust of the federal government and its politicians and bureaucrats was on the rise.[20] Many Americans felt that they were not getting enough governmental support and that their representatives were evasive rather than responsive. Other people believed that the federal government was doling out billions of dollars to undeserving groups and wasteful bureaucrats. In short, citizens were demanding more from government and, in their eyes, getting little satisfaction.

These tendencies were exacerbated in the late 1960s and early 1970s by public dissatisfaction with the Vietnam war, lying in high places, economic recession, revelations of political corruption and corporate bribery, and, of course, the Watergate scandal. High-placed intellectuals began to talk about the danger of "government overload" and the "crisis of democracy."[21] They struck a neoconservative chord, complaining that people wanted more than government could deliver and should scale down their expectations. High-placed politicians took up this theme and improvised with talk about an impending era of limits and the fiscal conservativism that promised cuts in welfare spending despite Americans' growing dependence on the government's social safety net. Jimmy Carter's words eventually gave way to Ronald Reagan's domestic budget-slashing in the early 1980s.[22] And it was now up to local officials as ambassadors from Washington, D.C., to administer not the largesse of welfare but the pain of cutbacks in programs that many people felt were their entitlements.

Yesterday's trade-offs increasingly seemed like swindles. Citizens now had less self-government in their communities and less welfare from the federal government. Local political officials and professionals now had less autonomy in their jurisdictions plus less access to federal funds and fewer career opportunities in the federal bureaucracy. And many of the people who felt swindled took action. With no outlet for their democratic energies *within* local government, they enrolled in backyard revolutions *against* local government. The choice made sense now that the local politicians and professionals were proximate representatives of a federal government that was failing to honor its side of the bargain. The rise of grassroots activism against local government posed a dilemma for local political officials. Should they join with activists in the hope of restoring their own autonomy and public service capacity? If so, should they use their administrative discretion to counteract federal social control mechanisms now that their career paths were less likely to lead them into shrinking federal agencies? Or should they ride out the storm of local protests by standing on professional objectivity and neutrality and by redefining public service in terms of minimizing the pain of cutbacks rather than maximizing happiness through social welfare? At least some practitioners of the new public administration cast their lots with the grassroots movements against federal social control.

This was more than a new calculus of consent. Growing interdependence between local administration and federal policymaking enhanced the importance of local events for national elites. Grassroots movements that contested local power indirectly contested the authority of federal government outposts. Thus they fueled a national legitimation crisis that made it increasingly difficult for national elites to plan for social control. Also, local officials and professionals who chose loyalty to grassroots movements and were willing to use their administrative discretion against federal control threatened a compliance crisis for national elites: local officials could channel citizen discontents against national elites and interpret federal mandates in ways that strengthened local initiatives against national policies. In theory, localities would be in a position to withhold consent and compliance as a lever for extracting democratic changes from the bottom up.

The Santa Monica left was in an ideal position to test the withdrawal of consent and compliance. The radicals not only led a grassroots movement against local government; they also took over local government and restaffed it. They might have built considerable public support in an affluent liberal community for contesting the authority of a conservative national government; and they could have tested the limits of federal laws and programs by reinterpreting them to fit more closely with their core values. But they did not recognize that they had won control of an outpost of federal government and they did not self-consciously test how much leverage this gave them against national elites. As we have seen, they tried to restore people's faith in local government by practicing good government instead of channeling distrust against higher political powers, and their appointed professionals mostly cooperated with the federal bureaucracy rather than experimented with discretionary powers that could be turned against it. Nevertheless, the Santa Monica radicals did *stumble* on one possibility for using local power in ways that threatened to overcome the barrier of federal control.

Liberated Public Space

"Almost in absent-mindedness," Maurice Zeitlin told me, "the movement in the city did invent a radical new governmental forum."[23] Zeitlin was referring to Santa Monica's rent control board, which grew out of the city's

1979 rent control charter amendment. He characterized the institution as

> an autonomous, democratically-elected rent board, empowered
> with comprehensive authority. . . . There is no other rent board
> quite like it, and it sets an extraordinary precedent—that not just
> the propertied but all people have inviolable economic rights, and
> that they also have the right and ability to participate fully in the
> major economic decisions affecting them.[24]

What was particularly unique about Santa Monica's rent control board was that it was a democratic institution exercising authority over one sphere of the marketplace with considerable freedom from control by local or federal political officials.

The rent control board was autonomous from local government and therefore from local officials administering federal guidelines in three respects. First, the rent board was a creation of a popular referendum written into the city charter rather than a creature of a city council ordinance. This enhanced the board's democratic legitimacy as an independent public body and insulated it from everyday city hall politics. The board was free to interpret its own public mandate and to employ its discretionary powers as it saw fit. Second, rent control board members were elected independently of other city officials. They were able to build an independent base of public support regardless of city hall actions and compromises. That Santa Monica's rent board members succeeded in building an independent constituency was evident in the April 1983 election, when all SMRR rent board candidates won their races by wide margins while all SMRR city council candidates were defeated. As a result, the rent board members had both principled and pragmatic reasons for distancing themselves from the council's "good government" brand of politics and from appointed professionals' "responsible" brand of public administration. Third, the rent board generated and controlled its own budget from landlord registration fees, hired its own staff, negotiated its own labor contracts, and consequently was free to pursue its own initiatives without fear of fiscal pressure from local or federal officials. This fiscal autonomy freed rent board members to experiment with new policies and guidelines rather than exercise restraint when pressured in the direction of moderation.

Operating in what might be considered liberated public space, the rent control board and its staff did exercise its freedom to promote radical democratic values and experiment with radical policies far more than the SMRR city council. Rent board people took the initiative to break SMRR's fortress mentality in the name of democracy when they publicly criticized the council's Israel resolution and its McDonald's leasing deal. They were also the ones who expressed public indignation when most SMRR councilmembers failed to stand up for the nuclear-free Santa Monica initiative and one SMRR councilmember stood up against it.

The rent board also generated the council candidacy of Gerald Goldman, who challenged SMRR's undemocratic internal organization and the coalition's refusal to take worker rights seriously. In effect, people connected with the rent board became the city's leftwing conscience, pointing out the gap between principles and practices and thereby keeping alive the tensions between dissent and consent as well as democracy and authority.

Furthermore, rent control board professionals demonstrated a remarkable willingness to test the limits of their discretionary powers. For example, they worked on a number of ways to extend rent control protections, even beyond the city charter, despite resistance from the SMRR-appointed city attorney, who claimed that such "political" activity constituted an illegal expenditure of public time and money. They also experimented with several controversial interpretations of the rent control law by hiring their own lobbyists, tripling landlord penalties for infractions, requiring rent reductions in specific instances, and strictly enforcing the ban on landlord demolitions of rental housing. As a result of their policies, tenant housing—one of the basic conditions for membership in Santa Monica's political community—became an issue that was largely removed from the marketplace and subjected to public decisionmaking.

SMRR rent control board radicals were no more principled than the coalition's city hall radicals, but they had the institutional autonomy from local and federal pressures that allowed them to adhere closely to the left's core values. Furthermore, the rent control board radicals *did not* pay a political penalty for promoting radical democratic values and policies, though the city councilmembers did lose some key support for having compromised their principles. SMRR's rent control board incumbents and candidates, to date, have won every single electoral contest whereas SMRR council incumbents and candidates have lost several important races. In short, the rent control board was a radical new governmental forum that facilitated the union of principles and pragmatism.

If the rent control board was vulnerable, it was in the courts, where the institution's autonomy and policies were challenged in hundreds of lawsuits. But rent control board members fought back in each case. When they lost some court battles, rent board activists protested against the efforts of extralocal officials to undermine local autonomy and, in instances, some succeeded in channeling residents' political distrust against judges who appeared to be in the pocket of landlord interests. Despite some legal ups and downs, rent control board autonomy and policies have largely been upheld in the courts. In March 1985, for example, the U.S. Supreme Court dismissed a landlord appeal of a California Supreme Court ruling that allowed the rent control board to continue its ban on the demolition of rental units.[25]

Part of the reason that the courts, especially the higher courts, have mostly supported the rent control board is that there is ample precedent in the United States to establish the legitimacy of fairly autonomous public spheres of authority. The federal government has often doled out public authority to independent agencies such as the Federal Reserve Board and to community groups through vehicles such as the Community Action Program of the 1960s. The franchising out of public authority, or what Alan Wolfe calls "the franchise state," usually has been built on a paradox:

> It renders civic life both more democratic and more elitist at the same time. On the one hand, more groups are brought into the affairs of state for the first time and are therefore much better off under these arrangements. But at the same time, the price paid is that decisions come increasingly to be made in a semisecret, informal manner, with all the important details being worked out by similar-minded elites.[26]

Historically, the democratic aspects of liberated public space have usually been neutralized. The most autonomous authority went to appointed officials who directly represented the interests of powerful elites. Sometimes, the authority went to professionals who, lacking an independent and organized public constituency, were vulnerable to the pressure group tactics and influence-peddling of powerful elites. In a few cases, franchises were given to agencies founded on genuine public participation. But as in the case of the Community Action Program, activists tested the limits of administrative discretion only to discover that they lacked independent budgetary control and were subject to fiscal constraints imposed by the federal bureaucracy.[27] Thus, powerful economic and political elites continued to control the key decisions.

Santa Monica's rent control board can be seen as a model local institution that circumvents elite control mechanisms. Its charter status maximizes its autonomy. Its board elections link it to a public constituency and insulate it from pressures mounted by local economic elites, city politicians, and professionals. And its ability to generate its own budget frees it from external fiscal constraints. It not only provides a congenial setting for radical democratic values and policy experiments; it also provides an ongoing forum for withholding local consent and compliance should higher government agencies and elites decide to gut local attempts to control the marketplace. At the very least, the existence of liberated public space and the threat of noncompliance would make it increasingly difficult for national elites to advance their interests or increase social control through a national tenant policy.

The Santa Monica radicals established this liberated public space "almost in absent-mindedness" and therefore did not self-consciously test whether it could be extended to other aspects of community life. The SMRR politicians did get involved in the creation of several nonprofit public corporations but the city council controlled their mandates, staffing, policy, and budgets, implicating them in the good government approach and professional harmony that marked city relations with the federal bureaucracy. Some SMRR radicals did talk about experimenting with a land use approach that would allow the city to build a public investment endowment, perhaps enhanced by the inclusion of public pension funds, that could be used according to local democratic standards for low income cooperative housing, municipal health care facilities, public childcare, job creation, and so forth, but the radicals did not follow through. Their land use policies were increasingly formulated and administered by city bureaucrats who stressed managerial efficiency and fiscal responsibility over politics as well as conventional social services delivery over citizen empowerment. Within two years of having come to power, SMRR's radical land use talk gave way to routinized, professionalized development policies that were nicely adapted to the interests of business and federal oversight. The rent control board, in short, was a unique part of Santa Monica's political landscape.

Still, one can imagine more experimentation with liberated public space, especially in matters of human welfare that define membership in the political community. Land use is a particularly fertile arena not only because it is crucial to residential living patterns but also because most American municipalities have considerable control over it. Local governments mostly determine "what kind" of development may occur in their jurisdictions, "where" it is permissible, and "whose" projects get the go-ahead. They can use their authority over zoning, development permit processes, and variances to decide if large factories will be allowed within city limits, if shopping centers may be located near residential neighborhoods, or if developers that discriminate against minorities or women or labor unions can do business in the city. Further, they can test the limits of their authority over land use to accumulate public funds through development fees and zoning trade-offs that could be used to enhance radical democratic experimentation in their jurisdictions. But as the Santa Monica experience suggests, they are unlikely to do any of this unless they liberate some public space, for example, by chartering a democratically elected, autonomous land use agency that insulates local policies from elite control.

The rent control board model of a democratic franchise points toward a potentially new relationship between local radicalism and national politics. The model provides insight into one institutional mechanism that allows radicals to wield some political authority and diminishes the pressure on them to compromise their values according to the political, bureaucratic, and legal standards ultimately set down by national elites. The model also suggests that particular sectors of public policy can be detached from national control, providing local radicals a forum for democratic experimentation and a local institutional basis for withholding consent and compliance from national elites. Were the model applied to several spheres of local life and then emulated in many cities, one can imagine grassroots movements gaining enough leverage to extract some democratic reforms on a nationwide scale.

From the Sunbelt to the Rustbowl

Joyce Rothschild-Whitt notes that an "alternative, participatory-democratic organization" is mostly likely to arise and endure where it has "a supportive and liberal professional base in its community" and "a hostile target institution that it can oppose."[28] Sympathetic, affluent professionals can provide resources, voluntary labor, skills, and contacts that help a free school, an alternative newspaper, or a people's clinic survive. Their help and activists' commitment can be strengthened if their alternative organization offers something distinct from and superior to mainstream institutions. These conditions certainly describe Santa Monica's experience with an alternative politics. The city's middle class radicals drew on the area's affluent tenant and professional base to mobilize people around issues such as rent control and limited development as alternatives to growth machine domination.

Does this mean that Santa Monica's experiment in middle class radicalism can be emulated only where similar conditions prevail? That is more or less the case in the Sunbelt. Berkeley and Santa Cruz radicals, for example, were able to win support from their towns' liberal university community for alternatives to landlord and developer dominated politics. More recently, middle class activists in West Hollywood, California, mobilized the area's affluent and mostly tenant population to incorporate as a city and to put pro-rent control and limited growth advocates on their first city council. The unusual factor in West Hollywood was that the reform movement contained a sizable gay contingent.[29] But most American cities are different. They do not have such high percentages of liberal professional residents; they do not have large tenant majorities; they do not suffer the throes of overdevelopment.

Ruth Yannatta Goldway told me that Santa Monica is like most American cities in one key respect:

> Developers are the largest single contributor to local government throughout the country. They basically control local government throughout the country. So when you have any group that makes its issue, "Hey, the people that live here want to decide what's nice for this city," that's a fundamental political change in our country, one that should be supported and encouraged.[30]

While rent control was the galvanizing issue in Santa Monica and other grassrooted California cities, it is merely one manifestation of a larger issue that exists in all cities: Will residents or developers shape the contours of community life? The overarching issue is community control, which can become focused in different ways across the country. Cities in the West might focus on rent control and ecology while cities in the East could generate coalitions around affirmative action, utility rate hikes, job opportunities, and low income housing.

Dave Lindorff, in his *Village Voice* report on early SMRR initiatives, suggested that the politics of community control versus developer interests could be the basis for an alternative politics in New York City. Lindorff imagined the application of Santa Monica's early development policies to the Big Apple:

> Clearly, mid-Manhattan is a goldmine for office tower developers. What if the city were to demand housing in return for each profitable office they wanted to erect? A 1.3 million square foot tower like the Citicorp building would require provision of 130 low-income housing units within walking distance if the same ratios were used as was applied to [Santa Monica's] Greenwood Development.[31]

However, applying Santa Monica's experience with middle class radicalism to "rustbelt" cities like New York, Boston, Philadelphia, or Chicago is hard to imagine for two reasons.

First, the middle class, liberal professionals who might support some variant of community control are the same people who are most likely to emigrate from rustbelt cities to satellite suburbs and towns where the problems of urban life are less compelling, where high tech employment is increasingly located, and where citizen access to political officials is less problematic. Meanwhile, the working class and lower class residents left in the central cities are less likely to enroll in a community control movement. They not only lack the middle class attributes that enhance participation; they also give lower priority to autonomy and control because they are faced with immediate material needs for jobs, housing, health care, and so forth. Where then is the political base that might support middle class radicals' alternative politics?

Second, most metropolitan residents are not in an ideal position to make demands on developers or growth machine interests. Many urban problems stem from underdevelopment and disinvestment: large numbers of unskilled and semiskilled people are confronted by factory shutdowns and runaway shops. Can local residents afford to exercise leverage against the business interests that can conceivably protect existing job opportunities and contribute to the tax base that underwrites needed social services? Or are they more likely to cede community control to the developers to ensure against further erosion of the urban economy? Facing economic decline, most big city people seek new developments and allow the growth machine to lead the way. This is the main reason

In These Times reporter Neal Goldberg concluded, "Santa Monica is ... too well-endowed, geographically and economically, to serve as a model for many American cities."[32]

While the reasoning is mostly sound, Goldberg's conclusion does not automatically follow. Consider the most recent chapter in the lives of middle class migrants to satellite towns. Their communities have been growing for up to forty years now. The farmland and green space that once separated these towns from the central city have largely been developed, sometimes to the point that one can drive the intervening fifty or sixty miles with housing and apartment complexes, hamburger outlets and gas station franchises, shopping centers, light industry, and warehouses lining the entire route. This gradual merging of countryside and big city brings to many affluent middle class communities the very urban crises that residents had hoped to escape: traffic congestion, pollution, overdevelopment, inflated real estate and rental prices, rising crime rates, pockets of indigence and homelessness, and so forth. Where is the middle class residents' next path of escape?

Nancy Eberle and her family took the pastoral tendency to its literal extreme.[33] They moved from the suburbs to a bona fide rural community more than one hundred miles from the metropolis. The Eberles gave up their professional careers to run a farm; they stowed away their urban lifestyles for the culture of rural simplicity. Most middle class families will not follow Eberle's example. They do not have the substantial savings necessary to subsidize such a move nor the deep desire to trade their cultural economy for a Thoreauvian existence. They will consequently have to face up to the deteriorating quality of life in their own communities and to the growth machine interests that feed further deterioration.

Their experience is remarkably similar to the evolution of Santa Monica. They may be the "supportive and liberal professional base" that can host a grassroots movement for some form of community control and it may be their children who take up middle class radicalism to lead the way. Precisely because Santa Monica is well endowed, it can serve as a political prototype for the affluent towns that circle every metropolis in the nation. And, as radical analysts often forget, these towns often host more people than the big city itself.

Furthermore, there is potential truth in *In These Times* reporter David Moberg's conclusion that Santa Monica "can still be a *partial* model for leftists in other cities who suffer not the agonies of growth but the tougher tribulations of decline."[34] The reason is that the significant changes in the American economy that explain capital flight from rustbowl cities also foster social conditions that enhance grassroots activism and weaken local developer interests. What follows is meant to be suggestive.

Since World War II, international investment patterns have favored the growth of large multinational corporations and high technology industries in the United States.[35] These patterns have hurried the destruction of many small- and medium-sized businesses in the competitive sector, "the groups on which the capitalist class has relied for electoral support."[36] The dominant capitalist elites have not found the survivors to be especially reliable allies. Many local business people want protective legislation to keep out international competition whereas multinational investors do not like trade barriers that inhibit the free flow of capital across political boundaries. Small and medium business people often adhere to a brand of conservativism that condemns government bailouts of big corporations as well as corporate investments in places like the Soviet Union and the People's Republic of China. And some competitive sector people are even attracted to grassroots movements founded on support for the small business economy and antipathy to monopolistic corporations. There are indications that corporate elites would like to reconstruct their domestic alliances, this time with members of the professional and managerial class. They are more cosmopolitan and appreciative of the international division of labor, trade, and investment; they are the ones who buy automobiles manufactured abroad and suffer least when local assembly plants are shut down and reopened overseas. Nonetheless, American professionals and managers as a class are not reliable allies. As we have seen, they harbor the middle class ambivalence that produces divided political loyalties.

The result is considerable disarray, both in economic elites' system of regional alliances and in the electoral coalitions at the base of America's two-party system. This disarray is a boon to grassroots movements in cities like Boston and Chicago as well as Santa Monica and West Hollywood. It means that grassroots mobilizations and electoral campaigns are likely to face highly fragmented opposition forces that have difficulty coalescing into cohesive competitors for municipal power. And to the extent that grassroots movements have a visible political impact in rust-bowl cities, they pose a dilemma for local developers. Do the developers try to make peace with local activists who threaten to enact reforms that will cut into profit margins? Or do the developers maintain their alliance with big business investors who regularly channel capital away from big Eastern cities and therefore threaten developers' profits?

Traditionally, developers have mediated the relations between city residents and large investors. The developers have been at the center of growth machines that win citizen support with promises of new job opportunities, tax revenues, and community amenities and that lure investors with political subsidies, incentives, and tax breaks. However, the internationalization of investment has weakened developers' ability to keep their promises to citizens because it has rendered developers' ability to lure investors nearly insignificant.

In the international marketplace, most investment capital will flow to where businessmen have the greatest competitive advantage and profit potential, and that means high technology. But high technology investments produce relatively few jobs and those mostly go to people in the professional and managerial class who live outside of the big cities. Investments that produce labor-intensive industries tend to migrate abroad. National dictators who rule over depressed labor markets in Third World countries can provide far greater incentives to investment than any American city could hope to match; they can guarantee starvation wage rates, military enforcement of labor discipline, cheap land, unregulated business practices, and parties at the palace.

Global factors such as trade patterns, currency markets, sales outlets, labor conditions, interest rates, natural resources, and political economic infrastructure are increasingly the major determinants of investment and disinvestment. On the one hand, Southern California cities like Los Angeles are still in the midst of an investment boom not because of incentives provided by politicians and their developer cronies but because of macroeconomic forces: the World War II aircraft industry that propelled the region into a high technology profile, massive U.S. defense spending in the area, and the recent shift of trade patterns from the Atlantic to the Pacific Rim. On the other hand, Eastern cities suffer disinvestment, depression-level unemployment, declining municipal and social services, and even fiscal collapse despite having offered incentives to investors. Cities simply do not have enough leverage to prevent multinational corporations from closing down steel mills, relocating manufacturing plants, and opening up new ventures overseas. The result is a persistent "rustbowl" recession with no end in sight. The victims are not only urban residents but also local developers who lack the mobility of international investment capital.

The rising fortunes of grassroots movements and the declining prospects of local developers suggest the possibility of applying Santa Monica's model of liberated public space within rustbowl cities. One can imagine popular mobilizations in behalf of a land use agency structured along the lines of Santa Monica's rent control board. The agency might cooperate with local developers to lure investment in labor-intensive industries that would provide desperately needed goods and services. The agency could also generate its own budget from development fees, business taxes, and perhaps pension funds and use that money to stimulate democratically determined investments. It could invest in small businesses that produce jobs, consumer dollars, and perhaps housing and health care for low income residents. It would be free to test methods of citizen empowerment, perhaps financing ventures in resident-owned cooperatives, neighborhood-run health clinics, or worker ownership of plants abandoned by runaway corporations. The popularity of such an agency, I suspect, would depend on the ability of activists to link community control to concrete material gains rather than to treat it as a middle class good in itself.

The risks of capital flight would be mitigated in several ways. First, the argument that community control would cause disinvestment loses much of its persuasion power when capital flight occurs regardless of local policies. Whether New York City offers incentives to developers or demands low income housing from them plays a relatively minor role in the calculations of investors looking at the global advantages of building office towers in mid-Manhattan. As in Santa Monica, community development fees become simply one among many factors that, taken separately, have little impact on final decisions. Second, although developers would surely raise fears about capital flight, they might do so with less forcefulness than in previous decades. Their warnings would be situated within a fragmented business community where at least some members might welcome public investments that boost small businesses and consumer spending. Also, developers' warnings could be compromised by their own ambivalence. It is conceivable that public investments in low income housing, for example, could provide the crucial infusion of capital needed to keep hard-strapped developers in business, albeit at reduced profit margins. Developers might be willing to deal with radicals in an effort to survive and yet minimize the reductions. If so, the result would be a variation on Santa Monica's theme of community control to prevent overdevelopment: rustbowl radicals would mobilize urban communities around community control to reverse underdevelopment.

Despite its shortcomings, the Santa Monica experiment can still be viewed as a prototype subject to modification or a partial model that can be adapted and emulated in many American cities. Middle class radicals in affluent satellite towns can learn from Santa Monica's grassroots mobilizations, electoral victories, and the successes and failures involved with running city hall. Activists working within America's major metropolises can explore the structural possibilities of Santa Monica's rent control board to meet their own democratic goals as well as the material needs of their own working class and lower class populations. Thus, the prospect of seeing variations on Santa Monica—"coast to coast"—is not unthinkable. But widespread emulation, at best, would still have a limited impact on democratic change in the United States.

Building a National Movement

Middle class radicals' optimism that local radicalism will spread to national politics is riddled with problems under the best imaginable circumstances. Localism will continue to provide a mixed civic education in the foreseeable future. Local enthusiasm for democratic reforms will continue to confront national checks and balances as barriers to change. Local residents, activists, and professionals who want to test the possibilities of withholding consent and compliance in order to extract some democratic concessions from national elites will continue to face political pressures to compete for even limited funding from the federal govern- ment and private foundations. Radicals who experiment with liberating public space from elite control will certainly encounter local resistance, legal battles, and bureaucratic constraints only to face the enormous economic pressures that will be mounted by corporate powers. And should middle class radicalism foster widespread emulation that could conceivably provide a mass base for a national democratic movement, we can be sure that America's dominant elites will not be disinterested observers. The civil rights movement and the antiwar movement of the 1960s fell far short of building a mass base for change, yet their modest challenge was met with considerable violence.

In one sense, the emergence of these problems would mean that mid- dle class radicalism had fulfilled part of its promise to change the nation's political agenda. Public dialogue over the meaning of civic education, the potential for democratic reforms, the restrictive nature of checks and balances, the nature of consent and dissent, and perhaps the value of some direct democracy could dramatically change the national political climate. The dialogue would expand "the politics of the possible" by legitimating experimentation with democratic values and policies; at the same time, it would diminish the capacity of national elites to contain political options and thus to plan and control for the future. Simply recognizing and facing up to these problems would empower the people and depower dominant elites.

We have witnessed this phenomenon on a small scale in the last few decades in the emergence of the environmental, feminist, and antinuke movements. Public dialogue over the relationship between ecological bal- ance and human health has opened up the question of who has authority over land use and it has forced public officials and private investors to add environmental impact to their calculations. Public dialogue over feminism has expanded the possible roles of women in American society while making it more difficult for national elites to take women's com- pliance for granted or to use women as a ready source of cheap labor. The antinuke movement has stimulated a national dialogue that simul- taneously justifies a linkage between national security and disarmament, and also places some barriers in the way of uncontested national defense policy. For example, Utah's Mormon Church was able to throw a wrench in the gears of U.S. government and military planning when it told national officials that it did not want the MX missile or the immoral arms race bunkered in its own backyard.[37] The expansion of "the politics of the possible" does not in itself dismantle elitist structures but it does widen the cracks in elite hegemony.

In another sense, the problems with projecting localism into the national arena are beside the point. The more immediate dilemma of middle class radicalism as an agent of democratic change is that it has yet to confront its own middle class biases. Santa Monica radicals won popular support by appealing to the self-interests of middle class residents who stood to gain from rent control, environmental protection, and controlled development. Santa Monica radicals used municipal power according to priorities that favored the middle class counterculture in Ocean Park, middle class rule in city hall, and middle class economic policies that did not empower low income residents. Overall, Santa Monica radicals gave precedence to the self-interests of middle class Santa Monica over other communities.

Suppose that the Santa Monica experiment were emulated from coast to coast. We might expect the following. Middle class radicals in affluent satellite towns would mobilize residents on local quality of life issues, sometimes cooperating with neighboring towns but often competing with them on a range of issues. These exurban middle class radicals would have little incentive to make common cause with rustbowl radicals dealing with the self-interests of workers, poor people, and minorities facing economic blight. Indeed, the potential for antagonism between middle class activists on the outskirts and leftists in the central cities would be great. As long as middle class radicals primarily represent the egalitarian promise of their own affluent class, they will have little hope of building a national movement that includes the majority of American citizens outside their class.

Suppose further that Committees of Correspondence, leftists in the Democratic party, or a new Green party could magically overcome the problems of regional and national coordination to become a significant force in American politics. Extrapolating from the Santa Monica experience, one would expect that such a movement would project into the larger national arena its own version of national self-interest. Middle class radicals might support a president who gives priority to environmentalism while neglecting the lower class interest in empowerment. Or they might give precedence to Americans' self-interest in full employment by supporting policies to rebuild the national economy in ways that eliminate many jobs overseas and close off domestic borders to political refugees. Without confronting what must be considered middle class selfishness, middle class radicalism on a national scale would be nationalism.

This raises a fundamental question: Is the promise of middle class radicalism really worth pursuing? Even if we could imagine middle class radicals winning the hearts and minds of millions of Americans and then building a national political movement, we must finally consider whether their democratic revolution has a place for the spirit of generosity that militates against creating a new middle class hegemony. Can middle class radicals be trusted, for example, when it comes to class, race, and gender? And can they be expected to guide the most powerful nation in the world toward a more humane foreign policy?

Conclusion
Class Privilege and Social Justice

A privileged person cannot evade an ongoing personal conflict between his pursuit of self-advantage and the demands of social justice.

Bruce A. Ackerman [1]

Santa Monica's affluent middle class is privileged. Its members have the
wealth and education that enable them to take full advantage of the individual freedom that exists in American society. They can set personal goals and then combine the resources, skills, and drive to achieve them. In general, they have the economic wherewithal to secure and increase their wealth even while others suffer a recession, and their solid financial base allows them to experiment with innumerable possibilities for self-expression and congenial lifestyles.

Moreover, Santa Monicans pass their privileges on to the next generation. They raise their own taxes to guarantee the superiority of their public school system.[2] They encourage their children, by example and instruction, to develop the sense of middle class efficacy that builds self-confidence and the experimental attitude toward learning and living that facilitates movement toward the cutting edge of culture and technology. The children of the affluent have the advantage of middle class social security, of knowing that family and friends can help out financially when it comes to putting a mortgage together or riding out hard times. They also have the educational credentials and social contacts that open the doors to a broad range of occupations. And they generally have the optimism and sense of unlimited choice that can be the basis for self-fulfilling prophecies.

Still, there are no guarantees that the younger generation will achieve economic success and psychological satisfaction in life. They are not young aristocrats whose inherited wealth, power, and status automatically guarantee access to nearly everything society can offer. Middle class youth must develop their capacities and put forth individual efforts in order to achieve personal goals. They are privileged in the sense that they have so many options for doing so. They can usually defer employment and long-term commitments to spend time testing their interests and talents among the many educational and occupational choices confronting them. They may be able to afford extensive travel, acquaint themselves with different ways of living, and even try out a few years of life in the counterculture.[3] Should politics arouse their interest, they have the self-confidence, skills, and connections that facilitate experimentation in that realm.

And even when they encounter barriers blocking the path to personal goals, they still have many possibilities for transforming apparent failures into temporary setbacks. They can change paths, perhaps going back to school to gain new educational credentials. They can shift lifestyles or try out new therapies now pervasive in the marketplace. Or like their parents, they can migrate to new careers and new cities in order to seek out more wealth or a better quality of life.[4] Middle class mobility is not only common; it is also taken as a sign of individual independence and a key to advancement in modern industrial society.

The very rootlessness of middle class youth—in terms of career choices, lifestyle choices, and residential choices—enhances their ability to engage in grassroots politics should they so desire. They can get involved in fighting city hall, engage in demonstrations and protests, and even get arrested for civil disobedience because they are strengthened by the attributes that come with being members of a privileged class. They have known relative success from birth and have the skills and confidence that produce more success. Theirs is the optimism that you can fight city hall and win. Furthermore, they usually have little to lose by engaging in grassroots politics. Their occupations and lifestyles provide opportunity for part-time political engagement. And if worse comes to worst, they can always change their commitments by investing in other callings and careers or by moving to communities where the political odds are more favorable to them.

Santa Monica's middle class radicals differed from their class cohorts only in their commitment to radical politics; otherwise, they were fairly typical. Santa Monica activists had the affluence, educational credentials, self-confidence, and social contacts familiar to their class. They were an extremely mobile group. Many of them had traveled extensively, experimented with an array of educational, career, and political pursuits in other cities, and only then expressed themselves through grassroots activism in Santa Monica. Their middle class backgrounds enhanced their excellence at organizing and political entrepreneurialism, and then minimized the risks of this mode of political self-expression. I recall one activist who helped to organize the tenants in his building against what he considered a greedy and vindictive landlord, all the while knowing that his wife's modest inheritance made homebuying an option should he be evicted. Meanwhile, some of Santa Monica's leading political figures discovered that their stint in radical government did not foreclose personal options but even increased them. Former SMRR councilmember Cheryl Rhoden went on to become the director of U.S. Senator Alan Cranston's Southern California office; Ruth Yannatta Goldway rebounded from her 1983 electoral loss to land a high-paying job as director of internal communications for a major health care conglomerate; and John Alschuler resigned from the city manager post to assume a partnership in a thriving public policy research firm. Overall, Santa Monica's middle class radicals had the class advantages that enhanced their chances for political victories, minimized the costs of political setbacks, and left future options intact.

Within this social context, it is not surprising that middle class radicalism focuses most clearly on individual choice and opportunity, that is, on individual freedom. Middle class radicals want to protect middle class autonomy, enrich it, and extend it to others. Thus their memories reach back to the ideal of the small businessman who can control his own worklife or the professional who is free to follow the thread of knowledge. Their loyalties go out to values such as individual freedom and rights,

self-reliance, voluntary participation, and economic independence, and
their antipathies are reserved for the avaricious who would achieve their own material goals by denying other people choices for self-fulfillment. Their political strategies follow suit. Or as Martin Carnoy and Derek Shearer put it, "Individual freedom and individual rights are an integral part of American culture. Any proposed reform that ignores this crucial ideological element could not gain support from many citizens."[5] Middle class radicals are most comfortable, articulate, committed, and unified when dealing with issues that directly involve individual freedom; after all, that is the class legacy that they ultimately defend.

However, the politics of individual freedom tends to discount issues related to social justice. Robert Bellah and his associates recently published a study of individualism in America and analyzed an interview with Santa Monica activist Wayne Bauer:

> His guiding ideal is simply to restore what he sees as the lost free-
> dom of everyone else. He wants to help give people back a sense
> that they are effective and can exercise some control over their lives.
> But his passionate commitment to economic and political democ-
> racy turns out to be strangely without content. He can envision
> freedom from what he sees as current forms of economic exploita-
> tion, but that freedom is, for him, a virtual end in itself. The legacy
> of freedom is still the right of each person to feel powerful, to strive
> after whatever he or she happens to want.[6]

But can freedom be an end in itself? What are the social conditions necessary that might allow everyone to take full advantage of freedom? And what kind of society should a free people choose? How should people distribute the scarce resources necessary for achieving individual and collective goals? And how should they resolve moral disputes that do not lend themselves to consensus or compromise? In other words, what is social justice? Bellah's analysis suggests that middle class activists have great difficulty thinking about these questions even though they are concerned about them.

In fact, middle class radicals rarely talk about social justice. In many cases, they operate in relatively homogeneous communities where it is easy to take for granted their own privileges and then assume that everyone is automatically in a position to take advantage of individual freedom. Often, they are political pragmatists involved in the entrepreneurialism and professionalism that avoid dealing with abstractions such as "the good society" and instead favor the concrete language and activity associated with mediation of conflicting interests or concrete problem-solving techniques. And because the majority of their movements and constituents are relatively affluent, they are not forced to face up to the scarcity of social and economic resources that make distributive issues compelling. Meanwhile, talk about social justice is politically dangerous.

It can bring back the ideological sectarianism that is pervasive in American left history and it can alienate the middle class base that, at best, is ambivalent about redistributive politics.

The major problem with middle class radicals' focus on individual freedom over social justice is that it produces a version of what Russell Jacoby calls "social amnesia."[7] Middle class radicals who struggle for more autonomy for themselves and their face-to-face communities tend to forget about their interdependence with the larger society. They often ignore the fact that their own affluence and education were not simply the result of individual efforts but were subsidized by privileged parents. And, in many instances, those privileges derived from businessmen who made their livings by employing the cheap labor of semiskilled and unskilled workers, minorities, and women or from professionals who earned healthy incomes by working for big businesses and bureaucracies that administered and constricted people's choices. Also, middle class radicals readily neglect the relationship between their community actions and their effects on outsiders. They have difficulty remembering that policies such as limited development or municipal grantsmanship may enhance the choices of local residents but simultaneously narrow the options of less affluent people living beyond city borders. This social amnesia allows middle class radicals to promote a politics for "the people" but practice a politics that gives priority to middle class self-interests.

That is largely what happened in Santa Monica. The local radicals were more interested in rent control to enhance middle class tenants' buying power than in the low income housing projects that would fulfill a pressing need for the poor. The SMRR activists were quicker to open up new avenues of political participation that draw more middle class residents into the public arena than to confront the social inequalities that keep minorities from winning direct representation in public policy matters. Santa Monica's city officials had a greater commitment to efficient public services administered by middle class professionals than to exploring ways to redistribute resources so as to empower women suffering the feminization of poverty. In terms of priorities, middle class radicalism mostly concerns the individual freedom of middle class Americans from their own elites.

This does not mean, however, that middle class radicals completely neglect social justice. Some of them still carry the New Deal legacy of commitment to labor, compassion for the poor, and concern for race and now gender equality. Many of them are children of the 1960s and bring into the 1980s an inchoate vision of a possible America where cooperation and mutual respect at home will characterize American relationships with people around the world. Most of them have an environmental consciousness, a sense that today's generation must take responsibility for the legacy that it leaves for tomorrow's citizens of the world. Thus, SMRR leaders such as Dolores Press and James Conn reminded their

colleagues that concern for individual freedom does not preclude commitment to values and policies that transcend a community of middle *Conclusion*
class self-interests.

Their reminders were sometimes heeded in the decisionmaking process. City officials, for example, did try to locate common ground between Ocean Park's middle class counterculture and the Pico neighborhood's low income, minority residents when setting up the Santa Monica Community Corporation. City hall radicals did improve political representation for poor people, blacks, Hispanics, and women through their support for public commissions and neighborhood organizations where social justice issues could be articulated. And to the extent that middle class radicals talked about economic democracy, empowering the powerless, and feminism, they helped to legitimate redistributive talk in community dialogues. Though Santa Monica's middle class radicals accomplished relatively little in the way of moving toward greater social justice, they did leave the city's least affluent groups in a better position to demand greater social justice.

What kind of democratic revolution is brewing where the rainbow ends? A successful middle class radicalism mainly promises to increase middle class support for political reforms that enrich the individual choices that middle class citizens are best able to explore; thus it primarily promises another bourgeois revolution. But this would still be a major accomplishment for three reasons. First, a successful middle class radicalism would extend citizen support for the individual freedom that has been slipping away in our increasingly market-dominated, elite-managed society. Invigorating individual freedom would not only enlarge the social space needed to contest the sovereignty of the marketplace and the hegemony of elites; it would also expand public possibilities for experiments in radical democratic values and policies. Second, another bourgeois revolution would conceivably reinforce the more benign, cooperative aspects of middle class culture and politics. Given the importance of middle class Americans in the nation's major institutions, their support for more democracy could be the enduring, powerful base for democratic change that radicals have long sought. Third, middle class radicalism might be infectious. It could draw into leftwing debates the less affluent Americans who often identify with middle class aspirations; and it could provide those outside the middle class with more operating room for organizing demands for greater social justice. Overall, the promise of middle class radicals' democratic revolution is to broaden "the politics of the possible" to encompass a greater plurality of egalitarian initiatives.

Still, middle class radicalism does not give priority to restructuring social life so that everyone is empowered to take full advantage of individual freedom. And it does not give primacy to renegotiating middle class morality to encourage the sense of human interdependence that is required for building an enduring democratic movement that cuts across class, race, gender, and national boundaries. Middle class radicals would like to believe that their version of enlightened middle class self-interests magically harmonizes with the demands of social justice. Sometimes that happens, for example, when greater individual freedom means destroying various kinds of discrimination that exclude powerless people from their portion of the American Dream. But harmony is not always the norm. Enlightened middle class self-interests can include investing scarce social resources in a better quality of life for the affluent rather than in job-creation, housing, and health care for the needy. As we have seen in Santa Monica, middle class radicals are all too ready to compromise the demands of the powerless and all too quick to defer the dreams of the less affluent. In general, I think that it is fair to say that middle class radicals are all too enamored of their own class to fulfill the Port Huron hope of building a middle class political movement that is able to absorb the democratic potentials of organized labor, minorities, and now radical feminists. These groups have good reasons to avoid absorption.

Middle class radicals ultimately lack a spirit of generosity toward people outside their own circles. They show little willingness to compromise middle class demands or to defer middle class dreams in behalf of social justice for other people. They do not have a systematic moral posture that transcends individual, community, or national self-interests; they do not cultivate a sense of responsibility or duty to humanity. They are not particularly sensitive to liberal philosopher John Rawls's argument that the least well-off should be the measure and immediate beneficiaries of public policy; they are not attuned to the marxist humanism that focuses attention on what human beings around the globe have in common.[8] Consequently, middle class radicals have no way to infuse their own individualism with a fuller sense of human community and connectedness needed to build a national democratic movement and a compassionate foreign policy perspective.

The irony is that middle class radicals do not draw on their own class's historical sense of generosity toward others. Middle class Americans have never been able to tolerate radical individualism for long without finding outlets for generosity in their families, churches, charities, voluntary organizations, and even occasionally in politics. They have demonstrated a persistent tendency toward some form of social service to the less fortunate and that tendency has been partly manifested in popular support for human solidarity during the New Deal, the New Frontier, and the Great Society as well as the civil rights and antiwar movements of the sixties. The recent Bellah study on individualism in America suggests that it coexists alongside social commitments:

> There is a profound ambivalence about individualism in America among its most articulate defenders. This ambivalence shows up clearly at the level of myth in our literature and popular culture.

There we find the fear that society may overwhelm the individual and destroy any chance of autonomy unless he stands against it, but also a recognition that it is only in relation to society that the individual can fulfill himself and that if the break with society is too radical, life has no meaning at all.[9]

In a society where the belief in radical individualism is pervasive, it is still conceivable that a politics of social justice can win popular support as a complement to the isolation of everyday life. If so, then perhaps the commitment to the human community can begin to replace private therapy as the preferred means of individual self-fulfillment; and perhaps the United States would be more prone to approach international relations as a partner rather than as a policeman. Even small steps in these directions could make a major difference in the lives of millions of people at home and abroad.

It remains to be seen whether middle class radicalism can delve deeper into its own class ambivalence to explore the tension between individualism and commitment or, on a political plane, class privilege and social justice. Shortcomings notwithstanding, however, middle class radicalism in Santa Monica suggests that the hope of mobilizing middle class America in the cause of radical democracy is more than a castle in the air. Santa Monica residents, activists, and politicians built some of the foundations. Their efforts should be applauded because they bear witness to an indigenous democratic legacy that reaches back to the nation's founding and stretches forward, hopefully, to a better future.

Notes and Index

Notes

Chapter 1

1. Ed Bradley, "Left City," on "60 Minutes," broadcast on CBS Television, August 8, 1982.
2. Figures from the 1980 census reported in the Santa Monica *Outlook*, April 30, 1983, and April 31, 1983.
3. Allan Heskin, *Tenants and the American Dream: Ideology and the Tenant Movement* (New York: Praeger, 1983), p. 94.
4. Santa Monica *Outlook*, April 30, 1983.
5. With few exceptions, Santa Monica's taxable sales increases have outpaced the state of California since 1981. In the first quarter of 1982, Santa Monica's taxable sales rose 11.5 percent, while the statewide increase was only 2.1 percent. During the third quarter of 1983, California's taxable sales soared 13.1 percent, but Santa Monica's taxable sales catapulted 22 percent. See the Santa Monica *Outlook*, July 12, 1982, and December 23, 1983.
6. See Maurice Zeitlin, "Tenant Power to Political Power," *The Nation*, July 4, 1981, pp. 15–17, and Dennis Zane, quoted in Neal Goldberg, "Santa Monica Tenants Get Revenge in Sweep of City Seats," *In These Times*, April 29–May 5, 1981, p. 5.
7. Louis Hartz, *The Liberal Tradition in America* (New York: Harcourt Brace and World, 1955), pp. 111–112.
8. See George Gilder, *Wealth and Poverty* (New York: Bantam, 1981), p. 4, where he argues that intellectuals do not like to defend capitalism directly.
9. Werner Sombart, *Why Is There No Socialism in the United States?* (White Plains, N.Y.: M. E. Sharpe, 1976), p. 106; see also John Laslett and Seymour Martin Lipset, eds., *Failure of a Dream?* (Garden City, N.Y.: Anchor, 1974).
10. I have dealt with these issues in far greater detail in Mark E. Kann, *The American Left: Failures and Fortunes* (New York: Praeger, 1982), esp. chaps. 1–2.
11. Cf. Daniel Bell, *The End of Ideology* (Glencoe, Ill.: Free Press, 1960), and John Kenneth Galbraith, *American Capitalism: The Concept of Countervailing Power* (Boston: Houghton Mifflin, 1952).
12. Cf. C. Wright Mills, *The Power Elite* (New York: Oxford University Press, 1956), and Herbert Marcuse, *One-Dimensional Man* (Boston: Beacon, 1964).
13. Much of this diversity is traced in Kirkpatrick Sale's exhaustive study *SDS* (New York: Vintage, 1973).
14. For example, see Herbert Marcuse, *An Essay on Liberation* (Boston: Beacon, 1969).
15. Jerry Rubin, quoted in Christopher Lasch, *The Culture of Narcissism* (New York: Warner, 1979), p. 44.
16. These options are drawn from Thomas Kuhn, *The Structure of Scientific Revolutions* (Chicago: University of Chicago Press, 1962). I have developed

their implications for political analysis in Mark E. Kann, *Thinking About Politics: Two Political Sciences* (St. Paul, Minn.: West, 1980).

17. Carey McWilliams, *Southern California: An Island on Land* (Santa Barbara, Calif.: Peregrine Smith, 1979), p. 273.

18. James Ring Adams, "Santa Monica's Suburban Radicals," *Wall Street Journal*, July 1, 1981.

19. Stephen Duthle, "Santa Monica: Ex-Detroiter's Worker Paradise," Detroit *News*, November 29, 1981.

20. Muriel Dobbin, "Santa Monica Renter Revolt: Is It the Wave of the Future?" Baltimore *Sun*, August 10, 1981.

21. Dave Lindorff, "About-Face in Santa Monica," *Village Voice*, December 2–8, 1981.

22. Harold Jackson, "Fighting Tenants Frighten Affluent Californians," Manchester *Guardian*, July 6, 1981.

23. Adams, "Santa Monica's Suburban Radicals."

24. Martin Kasindorf, "Santa Monica Tilts Left," *Newsweek*, January 4, 1982, p. 25.

25. Charles Krauthammer, "Stretch Marx," *The New Republic*, August 16–23, 1982, pp. 30–31.

26. Elaine Warren, "Ruth Goldway: A Dragon Lady or a Pussycat?" Los Angeles *Herald Examiner*, January 31, 1982.

27. Bob Kuttner, "Economic Jeopardy: Can One of These Whiz Kids Answer the Trillion Dollar Question?" *Mother Jones*, May 1982, p. 34.

28. Derek Shearer, "How the Progressives Won in Santa Monica," *Social Policy* 12, no. 3 (Winter 1982): 7–14.

29. Ruth Yannatta Goldway, "How Women Will Change American Politics," *Playgirl*, July 1982, pp. 30–32.

30. Zeitlin, "Tenant Power to Political Power," pp. 15–17.

31. Goetz Wolff and Allan Heskin, "Santa Monica Progressive Victory," URPE *Newsletter*, July/August 1981, pp. 9–10.

32. Heskin, *Tenants and the American Dream*, chap. 9.

33. At least part of the reason for this identification is that Derek Shearer uses the term populism in his works on economic democracy and on Santa Monica, and he is unquestionably the main intellectual link between local politics and the American left.

34. See Kann, *The American Left*, chap. 5, for a more detailed discussion of the growth of the new populism.

35. Perhaps the best study and survey of new populist movements is Harry C. Boyte, *The Backyard Revolution* (Philadelphia: Temple University Press, 1980).

36. See Mike Rotkin and Bruce Van Allen, "Community and Electoral Politics," *Socialist Review* 9, no. 5 (September/October 1979): 101–118.

37. Jeff Lustig, "Community and Social Class," *democracy* 1, no. 2 (April 1981): 96–111.

38. Cf. Jeff Escoffier, "Introduction," and Mark E. Kann, "Radicals in Power: Lessons from Santa Monica," *Socialist Review* 13, no. 3 (May/June 1983): 3–4, 81–101.

39. Goldberg, "Santa Monica Tenants Get Revenge in Sweep of City Seats," p. 5.

40. David Moberg, "From Rent Control to Municipal Power: The Santa Monica Story," *In These Times*, January 12–18, 1983, pp. 11–13, 22.

41. These arguments are made in greater detail by Margaret Cerullo, Dick Flacks, and Manning Marable in a symposium published in *Socialist Review* 9, no. 1 (January/February 1979): 91–120.

42. Carl Boggs, "The New Populism and the Limits of Structural Reforms," *Theory and Society* 12, no. 3 (May 1983): 56–57.

43. Ibid., p. 359. My critique of Boggs's thesis is included in the same issue. See Mark E. Kann, "The New Populism and the New Marxism," *Theory and Society* 12, no. 3 (May 1983): 365–373.

44. See Harvey Goldberg, ed., *American Radicals: Some Problems and Personalities* (New York: Monthly Review, 1957). The book includes essays on John Jay Chapman, Theodore Dreiser, Heywood Broun, Henry Demarest Lloyd, Robert M. LaFollette, John Brown, John Peter Altgeld, Vito Marcantonio, Eugene Debs, William Haywood, Daniel De Leon, Walter Weyl, Thorstein Veblen, and Charles Austin Beard—mostly a highly educated middle class male crowd.

45. Aileen Kraditor, *The Radical Persuasion, 1890–1917* (Baton Rouge: Louisiana State University Press, 1981), p. 13.

46. Richard Sennett and Jonathan Cobb, *The Hidden Injuries of Class* (New York: Knopf, 1972), pp. 38–39.

47. Cf. Stanley Aronowitz, *False Promises: The Shaping of American Working Class Consciousness* (New York: McGraw-Hill, 1973), and Alan Wolfe, "The Penalty of Having Politics," *The Nation*, July 19, 1982; on the left's love affair with Gramsci, see Mark E. Kann, "Antonio Gramsci and Modern Marxism," *Studies in Comparative Communism* 13 (Summer/Autumn 1980): 250–266.

48. Deirdre English, "We Oughta Be in Pictures," *Mother Jones*, August 1982, pp. 4–5.

49. Eric Mankin, "You *Can* Win City Hall," *Mother Jones*, December 1981, p. 66.

50. Jennifer Hochschild, *What's Fair? American Beliefs About Distributive Justice* (Cambridge, Mass.: Harvard University Press, 1981), p. 39.

51. George Orwell, "The English People," in Sonio Orwell and Ian Angus, eds., *The Collected Essays, Journalism, and Letters of George Orwell*, vol. 3 (New York: Harcourt Brace Jovanovich, 1968), p. 16.

Chapter 2

1. Quoted in James W. Lunsford, *Looking at Santa Monica* (Santa Monica: James W. Lunsford, 1983), p. i.

2. Rich Seeley, "Jones' Role in Founding SM Disputed," Santa Monica *Outlook*, January 3, 1983.

3. Ibid.

4. David Lavender, *The Great Persuader* (Garden City, N.Y.: Doubleday, 1970), p. 312.

5. See Ernest Marquez, *Port Lost Angeles: A Phenomenon of the Railroad Era* (San Marino, Calif.: Golden West, 1975), pp. 1–25; see also Joseph S. O'Flaherty, *An End and a Beginning: The South Coast and Los Angeles, 1850–1887* (New York: Exposition Press, 1972), pp. 149–150.

6. Marquez, *Port Los Angeles*, p. 11.

7. Ibid., p. 23; see also Lavender, *The Great Persuader*, p. 313.

8. Marquez, *Port Los Angeles*, p. 24.

9. Quoted in Robert Gottlieb and Irene Wolt, *Thinking Big: The Story of the Los Angeles Times, Its Publishers and Their Influence on Southern California* (New York: Putnam's, 1977), p. 59.

10. Marquez, *Port Los Angeles*, p. 114.

11. Lee Draper, "Santa Monica 'Saved the Houses,'" *Santa Monica Realtor*, November 1980, pp. 8, 11.

12. Quoted in Ed Moosbrugger, "Henshey Left Legacy of Involvement," Santa Monica *Outlook*, February 11, 1983.

13. For example, see Horatio Alger, *Ragged Dick and Mark, the Match Boy* (New York: Collier, 1962).

14. See C. Wright Mills, "The Middle Classes in Middle-Sized Cities," in Irving Louis Horowitz, ed., *Power, Politics, and People: The Collected Essays of C. Wright Mills* (London: Oxford University Press, 1963), pp. 277–280.

15. Garry Wills, *Confessions of a Conservative* (Middlesex, Eng., and New York: Penguin, 1979), p. 212.

16. Nancy Eberle, *Return to Main Street: A Journey to Another America* (New York: Norton, 1982), pp. 160–169.

17. Mills adds, "Big business doesn't have to compete and doesn't; little business sometimes has to and always hates it." See C. Wright Mills, "The Competitive Personality," in Horowitz, ed., *Power, Politics, and People*, pp. 266–267.

18. Lester Thurow, *The Zero-Sum Society* (Middlesex, Eng., and New York: Penguin, 1981), p. 125.

19. Sinclair Lewis, *Babbitt* (New York: Signet, 1961).

20. See Harvey Molotch, "The City as a Growth Machine: Toward a Political Economy of Place," in Harlan Hahn and Charles Levine, eds., *Urban Politics: Past, Present, and Future* (New York: Longman, 1980), pp. 129–150.

21. This analysis combines what marxists call the "instrumentalist" and "structuralist" theories of the state. For a more broad-gauged analysis, see Ralph Miliband, *Marxism and Politics* (Oxford, Eng.: Oxford University Press, 1977); for an excellent critique, see Isaac Balbus, *Marxism and Domination* (Princeton, N.J.: Princeton University Press, 1982), chap. 3.

22. Manuel Castells, "Local Government, Urban Crisis, and Political Change," in Maurice Zeitlin, ed., *Political Power and Social Theory: A Research Annual*, vol. 2 (Greenwich, Conn.: JAI Press, 1981), p. 6.

23. Quoted in Mills, "The Middle Classes," p. 283.

24. Joel Kotkin and Paul Grabowicz, *California, Inc.* (New York: Rawson Wade, 1982), p. 37.

25. For the fuller story, see Bradford Snell, "American Ground Transport," in Jerome Skolnick and Elliott Currie, eds., *Crisis in American Institutions*, 3rd ed. (Boston: Little Brown, 1976), pp. 304–326.

26. These figures are based on data found in Allan Heskin, *Tenants and the American Dream: Ideology and the Tenant Movement* (New York: Praeger, 1983), p. 40.

27. See Anne Morgenthaler, "SM Split into 7 Areas for Survey," Santa Monica *Outlook*, December 26, 1983.

28. Jane Bednar, "Census Tally Offers Peek into Future," Santa Monica *Outlook*, April 30, 1983.

29. Santa Monica Area Chamber of Commerce, "Community Economic Profile for the City of Santa Monica, County of Los Angeles, California," January 1982, pp. 1–4.

30. Barbara and John Ehrenreich, "The New Left: A Case Study in Professional-Managerial Class Radicalism," *Radical America* 11, no. 3 (May/June 1977): 7; a recent review of "new class" theories is Jean-Christophe Agnew's "A Touch of Class," *democracy* 3, no. 2 (Spring 1983): 59–72.

31. Henry F. May, *The Enlightenment in America* (Oxford, Eng.: Oxford University Press, 1976), pp. 211–212.

32. Thomas Jefferson, *Notes on the State of Virginia* (New York: Harper & Row, 1964), p. 157.

33. David Noble, "Present Tense Technology—Part One," *democracy* 3, no. 2 (Spring 1983): 23.

34. Lawrence Goodwyn, *Democratic Promise: The Populist Movement in America* (New York: Oxford University Press, 1976), p. 360.

35. David Smith, "Professional Responsibility and Political Participation," in J. Roland Pennock and John W. Chapman, eds., *Participation in Politics* (New York: Lieber-Atherton, 1975), p. 227.

36. See John Dewey, *Liberalism and Social Action* (New York: Capricorn, 1963), p. 81.

37. Ira Shor, "The Working Class Goes to College," in Theodore Mills Norton and Bertell Ollman, eds., *Studies in Socialist Pedagogy* (New York: Monthly Review, 1978), p. 110.

38. A nice survey of the professionalization of urban America is Harlan Hahn and Charles Levine, "The Politics of Urban American and the Study of Urban Politics," in Hahn and Levine, eds., *Urban Politics*, pp. 1–50.

39. A survey and critique of variants of New Deal liberalism that has withstood the test of time is Peter Bachrach, *The Theory of Democratic Elitism: A Critique* (Boston: Little Brown, 1967); see also C. B. Macpherson, *The Life and Times of Liberal Democracy* (Oxford, Eng.: Oxford University Press, 1977).

40. Louis Hartz calls this phenomenon America's "colossal liberal absolutism." See his *The Liberal Tradition in America* (New York: Harcourt Brace and World, 1955), chap. 11.

41. Alan Wolfe, "Presidential Power and the Crisis of Modernization," *democracy* 1, no. 2 (April 1981): 22.

42. Christopher Lasch, *The Culture of Narcissism* (New York: Warner, 1979), p. 385.

43. See Hannah Arendt, *Crises of the Republic* (New York: Harcourt Brace Jovanovich, 1972), pp. 10–13.

44. Murray Edelman, *Political Language: Words That Succeed and Policies That Fail* (New York: Academic Press, 1977), p. 75.

45. Sheldon Wolin, "The Idea of the State in America," in John P. Diggins and Mark E. Kann, eds., *The Problem of Authority in America* (Philadelphia: Temple University Press, 1981), p. 54; see also Richard Ohmann, *English in America* (New York: Oxford University Press, 1976), p. 187.

46. See Harry Braverman, *Labor and Monopoly Capital* (New York: Monthly Review, 1974), p. 87.

47. Cf. Thurow, *The Zero-Sum Society*, chap. 5, and Sheldon Wolin, "The New Public Philosophy," *democracy* 1, no. 4 (October 1981): 23–36.

48. Kirkpatrick Sale, *Human Scale* (New York: Coward, McCann and Geoghegan, 1980), p. 206.

49. Ibid., p. 21.

50. Much of this analysis is based on Robert Kargon, "The Future of American

Science: An Historical Perspective," in Mark E. Kann, ed., *The Future of American Democracy: Views from the Left* (Philadelphia: Temple University Press, 1983), pp. 140–161.

51. See Charles Schwartz, "Atoms for War," in Kann, ed., *The Future of American Democracy*, pp. 162–174, for an analysis of nuclear weapons research.

52. David Dickson, "Limiting Democracy: Technocrats and the Liberal State," *democracy* 1, no. 1 (January 1981): 71.

53. Quoted in Kargon, "The Future of American Science," p. 153.

54. Ibid., p. 155.

55. Anthony Fainberg, "Scientists, Humanists, and Militarism," *Humanities in Society* 5, nos. 1–2 (Winter/Spring 1982): 149.

56. Between 1970 and 1980, Santa Monica experienced a 10.7 percent leap in the percentage of working women residing in the city. We will see in a later chapter that their inability to buy homes was one important impetus behind local radicalism.

57. Celeste MacLeod describes in detail many of the difficulties that the children of the affluent have experienced in their job searches in recent years. See her *Horatio Alger, Farewell: The End of the American Dream* (New York: Seaview, 1980), chap. 11.

58. This disenchantment was documented in a city-funded survey reported in the Santa Monica *Outlook* series published in the last week of 1983. As we will see, it was also the source of several city task forces that were created in the 1970s and 1980s.

59. The city survey, mentioned above, also revealed considerable disenchantment with government and bureaucracy in homeowner areas where professionals live in the highest concentrations. As we will also see, radical city officials were well aware of skepticism of political authority.

60. See Jennifer Hochschild, *What's Fair? American Beliefs About Distributive Justice* (Cambridge, Mass.: Harvard University Press, 1981), chap. 8, "Ambivalence."

Chapter 3

1. Holly Near and Ronnie Gilbert, quoted in "Singing for Their Lives: An Interview with Holly Near and Ronnie Gilbert," *Socialist Review* 14, no. 1 (January/February 1984): 90–91.

2. The ensuing quotations are from Students for a Democratic Society, "The Port Huron Statement," in Robert A. Goldwin, ed., *How Democratic Is America?* (Chicago: Rand-McNally, 1971), pp. 1–15.

3. Barbara and John Ehrenreich, "The New Left: A Case Study in Professional-Managerial Class Radicalism," *Radical America* 11, no. 3 (May/June 1977): 8–9.

4. Dotson Rader, "More About Columbia," in Terrence Cook and Patrick Morgan, eds., *Participatory Democracy* (San Francisco: Canfield, 1971), p. 336.

5. Kirkpatrick Sale, *SDS* (New York: Vintage, 1973), p. 45.

6. See Richard Lemon, *The Troubled American* (New York: Simon and Schuster, 1970).

7. Ibid., pp. 28, 35, 202–205.

8. Ehrenreich and Ehrenreich, "The New Left," p. 10.

9. Peter Clecak, *America's Quest for the Ideal Self* (New York: Oxford University Press, 1983), p. 51.

10. See Ronald Gross and Paul Osterman, eds., *The New Professionals* (New York: Simon and Schuster, 1972), and Frank Marini, ed., *Toward a New Public Administration* (New York: Chandler, 1971).
11. Cf. Michael Harmon, "Normative Theory and Public Administration: Some Suggestions for a Redefinition of Administrative Responsibility," and H. George Frederickson, "Toward a New Public Administration," in Marini, ed., *Toward a New Public Administration*, pp. 172–189 and 309–331 respectively.
12. Ehrenreich and Ehrenreich, "The New Left," p. 16.
13. See Ronald Gross and Paul Osterman, "Introduction," in Gross and Osterman, eds., *The New Professionals*, pp. 19–23.
14. See Frank Marini, "The Minnowbrook Perspective and the Future of Public Administration Education," in Marini, ed., *Toward a New Public Administration*, esp. p. 348.
15. See Howard I. Kalodner, "Citizen Participation in Emerging Social Institutions," in J. Roland Pennock and John W. Chapman, eds., *Participation in Politics* (New York: Lieber-Atherton, 1975), pp. 161–185, for a discussion of community action programs in the 1960s.
16. For example, see Michael Best and William Connolly, *The Politicized Economy* (Lexington, Mass.: Heath, 1976), pp. 115–118.
17. This point is made in numerous ways in Charlotte Bunch et al., eds., *Building Feminist Theory* (New York: Longman, 1981).
18. This is one of the main assumptions of the Mid-Peninsula Conversion Project and the Economic Task Force for the National Freeze Campaign.
19. Ellen Schrecker, "The Missing Generation: Academics and the Communist Party from the Depression to the Cold War," *Humanities in Society* 6, nos. 2–3 (Summer/Spring 1983): 139.
20. See Theodore Mills Norton and Bertell Ollman, eds., *Studies in Socialist Pedagogy* (New York: Monthly Review, 1978).
21. Holly Henderson, "The New Businessman," Gross and Osterman, eds. *The New Professionals*, pp. 213–238.
22. Ibid., p. 219.
23. Kirkpatrick Sale, *Human Scale* (New York: Coward, McCann and Geoghegan, 1980), p. 340.
24. Ibid., p. 46.
25. See Harry C. Boyte, *The Backyard Revolution* (Philadelphia: Temple University Press, 1980), pp. 54–55; John Case and Rosemary Taylor, eds., *Coops, Communes and Collectives* (New York: Pantheon, 1979), esp. pt. 1.
26. Tom Hayden, *The American Future: New Visions Beyond Old Frontiers* (Boston: South End, 1980), p. 301.
27. Tom Hayden and the Tom Hayden for U.S. Senate Campaign, "Make the Future Ours," 1976 campaign document. The ensuing quotations are also taken from this document.
28. Cf. Jack Newfield and Jeff Greenfield, *A Populist Manifesto* (New York: Praeger, 1972), and Fred R. Harris, *The New Populism* (New York: Saturday Review, 1973).
29. Campaign for Economic Democracy, "Founding Statement of the Campaign for Economic Democracy," in Hayden, *The American Future*, p. 304.
30. This brief biography and the following ones are taken from a series of profiles

written by Rich Seeley for the Santa Monica *Outlook* and published there in late May and early June 1981.

31. Sale, *Human Scale*, p. 37.
32. Author interview with Maurice Zeitlin, Los Angeles, July 12, 1982.
33. Derek Shearer, quoted in Will Thorne, "Conservative Hues Tint Shearer's Radical Image," Santa Monica *Outlook*, July 30, 1981.
34. Author interview with Dennis Zane, Santa Monica, July 28, 1982.
35. Author interview with Vivian Rothstein, Santa Monica, July 7, 1982.
36. Author interview with Ruth Yannatta Goldway, Santa Monica, June 22, 1982.
37. Ibid.
38. Author interview with Derek Shearer, Santa Monica, June 17, 1982.
39. Zane interview.
40. Author interview with James Conn, Santa Monica, August 25, 1982.
41. Shearer interview.
42. Goldway interview.
43. Zeitlin interview.
44. Derek Shearer, "Foreword" to Mark E. Kann, *The American Left: Failures and Fortunes* (New York: Praeger, 1982), p. xi.
45. Terrence Cook and Patrick Morgan, "An Introduction to Participatory Democracy," in Cook and Morgan, eds., *Participatory Democracy*, p. 4.
46. Goldway interview.
47. Conn interview.
48. Zeitlin interview.
49. Derek Shearer, "How the Progressives Won in Santa Monica," *Social Policy* 12, no. 3 (Winter 1982): 8.
50. Conn interview.
51. Author interview with John Alschuler, Santa Monica, July 14, 1982.
52. Rothstein interview.
53. Author interview with "Anonymous," Santa Monica, July 21, 1982.
54. Zane interview.
55. Campaign for Economic Democracy, "Founding Statement," p. 306.
56. See Martin Carnoy and Derek Shearer, *Economic Democracy: The Challenge of the 1980s* (White Plains, N.Y.: M. E. Sharpe, 1980), pt. 2.
57. Zane interview, Zeitlin interview, and Maurice Zeitlin, "The American Crisis: An Analysis and Modest Proposal," in Mark E. Kann, ed., *The Future of American Democracy: Views from the Left* (Philadelphia: Temple University Press, 1983), pp. 116–136.
58. Goldway interview.
59. Santa Monicans for Renters' Rights, "Principles of Unity Between Members of the Santa Monicans for Renters' Rights Coalition, February 1981," internal document.
60. See C. B. Macpherson, *The Life and Times of Liberal Democracy* (Oxford, Eng.: Oxford University Press, 1977), pp. 18–19.
61. John Alschuler, quoted in Mark Fabian, "Alschuler Given 4% Raise, Bonus," Santa Monica *Outlook*, March 14, 1984.
62. Allan Heskin, *Tenants and the American Dream: Ideology and the Tenant Movement* (New York: Praeger, 1983), p. xii.
63. Ibid., pt. 2.

64. Robert Myers, "Rent Control: It Helps Curb Speculators; and It's Fair to Both Tenant and Landlord," Los Angeles *Herald Examiner*, May 26, 1981.

65. There is a distinct similarity between local activists' economic perspectives and those of Henry George's nineteenth-century Single Tax Movement.
66. Conn interview.
67. James Conn, quoted in Rich Seeley, "Conn: Reluctant Candidate Brings Sixties Enthusiasm to S.M. City Council," Santa Monica *Outlook*, May 28, 1981.
68. Conn interview.
69. Shearer interview.
70. Author interview with Dolores Press, Santa Monica, July 19, 1982.
71. Author interview with Kenneth Edwards, Santa Monica, July 22, 1982.
72. Ruth Yannatta Goldway, quoted in Rich Seeley, "Mayor Advocates Democracy with Small d," Santa Monica *Outlook*, April 29, 1981.
73. This theme runs through Hayden's *The American Future*, Carnoy and Shearer's *Economic Democracy*, and nearly every interview I conducted with Santa Monica activists. I have treated it in greater detail in Kann, *The American Left*, chaps. 1–2.
74. See Isaac Kramnick, "Tom Paine: Radical Democrat," *democracy* 1, no. 1 (January 1981): 128.
75. See James C. Scott, "Hegemony and the Peasantry," *Politics and Society* 7, no. 3 (1977): 267–296; related analyses have been done by E. P. Thompson and Harry Boyte.
76. Conn interview.
77. See E. F. Schumacher, *Small Is Beautiful* (New York: Harper & Row, 1973), pp. 21, 146–159; see also Sale, *Human Scale*, pp. 159–161.
78. See Kann, *The American Left*, chap. 6.
79. Philip Green, "Property Rights and Equality," paper delivered at the 1983 meeting of the American Political Science Association, Chicago, September 1–4, 1983.
80. See Daniel Yankelovich, *New Rules: Searching for Self-Fulfillment in a World Turned Upside Down* (New York: Random House, 1981), esp. chaps. 1, 24. Yankelovich's data and Clecak's argument in *America's Quest for the Ideal Self* are welcome counterweights to Christopher Lasch's "culture of narcissism" thesis cited earlier. Yankelovich and Clecak are more sensitive than Lasch to the currents of ambivalence and ambiguity that run through American culture.
81. This is particularly true of what Robert Maniquis calls marxists of the "hyphenated sort—Freudian-Marxists, structuralist-Marxists, Derridean-Marxists, Althusserian-Marxists." See his "Marxists and the University Introduction," *Humanities in Society* 6, 2–3 (Spring/Summer 1983): 133–137.
82. Frances Fox Piven and Richard A. Cloward, *Poor People's Movements* (New York: Vintage, 1979), p. xi.
83. This phenomenon does *not* describe groups like the Democratic Socialists of America (DSA) but does represent a persistent trend among leninist sects in America.
84. See Frances Fox Piven and Richard A. Cloward, *The New Class War* (New York: Pantheon, 1982), esp. chap. 5.
85. Zeitlin interview.

1. Maurice Zeitlin, "Tenant Power to Political Power," *The Nation*, July 4, 1981, p. 16.

2. Harry C. Boyte, *The Backyard Revolution* (Philadelphia: Temple University Press, 1980), p. 51; see also Martin Carnoy and Derek Shearer, *Economic Democracy: The Challenge of the 1980s* (White Plains, N.Y.: M. E. Sharpe, 1980), pp. 18–19, and Tom Hayden, *The American Future: New Visions Beyond Old Frontiers* (Boston: South End, 1980), esp. pp. 179–184.

3. See Tom Hayden and the Tom Hayden for U.S. Senate Campaign, "Make the Future Ours," 1976 campaign document, pp. 23–24.

4. In my interviews, I spoke formally with four local CED members and informally with several others. The Santa Monica chapter of CED, I was told, has never kept a written record of its proceedings; further, several CED members were reticent to speak about the internal politics of the chapter. Consequently, my analysis of CED's role in the Santa Monica left is based on individual recollections and comments that were crosschecked with other members wherever possible.

5. See Allan Heskin, *Tenants and the American Dream: Ideology and the Tenant Movement* (New York: Praeger, 1983), pp. 55–57.

6. Author interview with Kenneth Edwards, Santa Monica, July 22, 1982.

7. Author interview with Christine Reed, Santa Monica, July 19, 1982.

8. Heskin, *Tenants and the American Dream*, p. 65.

9. Santa Monica Rent Control Board, *Santa Monica Rent Control: A Guide for Tenants and Landlords* (Santa Monica: Santa Monica Rent Control Board, 1981), p. v.

10. See Derek Shearer, "How the Progressives Won in Santa Monica," *Social Policy* 12, no. 3 (Winter 1982): 8.

11. Author interview with Roger Thornton, Santa Monica, July 15, 1982.

12. See Zeitlin, "Tenant Power to Political Power," p. 16.

13. Shearer, "How the Progressives Won in Santa Monica," p. 14.

14. Ibid., p. 9.

15. Author interview with Dennis Zane, Santa Monica, July 28, 1982.

16. Shearer, "How the Progressives Won in Santa Monica," p. 12.

17. Author interview with William Jennings, Los Angeles, August 6, 1982.

18. Shearer, "How the Progressives Won in Santa Monica," p. 11.

19. See Chapter 3, note 4; see also Carnoy and Shearer, *Economic Democracy*, pp. 383–384, for their criticism of Hayden's role in CED.

20. C. Wright Mills, *The Power Elite* (New York: Oxford University Press, 1956), p. 11.

21. Author interview with Ruth Yannatta Goldway, Santa Monica, June 22, 1982.

23. G. William Domhoff, "State and Ruling Class in Corporate America," in Henry Etzkowitz and Peter Schwab, eds., *Is America Necessary?* (St. Paul, Minn.: West, 1976), p. 50.

25. Author interview with Derek Shearer, Santa Monica, June 17, 1982.

26. Reed interview; Jennings interview.

27. Ralph Miliband, *The State in Capitalist Society* (New York: Basic Books, 1969), chap. 6.

28. Author interview with Fred Allingham, Santa Monica, July 7, 1982.
29. Santa Monica Research Associates, Inc., *Santa Monica Research News* 1, no. 4 (April 1982): 1.
30. Allan Heskin, "After the Battle Is Won: Political Contradictions in Santa Monica," unpublished ms., pp. 12–14.
31. Author interview with John Alschuler, Santa Monica, July 14, 1982.
32. Author interview with Christopher Rudd, Santa Monica, June 29, 1982.
33. Shearer interview.
34. See Anne Morgenthaler, "Changes Come with Myers Administration," Santa Monica *Outlook*, February 21–22, 1982; Rick Martinez, "Police, Firefighters Like What They See," Santa Monica *Outlook*, October 6, 1981; and Kenneth Fanucchi, "Liberals' Budgeting Pleases Police Chief," Los Angeles *Times*, March 14, 1982.
35. Hamilton, Rabinowitz, and Szanton, Inc., "Review of California Fee Policies," March 1982, and "Review of Existing Santa Monica Development Fees," April 1982.
36. This language is taken from Santa Monica Ordinance no. 1220 adopted at the September 1, 1981, city council meeting.
37. Author interview with "Anonymous," Santa Monica, July 21, 1982.
38. Zane interview.
39. For example, see Robert Ross, "Regional Illusion, Capitalist Reality," *democracy* 2, no. 2 (April 1982): 93–99.
40. Aubrey Austin Jr., quoted in Charles Wallace, "Polarization of a City by Ballot Box," Los Angeles *Times*, June 15, 1981.
41. Barry Rosengrant, quoted in Dave Lindorff, "About-Face in Santa Monica," *Village Voice*, December 2–8, 1981.
42. Alschuler interview.
43. Barry Rubens, quoted in Ed Moosbrugger, "Bank Forming in SM," Santa Monica *Outlook*, July 9, 1982; see also Ed Moosbrugger, "SM Firm Rides Wave of New Banks, S&Ls," Santa Monica *Outlook*, January 31, 1983.
44. Author interview with James Conn, Santa Monica, August 25, 1982.
45. Reed interview.
46. Carl Boggs, "The New Populism and the Limits of Structural Reforms," *Theory and Society* 12, no. 3 (May 1983): 352.
47. Carnoy and Shearer, *Economic Democracy*, p. 384.
48. Quotation is taken from Radio KCRW broadcast of the April 19, 1983, meeting of the Santa Monica city council.
49. Author interview with Maurice Zeitlin, Los Angeles, July 12, 1982.
50. In different ways, this argument is made in Richard Sennett, *Authority* (New York: Knopf, 1980), and Christopher Lasch, *The Culture of Narcissism* (New York: Warner, 1979).

Chapter 5

1. E. F. Schumacher, *Small Is Beautiful* (New York: Harper & Row, 1973), p. 294.
2. Kirkpatrick Sale, *Human Scale* (New York: Coward, McCann and Geoghegan, 1980), p. 39.
3. Ruth Yannatta Goldway, quoted in Sam Hall Kaplan, "Paying for the Pier:

A Big Issue in Santa Monica," Los Angeles *Times*, March 23, 1983.

4. See Lisa Endig and Jane Bednar, "New Attractions Proposed for SM Pier," Santa Monica *Outlook*, September 14, 1982, and Kenneth Fanucchi, "Pier: Museum, More Fishing, No Cars," Los Angeles *Times*, September 12, 1982.

5. See Lisa Endig, "Pier Repair Work Taxing City's Staff," Santa Monica *Outlook*, March 16, 1983.

6. Dennis Zane, quoted in Lisa Endig, "Economic Concerns Color Pier's Future," Santa Monica *Outlook*, May 16, 1983.

7. See Anne Morgenthaler, "3 Experts Enlisted for Pier Panel," Santa Monica *Outlook*, July 18, 1983.

8. Ernie Powell, quoted in Endig, "Economic Concerns Color Pier's Future."

9. Maynard Ostrow, quoted in Jane Bednar, "Lessees Hail Nonprofit Pier Corporation," Santa Monica *Outlook*, May 11, 1983.

10. The SMRR councilmembers had a habit of telling people how "proud" they were of their various accomplishments. At at least one council meeting, the word was used so often that it generated laughter among councilmembers and audience. As we will see, such pride can be used as an excuse for holding on to power; and it does indeed cometh before the fall.

11. I am reserving a full discussion of the SMRR council's development policies for Chapter 7, where I discuss the radicals' approach to economic policies.

12. Author interview with John Alschuler, Santa Monica, July 14, 1982.

13. Sarah Tamor, quoted in Jennifer Smith, "Two-Day Art Conference Planned in Santa Monica," Santa Monica *Outlook*, April 28, 1983.

14. Kenneth Edwards, quoted in Jennifer Smith, "Forum Kicks Off Major SM Arts Program," Santa Monica *Outlook*, May 16, 1983.

15. Author interview with Dennis Zane, Santa Monica, July 28, 1982.

16. Debra Behr, "Santa Monica: Everything Under the Sun's in Santa Monica," Los Angeles *Times*, September 24, 1982.

17. City general services director Stan Scholl, quoted in Mark Fabian, "SM Weighs Gateway Project for Wilshire Boulevard," Santa Monica *Outlook*, October 25, 1983.

18. Mark Fabian, "A Clean Environment Top Priority in SM," Santa Monica *Outlook*, August 29, 1983.

19. Zane interview.

20. Author interview with James Conn, Santa Monica, August 25, 1982.

21. Ruth Yannatta Goldway city council speech broadcast over KCRW radio, July 27, 1982.

22. See the Ocean Park Community Organization (OPCO) Constitution available from OPCO, 237 Hill St., Santa Monica, CA 90405; see also "OPCO Is . . . ," an OPCO recruitment flyer.

23. Harvey Molotch, "The City as a Growth Machine: Toward a Political Economy of Place," in Harlan Hahn and Charles Levine, eds., *Urban Politics: Past, Present, and Future* (New York: Longman, 1980), p. 143.

24. William Tabb and Larry Sawers, "Editors' Introduction," in William Tabb and Larry Sawers, eds., *Marxism and the Metropolis* (New York: Oxford University Press, 1978), p. 14.

25. Harlan Hahn and Charles Levine, "The Politics of Urban America and the Study of Urban Politics," in Hahn and Levine, eds., *Urban Politics*, p. 35.

26. Author interview with Dolores Press, Santa Monica, July 19, 1982.

27. Author interview with Kenneth Edwards, Santa Monica, July 22, 1982.

28. Author interview with Herman Rosenstein, Santa Monica, June 30, 1984.

29. Author interview with Allan Heskin, Santa Monica, July 9, 1982.

30. Author interview with Fred Allingham, Santa Monica, July 7, 1982.

31. See Barbara Baird, "S.M. Study Finds Latinos Alienated," Los Angeles *Times*, May 29, 1983.

32. David O'Malley, quoted in Anne Morgenthaler, "Financing Plans to Rebuild Pier Unveiled," Santa Monica *Outlook*, April 7, 1983.

33. Author interview with Maurice Zeitlin, Los Angeles, July 12, 1982.

34. Sale, *Human Scale*, p. 188.

35. Milton Kotler, "An Interview with Milton Kotler," *Social Policy* 12, no. 3 (Winter 1982): 31–32.

36. "Recommendations of Citizens Task Force, Development Permit Processes and Neighborhood Planning, Adopted August 20, 1981," available from Santa Monica city hall.

37. Memorandum prepared by Joseph Eisenhut from city staff to the mayor and city council, dated October 27, 1981.

38. "Recommendations of the Citizens Task Force on Development Permit Processes and Neighborhood Planning, March 25, 1982," available from Santa Monica city hall. The ensuing quotations are taken from this document.

39. Author interview with Vivian Rothstein, Santa Monica, July 7, 1982.

40. Arrie Bachrach, "Letter to the Editor," Santa Monica *Outlook*, October 15, 1982.

41. Dennis Zane, Kenneth Edwards, and Mark Tigan, quoted in Lisa Endig, "Veto Power Proposal Draws Heavy Criticism," Santa Monica *Outlook*, May 23, 1983.

42. Conn interview.

43. Edwards interview.

44. Allan Heskin, "After the Battle Is Won: Political Contradictions in Santa Monica," unpublished ms., p. 25.

45. Like the word "proud," the word "responsibility" was a basic part of the SMRR councilmembers' daily vocabulary. The next chapter in particular will show how "responsibility" can become an excuse for not sharing political power.

46. Author interview with Ruth Yannatta Goldway, Santa Monica, June 22, 1982.

47. Mark Fabian, "Mid-City Neighbors' Newsletter Stirs City Hall Furor," Santa Monica *Outlook*, September 7, 1983.

48. Santa Monicans for Renters' Rights, "Principles of Unity Between Members of the Santa Monicans for Renters' Right Coalition, February 1981," p. 4.

49. See "Shaping Our Future," the program for OPCO's 3rd Annual Community Congress, November 14, 1982.

50. "Broadway Angels," OPCO *Newsletter*, April 1982, p. 5.

51. Author interview with Derek Shearer, Santa Monica, June 17, 1982.

52. Joe Miko Jr., quoted in Kenneth Fanucchi, "Farmers, Customers to Go to Market," Los Angeles *Times*, July 12, 1981.

53. See Ed Moosbrugger, "Need Cited for First-Class Hotel Rooms to Enhance SM Tourism," Santa Monica *Outlook*, March 9, 1984.

54. See Anne Morgenthaler, "New York City Official Named to Head Pier Restoration Corp.," Santa Monica *Outlook*, March 29, 1984.

55. See Lisa Endig, "Farmers Market Planned for Pico Area," Santa Monica *Outlook*, March 29, 1983.

56. Shearer interview.

57. Edwards interview; Shearer interview.

58. Joe Miko Jr., "The Incoming President's Message," in "Santa Monica Area Chamber of Commerce: 60 Years of Service to the Community," published in the Santa Monica *Outlook*, May 31, 1983.

59. See Mark Fabian, "Business Tax Action Delayed," Santa Monica *Outlook*, September 28, 1983, and "Council, Chamber See Eye-to-Eye on Tax Issue," Santa Monica *Outlook*, October 19, 1983.

60. See Jane Bednar, "Impending Boosts Spawn Talk of Commercial Rent Control," Santa Monica *Outlook*, January 12, 1983.

61. Robert Myers, Don Arnett, and Richard Chacker, quoted in Ellis Conkin, "Beach Vendors Upset by SM Bid to Increase Rents," Santa Monica *Outlook*, March 1, 1984.

62. See Mark Fabian, "Burger Pact OK'd," Santa Monica *Outlook*, April 11, 1984.

63. See Anne Morgenthaler, "SM Residents Favor 15 Foot Breakwater for Pier," *The Daily Breeze*, July 15, 1984.

64. Mark Tigan, quoted in Russell Snyder, "Suit Filed to Halt Moby Dick's Eviction," Santa Monica *Outlook*, January 26, 1984.

65. David Moberg, "Experimenting with the Future: Alternative Institutions and Socialism," in John Case and Rosemary Taylor, eds., *Co-ops, Communes and Collectives* (New York: Pantheon, 1979), p. 299.

66. Conn interview.

67. Frances Fox Piven and Richard A. Cloward, *Poor People's Movements* (New York: Vintage, 1979).

68. Ibid., p. xxi.

Chapter 6

1. Ruth Yannatta Goldway, "How Women Will Change American Politics," *Playgirl*, July 1982, p. 32.

2. Isaac Balbus, *Marxism and Domination* (Princeton, N.J.: Princeton University Press, 1982), p. 358.

3. Author interview with Roger Thornton, Santa Monica, July 15, 1982.

4. Author interview with Dennis Zane, Santa Monica, July 28, 1982.

5. Allan Heskin, "After the Battle Is Won: Political Contradictions in Santa Monica," unpublished ms., p. 8.

6. According to an author interview with Herman Rosenstein, Santa Monica, June 30, 1984, this logic worked itself out quite clearly in the candidate selection process preceding the April 1983 municipal election.

7. This information comes from several informal talks with activists. I might add that the compact minority strategy helps to explain the demise of democratic processes in many leftwing organizations.

8. Parke Skelton, interviewed on KCRW radio, April 12, 1983.

9. Zane interview.

10. The actual text of the resolution was reported in Lisa Endig, "City Council

Passes Resolution in Support of Israel," Santa Monica *Outlook*, June 30, 1982.

11. The partial text of Press's letter was published in Lisa Endig, "Press Raps Employees' Opposition to Israel Vote," Santa Monica *Outlook*, July 27, 1982; the full text was read over KCRW radio, July 27, 1982.
12. Curt Ullman and Margie Gillies, quoted respectively in Endig, "Press Raps Employees' Opposition to Israel Vote."
13. Christine Reed, quoted in Elizabeth Mehren, "Santa Monica Has Own Foreign Policy," Los Angeles *Times*, August 29, 1982.
14. Tom Hayden, quoted in Will Thorne, "Hayden Criticizes SM Foreign Policy," Santa Monica *Outlook*, October 6, 1982.
15. Author interview with Kenneth Edwards, Santa Monica, July 22, 1982.
16. Cheryl Rhoden, quoted in Charles P. Wallace, "Polarization of a City by Ballot Box," Los Angeles *Times*, June 15, 1981.
17. Santa Monica *Outlook* editorial, September 2, 1982.
18. Author interview with "Anonymous," Santa Monica, July 21, 1982.
19. It would be too cumbersome to cite the extraordinary number of instances in which the SMRR councilmembers used the word "responsibility" or expressed a sense of being "responsible" in the course of my interviews. Suffice it to say that they rarely strayed from responsibility when explaining their actions.
20. Author interview with James Conn, Santa Monica, August 25, 1982.
21. For example, see Sydney Verba and Norman Nie, *Participation in America: Political Democracy and Social Equality* (New York: Harper & Row, 1972).
22. Within an American context, a perfectly free system of political participation is likely to produce domination by lawyers. This is one of the criticisms of Bruce Ackerman's recent theory of social justice. See Ben Agger, "A Critical Theory of Dialogue"; Michael Mosher, "Illiberal Prospects"; and Emily Albrink Fowler, "Skepticism in Stasis," all in *Humanities in Society* 4, no. 1 (Winter 1981): 7–68.
23. For example, see Howard I. Kalodner, "Citizen Participation in Emerging Social Institutions" in J. Roland Pennock and John W. Chapman, eds., *Participation in Politics* (New York: Lieber-Atherton, 1975), pp. 161–185.
24. This information is taken from the program for OPCO's third annual congress, November 14, 1982.
25. This information is taken from an article called "Meet the PNA Board," published in the Pico Neighborhood Association *Newsletter*, no. 2, n.d.
26. Edwards interview.
27. This information came from a list that accompanied the Commercial and Industrial Task Force report, available from Santa Monica city hall.
28. Author interview with Christopher Rudd, Santa Monica, June 29, 1982.
29. Ruth Yannatta Goldway, quoted in Wallace, "Polarization of a City by Ballot Box."
30. The quotes come from the Commercial and Industrial Task Force report, revised to include planning commission recommendations before being forwarded to the city council, n.d., provided to me by the planning commission staff in Santa Monica city hall.
31. The texts of these council actions, dated respectively October 27, 1981, and June 1, 1982, are available from Santa Monica city hall.

32. See Lisa Endig, "Conn Proud of 'Fathering' Arts Panel," Santa Monica *Outlook*, July 30, 1982.

33. See Ed Moosbrugger, "Executive to Head Mall Revitalization," Santa Monica *Outlook*, July 26, 1984.

34. Zane interview.

35. Author interview with Dolores Press, Santa Monica, July 19, 1982.

36. Author interview with John Alschuler, Santa Monica, July 14, 1982.

37. Christine Reed and William Jennings, quoted in Jane Bednar, "Councilmembers Criticize Beach Club Lease," Santa Monica *Outlook*, August 20, 1982.

38. See Lisa Endig, "Council Accepts Sand and Sea Club Proposal," Santa Monica *Outlook*, August 18, 1982.

39. Conn interview.

40. Ibid.

41. See Anne Morgenthaler, "Beach Club Lease Plan Defended," Santa Monica *Outlook*, August 23, 1982, and Jane Bednar and Anne Morgenthaler, "Competing Interests Hit Beach at Sand and Sea," Santa Monica *Outlook*, August 28-29, 1982.

42. Conn interview.

43. John Alschuler, quoted in Lisa Endig, "SM Presses for Acquisition of Beach Club," Santa Monica *Outlook*, June 16, 1983.

44. See Mark Fabian, "Rules for Pier Board Sessions Discussed," Santa Monica *Outlook*, October 14, 1983, and "Alschuler Won't Fight Open Talks," Santa Monica *Outlook*, November 5-6, 1983.

45. Robert Myers, quoted in Mark Fabian, "Councilmembers Criticize Proposed Closed Session," Santa Monica *Outlook*, November 8, 1983.

46. Goldway, "How Women Will Change American Politics," pp. 30-31.

47. See Lisa Endig, "More Women Climbing City Hall Job Ladder," Santa Monica *Outlook*, October 11, 1982.

48. See Lisa Endig, "Fire Department Lacks Women," Santa Monica *Outlook*, September 22, 1982, and Lisa Endig and Jane Bednar, "SMFD Seeks More Women, Minority Recruits," Santa Monica *Outlook*, May 18, 1983.

49. See Lisa Endig, "SM Firefighters Back Hiring Plan," Santa Monica *Outlook*, June 15, 1983.

50. Jean Stanley and an unnamed secretary, quoted in Lisa Endig, "Reaction Mixed to SM Reclassification," Santa Monica *Outlook*, January 21, 1983.

51. The turf wars at times pitted Robert Myers against the rent control board staff and John Alschuler against city planning commissioners, but the lines of bureaucratic conflict over jurisdiction were far more complex. The results of these battles included mostly disenchantment but also a threatened public employees' strike and several resignations.

52. See Lisa Endig and Jane Bednar, "SM Preparing Alternatives to Parking Meters," Santa Monica *Outlook*, October 26, 1982.

53. I conducted a series of informal interviews with activists, task force members, and city staff people during the summer of 1984. I discovered a consistent thread of disenchantment with what most of the interviewees condemned as the professionalization of city politics. Several had felt this for quite a while but were only willing to express themselves publicly after the trend had progressed quite far.

54. I develop the implications of a crisis of political authority much more in

Mark E. Kann, "Consent and Authority in America," in John P. Diggins and Mark E. Kann, eds., *The Problem of Authority in America* (Philadelphia: Temple University Press, 1981), pp. 59–83.

Chapter 7

1. Tom Hayden, quoted in Marian Christy, "The New Tom Hayden," Boston *Globe*, February 3, 1980; see also Tom Hayden, *The American Future: New Visions Beyond Old Frontiers* (Boston: South End, 1980), chap. 1.
2. Jane Fonda, quoted in John Wilson, "See Jane Run," Los Angeles *Times*, April 29, 1984.
3. Author interview with Dolores Press, Santa Monica, July 19, 1982.
4. Lester Thurow, *The Zero-Sum Society* (Middlesex, Eng., and New York: Penguin, 1981), pp. 104–105.
5. Author interview with Maurice Zeitlin, Los Angeles, July 12, 1982.
6. Press interview.
7. An excellent analysis of the immediacy of the needs of low income people is Paul Jacobs, "Keeping the Poor Poor," in Jerome Skolnick and Elliott Currie, eds., *Crisis in American Institutions*, 3rd ed. (Boston: Little Brown, 1976), pp. 129–139.
8. Derek Shearer, interviewed on CBS's "60 Minutes," taken from the August 8, 1982, broadcast, "Left City."
9. Several good articles on the effects of rent control in Santa Monica are Frank Bies, "The Joys of Rent Control: House Hunting in the People's Republic of Santa Monica," *California Magazine*, January 1983, pp. 49–50; Alan Citron, "Santa Monica—Only the Elite Need Apply," and Ellie Kahn, "Treasure Hunting in Santa Monica," Los Angeles *Times*, April 8, 1984; and Mary Thompson, "Some Units Said Kept Off Market," Santa Monica *Outlook*, June 13, 1983.
10. David Shulman, "SM City Council: Conservatives Posing as Radicals," Santa Monica *Outlook*, July 23, 1981.
11. Dennis Zane, quoted in Kenneth Fanucchi, "'Radical' S.M. Council Branded Conservative in First 100 Days," Los Angeles *Times*, July 30, 1981.
12. Author interview with Allan Heskin, Santa Monica, July 9, 1982.
13. There were some earlier allocations, but the bulk of them materialized in late 1983 and early 1984.
14. For example, see Jane Bednar, "Design of Affordable Housing Units Unveiled," Santa Monica *Outlook*, July 8, 1982.
15. Superior Court Judge Laurence Rittenband, quoted in Anne Morgenthaler, "Curbs on SM Development Fees Reaffirmed," Santa Monica *Outlook*, July 13, 1982.
16. See Jane Bednar, "War Heating Up on Home Ownership Initiative," Santa Monica *Outlook*, December 10, 1982.
17. Ralph Nader, quoted in Mike Tipping, "Nader Denounces HOME Bid," Santa Monica *Outlook*, March 29, 1983.
18. See Allan Heskin, *Tenants and the American Dream: Ideology and the Tenant Movement* (New York: Praeger, 1983), pp. 183–185.
19. Dennis Zane, quoted in Mark Fabian, "Condo Conversion Measure Adopted in 'Landslide,'" Santa Monica *Outlook*, June 6, 1984.

20. Jane Bednar, "Call for City-Run Clinic Gets Cool Reception," Santa Monica *Outlook*, January 29–30, 1983.

21. See Sheldon Wolin, "The State of the Union," *New York Review of Books*, May 18, 1978, p. 31, and Christopher Lasch, "Democracy and the 'Crisis of Confidence,'" *democracy* 1, no. 1 (January 1981): 27.

22. Cited in Lisa Endig, "Ordinance Makes Landlord Abuses Open to Prosecution," Santa Monica *Outlook*, October 13, 1982.

23. Fred Allingham, quoted in Jane Bednar, "City Subsidy Held Key to Pico Area Market," Santa Monica *Outlook*, May 3, 1983; cf. Lisa Endig, "SM Weighs Opening Food Co-op," Santa Monica *Outlook*, August 4, 1982.

24. Ibid.

25. See Nancy McFarland, "CDBG Grantee Performance Report," August 26, 1982, available at Santa Monica city hall.

26. See Mary Love, "Senior Dana Deputy Sees That SM Gets Generous Slice of County Pie," Santa Monica *Outlook*, July 15, 1982.

27. For example, see Lisa Endig, "New SM Office Aids the Disabled," Santa Monica *Outlook*, February 17, 1983.

28. Author interview with Derek Shearer, Santa Monica, June 17, 1982.

29. Author interview with James Conn, Santa Monica, August 25, 1982.

30. For example, see Sean Hillier, "Cameras Roll as Cable TV Workers Picket Studio," Santa Monica *Outlook*, July 17–18, 1982, and "Cable TV Strikers Win Council Backing," Santa Monica *Outlook*, August 4, 1982.

31. Zeitlin interview.

32. Cheryl Rhoden, "Letter to the Editor," Santa Monica *Outlook*, July 14, 1982.

33. Press interview.

34. Rent control board chair David Finkel interviewed on KCRW radio, April 12, 1983.

35. Author interview with Dennis Zane, Santa Monica, July 28, 1982.

36. Author interview with Kenneth Edwards, July 22, 1982.

37. Salvatore Osio, quoted in Anne Morgenthaler, "Bankruptcy Move Laid to SM Policy for Development," Santa Monica *Outlook*, July 2, 1982.

38. John Kaufman, quoted in Ed Moosbrugger, "'Blue Ribbon' Developers to Shun SM," Santa Monica *Outlook*, May 9, 1983.

39. See Jane Bednar, "New SM Building Guide Displeases Some," Santa Monica *Outlook*, March 23, 1983.

40. Ruth Yannatta Goldway, quoted in Lou Siegel, "Santa Monica Demands More from Its Developers," Los Angeles *Herald Examiner*, October 26, 1981.

41. CeCe Bradley, quoted in Pat Alston, "Pico Community Backs Development Project," Santa Monica *Outlook*, March 19–20, 1983.

42. Dennis Zane, quoted in Lisa Endig, "Eased Growth Policy Seen in Project Approval," Santa Monica *Outlook*, June 15, 1983.

43. See Mark Fabian, "Staff Freeze on Development Pacts Disputed," Santa Monica *Outlook*, September 20, 1983.

44. See Mark Fabian, "SM Thaws Staff 'Freeze' on Developer Pacts," Santa Monica *Outlook*, September 21, 1983.

45. Robert Kleffel, quoted in Jane Bednar, "Rhoden, Kleffel Quit Planning Unit," Santa Monica *Outlook*, August 3, 1982.

46. See Mark Fabian, "Cadillac Project Approved," Santa Monica *Outlook*, October 26, 1983.

47. See Ed Moosbrugger, "Cadillac Dealership Kills Plans to Relocate in Santa Monica," Santa Monica *Outlook*, May 6, 1984.
48. Edwards interview.
49. John Alschuler, quoted in Jane Bednar, "Experts See Plenty of Room for SM Growth," Santa Monica *Outlook*, November 22, 1982; see also Jane Bednar, "Plant, Office Plan Urged for SM's Industrial Area," Santa Monica *Outlook*, April 5, 1983.
50. See Mary Thompson, "SM's Goals for Land Use Challenged," Santa Monica *Outlook*, June 21, 1983.
51. Jim Wannemacher, quoted in Anne Morgenthaler, "Revision of Land Use Plan Presented," Santa Monica *Outlook*, July 30, 1984.
52. Ken Genser, quoted in Anne Morgenthaler, " 'Hot Spots' Emerge in Land Use Plan," Santa Monica *Outlook*, August 29, 1984.
53. Mark Fabian, "Change in Land Use Proposals Hit by Planners," Santa Monica *Outlook*, October 9, 1984.
54. See Mark Fabian, "SM to Seek U.S. Funds for Aid to Becket Project," Santa Monica *Outlook*, January 25, 1984, and Ed Moosbrugger, "SM Bid for Grant Based on Economic Distress," Santa Monica *Outlook*, March 8, 1984.
55. See Mark Fabian, "$1.6 Million Housing Project OK'd," Santa Monica *Outlook*, December 14, 1983.
56. Zane interview.
57. Shearer interview.
58. Author interview with Ruth Yannatta Goldway, Santa Monica, June 22, 1982.
59. See Mike Tipping, "Renters' Group Accused of Plan for City-Ownership of Rentals," Santa Monica *Outlook*, March 12–13, 1983.

Chapter 8

1. Ruth Yannatta Goldway, quoted in Lisa Endig, "The Race Goes On: Now It's Council's Turn," Santa Monica *Outlook*, November 6–7, 1982.
2. Cheryl Rhoden, quoted in Moe Stavnezer, "Renters' Rights Setback in Santa Monica Election," Los Angeles *Catalyst*, June 1983.
3. Dennis Zane, quoted in Mike Tipping, "Zane Sees April Balloting as SMRR's 'Coup de Grace,' " Santa Monica *Outlook*, February 14, 1983.
4. Tom Hayden, interviewed on KCRW radio, Santa Monica, April 12, 1983.
5. Kenneth Edwards, interviewed on KCRW radio, April 12, 1983.
6. See Allan Heskin, "After the Battle Is Won: Political Contradictions in Santa Monica," unpublished ms., pp. 2–3.
7. Ruth Yannatta Goldway, quoted in Kenneth Fanucchi, "Santa Monica Renters Saw No Reason to Vote," Los Angeles *Times*, April 25, 1983.
8. Thomas Laramore, quoted in Robert Lindsey, "In 'People's Republic of Santa Monica,' Voters Turn to the Right," New York *Times*, April 17, 1983.
9. Ruth Yannatta Goldway and Kenneth Edwards, city council speeches broadcast over KCRW radio, May 19, 1983.
10. Editorial, Santa Monica *Outlook*, February 14, 1983.
11. William Jennings, quoted in Rich Seeley, "Pros, Cons of SM Renters' Group Dominate Forum," Santa Monica *Outlook*, March 7, 1983.
12. KerryAnn Lobel, quoted in ibid.

13. Ruth Yannatta Goldway, quoted in Mike Tipping, "Battle Lines Set in Council Race," Santa Monica *Outlook*, February 4, 1983.

14. Kenneth Edwards, interviewed on KCRW radio, April 12, 1983.

15. Mary Kay Kamath, quoted in Mike Tipping, "BEST Group Backs Slate for School Board," Santa Monica *Outlook*, February 9, 1983.

16. Christine Reed, quoted in Fanucchi, "Santa Monica Renters Saw No Reason to Vote."

17. Parke Skelton, quoted in ibid.

18. Author interview with Kenneth Edwards, Santa Monica, July 22, 1982.

19. Ruth Yannatta Goldway, quoted in Kenneth Fanucchi, "SM Candidates Gird for April 12," Los Angeles *Times*, January 16, 1983.

20. William Allen, quoted in Mike Tipping, "Activist Withdrawing from Political Arena," Santa Monica *Outlook*, February 7, 1983.

21. Author interview with Herman Rosenstein, June 30, 1984.

22. Derek Shearer tape, quoted in Mike Tipping, "Mailed Cassette of Goldway's Remarks Termed 'Misleading,'" Santa Monica *Outlook*, April 1, 1983.

23. Shearer tape, quoted in Will Thorne, "400 Help Coalition Rev Up Campaign," Santa Monica *Outlook*, February 28, 1983.

24. Parke Skelton, quoted in Tipping, "Mailed Cassette."

25. See Lisa Endig, "HUD Receives 2 Letters Dealing with Alleged Funding Violations," Santa Monica *Outlook*, March 30, 1983.

26. John Alschuler, quoted in Jane Bednar, "City Warns Community Groups on Federal Funding Violations," Santa Monica *Outlook*, June 1, 1983.

27. See Lisa Endig, "Budget Ax Cripples OPCO," Santa Monica *Outlook*, June 22, 1983, and Mike Tipping, "OPCO Faces Bleak Future After Council Cuts Funds," Santa Monica *Outlook*, June 23, 1983.

28. All quotations in this paragraph are from Heskin, "After the Battle Is Won," pp. 1–30.

29. I gave a number of talks in Santa Monica in the year following the election losses. Previous to the election, it was difficult to get people to be critical of SMRR in private; after the election, I listened to activists and people in the city bureaucracy criticize SMRR in public gatherings without hesitation.

30. Thom Poffenberger, quoted in "Slates Already Planning Next Election," Santa Monica *Outlook*, June 25–26, 1983.

31. Dennis Zane, quoted in ibid.

32. Kenneth Edwards, quoted in Will Thorne, "Infighting Threatens Future of Plan to Restructure SMRR," Santa Monica *Outlook*, October 20, 1983. It is significant to note that this was the first time since William Jennings bolted SMRR years earlier that the coalition's internal politics became public knowledge.

33. Marianne Boretz, quoted in ibid.

34. John Alschuler, quoted in Anne Morgenthaler, "Acting Director Handed Top City Planning Position," Santa Monica *Outlook*, August 20, 1984.

35. Robert Myers, quoted in Will Thorne, "Myers Backs Incumbent Judge over Ex-Colleague," Santa Monica *Outlook*, March 3–4, 1984.

36. Kenneth Edwards, quoted in Will Thorne, "SMRR-Supported Officials Explain Stand on Issues," Santa Monica *Outlook*, April 16, 1984.

37. Christine Reed, quoted in ibid.

38. Gerald Goldman, quoted in Mark Fabian, "Disillusioned SMRR Supporter

Seeks Council Seat," Santa Monica *Outlook*, October 17, 1984.

39. See Mark Fabian, "Willis Seeks to Represent Minorities on SM Council," Santa Monica *Outlook*, October 24, 1984.

40. Herb Katz, quoted in Mark Fabian, "Katz, Civic-Minded Architect, Runs for Council," Santa Monica *Outlook*, October 18, 1984.

41. Irene Zivi, quoted in Mark Fabian, "Zivi Walks, Climbs While Running for Council," Santa Monica *Outlook*, October 26, 1984.

42. Dennis Zane, quoted in Mark Fabian, "Zane Seeks Re-Election to Guard Rent Control," Santa Monica *Outlook*, October 25, 1984.

43. James Conn, quoted in Mark Fabian, "Airport, Art Special Concerns of James Conn," Santa Monica *Outlook*, October 15, 1984.

44. Ibid.

45. Dolores Press, quoted in Mark Fabian, "Press Tells Why She's Making Write-In Effort for Council Seat," Santa Monica *Outlook*, October 23, 1984.

46. Kenneth Edwards, quoted in Mark Fabian, "Edwards Leans on Talent as Catalyst in Re-Election Bid," Santa Monica *Outlook*, October 16, 1984.

47. Ibid.

48. Kelly Hayes-Raitt, quoted in "Toward Nuclear-Free Santa Monica," *Peace Conversion Times* 2, no. 9 (October 1984): 1.

49. Editorial, Santa Monica *Outlook*, October 24, 1984.

50. See Jan Stevens, "Proposition TT Gap Too Wide to Bridge," Santa Monica *Outlook*, November 13, 1984.

51. Stephen Rivers, quoted in Mark Fabian, "Santa Monica Power Drive Changes Gears," Santa Monica *Outlook*, November 7, 1984.

52. I have considered this phenomenon in great detail in Mark E. Kann, *The American Left: Failures and Fortunes* (New York: Praeger, 1982).

53. Michael Walzer, "Philosophy and Democracy," in John Nelson, ed., *What Should Political Theory Be Now?* (Albany: State University of New York Press, 1983), p. 75.

54. Author interview with Conrad Melilli, Santa Monica, September 30, 1984.

55. See Stevens, "Proposition TT Gap Too Wide to Bridge," and Kathy Rethlake, "Hispanic Involvement Pushed," Santa Monica *Outlook*, September 21, 1984.

56. See Anne Morgenthaler, "Press Disappointed She Let SMRR Down," Santa Monica *Outlook*, November 9, 1984.

Chapter 9

1. Martin Carnoy and Derek Shearer, *Economic Democracy: The Challenge of the 1980s* (White Plains, N.Y.: M. E. Sharpe, 1980), p. 403.

2. Carl Boggs, "The New Populism and the Limits of Structural Reforms," *Theory and Society* 12, no. 3 (May 1983): 356–357.

3. Jack Nicholl, "Dear Fellow Californian," Campaign for Economic Democracy mass mailing, April 1985.

4. Santa Monicans for Renters' Rights, *Year Seven* 1, no. 1 (Spring 1985): 1.

5. Paul Starr, "The Phantom Community," in John Case and Rosemary Taylor, eds., *Co-ops, Communes and Collectives*, (New York: Pantheon, 1979), p. 262.

6. Ibid., p. 263.

7. Jennifer Hochschild, *What's Fair? American Beliefs About Distributive Justice* (Cambridge, Mass.: Harvard University Press, 1981), p. 242.

8. Howard Zinn, *A People's History of the United States* (New York: Harper & Row, 1980), p. 59.

9. Sheldon Wolin, "The People's Two Bodies," *democracy*, 1, no. 1 (January 1981): 12.

10. See Walter Fisher, "Reaffirmation and Subversion of the American Dream," *Quarterly Journal of Speech* 59, no. 2 (April 1973): 160–167, for a discussion of the nation's two American Dreams.

11. See John P. Diggins and Mark E. Kann, eds., *The Problem of Authority in America* (Philadelphia: Temple University Press, 1981), chaps. 1–3.

12. See Louis Hartz, *The Liberal Tradition in America* (New York: Harcourt Brace and World, 1955), esp. chap. 5, which is entitled "The American Democrat: Hercules and Hamlet."

13. David Moberg, "Experimenting with the Future: Alternative Institutions and American Socialism," in Case and Taylor, eds., *Co-ops, Communes and Collectives*, p. 303.

14. Barbara Ehrenreich, *The Hearts of Men: American Dreams and the Flight from Commitment* (Garden City, N.Y.: Anchor, 1984), p. 151.

15. Ibid., 151–152.

16. One of the major criticisms of middle class radicalism is that its appeal is strikingly similar to that of new right populists. For example, see Al Szymanski, "A Critique and Extension of the Professional Managerial Class," in Pat Walker, ed., *Between Labor and Capital*, (Boston: South End, 1979), pp. 49–65.

17. I discuss this at greater length in Mark E. Kann, *The American Left: Failures and Fortunes* (New York: Praeger, 1982), chap. 2.

18. See Harry C. Boyte, *The Backyard Revolution* (Philadelphia: Temple University Press, 1980), pp. 162–164.

19. Barbara and John Ehrenreich, "Rejoinder," in Walker, ed., *Between Labor and Capital*, pp. 329–330.

20. For an excellent discussion, see Joel Kotkin and Paul Grabowicz, *California, Inc.* (New York: Rawson Wade, 1982), particularly chap. 4, which is titled "Jerry Brown and the New Class."

21. Michael Novak, *The American Vision: An Essay on the Future of Democratic Capitalism* (Washington, D.C.: American Enterprise Institute, 1978), p. 33.

22. Cf. Ralph Miliband, *The State in Capitalist Society* (New York: Basic Books, 1969), and Nora Hamilton, *The Limits of State Autonomy: Post-Revolutionary Mexico* (Princeton, N.J.: Princeton University Press, 1982).

23. Katherine Coit, "Local Action, Not Citizen Participation," in William Tabb and Larry Sawers, eds., *Marxism and the Metropolis* (New York: Oxford University Press, 1978), p. 298.

24. See Frances Fox Piven and Richard A. Cloward, *Poor People's Movements* (New York: Vintage, 1979), chap. 1.

25. Michael Walzer, *Spheres of Justice: A Defense of Pluralism and Equality* (New York: Basic Books, 1983), p. xi.

26. For example, one might consider the leadership question in the early American Socialist party. See Mark E. Kann, "Challenging Lockean Liberalism in

America: The Case of Debs and Hillquit," *Political Theory* 8, no. 2 (May
1980): 203–222.

311
Notes to
Chapter 9

27. Cf. Boyte, *The Backyard Revolution*, pp. 204–208, and Jerome Karabel,
"Revolutionary Contradictions: Antonio Gramsci and the Problem of Intellectuals," *Politics and Society* 6, no. 2 (1976): 123–172.

28. For example, see Nancy Hartsock, "Staying Alive," in Charlotte Bunch et al.,
eds., *Building Feminist Theory* (New York: Longman, 1981), pp. 111–122.

29. Author interview with James Conn, Santa Monica, August 25, 1982.

30. For example, the SMRR radicals constantly criticized homeowners despite
the fact that many of those who supported the tenant movement and the
SMRR politicians were tenants aspiring to become homeowners. But the
SMRR councilmembers were too busy practicing "good government" in city
hall to notice. See Allan Heskin, *Tenants and the American Dream: Ideology
and the Tenant Movement*: (New York: Praeger, 1983), p. 251.

31. See Allan Heskin, "After the Battle Is Won: Political Contradictions in Santa
Monica," unpublished ms., p. 14.

32. Eugene V. Debs, *Writings and Speeches of Eugene V. Debs*, ed. Arthur
Schlesinger Jr. (New York: Hermitage, 1948), p. 225.

33. For example, see Isaac Balbus, *Marxism and Domination* (Princeton, N.J.:
Princeton University Press, 1982), pp. 362–366.

34. Peter Bachrach, "Democracy and Class Struggle," in Mark E. Kann, ed., *The
Future of American Democracy: Views from the Left* (Philadelphia: Temple
University Press, 1983), pp. 246–247.

35. Boggs, "The New Populism and the Limits of Structural Reforms," p. 355.

36. Sandy Carter, "Class Conflict: The Human Dimension," in Walker, ed.,
Between Labor and Capital, p. 113.

37. Author interview with Derek Shearer, Santa Monica, June 17, 1982.

38. Santa Monicans for Renters' Rights, *Year Seven* 1, no. 1 (Spring 1985): 12.

39. Author interview with Vivian Rothstein, Santa Monica, July 7, 1982.

40. Michael Walzer, *Obligations: Essays on Disobedience, War, and Citizenship*
(New York: Clarion, 1970), p. 238.

41. In different ways, this argument is made in Richard Sennett, *Authority* (New
York: Knopf, 1980), and Christopher Lasch, *The Culture of Narcissism* (New
York: Warner, 1979).

42. I have explored why political education never quite meets the standards of
intellectuals in Mark E. Kann, "Political Education and Equality," *Teaching
Political Science* 8 (July 1981): 417–446.

43. Author interview with Dolores Press, Santa Monica, July 19, 1982.

44. Harlan Hahn, "Alternative Paths to Professionalization: The Development
of Municipal Personnel," in Charles H. Levine, ed., *Managing Human Resources: A Challenge to Urban Governments* (Beverly Hills, Calif.: Sage,
1977), p. 47.

45. Larry Hirschhorn, "Alternative Services and the Crisis of the Professions,"
in Case and Taylor, eds., *Co-ops, Communes and Collectives*, pp. 186–187.

46. Author interview with Ruth Yannatta Goldway, Santa Monica, June 22, 1982.

47. Walzer, *Spheres of Justice*, p. 109.

48. Ibid., p. 121.

49. Hannah Arendt, *Crises of the Republic* (New York: Harcourt Brace Jovanovich, 1972), p. 88.

50. Sennett, *Authority*, p. 168.

1. Maurice Zeitlin, "Tenant Power to Political Power," *The Nation*, July 4, 1981, p. 17.
2. William Appleman Williams, "The City on a Hill on an Errand into the Wilderness," in Harrison Salisbury, ed., *Vietnam Reconsidered*, (New York: Harper & Row, 1984), p. 11.
3. Tom Hayden, *The American Future: New Visions Beyond Old Frontiers* (Boston: South End, 1980), pp. 300–301.
4. Martin Carnoy and Derek Shearer, *Economic Democracy: The Challenge of the 1980s* (White Plains, N.Y.: M. E. Sharpe, 1980), pp. 396–402.
5. See James Weinstein, *The Decline of Socialism in America, 1912–1925* (New York: Vintage, 1967), pp. 94–102, 116–118.
6. Author interview with Ruth Yannatta Goldway, Santa Monica, June 22, 1982.
7. Harry C. Boyte, "The Politics of Community," *The Nation*, January 12, 1985, pp. 12–15.
8. See George Shulman, "The Pastoral Idyll of *democracy*," *democracy* 3, no. 4 (Fall 1983): 43–54. The journal *democracy*, while it lasted, was a rich source of debate over the strengths and weaknesses of localism.
9. See Jeff Lustig, "Community and Social Class," *democracy* 1, no. 2 (April 1981): 96–111.
10. Paul Starr, "The Phantom Community," in John Case and Rosemary Taylor, eds., *Co-ops, Communes and Collectives*, (New York: Pantheon, 1979), p. 259.
11. David Vogel, "On Democratic Investment," *democracy* 2, no. 3 (July 1982): 140.
12. Jack Nicholl, quoted in Alan Citron, "CED Shuns Its Radical Roots in Shifting to a New Agenda," Los Angeles *Times*, February 26, 1985.
13. William Appleman Williams, "Procedure Becomes Substance," *democracy* 2, no. 2 (April 1982): 102.
14. Ruth Yannatta Goldway, quoted in Muriel Dobbin, "Santa Monica Renter Revolt: Is It the Wave of the Future?" Baltimore *Sun*, August 10, 1981.
15. See Gordon Wood, *The Creation of the American Republic, 1776–1787* (New York: Norton, 1969), pp. 226–237, 319–328; Steven Ross, "Political Economy for the Masses: Henry George," *democracy* 2, no. 3 (July 1982): 125–134; and Carey McWilliams, *Southern California: An Island on Land* (Santa Barbara, Calif.: Peregrine Smith, 1979), chap. 14.
16. Manuel Castells, "Local Government, Urban Crisis, and Political Change," in Maurice Zeitlin, ed., *Political Power and Social Theory: A Research Annual* vol. 2 (Greenwich, Conn.: JAI Press, 1981), p. 4.
17. See Harlan Hahn and Charles Levine, "The Politics of Urban America and the Study of Urban Politics," in Harlan Hahn and Charles Levine, eds., *Urban Politics; Past, Present, and Future* (New York: Longman, 1980), pp. 1–50.
18. Castells, "Local Government, Urban Crisis, and Political Change," p. 10.
19. See Center for Research on Criminal Justice, *The Iron Fist and the Velvet Glove: An Analysis of the U.S. Police* (Berkeley, Calif.: Center for Research on Criminal Justice, 1977).
20. Cf. Richard Lemon, *The Troubled American* (New York: Simon & Schuster, 1970), and Robert Gilmour and Robert Lamb, *Political Alienation in Contemporary America* (New York: St. Martin's, 1975).

21. See Michel Crozier, Samuel Huntington, and Joji Watanuki, *The Crisis of Democracy* (New York: New York University Press, 1975).

22. See Robert R. Alford, "The Reagan Budgets and the Contradiction Between Capitalism and Democracy," in Mark E. Kann, ed., *The Future of American Democracy: Views from the Left*, (Philadelphia: Temple University Press, 1983), pp. 22–54.

23. Author interview with Maurice Zeitlin, Los Angeles, July 12, 1982.

24. Zeitlin, "Tenant Power to Political Power," p. 16.

25. See Philip Hager, "Challenge to Rent Control Dismissed: U.S. High Court Rejects Landlord's Appeal in Santa Monica Case," Los Angeles *Times*, March 19, 1985.

26. Alan Wolfe, *The Limits of Legitimacy: Political Contradictions of Contemporary Capitalism* (New York: Free Press, 1977), p. 152.

27. See Howard I. Kalodner, "Citizen Participation in Emerging Social Institutions," in J. Roland Pennock and John Chapman, eds., *Participation in Politics* (New York: Lieber-Atherton, 1975), pp. 161–185.

28. Joyce Rothschild-Whitt, "Conditions for Democracy: Making Participatory Organizations Work," Case and Taylor, eds., *Co-ops, Communes and Collectives*, p. 234.

29. For a good discussion of West Hollywood politics, see Andrew Kopkind, "Once Upon a Time in the West," *The Nation*, June 1, 1985, pp. 657, 672–675.

30. Goldway interview.

31. Dave Lindorff, "About-Face in Santa Monica," *Village Voice*, December 2–8, 1981.

32. Neal Goldberg, "Santa Monica Tenants Get Revenge in Sweep of City Seats," *In These Times*, April 29–May 5, 1981, p. 5.

33. Nancy Eberle, *Return to Main Street: A Journey to Another America* (New York: Norton, 1982).

34. David Moberg, "From Rent Control to Municipal Power: The Santa Monica Story," *In These Times*, January 12–18, 1983, p. 22.

35. I have discussed this in greater detail in Mark E. Kann, *The American Left: Failures and Fortunes* (New York: Praeger, 1982), chap. 6, which is titled "Cracks in Elite Hegemony."

36. Samuel Bowles, "The Trilateral Commission: Have Capitalism and Democracy Come to a Parting of Ways?" in Union for Radical Political Economics, ed., *U.S. Capitalism in Crisis*, (New York: Union for Radical Political Economics, 1978), p. 264.

37. See William Appleman Williams, "Radicals and Regionalism," *democracy* 1, no. 4 (October 1981): 87–98.

Conclusion

1. Bruce A. Ackerman, *Social Justice and the Liberal State* (New Haven, Conn.: Yale University Press, 1980), p. 377.

2. See Donna Prokop, "Emergency School Tax Approved," Santa Monica *Outlook*, June 6, 1984.

3. See Celeste MacLeod, *Horatio Alger, Farewell: The End of the American Dream* (New York: Seaview, 1980), chap. 11.

4. See Kirkpatrick Sale, *Human Scale* (New York: Coward, McCann and Geoghegan, 1980), p. 206.

5. Martin Carnoy and Derek Shearer, *Economic Democracy: The Challenge of the 1980s* (White Plains, N.Y.: M. E. Sharpe, 1980), p. 19.

6. Robert Bellah, Richard Madsen, William Sullivan, Ann Swidler, and Steven Tipton, *Habits of the Heart: Individualism and Commitment in American Life* (Berkeley: University of California Press, 1985), p. 25.

7. See Russell Jacoby, *Social Amnesia* (Boston: Beacon, 1975).

8. Cf. John Rawls, *A Theory of Justice* (Cambridge, Mass.: Harvard University Press, 1971), and Karl Marx, *The Economic and Philosophic Manuscripts of 1844*, ed. Dirk Struik (New York: International Publishers, 1964).

9. Bellah et al., *Habits of the Heart*, p. 144.

Index